JERRY GRAHAM'S BAY AREA BACKROADS

JERRY GRAHAM'S

Bay Area Backroads

by Jerry and Catherine Graham

PERENNIAL LIBRARY

HARPER & ROW, PUBLISHERS, NEW YORK
Cambridge, Philadelphia, San Francisco, Washington
London, Mexico City, São Paulo, Singapore, Sydney

Designer: Barbara DuPree Knowles

Cartographer: Ron Lang

Copy Editor: Bruce Emmer

Indexer: Sayre Van Young

Library of Congress Cataloging-in-Publication Data

Graham, Jerry, 1934–

Jerry Graham's bay area backroads.

Includes index.

1. San Francisco Bay Area (Calif.)—Description and travel—Guide-books. I. Graham, Catherine, 1955– . II. Title.

F868.S156G7 1988   917.94'610453   87-46142

ISBN 0-06-096194-5 (pbk.)

88 89 90 91 92 RRD 10 9 8 7 6 5 4 3

Contents

Beyond the Bay

Acknowledgments

This book exists thanks to the direct and indirect contributions of many people.

First of all, thanks to Bob Klein, executive producer of KRON-TV, San Francisco, who had the idea of creating a television series about the Bay Area's back roads, and then asked me to do it. Thanks also to Dave Wilson and Jim Smith, program director and general manager of KRON, for going along with the idea and providing all the necessary encouragement and resources to make it happen.

On a daily basis, much credit is due to the *Backroads* show staff that takes care of all the production details and keeps an eye out for new destinations. Thanks to Chris DeFaria, my coproducer, whose boundless energy and fertile mind make collaborating such a pleasure; to Jessica Abbe, who originally researched most of the destinations in the book; to Paul Ghiringhelli, who produced many of these stories for television; to Dave Vandergriff, Mike Morgan, and Susan Burgess-Lent, who did much of the television editing; to Stan Drury, whose camerawork made me discover once again the truth in the old saw that a picture is worth a thousand words, and to Peter Hammersly, who joined the show more recently as researcher.

Special thanks go to Jeff Pierce, who was the entire crew when we first set out to explore the back roads in the summer of 1984. He has been on every shoot since and is not only the main photographer and sound man, but a valuable story editor, idea person, and discerning restaurant critic as well. He is also a wonderful traveling companion.

Thanks to the entire staff of KRON-TV, many of whom have contributed to the success of the program.

Thanks, too, to the audience, who embraced the idea of the glories of the back roads and has watched the series faithfully. In my many years of television, I have never been associated with a program that has elicited such a warm and personal response.

As for this book, thanks to Lawrence Peel Ashmead, executive editor of the trade division of Harper & Row, for his enthusiastic support and his guidance. Thanks also to Larry's assistants, Margaret Wimberger and John Michel, and to the copy editor, Bruce F. Emmer.

Thanks to my collaborator on this book, my wife, Catherine. She is the real writer in the family and has helped me immeasurably in translating my impressions to the printed page. She is also my best critic and best friend. Without Catherine, there would be no book.

And finally, thanks to a man who has been my role model in my approach to seemingly ordinary people and places, Charles Kuralt. He opened America's eyes to the back roads.

Jerry Graham

INTRODUCTION: Read This First

OK, so you've seen the Golden Gate Bridge, Coit Tower, and the cable cars. What else is there to do around San Francisco?

Plenty. Whether you are visiting the area or have lived here all your life, you'll be amazed by what you'll find on the Bay Area's back roads. With this premise in mind, the television series *Jerry Graham's Bay Area Backroads* was born in the summer of 1984, and it's still going strong. Broadcast each Sunday at 6 P.M. on KRON-TV, San Francisco, it has consistently been among the top-rated locally produced television shows in the San Francisco Bay Area.

Each week, the show features three or four destinations plus recommendations of places to eat and sometimes places to spend the night. Our emphasis is the offbeat location and the unforgettable local character that most people could find if they took the time to slow down and look around for a while. The most often heard comment from viewers goes something like this: "I've lived here 25 years and you're showing me places I didn't know existed in my own back yard!"

This book is based on that series. We have included over 200 of our most memorable locations, arranged geographically. Like the show, this book is about the pleasure that is easily lost in our modern, fast-paced society, the simple joy of roaming around and just looking. It requires getting off the main highway, slowing down, and forgetting about time. Traveling the back roads is as much a state of mind as it is an activity; it means being a visitor or guest instead of a tourist.

The San Francisco Bay Area is the best place in the world to experience the back roads. We have lived in many parts of the United States and have traveled extensively around Europe and have yet to find anyplace that offers so much diversity within two to three hours of a major city. Whether one heads north to the wine country and the rugged Mendocino Coast, east to the Sacramento Delta and the Wild West towns of the Gold Country, or south to the beaches of Santa Cruz and Carmel, one can head out on the back roads every single weekend and yet never see everything there is to see.

This book is not a list of tourist sites. It is a companion guide to the guidebooks that point out the usual places to go. As often as possible, we've included places and people not mentioned in other books about the area. For places that are found in other guidebooks, we've tried to add a new perspective. We assume that our readers are like us, people who would rather cruise down a beautiful country road at 30 miles per hour than speed down the highway at 70, people who like to explore and are excited by the folks they happen to meet.

The best way to use this book is to pick no more than two or three destinations per day and then head out. In the introduction to each chapter we have included approximate driving times. Within each chapter, the stories are arranged geographically. Although maps are included in the book, it's a good idea to take along a larger, more detailed map that may show every road, no matter how small. Then take off and find some spots of your own.

Keep in mind that some of our destinations do not have street addresses. In some back-roads towns, the residents do not use them; the place you're looking for is "just down the block from the post office" or "one road beyond the stop sign." In fact, in Carmel, the official town policy is to have no numbers at all; addresses are the street name and nearest cross street. We've included directions to each destination; if you get into town and the location is not obvious, just ask a local. You might even make a new friend.

Some words of caution: The back roads are ever changing. Country property has a way of becoming prime real estate, and charm has a tough time competing with potential profit. A wonderful farm or inn can become a shopping center almost overnight. Also, most of the destinations in this book are mom-and-pop-type operations; they do not have the heavy financial backing of major tourist operations and franchised restaurants. As a result, hours can fluctuate, and if the kid at home gets sick, the business might be closed for the day. Please call ahead to see if hours, admission, or location have changed. We've provided a phone number for each destination (each one that has a phone, that is).

Finally, a word about the writing of this book. The television show *Jerry Graham's Bay Area Backroads* is about Jerry driving around in his convertible visiting places and meeting people. Though he is the field producer of most of the segments, the show is always a collaboration between his coproducer, the crew, and the research staff stuck indoors at the office. Writing the book version

The Bay Area

Sonoma
Napa
Yolo
Solano
Marin
Contra Costa
San Francisco
Alameda
San Mateo
Santa Clara
Santa Cruz

of the show was a similar collaboration. For simplicity, we decided the book should follow the format of the show and use Jerry again as the voice. Thus many of the stories you will read are written in the first person, the *I* meaning Jerry. However, the book was a collaboration in the truest sense. Jerry wrote the first draft of each story, and Catherine made it work on the printed page.

There is much to see out there, and we hope you find some new stories on your own. You'll be amazed by what you'll find on the Bay Area's back roads.

Jerry Graham
Catherine Graham

BERKELEY, CALIFORNIA
MAY 1987

JERRY GRAHAM'S BAY AREA BACKROADS

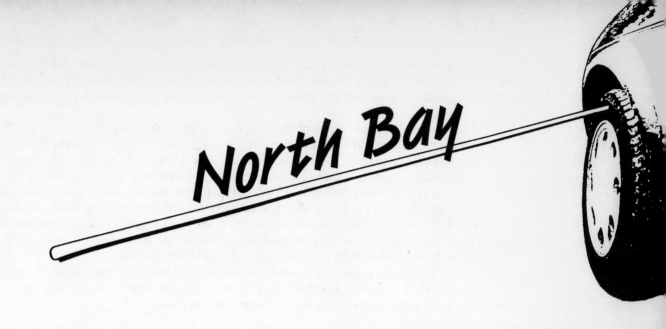

North Bay

When most of us head out for an adventure on the Bay Area's back roads, we travel north from San Francisco. A drive across the Golden Gate Bridge is an attraction in itself, but it is where the bridge takes us that provides the real treat. If you have time for only one trip out of town, make it to the north.

Marin and Sonoma counties feature unspoiled beaches, well-preserved parks, and hidden towns filled with interesting characters. Napa is famous as the center of the California wine country and also features some of the more entertaining and quirkier roadside attractions. And since one of the major industries is the tourist business, you will find wonderful places to eat and stay.

If you only have time for a day trip, you can reach many points in Marin, Sonoma, and Napa and still return to San Francisco for the night.

CHAPTER 1 Marin County

We'll begin by driving across the symbol of the San Francisco Bay Area, the Golden Gate Bridge, into Marin County. Just a few minutes from the city you can be in the famous waterfront town of Sausalito, and in an hour or so you can

AREA OVERVIEW

1

travel to the farthest points in the county. The two major roads are Highway 101, which is the freeway on the Marin side of the bridge that cuts inland until reaching the coast 300 miles to the north, and Route 1, which snakes its way along the coast.

Much has been made of the so-called Marin lifestyle. In an early-1970s NBC documentary, *I Want It All Now*, Marin was portrayed as a hedonistic haven for self-indulgent rich people who pamper themselves with hot tubs and peacock feathers. Certainly there are some residents who fit that stereotype, but the real Marin is a diverse mixture of folks in stylish towns like Sausalito, in working-class cities like Novato, and in small, woodsy villages like Inverness and Point Reyes Station. Perhaps most important of all, it is a county of exceptional beauty, a place where you can go from the beach to the mountains to an unspoiled redwood grove to the fanciest Mercedes dealership around.

The main population centers are near Highway 101; the farther west you travel, the more countrified it gets. We will visit both sides of the county, starting off in a part of Sausalito most visitors seem to miss.

BAY MODEL
(1)

This is an appropriate place to begin a back-roads tour of the entire Bay Area. In less than an hour you can walk around several counties, over bridges and above tunnels from Sonoma to San Mateo. This is the Bay Model, a replica of San Francisco Bay and its interconnecting bodies of water. It's like a giant three-dimensional map that gives you a sense of where everything is in relation to San Francisco.

It is the size of two football fields, housed in a two-acre warehouse near the famous houseboat community in Sausalito. The building was originally constructed in 1942 for producing World War II Liberty ships; in 1955 the Army Corps of Engineers took it over and built this hydraulic model for the purpose of studying San Francisco Bay.

Today the Bay Model is used by engineers, scientists, and planners to see how changes proposed by the government or private enterprise can affect the saltwater flows and water quality of the region. Schoolchildren come here on field trips to learn how everyday life in the Bay Area is affected by the tides and other conditions on the area's waterways.

Tours are self-guided, with the help of plenty of descriptive material. But if that's not enough, there are more exhibits upstairs, including films and slide shows explaining life in and on the Bay.

THE BAY MODEL, *2100 Bridgeway, Sausalito. Open 10 A.M. to 4 P.M. Tuesday through Friday, 9 A.M. to 4 P.M. Saturday. Admission: Free. Be sure to call ahead; sometimes the model does not have water! It would still be open, but not as much fun. Phone: (415) 332-3871. Wheelchair accessible.*

Marin

Point Reyes Station

Novato

101

Sir Francis Drake
Blvd.

San Rafael

Mill Valley

Sausalito

Tiburon

HOW TO GET TO THE BAY MODEL: *From San Francisco, take the Sausalito–Marin City exit off Highway 101, turn right off the ramp, and head south toward downtown on Bridgeway. At the third stoplight you will see the Big G supermarket; turn left and follow the signs to the Bay Model.*

MARIN HEADLANDS

It's difficult to describe the dramatic beauty of the Marin Headlands without sounding evangelical. This area just across the Golden Gate Bridge from San Francisco is a great place for a drive. You will see rugged cliffs with knife-sharp drops to the ocean, beaches, and, depending on the time of year, your choice of lush valleys, hillsides of blue and yellow lupine, orange poppies, eucalyptus, and sage, and maybe a fox or deer. And some of the best views of San Francisco are from the bluffs of the Headlands.

As an interesting contrast to the awesome natural beauty, you will also find scattered throughout the 15 square miles remnants of military bunkers that defended the Golden Gate from 1870 through World War II. Three forts exist on the land: Forts Baker, Cronkhite, and Barry. In Fort Baker, down on the east side of the Headlands facing the Bay, about 100 servicemen are stationed. (I have no idea what they do there, but there can be no better assignment.)

In 1972 the land became part of the Golden Gate National Recreation Area (which we will refer to several times in this chapter, from now on as the GGNRA). Under the mantle of the National Park Service, the GGNRA includes 45,000 acres of recreation area on both sides of the Golden Gate Bridge, nearly 40,000 acres of which are in Marin County. This means that this land is your land, this land is my land, protected forever from development. There is a visitor's center in Fort Cronkhite where you can get maps and be introduced to all the Headlands has to offer. Let me recommend three stops in particular: the Point Bonita Lighthouse, Hawk Hill, and the Marine Mammal Center.

But first, a word of advice: Wherever you go, bring along a sweater or jacket. Even on the warmest days it can get chilly out here.

✓ Point Bonita Lighthouse.   If a Hollywood producer wanted to shoot a movie that takes place in a lighthouse, this is the one he'd use. The Point Bonita Lighthouse looks like everybody's image of the lonely beacon welcoming ships in the night. It is perched solidly on a craggy cliff with seagulls circling overhead, and you can picture a grizzled Sterling Hayden character standing in its doorway.

Long before the Golden Gate Bridge was even dreamed of, the Point Bonita Lighthouse signaled sailors they were entering the San Francisco Bay Area. Built in 1877, it was one of the West Coast's first lighthouses and is now one of its last.

Getting to the lighthouse is part of the fun. After parking the car, you follow a path that takes you through hand-dug tunnels and finally out to the point. The ocean breezes are invigorating, and if the skies are clear, you have the strange sensation of being in the middle of nowhere, where no one lives, and, by contrast, looking across the bay at the bulging city of San Francisco. The final approach to the lighthouse is via a fairly new bridge. Before this was built, visitors had to risk life and limb by snaking around the cliff on a narrow dirt path, with nothing but a cold ocean below.

When you drop by, you might see a friendly-looking man wearing a captain's hat. Not exactly Sterling Hayden, but a reasonable facsimile. He's Wayne Wheeler, founder of the United States Lighthouse Society. Like the 2300 members of his club, he is crazy about lighthouses (the society even has members in such unnautical states as Kansas and Nebraska). Wayne says he doesn't mind being called a lighthouse nut, though there are those who would take offense and would prefer to be known as "pharosologists," named after the first lighthouse on the island of Pharos, off Alexandria, Egypt (which was one of the Seven Wonders of the World). Wheeler explains the fascination with these unique structures: "They are romantic symbols of security, a picket fence against that dark, evil sea."

Wayne is a walking library of Marin Headlands lore. He told me about the West Coast's first foghorn, established nearby (this foghorn was a cannon that had to be fired every half hour in the mist). He also told me more than I thought there was to know about giant Fresnel lenses, which provide the light for the lighthouse.

If you can't find Wayne for a personal tour, just take matters into your own hands and stroll on your own as far as you can down the path to Point Bonita and its lighthouse, or catch up with a tour group; you can go inside only during regularly scheduled times, and it's a good idea to have a reservation. Inside or out, weather permitting, you'll get a wonderful view of San Francisco.

✔ **Hawk Hill.** The very best view of the entire Bay Area can be found on Hawk Hill, high on a bluff looking down on the Golden Gate Bridge. On a clear day you can see Mount Diablo, more than 30 miles to the east, not to mention Alcatraz, Angel Island, Berkeley, San Francisco—in other words, forever!

So why are so many people on the hill ignoring the view and looking up at the sky?

They're looking for birds. This is one of the best places on the West Coast for watching concentrations of birds of prey, as many as 11,000 spotted in a single season. Every year in the fall, the largest migration of predatory birds in the West heads over this bluff, which has been nicknamed Hawk Hill.

In addition to avid birdwatchers and school groups, you're likely to run into Alan Fish (no kidding!). He's head of the project studying the migration. Fish is aided by volunteers and other knowledgeable ornithologists who will tell you all you need to know about what you're seeing overhead.

All you need is a pair of good walking shoes, some warm clothes (in case the fog rolls in), and a pair of binoculars. It's also recommended that you bring something to eat and drink since you'll probably want to hang around once you get up there. The crowd you'll meet is fun and fascinating. Every now and then somebody has to look up and say, "Look, it's a bird . . ." so someone else can chime in, "No, it's a plane. . . ." But soon, when a majestic hawk or a rare golden eagle flies by, the joking stops; the excitement is real and contagious.

On weekends in October, hawks are caught and banded for study, which is a chance to put down the binoculars and see the birds up close. And birds or no birds, there's always that spectacular view.

✓ **Marine Mammal Center.** The California Marine Mammal Center is in another section of the Headlands from the lighthouse and Hawk Hill. This is a hospital of sorts for sea lions, seals, and other oceanic creatures in need of medical attention. Wounded animals from as far north as the Oregon border and as far south as San Luis Obispo are brought there to be cared for until they are well enough to return to their natural environment.

At any given time you are likely to find 20 or more animals being nursed back to health. Some of the patients are cute and amusing as they recover from minor scrapes and bruises acquired while at play in the ocean. Other cases are heartbreaking, the victims of some act of human cruelty.

On a typical visit you will see volunteers cleaning cages, coaxing wounded animals to eat, encouraging them to play or get some needed exercise, and giving shots (this may sound simple, but it is no easy task to get a huge sea lion to sit still for a hypodermic needle, even if it is for his own good).

A trip to the Marine Mammal Center is a chance to get close to animals that grew up in the wild and will soon return there and to give encouragement to the center's staff and volunteers. Special tours can be arranged, particularly for school groups. It is a truly educational experience.

THE MARIN HEADLANDS, *just across the Golden Gate Bridge from San Francisco.*

HOW TO GET TO THE POINT BONITA LIGHTHOUSE: *From San Francisco, cross the Golden Gate Bridge and leave Highway 101 at Alexander Avenue. Stay to the right at the fork in the road. Turn right, drive for a quarter mile, and look for a left-turn lane; at a brown sign that says "Fort Baker/Fort Cronkhite/Fort Berry," turn left. Go under the freeway and follow the road until you reach the one-way tunnel. Go through the tunnel until you find Field Road; turn left and follow signs to the lighthouse. (Note: The tunnel is called the six-minute tunnel, because that's how long it takes for the light to change.)*

Point Bonita is open all year round and worth a visit anytime. The lighthouse is open at irregular times and requires an advance appointment certain times of the year. The best advice is for you to call ahead and get the current schedule. Phone: (415) 331-1450. You might want to join one of the walks at sunset and during the full moon, conducted by park rangers. Admission to the lighthouse and all tours are free.

TO GET TO HAWK HILL: *Follow the same directions to the lighthouse, but well before you get there look for an area where cars can pull off the road to park and a road marker for "Hill 129." You have a wonderful view of the Bay Area from the parking area. Hawk Hill is directly above and requires a steep climb. In the fall, that's where the experienced birdwatchers hang out.*

HOW TO GET TO THE MARINE MAMMAL CENTER: *From San Francisco, take the Golden Gate Bridge to the Alexander Avenue exit off Route 101. Follow the sign to Fort Cronkhite. Go through the tunnel and continue on Bunker Road all the way until you see the sign for the center. The Marine Mammal Center is open from 10 A.M. to 4 P.M. daily. Admission is free, but donations are appreciated. Phone: (415) 331-SEAL. Wheelchair accessible.*

In addition, the visitor's center and ranger station are both on Bunker Road near the Rodeo Lagoon in Fort Cronkhite. There you can get maps and information. The visitor's center is open from 8:30 A.M. to 4:30 P.M. daily. Admission: Free. Phone: (415) 331-1540.

The Marin Headlands Ranger Station is open from 8:30 A.M. to 5 P.M.; pick up maps of roads and hiking trails. Phone: (415) 561-7612.

UNKNOWN MUSEUM

When people ask me what kinds of places I visit on the *Backroads* show, I often use the Unknown Museum as an example. This unusual museum is the creation of Mickey McGowan, who has spent his life collecting what he considers to be the artifacts of American culture. As curator and artist-in-residence, Mickey creates mind-boggling displays using Mr. Potato Heads, lunch pails, vintage TV sets, car parts, puzzles, pocket books, toys, dolls, and just about every object ever made out of plastic. Each exhibit is a work of art in its own right, often involving some sort of visual pun. Add to this an audio tape collage—the sounds of 1950s television, Kennedy speeches, soap operas, sporting events, and K-Tel greatest hits offers—and you have a sensory experience you are not likely to forget.

Mickey calls it all "a visual newscast." I don't know what to call it, but the effect is at first staggeringly funny, then thought-provoking as you suddenly recognize forgotten objects from your childhood.

One reason the museum is called "unknown" is that Mickey spends his time at rummage sales and flea markets, collecting and curating instead of pinning down a permanent location. Originally the Unknown Museum was in downtown Mill Valley in a converted auto repair garage that is now a fancy garden supply shop.

Last time we visited, the Unknown Museum was set up in a house in which each room had its own theme. For example, upstairs in the Girl's Room was a mannequin dressed as a bride, lying on a bed of rice surrounded by a population of wedding cake figurines tying her down with strings; bordering the display was a collection of romance comic books, plus hundreds of wedding invitations and snapshots of unknown people. The kitchen was a homage to the products we saw advertised during our collective misspent youth.

I'm not sure where Mickey will be by the time this book is in print. He has talked about moving north to Stinson Beach and opening a small roadside café to accompany his museum. Wherever he is, his priceless collection is worth seeking out.

UNKNOWN MUSEUM, *at last report at 243 Blithedale Avenue, Mill Valley. Open Sundays only, but call ahead for current time and location. Phone: (415) 383-2726. Free admission, but donations are appreciated.*

ANGEL ISLAND/TIBURON
④

Mark Twain is quoted as having said, "The coldest winter I ever spent was a summer in San Francisco." Well, when the summer fog cools the City, many San Franciscans head to Sam's in Tiburon to warm up. It's a dockside restaurant with a huge deck where people go for the sun, not necessarily the quality of the food. It's also the view of San Francisco they're after and the opportunity to sit by the water enjoying the California art of "hanging out."

Sam's is located on Main Street, which in the 1800s was a tough waterfront strip of hotels, taverns, and heaven knows what else. Today it is a quaint little street, some buildings dating back to the Gold Rush, others constructed to look like they date back to the Gold Rush, where you can find cafés, art galleries, and fine clothing stores.

From Tiburon (which, by the way, means "shark" in Spanish), back-roads travelers can leave their car behind and take a 10-minute ferry ride to Angel Island State Park. This is the largest and one of the least explored islands in San Francisco Bay.

This is not to say you'll be alone. During those cold San Francisco summers, the island is often as toasty as the Caribbean, and private boats and public ferries take sun worshipers out in droves. Most people, however, never get past Ayala Cove with its picnic areas, snack bar, and rest rooms. It takes some hiking over the hill to get to the really interesting parts.

On the island, there are 740 acres with hiking trails. You can hike around the perimeter in about three hours—it's a 5-mile jaunt. There are also Civil War barracks, the Chinese immigration center, and many nooks and crannies where you can find solitude, even on a day when the main cove is jammed with tourists.

Angel Island was discovered in 1775, when the Spanish first entered the Bay. Captain Don Juan Manuel de Ayala anchored at the island, which he named Isla de Los Angeles, and landed at the location now known as Ayala Cove. During the War between the States, the Union Army built garrisons on the northwestern shore at Camp Reynolds. The purpose was to foil a Confederate plan to sail through the Bay to the Gold Country and steal gold to fund the war effort. The Confederates never made it, and there was never a cause to try the effectiveness of the many cannon, which still point out from land.

Near the turn of this century, Angel Island was called the "Ellis Island of the West." That's because on the eastern side of the island was the place where Asian immigrants would enter the United States. During World War II it was a detention center for Japanese and others considered "enemy aliens."

Visitors can see the remains of this island's checkered past on foot or by bicycle.

The island's most significant new development is the Angel Island Association, founded by Robert Noyes, a retired doctor from Palo Alto. Noyes and the handful of others who live on Angel Island have been restoring buildings in the Civil War barracks area to provide access for the elderly and disabled. Their projects include special docking facilities and special buses for tours of the island.

TO GET TO TIBURON, *take Highway 101 north from the Golden Gate Bridge to the Tiburon Boulevard–East Blithedale Avenue exit. Turn right off the freeway and continue until you can go no farther. Turn right, and you will be on Main Street, in the quaint, somewhat cutesy downtown of Tiburon. Parking is at a premium, so you will probably want to pull into a lot. The ferry entrance is on Main Street.*

TO GET TO ANGEL ISLAND BY FERRY FROM TIBURON, *park your car in town and head up Main Street to the pier. Look for the Angel Island State Park Ferry Company. The ferry leaves Tiburon every hour on the hour from 10 A.M. to 4 P.M. every day during the summer and on Saturdays, Sundays, and holidays during the rest of the year, weather permitting; always call ahead to check the schedule. The last ferry leaves Angel Island at 4:40 P.M. Round-trip price, which includes admission to the state park, is $2.50 for adults, $1.25, children 5 to 11; children under 5, free. Transporting a bicycle costs 50 cents for the round trip. Phone: (415) 435-2131.*

TO GET TO ANGEL ISLAND FROM SAN FRANCISCO, *check the schedule of the Red and White fleet, (415) 546-2815. They usually run half-hour ferry trips from Pier 43½, which is at the Embarcadero, near the end of Broadway. Phone for current schedules and rates.*

Other useful phone numbers: Angel Island State Park Ranger Station at Ayala Cove: (415) 435-1915. Angel Island Association: (415) 435-3522; this is the group that organizes tours for the handicapped, plus many other activities.

MUIR WOODS ⑤

This preserve of majestic redwoods is on everybody's list of places to visit in the Bay Area, as you will quickly realize when you encounter all the tour buses in the parking lot.

But there are back-roads ways to avoid feeling like you're in the thick of a crowd. First, you can go in the early morning or late afternoon when the crowds tend to thin out.

Second, you can find Lawson Brainerd, now in his eighties. He's been with the Forest Service since 1919. In fact, he's primarily responsible for Muir Woods being the wonderful place it is today. When Lawson arrived here after the Depression, the place looked more like an urban park than a virgin redwood forest. He became a man with a mission: to restore the awesome majesty of the park. Even though he's retired now, Lawson loves to hang out in the woods and tell stories. Engage him in a conversation and you're in for a treat.

In the 550-acre park you'll walk among giant coast redwoods, some more than 200 feet high (be sure to bring a sweater; even on hot days the shade can be chilly). You'll find trout and salmon running in the brook; look closely and you'll spot some deer running free. There are 6 miles of paved paths for easy walking, including a braille trail for the blind. But leave the picnic basket in the car; no snacking is allowed in the park.

Tip number 3: Remember all those tour buses? Well, the drivers are on a tight schedule, so the tour groups rarely go farther than a half mile into the redwood grove before turning around. So if you want to really enjoy the quiet of the woods, start your private tour deep in the forest and discover the area the bus passengers never see. You can stay as long as you like, but if you are trying to schedule your time, plan on a visit of at least an hour.

MUIR WOODS NATIONAL MONUMENT, *Mill Valley. Open 8 A.M. until sunset every day. Admission: Free. Phone: (415) 388-2595. Wheelchair accessible.*

HOW TO GET TO MUIR WOODS. *From San Francisco, head north on Highway 101. Take the Highway 1–Stinson Beach exit and follow the signs to Muir Woods. The route is well marked. Muir Woods is 17 miles north of San Francisco.*

TOP OF MOUNT TAM ⑥

Just above Muir Woods is Mount Tamalpais, which everyone in the Bay Area knows as "Mount Tam." Many others call the mountain by its nickname "The Sleeping Lady"; with a little imagination you can see this mountain range as having the contours of a reclining maiden.

Most Bay Area residents view Mount Tam from below. Surprisingly few people know how easy it is to get to the top.

You can drive almost to the summit, which is nearly 3000 feet above sea level. A beautiful road takes you to about a quarter of a mile from the peak. You leave your car in the parking lot; then, in good walking shoes, you climb to the summit on a fairly steep dirt road to the 1937 stone building that houses the fire lookout.

This building is not open to the public, but from the grounds below the lookout you will have a spectacular view. Quite conveniently, nature has furnished many comfortable boulders for sitting on what feels like the top of the world.

The last time I drove to the top of Mount Tam, it was one of those summer days when the fog blanketed San Francisco and the normally sunny parts of Marin. But as I made the final turn up the hill to the summit parking area, the sun was shining brightly. This is par for the course; it's a rare day when it's not warm and sunny at the top.

The main activities at the top are boulder sitting and hiking. If you enjoy the latter, you can take a fairly long hike to the old West Point Inn, which is a very secluded series of camplike buildings. Hikers can get fresh lemonade and rest in the shade; overnighters can get an inexpensive room if they're willing to forsake electricity and to bring their own provisions. A less vigorous trip would be simply to roam around the various paths near the top and wind your way back down to the parking lot. Or you may want to join a group led by the Sierra Club or the other organizations that offer nature walks.

When sitting or standing at the top, you can see the entire panorama of Marin County, from the densely populated areas around Highway 101 inland, past vast canyons and forests until you reach the ocean. Even though I have traveled many of these roads, I was amazed to see how much of Marin is still undeveloped. Much of it is protected by either the State Park System or the adjacent Golden Gate National Recreation Area.

In the early days of Marin, the Mount Tam summit was where the action was. There were grand hotels and taverns and a scenic railway to bring customers here. All this was before Prohibition. The rail line was abandoned in the early 1930s, and most of the structures have been removed; the above-mentioned West Point Inn is one of the few that remain from this era.

Now all the action is down below in the towns, and the summit has become one of nature's hideaways. The treasures to be found are of a spiritual and sensual kind. There is a feeling of magic here, and the sights and smells are wondrous.

On a more prosaic level, you might want to know that the parking area has rest rooms, phones, and a snack bar.

Other points of interest on Mount Tam include the Mountain Theatre, the outdoor site of a major musical production each spring, and, farther down, the Pantoll Ranger Station, where you can find a map and get your bearings.

Another way to enjoy Mount Tam is simply to drive on Ridgecrest Boulevard or along Panoramic Highway, which eventually winds down to Stinson Beach. Either way, stop at least once to get out of the car and discover what fresh air really is.

TAMALPAIS STATE PARK, *open 7 A.M. to sunset daily. Admission: Free. For general information about the park and group hikes, call the Pantoll Ranger Station: (415) 388-2070; for information regarding West Point Inn: (415) 388-9955.*

HOW TO GET TO MOUNT TAMALPAIS: *From San Francisco, take the Golden Gate Bridge to the Stinson Beach–Route 1 exit. Follow Route 1 until you come to Panoramic Highway, which is marked by a sign pointing to Muir Woods. Turn right and continue past the Mountain Home Inn to the intersection of Southside Road. This is the location of the Pantoll Ranger Station. To get to the summit parking lot, turn right on Southside Road and continue uphill to Ridgecrest Boulevard. Turn right to the summit parking lot.*

SLIDE RANCH

The Shoreline Highway, aka Route 1, which you will find off Route 101 in Mill Valley, is the quickest way to the area's most popular beaches, Muir and Stinson. Muir is closer to San Francisco and is also small and usually uncrowded. Situated in a cove, it doesn't have the long stretch of beach Stinson has, nor does it offer the amenities of a beach town like Stinson. It does, however, offer the curious contrast of a family beach (on the main section) with a nude beach (in an adjoining cove, out of view of the G-rated area).

If you continue north on Route 1 for a few miles, you will come to a driveway on the left with the big initials S.R. This is Slide Ranch, a unique demonstration farm where visitors can watch workers milk goats, shear sheep, pick vegetables, and—so that we have no romantic views of how we get our food—even slaughter chickens.

The director of the project is a warm, earnest man with the unlikely name Trout Black. His mission is to celebrate all forms of life and to help us understand all of life's interconnections. He is a joy to spend an afternoon with. When he took me into the chicken coop to show me an egg warm under its mother, he was as thrilled as if it were his first time. And when he pointed out each new flower or vegetable in the Slide Ranch's many gardens, it was like meeting his children.

The experience is more than just visiting a farm. Trout and his staff challenge us to think about our relationship to other creatures, what we eat, and what we wear—"letting people know where the source of their lives comes from," as Trout puts it. The experience made me feel like a kid again.

Trout, his wife, and four staff members live on the ranch, along with six farmhand interns. The activities range from afternoon visits to one-, two-, and three-day programs, for people of all ages, preschool to senior citizen, with a special emphasis on inner-city kids and the handicapped. Also, you can drop in just about any time during daylight hours to walk around the 164 acres of ranch property, which has hiking trails and tide pools and is adjacent to Mount Tamalpais.

SLIDE RANCH, *Muir Beach. Open during daylight hours all year. No admission charge for hikes or wandering around the land. For demonstrations of the working ranch, groups of 10 or more people can arrange for a guided tour; the cost is $6 per person, and you must call in advance. Phone: (415) 381-6155. Wheelchair accessible.*

HOW TO GET TO SLIDE RANCH: *From Highway 101, take the Stinson Beach exit and follow the signs to Highway 1. This is a curvy road that winds through the hills and gives you a spectacular view of the ocean. Stay on Highway 1, about a mile past Muir Beach, and look to your left for the driveway marked with the initials S.R. Go slow, as this turn is on a curve.*

AUDUBON CANYON RANCH

As a transplanted Midwesterner, it took me a while to realize one essential fact about California life: Not all the birds go away in winter. Birdwatchers get to enjoy looking through their binoculars all year round in various parts of the state.

Birdwatchers are in paradise in West Marin. Several species of rare birds thrive on the lagoons and forests that are thankfully protected from development.

One of the best places of all for seeing and learning about our fine feathered friends is at the Audubon Canyon Ranch. This 1000-acre wildlife sanctuary bordering the Bolinas Lagoon is a unique spot for birdwatchers: You get to watch birds from above, rather than below.

The land was originally purchased in 1961 as a cooperative effort of several environmental groups, including the Marin Audubon Society; in 1969 the place became a registered national landmark. Named in honor of the most famous bird lover of all, John James Audubon, the Audubon Canyon Ranch is run by a private, nonprofit organization that supports itself from the gift shop in the visitor's center and from donations.

There are several ways to take advantage of this special place. You can spend an hour or so at sea level, picnicking in the meadows, wandering through the exhibits to learn about egrets, herons, and other natives, or browsing in the bookstore. There are several miles of hiking trails, each varying in length and difficulty, including the relatively easy ¾-mile Harwell Nature Trail and the more formidable 3-mile Griffin Loop (it is steep, narrow, and often slippery). But I recommend the ½-mile Rawlings Trail, rising 250 feet to the top of the canyon. It is worth the effort. Each spring, the incredible great blue herons (which are 4 to 5 feet tall, with a 6-foot wingspan) come to nest in the tips of the redwood trees in Schwartz Grove on the east side of the ranch. By mid-March they are joined by their neighbors the great egrets (smaller creatures, with a 4½-foot wingspan). From the overlook you will have a unique view of the nesting pageant of the birds.

The Audubon Canyon Ranch offers weekend programs, some designed especially for families making use of the overnight accommodations in the bunkhouse, which boasts such alternative features as solar-heated water and wind-powered toilets (I was too timid to ask how they work). Participants provide their own bedding and food. Free docent-conducted tours can be arranged for groups, and pamphlets for self-guided tours of the ranch are available at the registration desk.

AUDUBON CANYON RANCH, *4900 Shoreline Highway, Stinson Beach. Open 10 A.M. to 4 P.M. on Saturdays, Sundays, and holidays, March 1 through July 4. Schools and other large groups can make arrangements to visit Tuesdays through Fridays. The ranch is closed all Mondays. Admission: Free. For appointments and information, call the ranch office on weekdays 9 A.M. to 5 P.M. at (415) 383-1644. Wheelchair accessible.*

TO GET TO AUDUBON CANYON RANCH *from Slide Ranch: Continue north on Route 1 past Stinson Beach. Look for the Audubon sign 3 miles north of Stinson. From San Francisco: Take the Golden Gate Bridge to Highway 101 North. Exit at Route 1–Stinson Beach and follow the road all the way. It's 28 miles from San Francisco and will take at least an hour by car.*

BOLINAS
⑨

One of the most intriguing towns in Marin County is Bolinas, a place made mysterious by the fact there is no sign letting you know where to turn to get there or even if you've arrived. As soon as someone puts one up, somebody else tears it down. This is not an official policy, but, you see, a lot of locals would prefer we didn't know about the place.

Bolinas *is* a charming town, well situated on bluffs overlooking the Pacific. There is not much in the way of public places—a bakery here, a café there; it's the physical setting that is its main attraction nowadays. However, near the turn of the century, it was the largest town in Marin, featuring 11 hotels and 9 saloons, and was both an artists' colony and a playground for Marin society. Its present character is reminiscent of the halcyon days of the 1960s. That's because much of its population migrated about that time from the famous Haight-Ashbury district of San Francisco. An oil spill off Bolinas threatened the environment and thousands of birds; the hippies answered the call of a San Francisco radio station and arrived in droves to help clean things up. Many of them never left. Today the town is a study in contrasts: the artists and craftspeople, wealthy retirees, authentic hippies, and just plain folks living quietly in a quaint town surrounded by incredible natural beauty.

And in spite of the town's reputation, a lot of locals welcome visitors. The welcome mat will surely be out at the Bolinas Museum, one of the smallest such establishments I've ever encountered (you can cover it all in a few steps). The museum specializes in collections of local residents. The day I visited, there was an exhibit of postcards and a collection of handkerchiefs on display. The idea behind the museum is to showcase personal memorabilia of real people, not impersonal artifacts of the distant past. It works. The good folks running the place will be glad to tell you all about the history of the town and direct you to other points of interest.

There's also a lovely little town park, a secluded beach that overlooks Stinson Beach, and some beautiful drives past impressive homes.

TO GET TO BOLINAS FROM AUDUBON CANYON RANCH: *Drive up Route 1 for a few miles and look for a big white farmhouse on the right. There should be a road to your left that is unmarked. That is the entrance route to Bolinas. From San Francisco: Take the Golden Gate Bridge to Highway 101 North. Take the Stinson Beach exit and follow Route 1 past Stinson Beach. The Bolinas Road is approximately 5 miles from Stinson.*

THE BOLINAS MUSEUM, *3 Olema-Bolinas Road, Bolinas. Open 11 A.M. to 5 P.M. Wednesday through Sunday. Admission: Free. Phone: (415) 868-1650. How to get here: Once you find your entrance to Bolinas, follow the road until you come to a T-intersection. Turn left, and as you head into the main part of town, the museum is well marked on the right side of the street.*

Entire books have been written about this part of the world, so I won't try to compete. But by way of introduction, let me say that Point Reyes ("Point of Kings") National Seashore is a 65,000-acre park that should not be missed; you can spend days here and not cover all it has to offer.

POINT REYES NATIONAL SEASHORE

Activities include beachcombing and swimming at the seashore's many beaches (though you'll most likely do more in the way of beachcombing, since it tends to be cold and windy and the water temperature will make your bones ache). Campsites are available, but only for hikers, not drive-in campers. There is also horseback riding, nature study, hang gliding, bird watching, fishing, and just getting away from it all.

Just as one brief description can't cover it all, don't expect to see all of Point Reyes in one visit. It is huge, and you can drive great distances simply getting from one beach to another. For example, it's a 22-mile drive from the entrance near Olema to the lighthouse at the end of Sir Francis Drake Road.

Among the many attractions are three separate visitor's centers, each offering maps, information, and educational exhibits. There's also a Miwok Indian village, an earthquake trail that traces damage on the fault line, and the lighthouse, which is a favorite spot for whale watchers in the winter. At the far northern end, near McClure's Beach, is the tule elk range. Here you can see scores of rare and majestic tule elk. Once on the brink of extinction with only two remaining, they have been nurtured and protected in their own range on the fringe of Tomales Bay.

Let me point out a couple of places I think deserve more detailed explanations: a unique hostel and a special breed of horse ranch.

✔ **Point Reyes Hostel.** Those who do not require luxury overnight accommodations might want to check out the Point Reyes Hostel, a part of the American Youth Hostel system. For $6 a night, you can stay near Limantour Beach *if* you do not mind sleeping on a bunk in a room with as many as 40 other guests of the same sex and sharing the bathrooms, kitchen, and chores.

The positive side is that the accommodations offer a chance to meet people from all over the world, and you will probably eat very well (guests tend to pitch in to create wonderful communal meals). You will stay within walking distance of the beach and can watch the sunset from the lodge room.

Clearly, hosteling is not for everyone, but the facility at Point Reyes is particularly inviting.

✔ **Morgan Horse Ranch.** The National Park Service operates this working ranch, where you can learn about the Morgan horse. Rangers will tell you the history of this very versatile work animal—the first American horse breed, in fact—and let you roam through the farm. More elaborate tours can be set up in advance, with riding and shoeing demonstrations, and you can observe firsthand the daily life on a ranch. Wait until you see the vet check the horses' teeth; you don't know what dentist phobia is all about until you've seen a horse get its teeth filed!

On most days there's a school tour in progress. I have found that a very entertaining way to learn about a new place is to simply join in with the kids, the younger the better. There is also a small visitor's center with historical photos and displays about the Morgan horse.

POINT REYES NATIONAL SEASHORE, *40 miles north of San Francisco off Highway 1, west of Olema. Open 8 A.M. to sundown daily. Admission: Free. Main information number: (415) 663-1092.*

The three visitor's centers for information are located at Bear Valley, Drake's Beach, and the lighthouse.

POINT REYES HOSTEL, *P.O. Box 247, Point Reyes Station, CA 94956. Phone: (415) 669-7414.*

HOW TO GET TO THE HOSTEL: *From San Francisco, take the Golden Gate Bridge to Highway 101 North. Take the Sir Francis Drake exit and follow it all the way to Olema. Turn right and look for the signs for the entrance to Point Reyes National Seashore. Head for Limantour Road and watch for the signs to the hostel.*

MORGAN HORSE RANCH, *near the Bear Valley visitor's center on Bear Valley Road. Open 9 A.M. to 5 P.M. daily, including most holidays (somebody's got to be there to feed the horses, and he or she can show you around). Admission: Free. Phone: (415) 663-1763. Large groups should call ahead. Most of the ranch is wheelchair accessible.*

HOW TO GET TO THE MORGAN HORSE RANCH: *Follow the directions for getting to the Hostel, but after reaching Olema and turning right at the T-intersection, turn left when you come to Bear Valley Road.*

INVERNESS

To get to the northern section of the Point Reyes National Seashore, you have to get back on Sir Francis Drake Road and drive through the town of Inverness, which borders Tomales Bay. It's a worthy destination on its own.

Inverness is one of my favorite towns in the Bay Area. It is lovely to look at all year round and filled with interesting and unusual places and people. Although only an hour from San Francisco, it has escaped being turned into a crowded tourist trap, probably because of the efforts of townspeople to keep things the way they are. There are many contradictions surrounding Inverness that somehow add to its charm. Although its name is Scottish, the three most notable buildings are two Czech restaurants and a domed Russian-style beach house. The town also offers several charming bed-and-breakfast inns, plus several bay-front motels. There are probably more writers living in the hills around Inverness than in any other town its size in California, which may explain the importance of the Inverness Library.

As you drive through town, on your right you will see a tiny red building near the heart of town. For years this was the home of the world's smallest library.

But in late 1986 Inverness gave up this claim to fame, and the library moved to a building four times the size of the old one. It is in the former home of the town's most famous historian and writer, Jack Mason, the man everyone in Marin used to call when they needed to know a fact about the county's heritage.

Mason died in 1986, and he willed his house to the community for use as a library and museum.

I never thought I'd wax enthusiastic about a branch of the public library, but librarian Nancy Hemingway (what a perfect name!) makes this place special. She has turned the library into an unofficial community center. Locals drop off their kids to read while they run errands or get information on who is available for housecleaning or babysitting services; visitors can find out about the best places in the area to eat and spend the night.

Even if you're not a resident of Marin County, the library is a comfortable place to read, do research, or get to know the town. You will be surprised how much more you can learn about a town in a library than at a place that caters to tourists, especially in this library, where it's OK to talk. That's because if you're disturbing someone who's reading, all you have to do is walk into another room of this converted house and you're in a museum where you can chatter to your heart's content.

This library and museum are in one of the first houses in Inverness. Built in 1894, it was called "The Gables." Its previous occupant, historian Mason, self-published seven books on Marin County history. Mason's books and his files chronicled the rich lore of the town. In one room you can explore the history of the town through historical photographs and the private papers of one man's passion for his community.

INVERNESS LIBRARY AND JACK MASON MUSEUM, *15 Park Avenue, Inverness. Open 3 to 6 P.M. Monday and Friday, 10 A.M. to 1 P.M. and 2 to 6 P.M. Tuesday and Wednesday, 10 A.M. to 1 P.M. Saturday; closed Thursday and Sunday. Admission: Free. Phone: (415) 669-1288. Wheelchair accessible.*

HOW TO REACH INVERNESS FROM SAN FRANCISCO: *Take the Golden Gate Bridge to Highway 101 North. Take the Sir Francis Drake exit and continue all the way until you come to a T-intersection at Olema. Turn right for a few miles and look for a turn on the left to Inverness. You will be back on Sir Francis Drake, which takes you directly into town.*

OYSTER FARM

Whether you say "oyster" or "erster," I am willing to bet you have never seen as many of these creatures in your life as you will find here. The Johnsons have been oyster farmers for generations. They cultivate the slimy delicacy using the traditional Japanese method of grafting tiny seeds onto shells, then taking them out into shallow waters of the Bay to hang them on racks. Eighteen months later, the Johnsons harvest them and sell them on the premises.

Papa Charlie Johnson is as crusty as one of those shells you'll see lying in a mound, and he's piled just as high with stories. He'll open one of his darlings for you with his knife and give you a lesson in eating them raw.

This is not a tiny operation. Several boats are being loaded and unloaded daily, and you have an opportunity to see quite a lot of action, such as watching workers haul oyster-filled nets out of the bay or visiting the incubation room to see how thousands of oysters are growing in huge tubs of warm water. After the cells have reached an appropriate size, they are ready to be taken out to the Bay. Johnson's appears to combine the latest technology in a setting that looks perfect for an old seafarer's movie.

JOHNSON'S OYSTER COMPANY, *11171 Sir Francis Drake Boulevard, Point Reyes National Seashore. Open 8 A.M. to 4 P.M. Tuesday through Sunday; closed Mondays. Admission: Free. Phone: (415) 669-1149.*

HOW TO GET TO THE OYSTER COMPANY: *Follow the directions to Inverness and continue through town on Sir Francis Drake. You will see signs to Johnson's Oyster Company once you enter the Point Reyes National Seashore.*

If you're driving around West Marin and hear a very loud cow moo, don't be alarmed. That just means that it's high noon in Point Reyes Station. This lovely little town near the Point Reyes National Seashore has several claims to fame, including the local newspaper, the *Point Reyes Light*, which made headlines itself in 1979 when it won the Pulitzer Prize. The media spotlight was turned on the town again in 1985 with the unveiling of its latest claim to fame, the town clock.

Judy Borello, who runs the Old Western Saloon in town, was the driving force behind the clock. She and several other locals wanted to preserve the cow-town image of the place lest it become yet another yuppified boutique town. She organized some supporters, and with the technical help of engineers from filmmaker George Lucas's company (whose headquarters at Skywalker Ranch is close by), a mooing clock was created.

While you're waiting for the clock to moo, there are some things to do in town. On the one main street, aptly called Main Street, you can pass your time in a wide range of shops, including bookshops and art galleries. Most interesting to me is Toby's Feed Store, which caters to both farmers and weekend city visitors; I was there once when they had a sale on baby chickens, and it was a great scene.

TO GET TO POINT REYES STATION: *Follow Sir Francis Drake Boulevard—Highway 1 north from Olema. Just south of town the road crosses a small bridge and then makes a sharp turn left onto Main Street/Highway 1.*

THE POINT REYES CLOCK *is located on the sheriff's substation, which is at Fourth and C streets (nobody uses street addresses in Point Reyes Station); however, the moo comes from a speaker atop the Old Western Saloon two blocks away, on the main drag of town at Main and Second. The clock moos twice a day, at noon and at 6 in the evening. Don't worry about missing it if you're in the area; the town moo is LOUD.*

PEDALING POINT REYES

While you're in the area, an adventure you might want to try is bicycling the back roads. Head over to the only bike shop in Point Reyes Station and leave your car in town while you pedal in the overwhelming quiet, past cattle grazing on hillsides, and on dirt roads at the seashore. The terrain is fairly flat, which makes it easy to get around. It is a relaxing and invigorating trip. Bicycles are available by the hour or by the day.

POINT REYES BIKES, *1143 Highway 1 (Main Street), Point Reyes Station. Open 10 A.M. to 6 P.M. Wednesday through Monday; closed Tuesdays. Phone: (415) 663-1768. Rental fees: Weekdays, $16 for a full day, $12 for four hours; weekends, $20 a day, $12 after 1 P.M.*

MARIN MANSIONS

Back on the inland side of Marin County, San Rafael is Marin's "big city," though anywhere else it would be considered a small town. Its downtown was used, practically untouched, as the setting for George Lucas's film *American Graffiti*. Though San Rafael does resemble Modesto, circa 1962, or a typical small town in the Midwest, it is the county seat and the place where many people go to shop.

But just two blocks above the downtown area you can be transported into another era. You see, after the Gold Rush, San Rafael became a fashionable town, with ritzy resort hotels and "good" neighborhoods where bankers, railroad barons, and others who struck it rich built elegant homes. Thirteen historic buildings have been restored in this neighborhood, which makes for a nice walking tour.

You can begin at Falkirk, the centerpiece of the neighborhood. Located on Mission Avenue between E and D streets, Falkirk is a gorgeous Queen Anne–style home that belongs to the citizens of San Rafael. Several years ago some developers tried to tear it down to put up condominiums; San Rafaelians rallied around the house and turned the 17-room historic mansion into a community cultural center.

Built in 1888, Falkirk is the former residence of shipping magnate Robert Dollar. Today the elegant parlor where the Dollars would entertain their guests is a community room, available for meetings, lectures, and weddings. The mansion also has three contemporary art galleries, open to the public during regular business hours. Throughout the house, the ornate wood paneling, elegant chandeliers and stained glass transport you back into an era of refinement and elegance.

Continuing east on Mission Avenue, you will see Maple Lawn, a Gothic-to-the-max mansion that is not open to the public but is nonetheless wonderful to gawk at. It was built in 1873 by two brothers who made a killing in the Comstock lode. Today it is an Elk's Club lodge.

Next door to Maple Lawn is the Gate House, a guest house the brothers built for their dear old dad. Today it is the home of the Marin Historical Museum. Here you can find on display the items that defined the Victorian era: gloves, high-button shoes, satin gowns, and stiff collars. You can also pick up a map that will lead you to the other points of interest on your walking tour.

FALKIRK COMMUNITY CULTURAL CENTER, *1408 Mission Avenue, San Rafael. Open 11 A.M. to 4 P.M. Monday through Friday, 10 A.M. to noon Saturdays. Admission: Free. Phone: (415) 485-3328. Wheelchair accessible.*

MARIN HISTORICAL MUSEUM, *1125 B Street (at Mission), San Rafael. Open 1 to 4 P.M. Wednesday, Saturday, and Sunday. Admission: Free. Phone: (415) 454-8538. The Marin Heritage Group sponsors docent-led walking tours of Marin's mansions. Call the Historical Museum for current information.*

HOW TO FIND MARIN'S MANSIONS: *From San Francisco, take the Golden Gate Bridge to Route 101 North to the Central San Rafael exit. Turn left on Fourth Street for a look at San Rafael's American Graffiti street, then turn right on E Street to Mission Street. Park on the street and begin your walking tour at Falkirk.*

One of the most remarkable structures in Marin County is visible from the freeway. Heading north on Highway 101, on your right you will see the blue-tiled roof of the Marin Civic Center, a long, low, graceful building designed by Frank Lloyd Wright; as a matter of fact, it was his last major project before his death in 1959. It is a prime example of the architect's visionary obsession with circles, half circles, and shapes attempting to become circles.

Inside, the civic center itself is the nerve center for the county; it houses the main branch of the library, a post office, the jail, and the courthouse where, in 1970, a famous shoot-out involving San Quentin inmates and smuggled guns took place; in 1985, fugitive attorney Stephen Bingham was tried here. Making your way around inside is a bit like Alice's adventures in Wonderland, so you might want to try to join a tour group; but if you would enjoy the challenge of finding your own way around, be forewarned that some sections of the building have three floors, others have four.

It is an amazing architectural feat. Exotic tropical and subtropical plants grow in many of the balconylike hallways, which are illuminated by skylights. Architecture buffs might be interested in seeing Wright's original model, on display on the ground floor. You might want to visit the cafeteria, which is open to the public and has pretty good food (one of my viewers wrote recently to say he and his wife enjoy having a cup of coffee there); the cafeteria opens up to an outside patio with a fountain. Outside the fourth floor on the south side of the building is a hillside garden of pine trees, geraniums, and succulents.

The back-roads traveler will also find the civic center worth a visit because the grounds are so special. The Marin Civic Center sits on 140 acres that include a landscaped lagoon complete with ducks and a hill with a panoramic view all the way to the Bay. You can walk around anytime and feel well removed from the hustle and bustle of the freeway. The annual county fair is held on the grounds each July.

Better yet, the farmer's market is held here twice a week. This is where the farmers of Marin and neighboring counties come to sell their produce directly to consumers. Not only can you buy tomatoes, carrots, and apples, but you will find rows and rows of vegetables you've never seen in your life: nopales, Lady Godiva squash (the ones with naked seeds), bok choy, 12 kinds of lettuce, 4 zillion kinds of peppers—all presented by the person who grew it. The food reflects the multicultural population of California. Here you can get an idea of what real California cuisine is all about.

MARIN COUNTY CIVIC CENTER, *San Rafael. Open 8 A.M. to 5 P.M. Monday through Friday; closed on legal holidays. Tours led by docents, most of whom are devotees of Frank Lloyd Wright, are available between 10 A.M. and 3:30 P.M. daily. There is no charge, and tours last about an hour. However, you must make arrangements at least three days in advance. Phone: (415) 499-7407. The tours and the civic center itself are wheelchair accessible.*

FARMER'S MARKET, *on the grounds of the Marin County Civic Center, in the parking lot of the Marin Civic Center Auditorium (also designed by Wright). Held from 9 A.M. to 1 P.M. Thursday and Sunday. Admission: Free. Phone: (415) 492-0122.*

HOW TO GET TO THE MARIN CIVIC CENTER: *From San Francisco, take the Golden Gate Bridge to Highway 101 North. Follow 101 past the main San Rafael exits and then turn right at the San Pedro Road exit. The civic center will be in full view, and there are signs directing you to the parking lot.*

CHINA CAMP (17)

At one time the Northern California coast was dotted with Chinese fishing villages. Like many fortune-seekers, the Chinese had come here for the Gold Rush in the mid-1800s. Unfortunately, many arrived too late and had to find something to do to make a living. Many of these immigrants were from the area around Canton, where they had fished the waters of the Yangtze and Pearl rivers for shrimp. After importing nets from the old country, these fishermen and their families set up 30 villages around the bays of San Francisco, where shrimp flourished.

Their business flourished, too, much to the dismay of American fishermen, who pressured legislators to pass discriminatory laws designed to end the Chinese fishing boom. By 1910 many Chinese had returned to their homeland or become absorbed into nearby cities. One by one, the villages faded away.

Today, only one of these fishing villages remains. It is the main attraction in China Camp State Park. The State Park Service acquired the land in 1977 and has restored many of the buildings and piers and has set up a small museum that tells the sad history of the Chinese and their camps.

According to the 1880 census, China Camp was the largest of all the fishing villages in the Bay Area, with a population of 500 residents. Today China Camp has only one resident, Frank Quan. His grandfather had been a storekeeper in the village in 1890; his father and uncle found a way to fish legally and started the shrimp business that Frank now operates. Every day, Frank is up before the crack of dawn, pulls shrimp out of the bay, then cooks them in huge vats by boiling them in very salty water, according to methods handed down from his father. He also operates a snack bar on weekends where you can taste what really fresh shrimp is like.

The Chinese fishing village is only one section of the 1500-acre state park. Other activities include hiking and picnicking; campers can walk to the primitive campground area and stay for $6 a night (no trailers or RV amenities, though).

CHINA CAMP MUSEUM AND STATE PARK, *San Rafael. Park is open sunrise to sunset daily. Admission: Free. The Chinese fishing village opens at 8 A.M. daily and closes at 5 P.M. November through March, 6 P.M. April and May, and 7 P.M. June through September. The museum is open most weekends year round, and rangers can arrange tours with advance notice. Phone: (415) 456-0766 or (415) 456-1286.*

HOW TO GET TO CHINA CAMP: *From San Francisco, take the Golden Gate Bridge and follow Highway 101 to the San Pedro Road exit. You will see the Marin Civic Center on your right at the exit. Go on San Pedro Road approximately 3 miles and you will enter China Camp State Park. Continue on the main road until you reach the fishing village.*

NOVATO HISTORY MUSEUM

The little town of Novato is fast becoming a bedroom community. During rush hours the freeway is jammed with Novatans going to and from work on the other side of the Golden Gate Bridge. The town joke is that Novato is a very safe place because so many San Francisco policemen live here.

But long before Novato served the housing needs of San Francisco, it had its own long and colorful history. After the Gold Rush, Novato became an authentic frontier town. Americans and European immigrants settled in the area and built stores, hotels, and saloons. They raised chickens and beef and dairy cattle. The climate was perfect for growing pears, cherries, and apricots; soon the world's largest apple orchard was growing in Novato. The timber industry supplied oak and laurel for the elegant Victorian homes in San Francisco.

Today several historic buildings have been put to good use by the community. City Hall is the town's original Presbyterian church (located at the intersection of De Long and Sherman avenues); the interior has been remodeled for office space, though several pews are available for sitting in a foyer. The exterior is painted red with white trim. Nearby, the church parsonage is now occupied by the city finance department.

Across the street from City Hall, at 807 De Long Avenue, is the Novato Chamber of Commerce, located in a Queen Anne–style cottage built in 1905, with additional offices built into a three-story water tank next to the house; here you can pick up a colorful brochure explaining other points of interest in town.

And next door to the C of C is the Novato History Museum, where you can really get a sense of what life has been like in this community over the years. The Novato History Museum is set up in the oldest house in town, built in 1850 for the town's first postmaster, who was murdered outside in the horse trough. The museum opened in 1976 as a temporary exhibit; but when the old-timers assembled their personal collections of memorabilia, they realized they were on to something too good to let pass.

Today the place is stocked like an antique store. Along with photographs depicting life through the decades there are the antique tools and artifacts, from branding irons to the old school bell. There are only a few rooms to visit, so you won't need to spend more than an hour.

But the best thing about a visit is the chance to chat with Jacqueline Moore, a lovely lady who looks and talks like everybody's favorite schoolteacher. She takes her role of curator seriously and breathes life into the exhibits of old photos and mementos of the days when Novato was a Wild West town.

If you happen to visit the museum with fidgety youngsters, just ask Ms. Moore to tell them the story about the postmaster's mysterious demise. She'll keep them entertained.

THE NOVATO HISTORY MUSEUM, *815 De Long Avenue, Novato. Open 10 A.M. to 4 P.M. Thursdays and Saturdays; groups admitted by appointment Monday through Saturday. Admission: Free. Phone: (415) 897-4320.*

HOW TO GET TO NOVATO: *From San Francisco, take the Golden Gate Bridge to Highway 101 and continue north past the city of San Rafael. Take the De Long exit and you will come to the museum before you reach the center of town.*

MIWOK MUSEUM

Before there was a hot tub or BMW in Marin, the area had its own definite lifestyle, one that bore little resemblance to the way the present inhabitants live in this beautiful country.

For centuries, Marin was the land of the coastal Miwok Indians, and the museum dedicated to their existence—past and present—is a must-see for all of the county's public school children; the local school board mandates that all its students be brought here as part of the curriculum.

But don't assume that this is just a place for kids. This tiny museum, tucked into the outskirts of Novato, is a real find for people of all ages.

Several things make this place special. First, the story of the Miwoks and how they lived is amazing. Their ability to live in harmony with nature and to live off the bounty of the earth is inspiring; they ground acorns for flour, tied strands of tule (an abundant type of bulrush) to make boats, and made coats for the chilly Marin nights out of rabbit pelts. The museum features hands-on displays where you can perform traditional activities with acorns, shells, stones, and antlers, play a game of chance—sort of a Miwok version of pick-up-sticks—and even ride in a boat made from tule.

Second, since it is a small museum with a very interested staff, you are almost guaranteed a personal guide as you wander through the small but well-presented exhibits. Program director Marilyn Englander took me through; holder of a Ph.D. in Native American studies, she regaled me with interesting stories, and I left feeling connected to the history of the area in a way I never had before.

Finally, the museum is important because it emphasizes that this is not a lost culture. To the contrary, you'll learn that many Miwoks still live in Marin and that they have an active role in setting up the exhibits.

MARIN MUSEUM OF THE AMERICAN INDIAN, *2200 Novato Boulevard, Novato. Open 10 A.M. to 4 P.M. Tuesday through Saturday, noon to 4 P.M. Sunday; closed in December. Admission: Free. Phone: (415) 897-4064.*

HOW TO GET TO THE MUSEUM OF THE AMERICAN INDIAN: *From San Francisco, follow the directions to the Novato History Museum. On De Long, continue west until you come to Novato Boulevard. Turn right and follow the road to the Miwok Park and Museum.*

MARIN FRENCH CHEESE COMPANY

From the Miwok Museum, if you take Novato Boulevard out of town, you will find yourself on one of the most beautiful roads in Marin. This is an area of rolling hills and lush dairy farms, very green most of the year, brown in the summer.

Just 9 miles south of Petaluma, at the junction of Novato Boulevard and the Point Reyes–Petaluma Road, you will be at a good place to stop for a picnic or a little bite to take on the road: the showroom and factory of the Marin French Cheese Company. You have probably seen or tasted their product, sold in stores all over the country under the brand name Rouge et Noir.

A French cheese company in Marin? It surprised me, especially since there are so few French people in the area. As it turns out, the Gold Rush attracted a contingent from France. They failed to strike it rich in the mother lode and eventually settled in these hills because they were reminded of Normandy. Louis Cantel started making camembert in his small dairy in Petaluma (believed to be the first to manufacture this soft-ripening cheese in the United States). In 1865 his neighbors, the Thompson family, started their own cheese factory, now operated by the fourth generation of cheese-making Thompsons.

In addition to camembert, three other types of cheeses are produced here: Brie, Schloss (sort of a pungent cross between Limburger and camembert), and "breakfast cheese," a buttery, soft white cheese to be sliced thin on toast or cut into cubes for salads.

When I went on a tour of the plant, I expected to see vats of boiling cheeses. Instead I saw a succession of spotless chilled rooms. As it turns out, these cheeses are not cooked; the process involves small round molds of cheese being turned and aged until ready to eat.

The tours are offered every day, ending with the opportunity to sample each kind of cheese. There is also a large retail outlet where you can purchase sandwiches, wine, fruit drinks, and more cheese for a picnic.

How does the Marin cheese compare to its European counterpart? Well, the Thompsons say theirs is better than the imported brands because it's not loaded with preservatives to ensure a longer travel and shelf life. They welcome comparisons by visitors familiar with the competition from abroad.

MARIN FRENCH CHEESE COMPANY, *7500 Point Reyes–Petaluma Road, Petaluma. Salesroom open 9 A.M. to 5 P.M. daily, though closed on some holidays; tours available 10 A.M. to 4 P.M. daily, closed on some holidays. Admission: Free. Phone: (707) 762-6001.*

HOW TO GET HERE: *From Novato, follow Novato Boulevard to the intersection of Point Reyes–Petaluma Road. From San Francisco, take the Golden Gate Bridge to Highway 101 North. Exit on Lucas Valley Road to Nicasio Valley Road. Turn right to the Point Reyes–Petaluma Road. Turn right and follow to the Cheese Company. This is a very scenic drive.*

CHAPTER 2 Sonoma County

AREA OVERVIEW Sonoma County is directly north of Marin, bordered on the east by Napa County and on the west by the Pacific Ocean. The nearest destinations to San Francisco, such as Petaluma, can be reached in less than an hour from the Golden Gate Bridge; some of the more distant stops, such as Fort Ross, require about a two-hour drive. As in Marin, Highway 101 provides the most direct inland route, and Route 1 takes you along the coast.

Sonoma is one of the best-kept secrets of the Bay Area. While next-door neighbor Napa draws visitors from around the world to its famous wine country, Sonoma goes about its quieter, less chic ways. There are just as many wineries in Sonoma as in Napa; they're just more spread out in Sonoma. In fact, there is probably a little bit more of just about everything in this large and scenic county, including ocean beaches, mountains, parks, resorts, farms, and boomtowns.

Santa Rosa, a solid hour's drive from San Francisco, is the major city; the towns of Sonoma, Petaluma, Sebastopol, and Occidental highlight unique facets of Sonoma life.

In almost any town, you can stop off at the local Chamber of Commerce or visitor's center to pick up a Sonoma Farm Trails map. This is a list of the farms

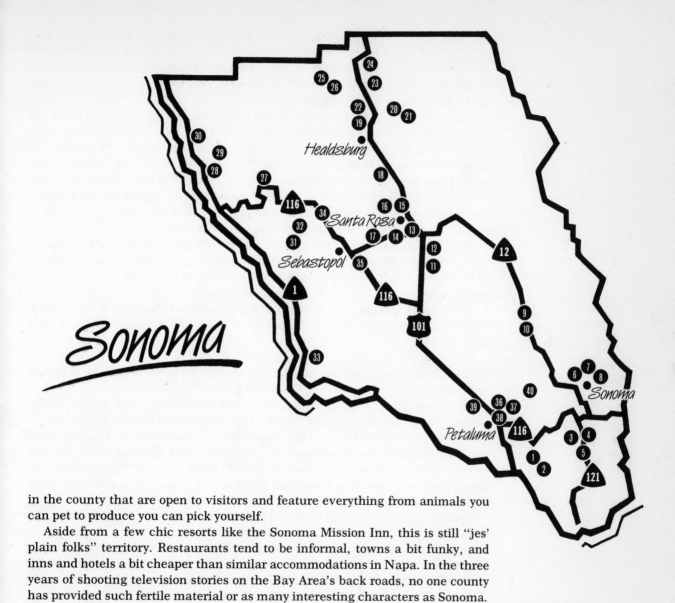

Sonoma

in the county that are open to visitors and feature everything from animals you can pet to produce you can pick yourself.

Aside from a few chic resorts like the Sonoma Mission Inn, this is still "jes' plain folks" territory. Restaurants tend to be informal, towns a bit funky, and inns and hotels a bit cheaper than similar accommodations in Napa. In the three years of shooting television stories on the Bay Area's back roads, no one county has provided such fertile material or as many interesting characters as Sonoma.

Not far from the town of Petaluma on the Lakeville Highway, you come to a place that defies description. The sign out front says "Gilardi's," but the owner is quick to tell you that's not the name of the joint. Another sign promises great beer and, get this, "weird" food.

PHYLLIS'S WEIRD FOOD

If you are not yet intrigued, wait until you are greeted by a friendly woman dressed in a warm-up suit and running shoes, talking to you as though you just returned after stepping out for an errand. This is Phyllis, and you are instantly welcome at her Lakeville Marina. It is a restaurant, bar, social club, athletic field, and home for wayward travelers.

You'll probably be invited to sit on the porch to watch the Petaluma River roll by out back. There is a real marina where lots of boat folks—as opposed to yacht people—stop by. Even more signs are there to inform you of the distance to places like Calais, Istanbul, and other points on the globe not served by the mighty Petaluma. If that's not enough to keep you entertained, check out Phyllis's seashell collection or the basketball court. Phyllis says basketball legend Hank Luisetti taught her hoops (in case you were born after the 1950s, Luisetti was the Stanford great who invented the one-handed shot).

After you get to know Phyllis, step inside and try her food. She calls it "weird" because, as she puts it, "It's not plastic, and today people think that's strange." The menu depends on her mood. A typical day might feature tripe, spanikopita, pork in green sauce, and "burgers for my rednecks," she says affectionately.

All cultures and age groups mix well here, under the guidance of our hostess. There's even a kids' corner with toys for the tots and a player piano for their parents.

The food, by the way, is very tasty and inexpensive. The Lakeville Marina is open daily for lunch and dinner. Sundays feature jazz concerts by local groups with occasional visits from San Francisco greats like Stan Getz.

One other point is worth mentioning: Even though the place is a bit funky, the rest rooms are immaculate. Phyllis says she learned how important it is to keep the facilities spiffy when she was a market researcher working for an oil company. Most of the respondents to a question about why customers chose to buy gas at her client's stations said it was because of the clean rest rooms. She swore then and there that if she ever had her own place, she would have great bathrooms.

LAKEVILLE MARINA, *588 Lakeville Highway, Petaluma. Open 9 A.M. to 9 P.M. daily. Phone: (707) 762-4900. Wheelchair accessible.*

HOW TO GET TO THE LAKEVILLE MARINA: *From San Francisco, take the Golden Gate Bridge to Route 101 North. Take 101 to Route 37, which is also marked as the turnoff to Vallejo and Napa. Follow 37 east a few miles until you come to the Lakeville Highway. Turn left and after a few miles, watch on the left for the sign that says "Gilardi's."*

Just down the road from Phyllis's is a place that looks perfectly normal from the entrance, with a wooden arch over the road announcing "Winner's Circle Ranch." In fact, as you take the long drive up to the stables and main buildings, everything looks typical—until you see the horses.

They are midgets.

Actually, they are a special breed of miniature horse, with a blue-blood lineage that dates back 400 years to the royal stables of merry old England. Not much bigger than a good-sized dog, these horses were bred for the royal children to ride; soon the French caught on and started breeding them for their aristocracy. Not only were they small, but they were a docile, affectionate breed that was easy to train.

These are advantages even today. Barbara Norman, who runs Winner's Circle Ranch, points out another advantage: They eat more like a bird than a horse (in other words, they eat less than a normal-size horse—very economical). Barbara breeds these miniatures to sell as pets or as show horses.

The ranch is a good place to visit if for no other reason than the rare opportunity to look down on a fully grown horse. They even put on a show for you. The trainers will put their diminutive steeds through a variety of exercises and runs, including pulling a carriage around a large track. On weekends, carriage rides are available for the kids, and at all times there are picnic tables and a snack bar.

Oh, yes, there are souvenirs, too, the most popular item being bags of powdered miniature horse manure, which Barbara says is great for fertilizing houseplants.

WINNER'S CIRCLE RANCH, *5911 Lakeville Road, Petaluma. Open June through October, Wednesday through Sunday from 10 A.M. to 4 P.M.; shows are at 11 A.M. and 2 P.M. Admission: $5 for adults and children over 12, $3 for children 3 to 12, $3 for senior citizens; groups of 10 or more get a discounted price. Phone: (707) 762-1808. Wheelchair accessible.*

TO GET TO WINNER'S CIRCLE RANCH: *From San Francisco, follow the directions to the Lakeville Marina, but look on your right on Lakeville Highway for the entrance to the ranch. It's well marked with an archway. If you reach the Lakeville Marina, you've gone too far. Don't worry. Phyllis can send you back to the right place.*

This is the first winery we come to in this book, so let's celebrate with champagne. Gloria Ferrer is one of the newest wineries in Sonoma Valley, though the Ferrer family has been making wine in Spain since the twelfth century. The family owns the company that makes Freixenet (pronounced "fresh-a-net"), the champagne that comes in the black bottle, and is one of the largest producers of wine made by the *méthode champenoise*, the time-honored way champagne is made in its namesake region in France.

With so many wineries in the Bay Area, I try to find places that offer something unique. Gloria Ferrer Champagne Caves fills the bill in several ways. First of all, it is the first Spanish winery in the area since the Mission days. But even more important is the tour, which includes the opportunity to see the unusual caves wedged in the mountainside and a collection of antique winemaking tools on display. This machinery, used 100 years ago, was 20 times slower than the modern operation you see today, yet the actual process of making the champagne remains much the same.

The winery building is an elegant structure, designed to create the feeling of Barcelona. Flags of California and Catalonia fly out front. The facility, which opened in September 1986, sits on 250 acres planted with several sparkling wine varieties, including Pinot Noir and chardonnay.

The wine produced here is Gloria Ferrer Brut, named for the wife of Freixenet president José Ferrer (not the one who played Cyrano). Keeping in the tradition of honoring women, the little old winemaker on the premises is Eileen Crane, formerly of Domaine Chandon.

Tours are free, but to sample the wine it will cost $2.50 for a full flute of Brut and some snacks. Then you can relax and enjoy it in their Sala de Catadores or on a patio overlooking the hills of Sonoma.

GLORIA FERRER CHAMPAGNE CAVES, *23555 Highway 121, Sonoma. Open 10:30 A.M. to 5:30 P.M. daily; last guided tour begins at 4:30 P.M. Admission: Free. Phone: (707) 996-7256.*

HOW TO GET HERE: *From San Francisco, take the Golden Gate Bridge to Highway 101 and follow it north to Route 37. Turn right on Route 37 to Route 121. Turn left and head north on Route 121 approximately 5 miles. The entrance is well marked, on the left of the road.*

WORLD OF EXOTIC BIRDS
④

It's one of those nondescript places I've driven by dozens of times, so nondescript I eventually had to check it out. What you see from the road is just an average one-story building with a parking lot and a sign with the slogan "Our business is for the birds." Inside, you are suddenly overwhelmed by the sight and sound of hundreds of birds of every size, shape, and color.

Even if you have little interest in feathered fauna, it's worth a visit to meet owner Pat Barbera. The license plate on her car is "BIRD MA." Sure enough, Pat hatched most of the gang you will find here, and she stays up all night with them when they are sick, feeding them with eyedroppers. If you play your cards right, she'll talk with them while carrying on a clear and concise conversation with you at the same time.

Let me make it clear that Pat takes no guff from her brood. While telling me how friendly and harmless a favorite parrot of hers is, the bird kept chewing on her sleeve. She simply looked the bird in the eye and warned, "Parrot soup, parrot soup . . ." The bird behaved.

Save some time for a visit here. There are so many birds to see and Pat has so many stories you'll want to hang around for a while. Be sure to go into the back room to see the prize macaws with spectacular plumage. There is also a pond with swans (also for sale), and out back on the 10 acres that surround the place, you'll see a herd of llamas (also for sale).

The birds come in all sizes, colors, and prices—from $22 to $9000. If that sounds like a lot of dough for one pet, just remember: it will probably outlive you and me.

WORLD OF EXOTIC BIRDS, *23570 Highway 121, Sonoma. Open 10 A.M. to 5 P.M. daily. Admission: Free. Phone: (707) 996-1477.*

TO GET TO THE WORLD OF EXOTIC BIRDS: *From San Francisco, follow the directions to the Gloria Ferrer Champagne Caves, but enter on the right almost directly opposite the winery.*

AIRBORNE ANTIQUES

If you get no kick from champagne or birds, you might want to stop down the road from the World of Exotic Birds at the Schellville Airport. The place is like a museum of aircraft; at least 150 antique planes—all of them still in use—are parked here by their owners. The skies in this area are to pilots what back roads are to drivers, so removed from populated areas that pilots can simply take off when they feel like it, soar in peace, and enjoy the wild blue yonder unencumbered by control towers, clearances, and radios—just like the good old days when planes were new.

If you're feeling adventurous, Christopher Prevost will take you up in a 1941 biplane. Christopher runs the flying service at Schellville Airport and is an interesting story on his own. He fell in love with antique planes on his fourteenth birthday when his mother bought him a ride in one. Now in his twenties, Christopher repairs and services vintage aircraft and does stunt flying for movies and television as well as for his own enjoyment. For $60 he'll take you up for a 20-minute ride. You have a choice of two kinds of rides: scenic or acrobatic. The scenic ride offers a unique and splendid view of the Sonoma Valley. The acrobatic ride makes every roller coaster in the world look tame. People less faint-hearted than I seem to love it, and weekends can get pretty busy.

But even if flying too high with some guy in the sky is your idea of nothing to do, the airport is worth a quick visit, just to see the planes. (My apologies to Cole Porter.)

SCHELLVILLE AIRPORT, *23982 Highway 121, Sonoma. Open during daylight hours every day, all year. The plane rides can be tailored to your spirit of adven-*

ture, with a little bit of air acrobatics, lots of air acrobatics, or none at all. The cost is $60 per person for 20 minutes. Phone: (707) 938-2444.

HOW TO GET TO THE SCHELLVILLE AIRPORT: From San Francisco, follow the directions for Gloria Ferrer Champagne Caves. The airport is across the street from the winery and just down the road from the World of Exotic Birds.

HISTORIC SONOMA PLAZA
⑥

One of the most intriguing figures in California history is General Mariano Guadalupe Vallejo. A gentleman, a scholar, and an entrepreneur, Vallejo was born in Monterey in 1807 and became an influential statesman. When Alta (Northern) California was under the rule of Mexico, he was put in charge of San Francisco's Presidio, with civil power that extended north to Sonoma.

A mission was established in Sonoma in 1823; Vallejo was not far behind with a garrison and plans to build himself a lovely home. The Sonoma Plaza was where all the action was: the Mission San Francisco Solano de Sonoma; barracks for the soldiers; a hotel called the Blue Wing Inn, owned and operated by Vallejo (and visited by such nineteenth-century superstars as Kit Carson, U. S. Grant, and William T. Sherman); and La Casa Grande, Vallejo's home.

In June 1846 the Plaza was the site of the famous Bear Flag Revolt. Rebellious settlers captured General Vallejo in his Casa Grande (the legend is that he took this intrusion in stride and offered them Cognac); then they hoisted the flag of the new Bear Republic above the Plaza as a declaration of independence from Mexico.

California remained an independent nation for only a few months before joining the United States, living happily ever after as a state. Meanwhile, Vallejo continued to enjoy a long and prosperous life. He bought an estate just a few blocks from the Plaza and built a home that looked like a place you'd find on Cape Cod, with a steep-pitched roof, ornamental eaves, and dormer windows. He lived there with his wife and 10 of their 16 children until his death in 1890.

Today a visit to the Sonoma Plaza and General Vallejo's estate is a wonderful way to spend the day. The Plaza itself is a grassy park with shade trees and picnic tables. It's also the largest town plaza in the state. It is bordered by wonderful places to buy picnic supplies and historic settings that include the mission, the Blue Wing Inn, and the monument where the rebellious settlers raised the Bear Flag.

One ticket is good for admission to the Sonoma Mission and three surviving creations of Vallejo: the Sonoma Barracks, what's left of Casa Grande (most of it was destroyed in a fire), and Lachryma Montis, General Vallejo's bucolic retirement estate.

This estate was 20 acres that came with an abundant water supply and an Indian legend about a jilted princess who cried so long and hard that her tears created the springs of water. Always the scholar, Vallejo gave his estate a Latin name, Lachryma Montis, "Tear of the Mountain." Always the entrepreneur, Vallejo sold his water to the city of Sonoma; in fact, he owned all the water rights to the area. From this estate he would send the townspeople their H_2O via redwood pipes.

Today the Sonoma State Historic Park Commission and the Sonoma Water Works bottle the water from Vallejo's springs and sell it on the premises under the Lachryma Montis label. The sale of this spring water provides revenue for restoration of Vallejo's home.

Visitors can go inside the Atlantic seaboard–style dwelling, complete with the furnishings, antiques, and clothing used by the Vallejo family; in fact, were it not for the iron railings that bar entry into the rooms, you might believe that the family still lives here. On the grounds is a Swiss chalet–style building that was used for storing olives, wine, and produce and is now a museum of General Vallejo's history.

But the grounds are the best part of the visit. Vallejo was fond of flowers—he was a member of the state's first horticultural board—so today you can walk and picnic in a lovely garden that is no doubt watered by the tears of the mountain.

LACHRYMA MONTIS, SONOMA. *Open 10 A.M. to 5 P.M. daily; closed Thanksgiving, Christmas, and New Year's Day. Admission: 50 cents for adults, 25 cents for children, ticket also good for admission to the Sonoma Mission, Sonoma Barracks, and La Casa Grande in Sonoma Plaza. Tickets for sale at the Sonoma Mission, Spain Street at First Street East. For information, call the Sonoma Park and Recreation Department: (707) 938-1519.*

HOW TO GET TO SONOMA: *From San Francisco, take the Golden Gate Bridge to 101 North. Exit at Route 37 and bear to the right (east). Follow Route 37 to Highway 121. Turn left on Route 12, and continue to the town of Sonoma.*

HOW TO GET TO LACHRYMA MONTIS: *From Sonoma Plaza, head west on Spain Street until you get to Third Street West. Turn right and continue about a half mile. Signs will direct you into the parking lot.*

CALIFORNIA'S OLDEST WINERY

If you glance at the names of most of the wineries in the Sonoma and Napa valleys, you would logically assume it was the Italians or the French who started this booming industry in Northern California. But would you believe it was actually a Hungarian?

Colonel Agoston Haraszthy is credited as the "father of California viticulture." It says so on a plaque in downtown Sonoma. Haraszthy, a career diplomat, migrated from Hungary in 1840 and had a colorful career before arriving in Sonoma, where he founded the Buena Vista Winery. Arriving with grapevines from the old country, Haraszthy first founded a settlement in Wisconsin; his crop did not fare well there, so he moved on to the sunnier climes of San Diego, where he was elected county sheriff and became a member of the state legislature.

Then in 1857 the colonel moved north and planted the first large vineyard in Northern California. The crop thrived, and the rest is history.

Today California's oldest premium winery is owned and run by one of the youngest teams in the Sonoma Valley. The owners and their winemaker are barely in their thirties. The winery and the surrounding grounds are beautiful, with an ivy-covered, cavelike tasting room and plenty of outdoor tables for picnicking. Even though it's just a few minutes from Sonoma Plaza, there is a feeling here of being miles away, in gorgeous country.

By the way, the colonel's colorful history did not stop with the founding of the Northern California wine industry. After both his sons married daughters of General Vallejo, the elder Haraszthy moved to Nicaragua and became a successful sugar manufacturer. According to legend, he died attempting to cross a stream near his plantation; the alligators left not a trace.

BUENA VISTA WINERY, *18000 Old Winery Road, Sonoma. Open 10 A.M. to 5 P.M. daily; tours around the historic cellars are self-guided. Admission: Free. Phone: (707) 938-1266.*

HOW TO GET TO BUENA VISTA: *From San Francisco, follow the directions to Sonoma Plaza. At the plaza, turn right onto East Napa Street and continue until you come to Old Winery Road. Turn left and follow the signs to Buena Vista.*

CALIFORNIA'S UNPRONOUNCEABLE WINERY ⑧

Another of the oldest wineries in the Sonoma Valley is also one of the hardest to pronounce. For me, the fact that Jim Bundschu has resisted all temptation to change the name and make life easier for everyone makes the place worth a visit. But even better, I find Gundlach-Bundschu a very pleasant stop.

Jim is the young, personable boss of the operation. He is a member of the fifth generation of Bundschus to operate the vineyard at this very location. His ancestor, Charles Bundschu (pronounced "bund-shoe") came from Bavaria with his friend Jacob Gundlach (pronounced "goond-lock") to strike it rich in the California Gold Rush. However, they arrived in 1856, a bit too late. Like the Chinese and French in Marin, they decided to stay and do what they knew best. They found a spot in Sonoma that reminded them of the Bavarian hills and began making wine.

If this is what Bavaria looks like, I'm going there soon. The winery overlooks a small lake, with rolling hills in every direction. After you park your car, you walk down a lovely flower-lined stone path to a stone-and-wood building that houses the winery. It's a small operation, much smaller than its neighbor, Buena Vista. One look inside will reveal the tasting room to the left, the storage barrels to the rear. It's not uncommon to find Jim's wife and daughter labeling bottles in the corner.

Everything is informal and folksy. Outside the winery building is a shaded picnic table, plus more secluded picnic areas up on the vine-covered hillside.

The tasting room has a big drain in the middle of the floor. Jim encourages visitors to taste the wine and then spit it out into the drain. Like many other winemakers, he is concerned about tourists overindulging on winery tours by trying to take in too many wineries in one day. His advice: Stay in the area for a few days, take time to see other attractions the area has to offer, and visit only a few wineries each day. When tasting, avoid swallowing. Look for a dump bucket or drain, and don't worry about not appearing chic or elegant. Highway patrol officers are out there waiting.

GUNDLACH-BUNDSCHU, *2000 Denmark Road, Sonoma. Open 11 A.M. to 4:30 P.M. daily; closed on major holidays. Admission: Free. Large groups should call in advance. Phone: (707) 938-5277.*

HOW TO GET TO GUNDLACH-BUNDSCHU: *From San Francisco, take the Golden Gate Bridge to 101 North. Exit at Route 37 and bear to the right (east). Follow Highway 37 to Highway 121. Turn left on Route 12 and continue to the town of Sonoma. At the town plaza, turn right on East Napa Street. Turn left at Eighth Street and go 1 mile. Turn left on Denmark Road and follow for about a mile to the winery.*

JACK LONDON STATE PARK ⑨

Once upon a time—at the turn of the twentieth century, to be exact—Glen Ellen was *the* place to bring your family for the summer. Two railways chugged into town, bringing fashionable people from all over the Bay Area to the lovely hotels, quaint cabins, and lively saloons.

One summer, Jack London, "America's first millionaire author," came up from Oakland and decided to stay. He started buying parcels of land, eventually totaling 1400 acres, that he named Beauty Ranch. Jack's dream was to build a house for himself and his wife Charmian and to create a utopian community for the ranch workers; each worker would get a parcel of land to call his own, and there would be a school on the property, so each ranch child would be educated.

London's dream never came true. In 1910 he started construction on Wolf House, a 26-room, four-story mansion, complete with accommodations for London's 18,000-book library. Shortly before construction was complete in 1913, a mysterious fire destroyed the house. The cause has never been determined; some say it was a tragic accident, others that arsonists destroyed the place in angry response to London's socialistic politics. Jack and Charmian spent the next few years traveling and writing; Jack died in 1916.

Fortunately for us, 49 acres of London's Beauty Ranch has been preserved as a state historic park. It is one of the loveliest and most accessible parks in the Bay Area, complete with a hilltop lake, riding stables, and picnic tables. There are beautiful nature trails, ranging from a difficult 3.3-mile trek up to the summit of Mount Sonoma to the easy 1-mile stroll on a path through the woods, which can take you to the ruins of Wolf House.

I recommend that you begin your visit to Jack London State Park at Wolf House. The foundations are still intact, and diagrams show the construction plans; you can see the grandeur of the plan and the kind of life the writer had in mind for himself. Enough of a structure remains to give you an idea of the layout and scope of the project. Walkways take you to second-level overlooks, which provide good views of the ill-fated dream house. Being a contemporary California homeowner, I was stunned to learn that the house cost only $80,000 to build. But then, that was 1910. . . .

On your way back, you can take a slight detour along the way to visit Jack's grave, a lovely hillside spot where you can take time to pay your respects and to admire the peaceful and untouched surroundings (may we all end up in such a spot!).

Above the parking lot where you left your car is the House of Happy Walls, the place the widowed Charmian built in honor of her late husband. The house is full of memorabilia from their global travels and contains such items of interest as Jack London's desk and files. The house is now operated by the state parks department as a museum featuring displays of original manuscripts. Upstairs, Charmian's belongings are also on display; for someone with socialist ideals living in the woods of Northern California, this lady had some fine dresses!

JACK LONDON STATE HISTORIC PARK, *Glen Ellen. Open 8 A.M. to sunset daily. Museum open 10 A.M. to 5 P.M. daily. Admission: $2 parking fee. Phone: (707) 938-5216.*

HOW TO GET HERE: *From San Francisco, take the Golden Gate Bridge to Highway 101 North. Take 101 to Route 37 East and continue to Route 121. Turn left on Route 121. Turn left on Route 12 and continue and follow it into the town of Sonoma. When you reach the plaza, turn left on West Napa Street, which is Highway 12. Continue about 6½ miles to the town of Glen Ellen and follow the signs to the park.*

JACK LONDON BOOKSTORE (10)

The sign may seem routine, but you will quickly realize that this is no ordinary bookstore. First of all, you will be greeted by Brewster the Rooster, a friendly bird that strolled into the bookstore about seven years ago and decided to stay. Nobody's bothered to tell him he's not a human (he probably wouldn't listen anyway).

Then you might see an elderly woman exploring the bookshelves. She's Becky London, the 84-year-old daughter of the author, for whom the bookstore is named. Becky lives with the remarkable couple who runs the bookstore, Russ and Winifred Kingman.

Russ Kingman has devoted his life to knowing everything about Jack London. He even has a card file, cross-indexing every single day of the writer's life between 1904, when he met his wife, Charmian, and his death in 1916. Ask King-man what London was doing on July 17, 1907, and he'll tell you.

Russ used to be an advertising man in the Bay Area. One of his accounts was a tourist attraction in Oakland called Jack London Square. While doing some research to promote the place, Russ got hooked on the subject. In 1973 he quit the advertising game and moved to Glen Ellen to run his bookstore.

But as I said before, this is no ordinary bookstore. It is also a museum dedicated to the art and life of Jack London, with research materials that attract literary scholars from all over the world. If it was written by or about Jack London, you'll find it here.

JACK LONDON BOOKSTORE, *14300 Arnold Drive, Glen Ellen. Open 11 A.M. to 5 P.M. daily. Phone: (707) 996-5288.*

TO GET HERE: *From Jack London State Park, the bookstore is about a mile and a half south on Arnold Drive.*

HIGHWAY PATROL COWS

While driving through Sonoma County, particularly in the area near Penngrove, you can get the paranoid feeling that there are highway patrol cars everywhere. Look again; what you're seeing out of the corner of your eye might be highway patrol cows.

Dick Gray breeds this unique type of cattle that look painted to Highway Patrol specifications: black at the front and rear, white in the middle. Actually, they are a crossbreed of Holstein and a kind of Dutch cow. Gray says he breeds them not for their looks but for the milk they produce.

If you would like to see a lot of Highway Patrol cows, and maybe take a snapshot for the folks back home, drive down Roberts Road off Route 101 north of Penngrove. That's the site of the main Gray farm, but the cows are also grazing in several other locations in the general Petaluma area.

CRANE MELONS (12)

Heading toward Santa Rosa on Petaluma Hill Road near Rohnert Park, you will notice that the name Crane is prominent in these parts: Crane Road, Crane Hill, Crane Farm Stand. This is the home of the Crane melon, developed by the Crane family, which has been farming this land for six generations.

Today fourth-generation George Crane is the patriarch of the family. His great-great-grandfather was a pioneer who came to Sonoma from Missouri on a wagon train in 1852; his grandfather developed the melon bearing the family name. The Cranes still live in the family house, built in 1868, with the melon patch next door, plus 80 more acres down the road.

So if it's melon season, which is mid-August through November, you ought to stop to try some of the best fruit you've ever tasted. Outside, Crane melons look like a cross between a giant cantaloupe and a honeydew. Inside, they have a soft orange flesh. Folks come from all over the Bay Area just to buy them, and they're shipped all over the world.

George says the secret is dryland farming. Other melons are irrigated, which he says reduces the flavor. The Cranes water their seeds only once, and from then on they're on their own. Apparently, it works.

At the family farm stand, the Cranes sell various items raised on their ranch, including string beans, corn, tomatoes, and a special yellow-fleshed watermelon. Years ago, a relative brought one seed of this unusual fruit from Texas; today the yellow melons of Texas thrive in Sonoma.

CRANE MELON BARN, *4947 Petaluma Hill Road, Santa Rosa. Open 10 A.M. to 6 P.M. from approximately August 10 through the week of November 15, depending on the readiness and availability of the melons. Phone: (707) 584-5141.*

HOW TO GET TO THE CRANE BARN: *From San Francisco, take the Golden Gate Bridge and follow Highway 101 North, past the Petaluma exits to the Rohnert Park exit. Turn right and go to the end of the road. Turn left on Petaluma Hill Road, and the barn will be on the left, 2½ miles down the road.*

LUTHER BURBANK'S HOUSE AND GARDENS ⑬

I remember learning about Luther Burbank in school. I knew that he was America's most famous fruit and vegetable man, inventing new plants by crossbreeding.

What I didn't realize is what a giant he was in his day. I came to appreciate this fact when I stopped at the Luther Burbank Home and Gardens in Santa Rosa. Burbank was regarded as the Henry Ford of horticulture, the Thomas Edison of the tomato. Burbank moved to Santa Rosa from Massachusetts; he thought the area offered the ideal climate for growing things.

Burbank would probably be shocked to find that Santa Rosa is now a bustling city—in fact, one of the fastest-growing in Northern California. But he'd be pleased to discover that the folks haven't forgotten their man of many roots.

Burbank arrived in Santa Rosa in 1875 and lived here for 50 years. Though the town was devastated in the famous 1906 earthquake that rocked San Francisco, his greenhouse withstood the shake. The home, however, did not and had to be rebuilt. While living in Santa Rosa, Burbank created over 800 varieties of fruits, vegetables, and flowers, including the russet potato, the Santa Rosa plum, the Shasta daisy (which took him 17 years to perfect), and the spineless cactus, which he developed with the help of his friend, writer Jack London, who was interested in producing a new kind of cattle feed.

The house itself is a modest, two-story dwelling, furnished with the belongings Burbank brought with him from back East. It is filled with photos and memorabilia that illustrate the scientist's fame. It's a warm and cozy home, nicely decorated, but hardly the mansion one would expect of someone of Burbank's standing. The greenhouse, included in the tour of the home and gardens, is where Burbank started his plantings; for larger experiments he had an 18-acre farm in Sebastopol. But the highlight of the visit is the beautiful outdoor garden, filled with the plants developed by Burbank.

LUTHER BURBANK HOME AND GARDEN CENTER, *204 Santa Rosa Avenue (at Sonoma Avenue), Santa Rosa. Gardens open 8 A.M. to 5 P.M. daily all year. Home and museum open 10 A.M. to 4 P.M. April 1 to the first week of October only. Admission to the gardens is free, but it costs $1 to visit the house. The gardens, greenhouse, and downstairs of the home are wheelchair accessible. Phone: (707) 938-8534.*

HOW TO GET HERE: *From San Francisco, take the Golden Gate Bridge to Route 101 North and continue all the way to Santa Rosa. Take the Third Street exit and follow the signs to the Burbank Home and Garden Center.*

THE CHURCH BUILT FROM ONE TREE

Believe it or not, just a few blocks from the Burbank home is a place dedicated to Santa Rosa's most famous native son, Robert Ripley. The building that houses the Robert L. Ripley Memorial Collection is itself like an item out of Ripley's famous "Believe It or Not" column: a church built entirely from just one redwood, felled in nearby Guerneville. This is the church Ripley attended as a young boy.

However, let me make it clear that this is not a "Believe It or Not"–type tourist attraction, like the kind you can find on San Francisco's Fisherman's Wharf. This museum is dedicated to the man himself: his life, his career, his writing. Ripley was an avid sports fan; he even played semipro baseball in his hometown. He was a shy man and an eccentric; for example, he owned several automobiles yet never learned to drive. He collected oddities (such as the famous fur-bearing trout).

He also liked to draw, and he started his career as a sports cartoonist for a New York paper. For his own amusement he collected odd facts about sports. The first "Believe It or Not" column came about on a slow day, when nothing very interesting was happening in the wide world of sports. To break the doldrums, Ripley drew and published a series of cartoons called "Champs and Chumps." The editor loved the cartoon but hated the name. On display in the museum is the original drawing with the title "Champs and Chumps" crossed out and replaced by the title that became famous, "Ripley's Believe It or Not."

While you're here, see if you can find curator Shirley Carter. She really knows the life of Ripley and recently completed her doctoral dissertation on the man.

THE ROBERT L. RIPLEY MEMORIAL COLLECTION, *located in the Church Built from One Tree, 492 Sonoma Avenue, Santa Rosa. Open 11 A.M. to 4 P.M. Tuesday through Saturday in June and August; 11 A.M. to 4 P.M. Wednesday through Sunday in September, October, November, March, April, and May; closed December 16 through February 28. Admission: 75 cents. Phone: (707) 576-5233.*

HOW TO GET HERE: *From the Luther Burbank Home and Gardens, cross Santa Rosa Avenue and go down Sonoma Avenue approximately one half block to the Church Built from One Tree. I recommend walking from the gardens, where there is better parking for visitors.*

PEANUTS ON ICE
⑮

If Luther Burbank and Robert Ripley were Santa Rosa's most famous citizens of the past, Charles Schulz is surely the most famous citizen of the present. In case you can't place the name, think "Peanuts." That's right, Charles Schulz is the father of Snoopy, Charlie Brown, and the rest of the gang.

Schulz is also one of America's most published creators. For nearly 40 years he's drawn the Peanuts gang for newspaper strips, books, drinking cups, sweatshirts, and the like. Schulz lives and works in Santa Rosa but spends every spare minute he can visiting the site of his true love, his Redwood Ice Arena. It must be love; the place loses a fortune every year, and the cartoonist must work like crazy just to keep the doors open.

Schulz, whose studio is located in a small cottage behind the ice arena, has his breakfast every day in the coffee shop. He also plays hockey at the rink as many nights as he can, a holdover from his childhood days in Minnesota. He bought the arena in the late 1960s, when he learned it was about to go out of business. He refurbished the place, so now it is an entertainment complex. Inside there's the ice rink and a coffee shop, which have become an unofficial community center; outside there are picnic grounds. It's one of those rare places where you can find both young and not-so-young people enjoying themselves.

Every year Schulz and skating champion Karen Kresge write the script for an ice show that is produced at the Redwood Ice Arena. According to Sparky (which is what Schulz's friends call him), this is one of the most impressive shows on ice. Not only does it attract big-time skating stars like Scott Hamilton, but the show is made more special by the intimacy of the 1000-seat theater; unlike going to a show at a giant arena, there isn't a faraway seat in the house at the Redwood.

Next door to the rink is a large gift shop, which features what I assume is everything ever made with the likenesses of the Peanuts characters: neckties, golf tees, stuffed Snoopys, and tiny Linuses. But if you're more of a historian than a shopper, go upstairs to the gallery, which is a graphic museum of Schulz's career. You can see the evolution of the characters, magazine spreads, and correspondence from some of the most famous people of our time, giving you an idea of the wide range of lives Sparky and his Peanuts gang have touched.

REDWOOD ICE ARENA, *1667 West Steele Lane, Santa Rosa, on the northwestern side of town. Hours vary each day and each season; it is best to call ahead: (707) 546-7147. The arena complex, including galleries and gift shop, is wheelchair accessible.*

HOW TO GET HERE: *From San Francisco, take the Golden Gate Bridge and continue up Route 101 North to the West Steele Lane exit, past the town of Santa Rosa. Stay in the middle and turn left off the freeway; stay in the right lane after the turn and continue past two stoplights. The road will fork; stay to the right. After you cross Range Avenue, the Redwood Ice Arena will be the third driveway on your right.*

JAPANESE GOLDFISH AND GARDENS

Just a few minutes' drive from the Redwood Ice Arena you can have another cultural experience, as far removed from the Americana of an ice arena and the Peanuts gallery as you can imagine.

Like the Redwood Ice Arena, the Kyoto Koi Garden is the fulfillment of a dream. But this time the dreamer is a burly former real estate developer named Paul Pattingale. A couple of years ago Paul bought a house, and while clearing away overgrown foliage he discovered a Japanese garden on his property. He became curious about the little bonsai trees and about the Japanese culture that created the art form. Curiosity led to obsession, and Paul opened the Kyoto Koi Garden as both a business and a place of serenity to share with others.

From the parking lot, you may think you're about to enter a plant nursery. You will see hundreds of bonsai trees, plants that are dwarfed according to the practice of an ancient Oriental art. For me, the major attraction was watching the bonsai master at work. Hiroshiko Suzuki gives demonstrations daily. He sits on a pedestal, surrounded by attentive students, and snips a branch here, binds a limb with wire there. Without the master's attention these trees would grow to be 60 to 80 feet tall; by careful shaping, pruning, and binding, the trees are allowed to grow only a foot or so high, as if all the energy of an entire tree gets packed into the beautiful miniature.

After taking your time admiring the trees, you can visit the *koi* tanks. *Koi* are orange, red, white, black, and gold fish, descendants of Japanese carp, and are as prized as the bonsai trees. They are also another of Paul's obsessions, on display in several waist-high tanks. For a quarter you can buy a handful of fish food and feed the *koi;* they will swim up and nibble from your hand. The larger and older the fish, the more it is worth; the jumbos sell for $500 to $10,000 and often live to be 200 years old.

You get to top off the visit with a stroll around the formal Japanese garden, complete with stone paths, ponds, footbridges, statuary, and dramatic waterfalls that completely mask the sound from the road just over the wall. Though the bonsai trees and the fish are for sale, there is nothing for sale in the garden. It is provided for tranquility and peace, a place of refuge from the hustle and bustle of the city, and you are invited to simply enjoy it.

KYOTO KOI AND GARDEN CENTER, *2783 Guerneville Road, Santa Rosa. Open 9 A.M. to 6 P.M. daily. Phone: (707) 575-9223.*

HOW TO GET HERE: *From San Francisco or any point north of the Golden Gate Bridge, take Route 101 to the Guerneville Road exit. Take Guerneville Road west until you come to Kyoto Koi.*

THE GOAT CHEESE REVOLUTION STARTED HERE ⑰

One of the hallmarks of California cuisine is goat cheese, and Laura Chenel is the person responsible. In the late 1970s she moved to a farm where there were several goats. She tried making some cheese, and by her own admission, it was dreadful. So Laura went to France to learn from the masters. Four years later she was back in Northern California peddling her product to a few choice restaurants. It was such a hit that not only was her cheese served at Chez Panisse and other California gourmet meccas, but these places even included her name on the menu.

Today at least seven or eight other goat cheese makers have set up shop in Northern California to keep up with the demand. But Laura was the first, and she has customers nationwide. She is also the first to take a cue from the wine industry and set up a tasting room.

An attractive, bubbly young woman who looks like she'd be just as comfortable at a chic cocktail party as she is working on the farm, Laura makes her famous cheese in a modest little building in a residential neighborhood outside Santa Rosa. From these cramped quarters, 13 varieties of Laura Chenel *chèvre* (aka goat cheese) are made. It's a fairly simple process. After the milk is pasteurized, a culture and coagulants are added. The mixture sits overnight to thicken. The next day the yogurtlike substance is ladeled into molds, some roundish, others tubelike. As the excess liquid drains out, the cheeses are turned each day by hand and individually handled until they achieve the right age and consistency. When ready, some are rolled in pepper or herbs; others are preserved in olive oil or grated like parmesan.

Unfortunately for now, the manufacturing area is too small for organized tours. But since so many people seem interested in seeing the process, Laura has plans to open a larger showplace somewhere in Sonoma. In the meantime, she has set up the informal tasting room in a little building outside the manufacturing plant where you can sample a variety of goat cheese, ask questions about the process, and purchase an attractive package or two for an afternoon picnic. Laura also does a brisk mail-order business, so you might want to add your name to her mailing list.

Be advised to call ahead for an appointment; Laura buys her milk from about a dozen goat farmers in the area and is often out on a run.

LAURA CHENEL CHÈVRE, *1550 Ridley Avenue, Santa Rosa. Phone: (707) 575-8888.*

HOW TO GET HERE: *From San Francisco or any point north of the Golden Gate Bridge, take Route 101 to the Steele Lane–Guerneville Road exit. Take Guerne-*

ville Road west approximately 1½ miles and turn left on Ridley Avenue. Continue on Ridley past Jennings Street, and turn into the driveway between the fourth and fifth houses on the left. The tasting room is in a little shack next to the main building.

JOHNSON'S EGG RANCH

Before you drive up to Johnson's Egg Ranch near the town of Windsor, you should know a few things about my taste. I am fascinated by what I call "industry on parade" images. One time in a movie theater I saw a short subject that was simply the story of how light bulbs are made. I watched how those delicate glass objects were put together by machines, then sent along a mechanized road to completion. I was fascinated.

So, imagine a similar process with eggs—thousands and thousands of eggs. Also imagine the entire operation being run by three novice farmers who moved from the city after working as a teacher, a Fuller Brush salesman, and a manager of a Sears store. Add all that up and you have what is for me a must stop.

As you enter Johnson's Egg Ranch, you go first into the processing part of the operation. What you see is a contraption that would make Rube Goldberg envious. Suction cups pick up 30 eggs at a time and move them to an area where they are scrubbed and brushed. They are then loaded, sorted, and weighed without shaking the yolk or cracking the shell (well, that is the ideal).

This operation was the result of much trial and error on the part of the Johnsons. It was designed to help solve the problem of how to get all those eggs from the hens to the stores of the Bay Area in five days, intact. Jean Jaeger, who used to be named Johnson and used to be the schoolteacher, will tell you this is only one of the challenges unforeseen by her parents (her father was the Fuller Brush salesman) and husband (from Sears) when they decided to move to the country. Jean gives tours of the operation and is happy to compare the realities of farm life to the fantasies they had when they first moved here 10 years ago. She says she likes giving tours of the place because it reminds her of the good old days of being a teacher.

Jean can also answer almost any question you might have about eggs. "How long will they keep in the refrigerator?" you might be wondering. Up to six months, says Jean, as long as they are kept at a constant cold temperature. "Any difference in taste between brown and white eggs?" None. "Which came first, . . ." Never mind.

There is more than eggs to see at Johnson's. Chickens, for example—at least 20,000 of them. A walk through the barn is an unforgettable experience in sensory overload as far as sight, sound, and smell are concerned.

There are other farm animals to be seen, including some unusual and quite affecting pygmy goats.

JOHNSON'S EGG RANCH, *259 Arata Lane, Windsor. Open 11 A.M. to 4 P.M. Mon-*

day, Tuesday, Thursday, Friday, and Saturday; closed Wednesday, Sunday, and holidays. Admission: Free. Phone: (707) 838-2429.

HOW TO GET TO JOHNSON'S EGG RANCH: *From San Francisco, take the Golden Gate Bridge to Highway 101 North to the Shiloh Road exit in Windsor, which is between Santa Rosa and Healdsburg. Exit right onto Shiloh Road and turn left at the Old Redwood Highway. Stay on Old Redwood Highway until Brooks Road, then turn right and continue to Arata Road. Turn left and look for the entrance.*

HOP KILN WINERY

Long before a bottle of wine was sold in this part of Sonoma, this was beer country. Up until World War II, hops were grown on farm after farm near Healdsburg, then sent to breweries for the production of beer. All that changed in the 1950s when a disease hit the crop and large breweries switched to rice instead of hops. This produced a lighter beer that not only sold well but was cheaper to produce. And so marked the end of the hop-growing industry in this region.

The hop farms dried up and the land was put to other use. But many of the old buildings remain. One of the most striking has been turned into a winery.

Though I had never seen a hop kiln in my life, I knew I had arrived at Hop Kiln Winery when I saw from the road three huge chimneys growing out of a barn. As I soon learned, these towers were for drying the hops. They would be hung near the top of the chimney. Inside the building, at ground level, fires would burn in huge furnaces with grates carrying the heat outside. This hot air would rise up through the hops for the drying process. It took eight hours to dry a load of hops.

The source of this information was Marty Griffin, owner and chief storyteller at Hop Kiln. He is also a practicing physician. He runs the winery as a way to unwind, though he'll be the first to tell you that the wine business is basically farming and involves hard work and long hours.

But as you will learn from visiting any small winery in California, there is something about the business that hooks people. A look at Marty's home may provide a clue. Right behind the winery is the marvelous two-story frame farmhouse where he lives, complete with a huge porch overlooking acres of vineyards and a pond filled with ducks and geese. It was built in 1873 and used to be 20 miles away; in order to move it to its present location, it had to be cut into four sections and rebuilt. It is an official Sonoma County landmark building.

The home is not open for public tours, but it is in clear sight when you visit the property, and there are public-use picnic tables in front of it (and more around the pond). The winery/hop kiln/barn, originally built in 1905, has been restored nicely and features photographs showing the old days of hop farming. Tours are self-guided, and you will see basically the same things you will see at any small winery. You will see storage tanks and bottling lines; if you happen to be there at harvest time in the fall, you will see a crush. Most people make a quick circuit and end up at the wine-tasting bar, where you can sample several of the Hop Kiln varietals. One speciality is a rare German Christmas wine called Weihnachten; try it if you like sweet wine or have the spirit of Christmas.

For your edification, you may wish to know that *The Magic of Lassie* with James Stewart, Mickey Rooney, Alice Faye, and America's favorite canine was filmed here in 1977. Stewart is said to have become quite fond of the winery's French Colombard; Lassie abstained. You may also wish to know that Westside Road, where Hop Kiln is located, is one of my favorite drives in the wine country; plan to spend several hours in the area.

HOP KILN WINERY, *6050 Westside Road, Healdsburg. Open 10 A.M. to 5 P.M. daily. Phone: (707) 433-6491.*

HOW TO GET THERE: *From San Francisco, take the Golden Gate Bridge to Route 101 North. Follow Route 101 to the town of Healdsburg and take the second exit. Make an immediate left turn onto Mill Street, which becomes Westside Road. Follow Westside Road approximately 6 miles to Hop Kiln Winery.*

LIVE FROM JOHNSON'S OF ALEXANDER VALLEY WINERY

As I said earlier in this section, with so many wineries in the area, I always try to find those that are one of a kind. The Johnsons' place certainly fits that description. As far as I know, it's the only winery in the world with a pipe organ in its tasting room.

And this is no ordinary pipe organ. Built in 1924, it was originally intended for use in a theater. It is the prize possession of the Johnson brothers, who own this small, family-run business. They owned the organ long before they went into the wine business in 1975; when they decided to open a winery, the brothers had the tasting room built around the musical instrument.

Once a month, Joan Shaffer comes from Santa Rosa and performs a Sunday matinee concert. She plays pop standards with a bounce, including a rousing rendition of "Beer Barrel Polka." Joan will also play requests and has the patter of a lounge performer. As you can imagine, the workings of such an instrument take up a lot of space, and you can get a close view of the various pipes and percussive devices in operation through glass windows in the walls.

The winery is also located in one of the least crowded valleys in Sonoma County. The Alexander Valley is said to have a climate similar to that of the Bordeaux region of France. It is quite warm in the summer and mild in the winter when it's not raining.

The winery is located in a barn with lots of antique farm equipment casually decorating the grounds. It's a small operation, so there is no organized tour; your visit here will be to enjoy the scenery, relax on the picnic grounds outside, and maybe catch an organ concert.

If your timing is right, you might have an additional treat. On one of my visits, I was entertained by a dozen playfully rambunctious basset hound puppies. You see, the Johnsons also breed bassets and sometimes display the latest litter on the winery grounds.

I should mention that there is another Alexander Valley Winery down the road. It's also a nice place to visit but not the one with the organ.

JOHNSON'S OF ALEXANDER VALLEY WINERY, *8333 Route 128, Healdsburg. Open 10 A.M. to 5 P.M. daily. Phone: (707) 433-2319.*

HOW TO GET TO JOHNSON'S: *From San Francisco, take the Golden Gate Bridge and continue north past Santa Rosa to the town of Healdsburg, approximately a 90-minute drive from the bridge. Exit onto Healdsburg Avenue and continue to Alexander Valley Road. Turn right. The winery is another 20 to 30 minutes from Healdsburg. From the Napa Valley: Take Route 128 West all the way from Calistoga. This is a long and beautiful drive.*

HORSE AND BUGGY RIDES ㉑

Another way to Johnson's Alexander Valley Winery is by horse and carriage. A business called Five Oaks Farm Horse-drawn Vineyard Tours offers rides around the Alexander Valley in a genuine surrey with red fringe on top. It's a lot of fun. You get to get off the back roads onto the back dirt roads of the wine country with somebody else doing the driving. This operation is run by Greg and Sue Hannan, a married couple who are both emergency care nurses at a local hospital. Plodding along and holding the reins of their Percheron draft horses is their idea of a perfect way to relax. Though the Hannans offer moonlight rides and dinnertime tours, their main business is daytime wine-tasting excursions that can either begin or end with a picnic at Johnson's Alexander Valley Winery.

I should mention that there are two other similar businesses servicing Sonoma County. Another is Carriage Charters, headquartered in Sebastopol, and the rides are tailored to individual interests; so if you don't give a hoot about wine but want to see apple orchards, the driver will take you there in a 100-year-old surrey. The third carriage charter company is called Stage-a-Picnic, which features rides in an antique milk wagon or an 1882-vintage stagecoach made by Studebaker; rides begin and end at the Hope-Bosworth House, a beautifully restored Victorian bed-and-breakfast inn in Geyserville.

How to choose one? Well, prices are competitive (around $40 a person for a daytime excursion that includes food), so the only advice I can offer is to look for a driver who doesn't talk much; out here, silence is golden. I found the sound, or rather the lack of motor noises, to be one of the most soothing and hypnotic parts of the ride; you can always ask questions and have a conversation at lunch. Take note that reservations are necessary and you are expected to pay in advance; you must cancel at least seven days in advance for a refund.

FIVE OAKS FARM, *Alexander Valley. Phone: (707) 433-2422. This service operates from May 1 through December 1, and the rest of the year, weather permitting.*

CARRIAGE CHARTERS, *Sebastopol. Phone: (707) 823-7083. Open all year, weather permitting.*

STAGE-A-PICNIC, *Geyserville. Phone: (707) 857-3619. Open May through October.*

One of the most appealing antique stores I've ever come across happens to be run by the Salvation Army. It's not like any other Salvation Army store you've ever seen. This one is situated in one of the most beautiful spots in all Sonoma County, on the site of a farm and former hot springs resort. There are three Salvation Army–run stores on the property, but Sallie's is the real find.

SALLIE'S ATTIC

Sallie's Attic is not really an attic. There are no stairs to climb. It is an old building with several rooms, which are filled with old furniture, clothing, books, glassware, china, and other vintage treasures—the cream of the crop of all donations made to the Salvation Army of Sonoma. The stock changes often; regular customers who come from as far away as San Jose and Eureka see to that.

Proceeds from the store help operate the farm, which is a rehabilitation center for men addicted to alcohol or drugs. The men enrolled in the rehab program care for the several acres of beautiful grounds, which include a public fishing pond. They also tend the cows that are later sold for beef at auction.

In case you're wondering how the Salvation Army ended up with such a paradise, the property was acquired for a song after the hot springs resort went belly up. At first it was used as a home for boys, but recently it was converted to an adult center.

By the way, though she sounds like somebody's lovable old grandmother, the "Sallie" in Sallie's Attic is a pet name for the Salvation Army. The other stores on the property are a thrift store and an as-is shop. If some members of your party get tired of browsing, they can roam the property or go fishing while the others rummage through the shops.

SALLIE'S ATTIC, *200 Lytton Springs Road, Healdsburg. Open 10 A.M. to 5 P.M. Monday through Saturday; closed Sunday. Phone: (707) 433-5177.*

HOW TO GET TO SALLIE'S ATTIC: *From San Francisco, cross the Golden Gate Bridge and take the Lytton Springs Road exit off Highway 101 (it is the first exit north of Healdsburg). Cross under the freeway and look for the signs for Sallie's. You will actually see the grounds on the left from the freeway before leaving Highway 101.*

ISIS OASIS

In the Fabulous 1960s, thousands of people seeking a new lifestyle came to San Francisco, literally or figuratively wearing flowers in their hair. Today the city streets that once were a haven for the flower children now feature croissants, cappuccino, and haute cuisine, and many of the hippies have become yuppies.

But there still are havens for those who have not forsaken the New Age, and one is nestled in the little town of Geyserville. The sign that greets you at Isis Oasis tells most of the story. It advertises bed and breakfast, with therapy, massage, tarot reading, past-life excursions, dance, theater, and the availability of various spiritual and corporeal experiences.

The "oasis" was founded by Lora Vigne, who must be the world's most unusual innkeeper. She calls herself an artist, New Age minister, and tarot reader, wears her hair à la Elizabeth Taylor in *Cleopatra*, and wears clothes that evoke the feeling of Egypt. She is particularly devoted to the Egyptian goddess Isis, goddess of fertility.

Her partner, Paul Rames, is equally interesting. He is a gestalt therapist and past-life guide. Together Paul and Lora have created "a retreat for body and spirit" on 8½ acres of woods and meadows where exotic animals (including an ocelot, a llama, and an emu, a huge flightless South American bird) mingle with artists, New Age spiritualists, and curious visitors.

Folks who spend the night or a week here have a choice of accommodations. The main lodge has several common rooms and individual bedrooms; guests share a large bathroom with showers. There are also tepees; the wine barrel room, which is a tiny bedroom in an actual barrel; and last but not least, yurts. (At the risk of underestimating your housing knowledge, I will explain that a yurt is a large, round Afghan structure, similar to a tepee.)

Food in the dining hall tends to be along the health food line, with mostly vegetarian and herbal tea–type offerings. Even though the place might make you think you've been transported back to the Age of Aquarius, Lora and Paul believe they are very much a part of the future. There is in fact a very quiet and peaceful feeling about the place. You can be part of a group or be by yourself. You can spend all your time alone by the swimming pool or hot tub or just take part in the activities that appeal to you. How about a massage in a room designed to look and feel like a womb?

Room rates are downright cheap. The top rate is $50 a night for two, including a country breakfast. Massage, readings, and various therapies are all extra.

ISIS OASIS LODGE AND CULTURAL CENTER, *20889 Geyserville Avenue, Geyserville. Phone: (707) 857-3524. If you're planning to drop by, call first so that someone can come down and open the gate.*

HOW TO GET TO ISIS OASIS: *From San Francisco, take the Golden Gate Bridge to Highway 101 North. Continue for about 90 minutes to the town of Geyserville.*

Take the Geyserville Avenue exit at the northern end of town and turn right. Geyserville Avenue is the frontage road that parallels the highway. Continue south on Geyserville Avenue, drive through the small commercial area of town, and you will come to a sign on the right for Isis Oasis.

One of the most inviting and fun wineries in the Bay Area is operated by the comedian Pat Paulsen, who rivals Harold Stassen for the record of running for president.

The Paulsen Winery is in the tiny town of Asti, which sits in the shadow of the huge Italian Swiss Colony plant. The village is so tiny, in fact, that it consists entirely of the Paulsen tasting room, a store (which, by the way, serves great sandwiches and homemade soups), and several buildings in various states of use and disrepair. Since Paulsen owns it all, he proclaimed himself mayor and has even established a "city hall." It's a one-room, barely standing shack with a desk, a phone (not yet connected), a light that won't work (there is no electricity), and several other gags that show you how seriously he takes his position as mayor. Security is at an absolute minimum, and anyone can get into the city hall and go through the mayor's desk. This "office" is also the headquarters for his next presidential campaign.

Paulsen is from the Bay Area, sort of. He grew up in Washington but moved to Northern California in time to attend Tamalpais High School in Mill Valley. In the early 1960s Paulsen tried his luck as a stand-up comedian and performed at San Francisco's Purple Onion, the nightclub that launched the careers of the Kingston Trio, The Limelighters, Phyllis Diller, and the Smothers Brothers. When the Smothers Brothers got their prime-time TV show on CBS in the 1960s, Paulsen and his dry, offbeat sense of humor joined the cast.

In the early 1970s Pat and his wife Jane planted a vineyard and soon thereafter established a winery. (The Smothers Brothers also have one nearby in Kenwood.) Pat Paulsen Vineyards now produces 20,000 cases of premium wine annually and has won numerous awards.

The tasting room is loaded with memorabilia from the comedian's career and various political campaigns. Outside you'll find picnic tables with nice views of the valley. You can bring your own food or get what you need in the general store.

The wine is really quite good, from a seriously competitive premium chardonnay to the humorously labeled American Gothic Red, a good jug wine with a cause: A dollar from the sale of each jug is sent to the National Farm Relief Program.

This is a family-run operation, with the Paulsen home and vineyard across the Russian River from Asti and not open to the public. Pat's daughter Terri runs the operation. Pat can be spotted around the place when he's not traveling around the country performing, he says, to pay the bills from the winery (he's probably not kidding).

PAT PAULSEN TASTING ROOM, *26155 Asti Store Road, Asti. Open 10 A.M. to 6 P.M. daily. Phone: (707) 894-2969. Tasting room is wheelchair accessible.*

HOW TO GET TO THE PAT PAULSEN WINERY: *From San Francisco, take the Golden Gate Bridge to Highway 101 North. Stay on Route 101 until you come to the Asti exit, which is between Geyserville and Cloverdale. It is well marked. The Paulsen Winery tasting room is an immediate right turn after the exit.*

LAKE SONOMA

When visitors to the Bay Area are in the mood for the water, they usually head to the Pacific Ocean. These beaches are indeed beautiful, but there's one problem—even during the warmest weather, the water is usually freezing cold. Those who like to take a dip and linger awhile are advised to visit one of the several lakes close to the Bay Area, the newest being Lake Sonoma.

This artificial lake and recreational area has been in operation since 1982, with the completion of the Warm Springs Dam. With each rainfall, what was once the Dry Creek Valley fills up higher and higher. It is a lovely body of water, with one major wide area and five fingers each leading to more secluded spots. Most of the use now is for fishing and waterskiing; as for swimming, the water is brisk but much more tolerable than the ocean, especially in summer, when the air temperature at the lake hovers around the 100-degree mark.

Nearly 50 years passed from the time the dam and lake were first proposed until the dam was finally completed. Plans call for resort hotels, fancy restaurants, theaters, and other tourist-oriented attractions. But at last check, the facilities were minimal. There are a few boating docks for launching motorboats and sailboats, a snack bar, and, high above the lake, an overlook with a spectacular view. The overlook is in a parklike setting, with picnic tables, rest rooms, and a pay phone.

LAKE SONOMA MARINA *is the headquarters for the various activities. For information about launching boats, swimming, and other facilities, call (707) 433-2200. There is a $2 parking fee.*

HOW TO GET TO LAKE SONOMA: *From San Francisco, take the Golden Gate Bridge to Route 101 North to Healdsburg. Exit at Dry Creek Road and follow the signs to the lake.*

FISH HATCHERY

When visiting Lake Sonoma, you might want to stop next door and see what's been created because of it. The Warm Springs Fish Hatchery is not only a fascinating place, but it is also a symbol of our new awareness of responsibility when we alter the course of nature.

Thanks to environmental laws, in order to build the Warm Springs Dam that created Lake Sonoma, the Army Corps of Engineers also had to build a fish hatchery. You see, before the dam, migrating salmon and steelhead came to the fresh water of Dry Creek to deposit their eggs. Since the dam would block Dry Creek and its tributaries, a new environment for spawning had to be created; hence the hatchery. It's probably not the salmon's idea of a romantic honeymoon setting, but it works, and the public is invited to see the operation.

After parking in the ample lot, you cross over a bridge to the visitor's center, a very attractive structure that looks like a museum. Inside you are given an illustrated brochure for the self-guided tour. This is a large operation, and you can spend a few hours here or just breeze through after a bit of salmon sex education.

I won't attempt to tell you everything you'll see if you go through the entire process, but some of the various stations on the tour show fish being tranquilized and workers from the California Fish and Game Service removing eggs and sperm from the drugged salmon and steelhead. Depending on the time of year you visit, you can witness live artificial insemination, incubation, and finally tanks of baby fish awaiting release back into the creek as soon as they're large enough. All year you can watch the entire process on video.

The hatchery's goal is to produce a million fish per year. Though the tour is self-guided, state park rangers are on hand to answer any questions you may have.

WARM SPRINGS FISH HATCHERY, *Lake Sonoma. Though spawning season is November through March, the visitor's center is open all year round. Open from 9:30 A.M. to 4 P.M. Monday, Thursday, and Friday and from 10 A.M. to 5 P.M. Saturday and Sunday; closed Tuesday and Wednesday. From Memorial Day to Labor Day the hatchery is open from 10 A.M. to 6 P.M. seven days a week. Admission: Free. Wheelchair accessible.*

HOW TO GET HERE: *From San Francisco, take the Golden Gate Bridge to Route 101 North to the Dry Creek exit, north of Healdsburg. Follow Dry Creek west (left) until it ends at the dam. An alternative is to take Canyon Road out of Geyserville, which intersects with Dry Creek Road. This is at least two hours from San Francisco.*

RUSSIAN RIVER AREA

The Russian River is the name given to the resort area centered around the community of Guerneville. The river itself runs from just south of Healdsburg and empties into the Pacific just below the town of Jenner.

The only constant in this area is change. Perhaps the central community of Guerneville should have been called Phoenix, because it keeps rising from the ashes of one disaster after another. There have been three town-destroying fires and two floods, but still the town and the area keep coming back.

This used to be redwood forest country until major logging companies moved in. Their rail lines went throughout western Sonoma, first for logging, then for bringing tourists up from San Francisco. While the super-rich went to Marin and Tahoe, working-class families came to the Russian River. In fact, it used to be called "Little Mission," named after the modest neighborhood in the City. When the trains stopped coming to town in the 1940s, tourism died. In the 1960s the hippies discovered they could live a less hassled life here than in the City and moved up. Then in the late 1970s the Russian River resorts became a haven for San Francisco's gay population.

But just as the area was coming back to life, two disasters struck. The first was the devastating flood of 1986, destroying many homes and businesses. Then the growing concern about AIDS frightened many customers away from the area, forcing some facilities catering to gay clientele out of business.

Still, the area keeps bouncing back and is worth seeing. A drive on River Road will show you the remnants of all the above-mentioned cultures. You will see old hotels, modest cabins in the woods, and new condos designed for an influx of yuppies. You will see middle-class families and people who look like the cast of *Easy Rider,* and you will see men walking hand in hand with other men and women walking hand in hand with other women.

The town of Guerneville is the best place to begin a visit to the Russian River resorts. The visitor's center in the downtown section is a good place to stop for a map and information about the latest developments in the area. Downtown you'll find the year-round residents mingling with the tourists, supermarkets and shoe repair stores next to the shops catering to the tourist trade.

In town you might even happen upon a world leader or two. That's because in the summer the most powerful men in the world flock to nearby Bohemian Grove, a private and well-guarded club, a sort of summer camp for elected officials, stars, corporate leaders, and other kinds of millionaires. The stories of what really goes on at the Grove are legion. You can probably pick some of them up by stopping for lunch or a drink at the Northwood Golf Club restaurant, between Guerneville and Monte Rio on River Road. Many of the "Bohemians" are rumored to hang out there at night, hoping to meet some ladies looking for, let us say, part-time work. Boys, even old rich ones, will be boys.

The Russian River has its share of wineries to visit, too. The most famous and appealing of these is the Korbel Champagne Cellars, also on River Road in Guerneville. Korbel is located in a 120-year-old ivy-covered building, surrounded by redwoods and a beautiful rose garden, with the Russian River flowing by. Free tours of the winery are given daily, every 45 minutes, and the garden is in bloom from April through June.

Heading toward the ocean, west on Route 116, there is a town that looks like a movie set for an old lumber town. This is Duncan's Mills, population 20. A couple of years ago the town voted unanimously to restore this former lumber village in hopes of catching some of the tourist trade. It is a charming place to stop. The centerpiece of the town is a small museum located in the old railroad depot, the last remaining depot from the once-active Western Pacific Coastal Line, which ran from Sausalito to Cazadero. The depot doubles as a reception office for the town campground. There is also an area with shops, including the town's original general store, which has been restored, and several buildings built to look like they existed in the late nineteenth century. They sell tourist-oriented items, from handicrafts to candy, and you can pick up picnic supplies.

THE VISITOR'S CENTER IN GUERNEVILLE *is located at 14034 Armstrong Woods Road, Guerneville. Phone: (707) 869-9009.*

KORBEL CHAMPAGNE CELLARS AND ROSE GARDEN, *13250 River Road, Guerneville. The tasting room is open from 10:30 A.M. to 4:30 P.M. daily. Phone: (707) 887-2294.*

HOW TO GET TO GUERNEVILLE: *From San Francisco, take the Golden Gate Bridge and follow Route 101 North to the River Road exit. Follow the signs all the way to Guerneville. Plan on at least a two-hour drive from the bridge.*

DUNCAN'S MILLS *is on Route 116, west of Guerneville, as you head toward the ocean.*

FORT ROSS

The more you explore Northern California, the more it becomes apparent that some of the best real estate is owned by the military. The Presidio in San Francisco and Fort Ord in Monterey are certainly prime examples. And you will discover that this was true even as far back as 1812, when the Russians held forth in this neck of the woods.

Many visitors to the area are surprised to learn that there was a considerable Russian presence in these parts (hence, the name Russian River). Near the turn of the nineteenth century the Russians expanded their Alaskan fish and fur interests as far south as Fort Ross, an oceanfront outpost about 11 miles north of the modern town of Jenner. Within the wooden fortress walls was an active community of 700 colonists led by a Russian commandant and his princess wife.

The Russians' original plan was to stick around awhile. However, they unexpectedly killed off the sea otter population (valued for their silky pelts), gophers ruined their crops, and the Mexicans who got there first were making them feel unwelcome. In 1821 the Russians sold the land and buildings to Captain Johann Sutter (of Gold Rush fame) and went home.

A visit to Fort Ross, which is now a state historic park, is a low-key stop along the way up or down the coast. The tour of the grounds is self-guided and involves the use of white telephone-like objects that sit on stakes in front of various points of interest; you listen to a recorded message, complete with background music, that tells the story of Russian life in these parts. You will see the stockade, a Russian Orthodox chapel, a tower with cannon, and the officers' barracks, which is also an information center where you can ask questions not answered by the telephones. You should plan to stay about an hour for the tour and to enjoy the magnificent ocean view. As I said before, the military always gets the best real estate.

FORT ROSS. *Open 10 A.M. to 5 P.M. Admission: $2 per car. Phone: (707) 847-3286.*

HOW TO GET TO FORT ROSS: *From San Francisco, take the Golden Gate Bridge to Route 101 North. Past Santa Rosa, take the River Road exit and follow River Road all the way through the Russian River resort area until you connect with Route 1 heading north at Jenner. Follow Route 1 to Fort Ross.*

BRUCE JOHNSON'S SCULPTURES

One day while driving up Seaview Road, a winding country drive up the hill from Route 1 near the town of Timber Cove, I suddenly saw a remarkable sight, a field covered with giant . . . things. I pulled over to take a look. These 8-foot-tall objects turned out to be sculptures made from redwood, fieldstones, and steel rods.

After knocking on a few doors, I found the artist. He's Bruce Johnson, a big, blond, friendly guy who lives across the road and uses the field as his studio. He moved up here 15 years ago to work on the historic restoration of Fort Ross and decided to stay. Taking advantage of the redwood stumps in the neighborhood, Bruce used a chainsaw as his chisel to create abstract shapes reminiscent of the work of Henry Moore. Bruce has gained some notoriety as a California artist, with examples of his works displayed at the Oakland Museum and commissioned by the cities of Palo Alto and Santa Rosa.

Bruce welcomes people to stop by and watch him work, as long as he doesn't have to stop what he's doing.

Bruce Johnson's sculptures can be seen most times of the year on Seaview Road.

HOW TO GET THERE: *From San Francisco, follow the directions to Fort Ross. On leaving Fort Ross, head north on Route 1 a mile or so to Timber Cove Road. Turn right and head up the hill. At the top of the hill, turn right on Seaview Road and look on the right in the fields for huge wooden sculptures. Once you're there, you can't miss it.*

KRUSE RHODODENDRON STATE RESERVE 30

If you're making your way back to Route 1 and it happens to be between late May and early July, you're in for a treat. Seaview Road will take you north to the town of Plantation, where you will catch Kruse Ranch Road down to the ocean. Suddenly you will be in the midst of a huge rhododendron preserve. If so inclined, you can pull off the road and take a walk on trails through 317 acres of lush fern canyons and redwoods, amid clusters of white, pink, red, and purple rhodo blossoms.

KRUSE RHODODENDRON STATE RESERVE, at the intersection of Highway 1 and Kruse Ranch Road, about 8 miles south of Stewart's Point. Open sunrise to sunset all year. Admission: Free. Phone: (707) 865-2391.

OCCIDENTAL

The only town in America to be named Occidental lies just a few miles from the Pacific Ocean, the gateway to the Orient. The main street is the hub for the roads leading to the Russian River resorts to the northwest, Bodega Bay to the west, Petaluma and Sebastopol to the southeast, and Santa Rosa to the northeast. Just outside of town on Coleman Valley Road there are several lovely attractions, including a small cactus garden, a lovely hillside nursery, and a breathtaking drive into Bodega Bay.

But what brings people to town? Food.

Yes, Italian food, and lots of it. For years, family-style restaurants have been drawing folks to Occidental. There are three big restaurants in town, each one capable of seating the entire population of permanent residents with plenty of seats left over. This is not the sort of fare you will find in the pages of *Gourmet* magazine, nor is it what you would call "spa cuisine." The meals are down-home affairs, often starting with a big bowl of minestrone, followed by mounds of homemade ravioli, then a meat or chicken course served with vegetables, followed by dessert. Everything is served family-style, and the portions are huge. It is also inexpensive.

The Union Hotel on the main drag is the oldest establishment in town. But it's not a hotel at all, it's a 500-seat restaurant with a saloon and the Bocce Ballroom with even more tables and a place to hear live music. The Gonella family runs the Union Hotel; in fact, they pretty much own the whole side of the street, including the town grocery, and a Christmas wreath-making business outside of town. The family patriarch, Dan Gonella, is known as Dan Mahoney. That's because when he was a kid, there were two Dan Gonellas in town, this Dan and his cousin Dan. So everybody could keep them straight they got nicknames that stuck: Dan McGee and Dan Mahoney.

Across the street from the Union Hotel you'll find Negri's, where 500 more people can sit down for dinner all at once. A sign proclaims it to be the town's "original" Italian restaurant. You'll probably find Joe Negri behind the bar and his mother, Theresa, will probably be in front of the bar watching a TV quiz show along with the regular customers. Joe looks like he could be the bouncer at the toughest club in New York City, but his mom says he's just a shy pussycat. Joe's wife does the talking for both of them. She comes out of the kitchen, wise-cracking, "You marry an Italian, you do all the work."

The Negris also own racehorse stables down the road and Negri's Occidental Lodge, a motel with a swimming pool. The Gonellas also own a motel, the Union Hotel Motel, and it, too, has a pool. (I should mention that it gets very warm here in the summer, and after pasta and wine at Union Hotel, Negri's, or the town's third competitor, Fiori's, many people feel like turning in for the night or taking a dip.)

In case you haven't guessed, there's an air of rivalry in this town. The Gonellas stay on their side of the street, the Negris stay on theirs. For the rest of us, that means both are competing for our business.

There are a few other things to do in town: shopping at some nice small stores, and coffeeshops for those who don't feel like a major mealtime production. If you take Coleman Valley Road a few miles out of town, toward the ocean, you will come to a cactus garden and a lovely nursery.

But the town's main attraction continues to be the dueling Italian restaurants. Reservations are recommended for weekends during the summer months especially.

UNION HOTEL, *Occidental. Phone: (707) 874-3662.*

NEGRI'S, *Occidental. Phone: (707) 823-5301.*

FIORI'S *Occidental. Phone: (707) 823-8188.*

HOW TO GET TO OCCIDENTAL: *The easiest way from San Francisco is to cross the Golden Gate Bridge and take Route 101 North to Route 116 West, an exit you pick up after you pass the Petaluma exits (it seems a bit confusing, but Route 116 West is several miles beyond the turnoff for Route 116 East). Take 116 West to the town of Sebastopol; then follow the signs to Bodega until you come to the Bohemian Highway and the town of Freestone. The Bohemian Highway will lead you into Occidental. An alternative route is to take 116 from Sebastopol to Graton Road and turn south; this will also lead into Occidental.*

RENT-A-BUNNY

A few weeks before Easter, I noticed a small ad in a Sonoma County newspaper offering a rent-a-bunny service. This sounded like an interesting idea worth investigating.

As it turns out, the service is the brainchild of a schoolteacher, Sharon Cahn of Buzzard's Roost Ranch. The idea is simple. Sharon feels that taking care of an animal is a serious responsibility. Sometimes around the holidays, families will buy a cute little bunny for the kids, but when the novelty wears off, or the rabbit grows up (whichever comes first), pets often fall victim to neglect. So Sharon decided to rent her rabbits; if family and beast turn out to be compatible, she will sell the bunny so everyone can live happily ever after.

But a visit to Buzzard's Roost Ranch offers even more. This is a working farm with sheep, chickens, pigs, organically grown vegetables, and herbs. Sharon loves to show people around (once a teacher, always a teacher) to let city slickers see what life on the farm is like close up. Because this is a small, family-run farm, operated just by Sharon and her husband Gene, you can imagine what your life might be like if you lived here.

But Sharon really loves her rabbits. Her prize pets are Angoras, from which she makes scarves and sweaters (which are for sale, by the way). She will set up a spinning wheel on the deck of the farmhouse and you can watch her pluck the rabbit and spin the yarn right there; it is quite a sight. The rabbits need plucking every two weeks anyway, so it is a happy marriage of necessity and enterprise.

BUZZARD'S ROOST RANCH, *1778 Facendini Lane, Occidental. Open noon to 6 P.M. Saturday and Sunday; closed mid-July through mid-August. Phone: (707) 823-2799.*

HOW TO GET TO BUZZARD'S ROOST RANCH: *From San Francisco, take the Golden Gate Bridge to Highway 101 North to Route 116 West. Take 116 West into the town of Sebastopol. In the center of town, turn onto Route 12 West toward Forestville. A few miles from Sebastopol, turn left on Occidental Road and continue for several miles to Facendini Lane on the right. If you have reached the town of Occidental, you've passed the turn. From Occidental, take Occidental Road a few minutes out of town to Facendini Lane and turn left.*

THE BODEGAS

The Bodega Highway winds through rolling hills dotted with sheep and cattle as you head from Sebastopol or Petaluma toward the ocean and to the "twin towns" of Bodega and Bodega Bay. These twins are fraternal rather than identical; in fact, the only things they have in common, really, is the similarity in name, phone area code, and the fact that Alfred Hitchcock used both places to film *The Birds* in 1963. There the similarities end.

Bodega is a small, quiet town, and everybody there likes it that way. Visitors are welcome, but they are not actively pursued. This is not a tourist town. There are a few stores along the main highway, businesses that cater to the many farm families that live in the area. The big event around here is the annual spring auction of the town quilt. Ladies from town work all year to make the huge bedspread; the proceeds from the auction benefit the volunteer fire department.

Just before you round the curve into town, you will notice an old schoolhouse on a hill to the left. If you're a movie buff, you will probably recognize it as the place the birds attacked the schoolchildren in Alfred Hitchcock's thriller. It hasn't been a schoolhouse for several years. Actually, the scariest thing you're likely to find in Bodega is the ghost story told by a lady named Charlene, who operates the only business in town geared for visitors.

She's easy to find. Right on the highway, on the right side of the road before entering town (with the abandoned schoolhouse off in the distance), you will see a sign for Charlene's Country Treasures. Behind her home is a long garden and several buildings jammed to the rafters with stuff for sale. "I keep what Grandpa threw away," says Charlene, who appears to have cleaned out several flea markets. Visitors are invited to roam and can regard her collection as either a store or a museum. Her motivation is to preserve a part of America's past.

Now, about that ghost story. I was told by people in town that Charlene has a ghost living in her house. She was glad to talk about it. She says that it's not a bad ghost, it's just there. Sooner or later, the subject just seems to come up, and Charlene loves to tell visitors what she's seen and heard and then watch the reactions. She says everybody is interested in ghosts, and everyone has a ghost story to tell her.

The town of Bodega Bay is another story entirely. This is fast becoming a tourist destination. Situated on the harbor just a few miles beyond Bodega on Route 1, Bodega Bay is a town of fishing wharves, restaurants, and inns. This is where you can go to eat or spend the night. The ocean is just beyond the spit of land called Bodega Head; it lies directly to the west of the bay. Within easy driving to the north are several beaches with access from the coastal highway (Route 1). Residents like to boast that Bodega Bay is the town with a hole in its head. That's because the citizens blocked a planned nuclear power plant on Bodega Head, even after the power company had dug the hole for the foundation. Now the hole remains as a reminder that the town chose to grow with tourism rather than nuclear power.

In addition to seeing many new motels and inns, the main street, which is Route 1, features several tourist-type shops. There is also camping nearby at the Bodega Dunes.

HOW TO GET TO BODEGA BAY: *From San Francisco, take the Golden Gate Bridge to Highway 101 North to the Central Petaluma exit. Take Bodega Avenue west to Valley Ford Road, which eventually goes into Route 1 and on into Bodega Bay. To get to Bodega, turn right onto the Bodega Highway. Charlene's Country Treasures is on the Bodega Highway, as you head out of town, traveling east. If you're coming from Occidental, take the Bohemian Highway south to the Bodega Highway and turn right into Bodega. Then continue until you hit Route 1 and turn right for Bodega Bay.*

KOZLOWSKI FARMS

If you like jams and jellies, chances are you've come across the name Kozlowski. Supermarkets across the country sell this family's sugarless preserves. But as you will quickly see when you visit their headquarters, the Kozlowski operation is a far cry from Smucker's.

The Kozlowskis live and work in the heart of Sonoma apple country, on the appropriately named Gravenstein Highway, no less. For years the family had sold the berries and apples raised on their farm at a little stand in front of the family house. One year they were overwhelmed by raspberries. Mrs. Kozlowski made a batch of jam in the kitchen and sold it as yet another Kozlowski farm product. Another year they were overwhelmed by apples. Mrs. Kozlowski used them instead of sugar to sweeten her jam. As it turns out, many of her regular customers were cutting down on sugar anyway, and soon she had a popular product. Sometimes she couldn't get a batch onto the shelves; people were buying it still warm from the kitchen.

Now production has expanded to fill the need, but Mrs. Kozlowski insists her jams and jellies are still made the old-fashioned way. Other products have been added to the Kozlowski line, such as vinegar, juices, and syrups.

Yet despite their success and wide distribution, the farm still has the look and feel of a family operation. As you drive in, you pass by Gravenstein apple orchards and berry patches on the long driveway that leads to the farm buildings. On one side is the modest but comfy-looking farmhouse; on the other side is the huge barn, which doubles as the retail outlet. You can roam the grounds, but most people make a beeline for the barn.

Inside, you are likely to meet Mrs. Kozlowski or several of her children, all of whom work in the family business. Depending on the season, there will be fresh berries or apples for sale, plus the various Kozlowski products. They even have a tasting room, but instead of wine you get jam on a cracker.

KOZLOWSKI FARMS, *5566 Gravenstein Highway (Route 116), Sebastopol. Open 9 A.M. to 5 P.M. daily; closed major holidays. Spring and summer are the best times of the year to get fresh berries, but frozen berries are available all year. Phone: (707) 887-2104 or (707) 887-2105.*

HOW TO GET HERE: *From San Francisco, take the Golden Gate Bridge to Highway 101 North. Follow Route 101 to the Route 116 West exit, which is several miles past the exit for Route 116 East. Turn left off the exit and take Route 116 West past the town of Sebastopol. After several miles, look on the left for the entrance to Kozlowski Farms.*

ANTIQUE ROW

It is difficult for transplanted Easterners to think of antiques in California. For many, a true antique must date back at least to 1830, before the Industrial Revolution, when things were made by hand and thus were one of a kind. Others have a more lenient definition and call an antique anything that dates back 100 years or more. Since California history more or less began with the Gold Rush, there are few items that could be considered antiques according to the first definition.

Yet that doesn't stop people from loving to shop for vintage items, no matter what they're called—antiques, collectibles, or "historic merchandise." For reasons unknown to me, there is a stretch of shops selling all the above in the little town of Sebastopol. At least a dozen shops are in business within a few blocks, each with its own unique personality. I honestly don't know if there are bargains to be found in Sebastopol, but if you want to pass some time browsing around various kinds of collections, from campaign buttons to large furniture pieces, the antique stores of Sebastopol offer a low-key, pleasant excursion.

For example, take Joel and Margaret Watson's American Country Furniture.

They sell to passers-by and to San Francisco dealers who come up country looking for bargains. They also make reproductions of historic pieces, such as George Washington pantry shelves (like the ones our first president had at home in Mount Vernon) and Rowland cabinets (like the ones brought over on the *Mayflower* as an all-purpose storage unit).

The Watsons are transplanted New Englanders who started building their own reproductions because they couldn't afford to buy originals. This led them to study the antiques of both coasts and to become a good resource of history and folklore. Margaret likes to think of her products in terms of our contemporary lifestyle. She showed me all I need for an early American equivalent of the Cuisinart: a grinder, a ricer, and a turn-of-the-century milkshake maker and juicer—all hand-powered, of course.

She offers a tip for amateur shoppers. She advises studying a piece well to know if it's a new piece or a genuine antique. New pieces are usually too clean or will have modern screws or maybe a trace of glue. Behind an authentic old desk drawer there should be old dust. If not, bargain accordingly.

As for prices, most of the dealers arrive at figures by referring to one of the many books published about antiques and the going market. Margaret recommends picking one up and deciding for yourself what you think something is worth before trying to bargain.

ANTIQUE ROW *is located about 3 miles south of the heart of Sebastopol, on Route 116 West, near the intersection of Lone Pine Road.*

HOW TO GET HERE: *From San Francisco, take Highway 101 North to the Route 116 West exit, which is several miles past the exit for Route 116 East. Follow Route 116 West (also called Gravenstein Highway) toward Sebastopol. As you approach town you will begin to see antique stores on both sides of the road. Though some stores are open seven days a week, many are closed on Monday.*

PET-A-LLAMA IN PETALUMA

Many futurists say that national trends start in California. If that's true, then, no matter where you are, there's probably a llama in your future. I know of at least three llama farms that have cropped up in the past year or so, and the llamas are selling like tortillas, or whatever it is they use for pancakes in Peru, where these creatures come from.

Why llamas? Well, one of the best people to answer that question is Chuck Warner, who runs the Pet-a-Llama Ranch in Petaluma. He's an entertaining character who became fascinated with the Andean work animals and decided to make his fortune in llamas. A transplanted New Englander (as you can quickly tell by his accent), Warner seems to like nothing more than to talk llama. He'll tell you that they are a great investment as well as a versatile work animal or pet. He can tell you their history—that they originally thrived in the 15,000-foot altitude near Lima, that the Incas domesticated them, that their wool is good for clothing and making rope, that William Randolph Hearst was the first to bring them to the United States, and that they seem to adapt to all altitudes and climates (you can find them in Alaska, Florida, and Texas, too).

As for the animals themselves, they are intriguing: friendly, big-eyed, with sweet faces and long necks. Believe me, growing up in Indiana, I for one never saw anything like them. They spend most of the day peacefully munching alfalfa, hay, and other native California cuisine. Trained to kneel, they are easy to load for use as pack animals. They are also relatively quiet and very strong. In fact, Chuck will take you for a ride in a buggy pulled by a pair of llamas.

Also on the premises is a small gift shop featuring sweaters and other apparel made from llama wool.

For the record, the proper pronunciation for *llama* in Spanish is "yama." Most Americans call them "lamas," though.

PET-A-LLAMA RANCH, *215 Gossage Way, Petaluma. Open by appointment. Phone: (707) 762-6979.*

HOW TO GET THERE: *From San Francisco, take the Golden Gate Bridge to Highway 101 North to the Washington Street exit in Petaluma. Turn left at the light on Washington Street, go back across the freeway, and continue to Petaluma Boulevard North. Turn right and continue to Gossage Avenue, which will be on the left. After a left turn onto Gossage, continue up over a hill to Gossage Way. Turn right, and Pet-a-Llama is the third driveway on the left.*

CINNABAR THEATRE

Petaluma is not known as an international cultural center. However, it was known for its chickens, having the nickname Chick-a-luma. For years Petaluma was known as the poultry capital of the world. Then developers convinced the farmers that the dollar came before the chicken *and* the egg. Now Petaluma's claim to fame is its annual arm-wrestling and ugly dog competitions.

Petaluma has a lot more going for it. Fancy and imaginative restaurants are opening, the local high school girls dress as stylishly as their San Francisco counterparts, and there is live theater almost year-round at the Cinnabar Theatre.

What makes the Cinnabar so interesting is that at any moment you expect Judy Garland and Mickey Rooney to pop out of the woodwork and say they've got the barn and the talent, so why not put on a show!

Here at the Cinnabar, the Mickey Rooney part is played by Marvin Klebe, a former singer with the San Francisco Opera. Years ago he decided to leave the bureaucracy of a big company and move to the country to start his own place.

Marvin and his family moved to Petaluma, buying the old Cinnabar School building, high on a hill a few blocks from the main part of town. With the help of his wife and four sons, Marvin converted the classrooms into an unusual combination of living quarters and 150-seat theater.

With a small staff and many volunteers, Marvin now fulfills his artistic dreams, offering programs ranging from Wagnerian opera to an updated version of Menotti's *Consul* (in which the setting is changed from a Soviet Bloc nation to Latin America). There are also frequent showcases for new talent and a wide variety of ambitious productions.

Because of Marvin's eclectic programming, reasonably free of the economic restraints of most big-city theaters, the Cinnabar draws an audience from around the Bay Area. It's a good idea to check on ticket availability before making the trip.

CINNABAR THEATRE, 3335 *Petaluma Boulevard North, Petaluma, near the intersection of Skillman Lane. Phone:* (707) 763-8920.

HOW TO GET HERE: *From San Francisco, take the Golden Gate Bridge to Route 101 North to the Penngrove exit, above Petaluma. At the exit, go left over the freeway and continue on the Old Redwood Highway approximately 1½ miles. The theater is on a hill to your right.*

MILLIE'S CHILI

There is a trend around the country to re-create diners of the 1950s, and suddenly people are rushing to stand in line for meatloaf sandwiches, mashed potatoes with gravy, and BLTs. Well, in Petaluma, just south of the main drag, is such a place that is not a re-creation; it is the real thing.

I first heard of Millie's Chili from the film crew working on Francis Coppola's film *Peggy Sue Got Married*. They used the place as a 1950s doughnut shop, changing the name and the food. Pity; you can't improve on the genuine article, and you could probably make the most entertaining movie ever made just by watching Millie and her twin sister Vickie in action.

Millie and Vickie live in back of the diner. They're in their late sixties, maybe early seventies now. They're up by 5:30 A.M., getting the chili on the stove, making salads, peeling onions. By opening time (11 A.M.) you'd better be ready to operate at their pace. Millie stands behind the little cooking area, flipping burgers and stirring her chili; Vickie's right there, order pad in hand, ready to take your order. All the time, they go at each other, bickering, teasing, laughing, and having the time of their lives. If they're really busy they'll tell you not to bother them; they have to concentrate!

It seems that no matter what you order, it's going to have chili on it. I'm not going to tell you this is the best chili in the world, but I promise you won't ever forget a visit with these memorable people. By the way, make sure you eat everything on your plate or else Vickie will give you the dickens.

MILLIE'S CHILI BAR, *Petaluma Boulevard South, at H Street, Petaluma. Open 11 A.M. to 3 P.M. Monday through Friday; closed weekends. No phone.*

HOW TO GET HERE: *From San Francisco, take the Golden Gate Bridge to Highway 101 North to the South Petaluma Boulevard exit in Petaluma. Millie's is a mile or so from the exit, on the left.*

KROUT'S PHEASANT FARM

While trying to come up with an unusual angle for our first Thanksgiving show, the staff and I decided to look for a back-roads alternative to the frozen supermarket turkey. That's how I happened upon Krout's, a delightful place to visit anytime from late summer to early winter.

Verna and Jack Krout run their farm, which is north of Petaluma, with the help of their friendly and talented dog, Max. The Krouts originally started raising pheasants more than 30 years ago as a hobby and as a way for their children to have the experience of watching an animal grow up. In 1960 the Krouts purchased the farm where they live now. The previous owner had 24 pheasants he didn't know what to do with. The Krouts said to include them in the price of the property and they'd take care of them; after all, if they had done it once, they could do it again.

The sideline grew into a full-time business. Last year the Krouts hatched more than 200,000 pheasants, most of them sold to consumers right from the premises.

When I arrived at the Krouts', I was greeted enthusiastically by Max, of the wagging tail. Past the picturebook white frame farmhouse to the back, I was suddenly confronted by thousands of birds in pens: pheasants, chukar partridges, guinea hens, wild turkeys, and, in special cages, some gorgeous birds with multicolored plumes from Southeast Asia and Latin America.

Even if you do not happen to be shooting a television show, you are invited to roam around, or you can get right down to business and choose a bird for dinner. You are also invited to try to catch it yourself, which is no mean trick. Verna will show you how to take a net and swoop down to capture your prey, then hold its feet to pull it out of the net. After that, the Krouts will take the bird inside to prepare it for the oven, a process you may not care to watch.

The Krouts are well aware of the difference between the realities of farm life, such as the butchering of the food we eat, and the romantic fantasies that many city dwellers have. They told me that when they moved to this farm, it really was the country. Now they are surrounded by prime real estate purchased by neighbors who are often not prepared for country life. The message to all of us, I think, is that living in the country means the smell of manure, the nightlong sound of sick animals, and the early morning sounds of farm equipment. The Krouts would like visitors to return home with an appreciation of real country living.

As for that Thanksgiving program, I ended with the rather obvious question, "What are you going to have for dinner?" Jack said he would like partridge, they ought to have pheasant, but they would probably have turkey.

KROUT'S PHEASANT FARM, *3234 Skillman Lane, Petaluma. Open 1 to 5 P.M. Tuesday through Saturday, September 15 through January 1; closed Sunday, Monday, and holidays. Phone: (707) 762-8613.*

HOW TO GET HERE: *From San Francisco, take the Golden Gate Bridge to Route 101 North. Exit at Washington Street, about 45 minutes from San Francisco. Turn right on Petaluma Boulevard and continue north to Skillman Lane, then turn left.*

PETALUMA ADOBE

In Northern California you can see just about every style of architecture imaginable. But at one time the dominant style was the adobe. Today only a few remain, and none is so striking or important as the Petaluma adobe, now a state historic park.

Remember our friend General Vallejo (of Sonoma Plaza and Lachryma Montis fame)? Well, this was the headquarters of his enormous ranch, some 66,000 acres of farmland with nearly 2000 inhabitants. The adobe was a community center of sorts, where workers and their children would gather and make clothing, tools, flour, and candles for use on the ranch and for export. The original quadrangular adobe was huge, with the foreman of the ranch occupying one wing, Vallejo's living quarters on the second floor, and, on the ground floor, kitchen and eating areas, a milling room, and yet another wing for tanning leather and making tallow.

Only about half of the original two-story structure remains now, but it is still an imposing hillside edifice with 3-foot-thick adobe walls and balconies that run the entire length of the second floor.

This is the sort of historic spot that could be drab and lifeless, the tourist-stop equivalent of taking medicine. Fortunately, Fred Welcome got the assignment of park ranger. Over the past several years Welcome and his family have devoted their energy and talent to making the historic park into a living place. It's a wonderful destination to bring children because there is lots to do and acres of hillside parkland for burning off all that energy they store up sitting in the back seat of the car. There are also loads of farm animals roaming freely; in fact, you may be greeted by a sheep or two in the parking lot.

The best time to visit is on weekends or holidays, when you will encounter ladies dressed in costumes of the 1850s, working at spinning wheels or baking bread as they did in Vallejo's day. Many hands-on activities are set up, allowing you to try your hand at dipping candles, churning butter, or performing whatever other activities are featured that day.

Though most of the action is outside in the courtyard, the inside of the adobe is interesting, too. You can get a good idea of what life must have been like in the community.

PETALUMA ADOBE STATE HISTORIC PARK, *3325 Adobe Road, Petaluma. Open 10 A.M. to 5 P.M. daily, though weekends are when most of the action takes place. Admission: 50 cents for adults, 25 cents for children. Phone: (707) 762-4871.*

HOW TO GET TO THE PETALUMA ADOBE: *From San Francisco, take the Golden Gate Bridge to Highway 101 North toward Petaluma. Exit at Route 116 East. At Frates Road, turn left and continue for a few minutes to Adobe Road. Turn left, and the adobe is on your right. Directions are well marked from Route 101.*

CHAPTER **3** Napa County

AREA OVERVIEW

Napa County is sandwiched between Sonoma County on the west and Solano County to the south and east. The closest destination from San Francisco is the town of Napa, about an hour's drive from the Golden Gate Bridge. It will take another 45 minutes in moderate traffic to get up to Calistoga, home of popular hot springs and health spas. The county includes a few lakes and valleys to the east and, to the west, a small mountain range that separates Napa from the Sonoma Valley. Most of the action, however, is concentrated along the center of the Napa Valley.

The Napa Valley is the place you're most likely to run into a crew from a show like *Lifestyles of the Rich and Famous.* They're interested in some of the more expensive resorts and restaurants in the area, as well as the wealthy winery owners who entertain lavishly. Don't be intimidated. There are plenty of places that cater to all tastes and price ranges.

Route 29 is winery row. You can't drive very far without bumping into yet another little old winemaker. Pace yourself; there are more places than you can visit in one day. The major tourist draws are the large and famous operations like Domaine Chandon, Robert Mondavi, Beringer, and Sterling. These places offer tours through beautiful and interesting facilities. At Sterling, for example, you take a tram ride up to their hillside headquarters. By all means visit all the wineries that appeal to you, but don't miss the smaller operations or some of the other attractions available. In this chapter we will concentrate on the latter, with a unique winery thrown in here and there.

Despite the size of its international fame, Napa is one of the smallest counties in the Bay Area. Because it's little and because the wineries are concentrated along one main road, Napa is also one of the easiest places to visit. Unfortunately, there are times it seems everyone in Northern California is on that road, Route 29, but fear not; there are back roads that can take you away from the crowds.

A few general tips: As you travel north and south through the valley, you can avoid the crowds by taking the Silverado Trail, which runs parallel to Route 29. You can pick it up by heading east on any major crossroad, such as the Yountville or Rutherford crossroads. Then you can wander through the many back roads that are between Route 29 and the Silverado Trail. The best time of year to visit is the fall, when the weather is ideal and the annual grape crush is on. This is when the wineries are bustling with energy and the grapevines themselves light up the roadside with brilliant reds and yellows. Finally, as we mentioned in the Sonoma County chapter, if you're tasting wine and planning to continue behind the wheel, don't swallow the samples. Each winery provides buckets or drains so you don't have to drink and drive.

NAPA'S MAIN STREET
①

Before there was a highway to the Napa Valley, the main thoroughfare around here was the Napa River. During the nineteenth century, Napa was a bustling port town; ships, ferries, and railways carried passengers and dry goods to and fro. The main street of town grew up along this river and was a lively district for commerce and social activities.

But after World War II came so-called progress, and in the name of redevelopment much of the downtown district was abandoned in favor of shopping centers on the outskirts. Thus was born an irony. Though many people started coming to visit the Napa Valley, few stopped to visit Napa, the city. Even today most visitors continue past Napa and head straight to the more publicized towns of Yountville, Saint Helena, and Calistoga.

But the good citizens of Napa, undoubtedly tired of watching all the traffic pass them by, have decided to change things. They're proud of their history and are hell-bent to resuscitate their downtown. Today you can walk up Napa's Main Street and have a good cup of cappuccino, sample wine from a 100-year-old winery, and feast your eyes on recently restored vintage buildings that have been given a new lease on life.

It's a very attractive project, similar to many "old towns" in cities throughout the country. What makes this one so appealing is that it is not loaded with tourist shops selling the same trinkets that are sold all over the world. Instead, Napa's Main Street feels like it's designed for the community.

A good place to start a walking tour of Napa's Main Street is at the river at the far south end, where you'll find the huge Old Mill Building. It's been empty for years, but plans are to make it into an office/restaurant/theater complex. From the Old Mill as you walk up Main Street, you'll pass the lovely glazed-tile façade of the Main Street Bar and Grill (originally the Oberon Bar, built in 1880)

Napa

Calistoga
St. Helena
Yountville
Napa

and, across the street, the terracotta façade of Faginai's Liquor Store. One stop might be the Napa Valley Coffee Roasting Company (at the corner of Main and First). Here's where you'll find out what's happening in town, accompanied by the incredible smell of the coffee beans being roasted right there behind the counter. The building was originally designed in 1888 as a doctor's office.

Around the corner on First Street you can see the Semorile Building, built the same year for an Italian grocer and featuring an unusual combination of brick, stone, and wrought iron on the façade.

Continuing up Main Street, between First and Pearl streets, you'll find one of the most ambitious projects in town, the restoration of the old Napa Opera House. In its day it was a popular spot, though more often used for vaudeville acts than productions of *Tristan und Isolde*. The once elegant building with classical columns and triple-arched windows has been vacant for 50 years, but a group of citizens has formed a corporation to restore the place as a community center. At last check, renovation and fund-raising were still in progress.

At Main and Clinton, the two-story sandstone building that was once the town brothel is now the Andrews Meat Company and Deli—in other words, still a meat market. Today, however, the featured attraction is take-out sandwiches. And four blocks farther (at Main and Yount) is the only winery in town, Joseph Matthews, which dates from 1878. Three buildings remain from the original operation, and all have been restored and expanded to include a tasting room, a good restaurant (the Sherry Oven Restaurant and Seafood Bar), and a lovely bed-and-breakfast inn called Hennessey House.

The town of Napa also features some fine examples of Victorian homes. The Chamber of Commerce sells for $1 a packet of pamphlets on self-guided walking tours of the residential districts and of Main Street historical buildings.

NAPA CHAMBER OF COMMERCE, *1900 Jefferson Street, Napa. Open 8:30 A.M. to 5 P.M. weekdays, 11 A.M. to 3 P.M. weekends. Phone: (707) 226-7455. Napa County Landmarks, Inc., can arrange guided tours of Napa's Main Street given a week's notice; the charge is $5 per person. Phone: (707) 255-1836.*

HOW TO GET TO NAPA'S MAIN STREET: *From San Francisco, take the Golden Gate Bridge to Highway 101 North. After San Rafael, begin looking for the Route 37 exit to Vallejo. Go right (east) on Route 37 until you come to Route 29. Turn left (north) on Route 29, then branch right onto Route 121 and follow the signs to Main Street.*

From the East Bay, take Route 80 to the Highway 37–Vallejo turnoff, which is also the exit for Marine World/Africa USA. Follow Route 37 until you come to Route 29 and turn right. Then take Route 121 into central Napa.

THE NAPA VALLEY SHOW ②

The town of Yountville is named for George Yount, a former trapper who hung out with Kit Carson and became Napa Valley's first pioneer settler. He is also the father of the local wine industry, the first to plant grapevines in the area. Yountville exists now primarily for tourists. The biggest crowds will be at Vintage 1870, a huge shopping center fashioned out of an old winery building. Don't be discouraged by all the cars. There is an attraction here that is a great introduction to the valley.

The attraction is called the Napa Valley Show, a slide presentation of beautiful photographs accompanied by classical music. There is no narration; the images tell you all you need to know for preparing your own exploration of the valley. With the help of Vivaldi, this is photographic evidence that there are indeed four seasons in Northern California.

The Napa Valley Show is the creation of Keith Rosenthal, a photographer who spends much of his time combing the valley for his shots. He is on hand to answer questions from the audience and is happy to provide photo tips for your own snapshots. He also has a gallery on the premises to sell his photographs.

Keith himself is an interesting story. Originally from Pennsylvania, he spent 10 years as a long-haired, unshaved nomad named "Boof" (which was an acronym for "Brain out of Focus"), working his way around the world doing odd jobs and taking pictures. This was during the 1960s and 1970s, when a lot of young people were trying to find themselves. He found himself in the Napa Valley, and now there is not a grandmother around who wouldn't agree Keith is a clean-cut, attractive young man. Keith's beautiful photography is enjoyed by hundreds of appreciative viewers every week. The Napa Valley Show is presented in a comfortable theater and offers the opportunity for rest and reflection.

THE NAPA VALLEY SHOW, *in the Keith Rosenthal Theater and Gallery, located in the Vintage 1870 Building, 6525 Washington Street, Yountville. The 15-minute slide show begins on the hour and the half hour, 10 A.M. to 5:30 P.M. daily. Phone: (707) 944-2525. Admission: $2 to the Napa Valley Show; no admission charge to the gallery. Wheelchair accessible.*

HOW TO GET TO THE NAPA VALLEY SHOW: *From San Francisco, take the Golden Gate Bridge to Highway 101 North. Exit at Route 37 and head for Vallejo, which is to the east. Route 37 eventually comes to Route 29. Turn left on Route 29 and follow the signs to Calistoga. Take the first exit for Yountville, turn left, and you will come to the Vintage 1870 Building. There is a huge parking area. The Napa Valley Show is on the eastern side of the building, facing the Napa Valley Railway Inn.*

During the peak seasons, the people who operate the wineries, restaurants, inns, and stores can get pretty swamped by curious and demanding tourists, and even the kindest of them can get a bit testy. Consequently, it is possible for the visitor to feel a bit unappreciated.

This will never be the case at the Yountville Veterans' Home, where they are always thrilled to have visitors. I realize this is not the sort of attraction that normally draws people to the Napa Valley, but it is as inviting a spot as you'll find anywhere, and the buildings are of historic importance. I'm sure you will be surprised and rewarded here.

Located across the highway from the busy tourist attraction Vintage 1870,

VETERANS' HOME

the Spanish-style Veterans' Home was built over 100 years ago to accommodate Civil War veterans. Later it would house survivors of two world wars. The chapel is now a museum, devoted primarily to World War I memorabilia: bugles, posters, and newspaper clippings, all lovingly assembled and cared for by the residents, some of whom served in the "Great War."

On my visit, I was shown around by two veterans of World War I, 91-year-old Irv Hazeltine and 88-year-old John Ryan. They moved slowly, but their minds were quick and alert, and their eyes lit up when they told the stories of their lives and loves. (Irv has since died; his daughter wrote to ask for a copy of the television interview with him as a family heirloom. She said he loved being on TV.)

Indeed, the most rewarding part of the visit is the reaction you will get from many of the residents. They are very happy to see someone actually take the time to detour from wine tasting, and they will regale you with stories from Over There. You will feel appreciated.

YOUNTVILLE VETERANS' HOME, *Highway 29, Yountville. The grounds are open to the public 8 A.M. to 4:30 P.M. seven days a week. The museum is open noon to 4 P.M. If you would like a guided tour, call 24 hours in advance. Phone: (707) 944-4000. Wheelchair accessible.*

HOW TO GET TO THE YOUNTVILLE VETERANS' HOME: *From San Francisco, follow the directions to Yountville, but at the exit, go back under the highway and follow the signs to the veterans' home. It's well marked.*

SNAIL LADY
(4)

Everyone who has ever tended a garden should visit a lady in St. Helena named Francis Herb (pronounce the *H*). Unlike everyone else, Francis loves snails. Those pesky, slimy, repulsive creatures that most people try to get rid of are Francis's companions. What's more, they have made her a tidy profit over the past several years.

Francis has about 70,000 snails in her back yard. She raises them from babies, cares for them, then sells them to the many gourmet restaurants in the area. For example, if you try the squash blossoms stuffed with snails on the menu at Rose et Favor, you will be eating *escargot* raised by Francis.

The Herb garden is in the back of a sweet little house on a quiet residential street. You're most likely to find Francis out back feeding her snails. They like green leafy things (as gardeners know all too well), with the possible exception of spinach. According to Francis, snails are gregarious, playful, even adventurous. Seen through her eyes, they seem to be having a splendid time, climbing all over each other, napping, munching. She says she likes having them around because they don't make any noise.

Francis is also an encyclopedia of snail facts. How do you keep them away from your garden plants? Francis says just donate part of your garden to them; give them their own lettuce section and they'll stay there. Are snails native to

California? No, the French brought them over. How long does it take to raise one? It takes two to three years for a snail to grow to full size.

And could your own garden snails become a delicacy like *escargots*? Sure, if they're properly fed and old enough to be eaten. Francis says a good snail should taste like a good mushroom, with a woodsy flavor.

FRANCIS HERB'S SNAIL GARDEN, *1213 Stockton Street, St. Helena. Francis will let you see her garden and greenhouse if you call ahead. Phone: (707) 963-5113.*

HOW TO GET HERE: *From San Francisco, take the Golden Gate Bridge to Highway 101 North. Exit at Route 37 and follow the signs to Vallejo. At the intersection of Route 29, turn left (north) and follow Route 29 directly into the town of St. Helena. In town, turn left on Spring Street and then right on Stockton to 1213. There may even be a slime trail in front of the house.*

As you drive through the Napa Valley, several homes will remind you of Jane Wyman's place on the TV show *Falcon Crest*. A prime example is the beautiful Beringer showplace on Route 29 in St. Helena. But the real place used on *Falcon Crest* is tucked away on Spring Mountain Road outside the town of St. Helena.

FALCON CREST HOUSE

The house has a history even more interesting than anything the writers of *Falcon Crest* have dreamed up. This grand Victorian mansion was built in 1885 by a young wag named Tiburcio Parrot, the bastard son of a wealthy San Francisco businessman. Tiburcio was the black sheep of the family, which owned much of downtown San Francisco. To keep Sonny out of the way, Dad gave him 800 acres on Spring Mountain, and Sonny lived the life of an eccentric bachelor on his $5,000 a month allowance, a very tidy sum in the late 1800s (and not bad now). Tiburcio called his home Villa Miravalle. After Tiburcio died in 1894, the mansion was abandoned for years. Kids from town would break in to roller-skate on the hardwood floors, occasionally stumbling on a possession of one of Tiburcio's many lady friends.

The place didn't have a permanent resident until 1974, when a wealthy San Francisco builder named Michael Robbins bought the crumbling mansion and renovated it. In addition to sprucing up the house, Robbins built a winery and began making premium chardonnay and cabernet sauvignon bearing the label Spring Mountain.

Then location scouts from Hollywood came to the Napa Valley to find the perfect setting for a new TV series about a winery dynasty. You can probably predict the rest. Soon Spring Mountain Winery became better known as the "*Falcon Crest* House" than for its cabernet. So many winery visitors were sneaking up to the home where the Robbinses live that regular tours of the grounds were organized.

The house itself is not open to the public; the Robbinses prefer keeping their home to themselves (and, anyway, the TV show uses only the grounds; interiors are shot on a set in Tinseltown). The winery building, which is the first place you see, has a tasting room and many historical photos. It's also the business quarters for Spring Mountain, as well as the place where wine is stored in barrels. You can taste the many varieties of Spring Mountain wine, including one called Falcon Crest.

There are actually two ways to see the place. If you want simply to see the winery operation and taste some of the product, there is no charge. If, however, you want a guided tour of the 259-acre estate, complete with an outside look at the home used on *Falcon Crest*, including the swimming pool, gardens, and the guide's stories about the making of the series, there is a charge of $4.

If watching a TV crew at work is your interest, the series shoots occasionally at the location in summer; the rest of the year the series is shot in studios in Los Angeles. You might get lucky and bump into Lorenzo Lamas or Susan Sullivan, but don't plan your trip around it.

SPRING MOUNTAIN WINERY, *2805 Spring Mountain Road, St. Helena. The tasting room is open 10 A.M. to 5 P.M. weekdays, 10 A.M. to 6 P.M. Saturdays and Sundays throughout the year. Winery tours are popular, so be sure to make an appointment in advance. Phone: (707) 963-5233. Limited wheelchair access.*

HOW TO GET TO SPRING MOUNTAIN WINERY: *From San Francisco, take the Golden Gate Bridge to Route 101 North to the Vallejo–Route 37 exit. Take Route 37 until it connects with Route 29. Route 29 then goes all the way through the Napa Valley and is the main thoroughfare of St. Helena. When you reach St. Helena, turn left on Madrona Avenue. Go three blocks and look for Spring Mountain Road. Turn right and you'll come to the Spring Mountain entrance on the left.*

SILVERADO MUSEUM ⑥

If Sonoma Valley is the province of Jack London, Napa is Robert Louis Stevenson country, and the Silverado Museum is dedicated to the works of the Scottish author. As you enter this small and comfortable building, you will probably be greeted by the curator, Ellen Shafer. The first thing she'll do is put you at ease by explaining that the price of admission is your signature on the guest register. After that, you can browse on your own or engage Ms. Shafer in conversation. I recommend the latter, since she is a storehouse of stories and information.

According to Ellen, though Stevenson lived for less than two months in Napa Valley, he made an enormous contribution to the history of the area through his writing. In 1884 Stevenson published a book called *The Silverado Squatters,* an account of his honeymoon in an abandoned bunkhouse near the Silverado Mines of Mount St. Helena. Unlike the well-paid Jack London, Stevenson was broke; he and his bride could not afford to stay at one of the warm spring spas in Calistoga. Instead they carved out an idyllic, albeit humble, little vacation spot on the slopes of Mount St. Helena. *The Silverado Squatters* turned out to be one of the best histories of life in early Napa, and it includes Stevenson's observations about the fledgling wine industry and his visit to the nearby petrified forest (see item 14). After Napa, the Stevensons headed for the South Pacific, where Robert Louis continued to write until his death in 1894.

Today the author is remembered in Napa County with Robert Louis Stevenson State Park and the Silverado Museum in St. Helena. The museum was started by an advertising titan, Norman Strouse, who was chairman of the board of the world's largest agency, J. Walter Thompson. Strouse read *The Silverado Squatters*, loved it, and began collecting Stevenson's writings. When he retired, Strouse moved to St. Helena to create a Stevenson museum and a foundation to support it. He also recruited Ellen Shafer from Philadelphia to run the place.

On display are personal belongings of the author, including original manuscripts and toy soldiers from his childhood (the same toy soldiers that were immortalized in *A Child's Garden of Verses*). It's a good bet you'll come across a book or two that played an important part in your childhood. Remember *Treasure Island? Dr. Jekyll and Mr. Hyde?*

THE SILVERADO MUSEUM, *1490 Library Drive, St. Helena. Open noon to 4 P.M. Tuesday through Sunday; closed Monday and holidays. Admission: Free. Phone: (707) 963-3757. Wheelchair accessible.*

HOW TO GET HERE: *From San Francisco, follow the directions to St. Helena. Turn right when you get to Pope Street, then left on Railroad and right again on Library Lane. The Silverado Museum is next to the town library.*

Route 19, the main road through the Napa Valley, can get pretty hectic during the peak tourist times with wine tasters bouncing from winery to winery. Fortunately, two adjoining parks between the towns of St. Helena and Calistoga offer a chance to get away from the action, with activities for the whole family.

BY THE OLD MILL STREAM

Bothe–Napa Valley State Park offers picnicking, hiking, camping, and even a good-sized swimming pool, which can be very welcome during the summer when the valley temperature hovers in the 90s. The 50 campsites are often in great demand, so it's a good idea to reserve as far in advance as possible.

There's a trail in the park that leads next door to the Bale Grist Mill State Park. Here you get an idea of what this valley was like before the first grapevine was ever planted. Back in General Vallejo's time, this area was the breadbasket of Northern California. Wheat and corn fields flourished, and an English doctor named Edwin Bale (who also happened to be Vallejo's brother-in-law) capitalized on the crops by building a huge mill for grinding flour.

The Bale gristmill became a community center. While locals ground their flour, they'd exchange gossip and get to know one another.

Today folks can still gather there to meet one another, though the gossip is most likely to be about which winery offers the best tastings and where you can get a good meal for less than 20 bucks. Situated on Mill Creek, the wooden structure itself is very impressive and inviting, featuring a 36-foot waterwheel. Inside, a museum has been set up to introduce you to the history of the mill and the area.

The grounds are quite lovely. You feel like you are miles away from the highway when in fact you are just minutes away from bustling Route 29.

BOTHE–NAPA VALLEY STATE PARK, *3601 St. Helena Highway North, St. Helena. Open 8 A.M. to sundown daily. Admission: Free. For camping reservations and more information, call (707) 942-4575. Adjacent Bale Grist Mill State Park is open 10 A.M. to 5 P.M. daily. Admission: Free. Phone: (707) 942-4575. Wheelchair accessible.*

HOW TO GET HERE: *From San Francisco, take the Golden Gate Bridge to Route 101 North. Exit at Route 37 for Vallejo and Napa. At the intersection of Route 29, turn left, and stay on Route 29 until a few miles north of St. Helena. Look for the entrance on your left. There are separate entrances to the parks, but they are connected by trails.*

HURD'S CANDLE FACTORY ⑧

When you're driving up Route 29 in the Napa Valley, there is never any doubt you're in wine country. From Yountville to Calistoga there are countless wineries along the road, from the big and famous like Mondavi and Beringer to the boutique wineries like Frog's Leap and Grgich Hills Cellars.

OK, now what goes with wine? Cheese? Yep, you'll find several cheese shops along the way, and some wineries even sell cheese to accompany any spirits you might purchase. How about candlelight? For that there is a very inviting shop and "factory" located in the Freemark Abbey winery complex between St. Helena and Calistoga.

The Hurds started making candles in their garage in the East Bay town of Concord. When the business got big enough, the family moved the operation to the Napa Valley. There they hired a team of local candlemakers and spend their own time in partial retirement.

As you enter Hurd's Candles, it looks like your typical tourist gift shop, except almost all the items are beeswax candles of varying sizes, shapes, and colors. Continuing into the next room there are still more candles, plus a friendly group of women at work making candles. This is the "factory," which looks more like my image of Santa's workshop. At one station, a worker will take a sheet of parchment beeswax, which resembles a lasagne noodle, soften it in an electric frypan, then hand-roll it into the desired thickness. At another station, six or seven women will be adding decorations to the candles, using such implements as hair curlers and eyedroppers. At yet another table, another group is adding leaves to the candles, making a candle tree. It's a very homey operation.

You are welcome to come and watch. I chatted for quite a while with the staff, and they genuinely get a kick out of their work, each other, and showing others how they make their wares. It makes for a nice visit. They have more candles than you can shake a wick at. (And, if you need another stupid pun, you can always use "It's none of your beeswax.")

HURD'S CANDLES, *in the Freemark Abbey complex, 3020 St. Helena Highway North, St. Helena. Open 10 A.M. to 5 P.M. daily; closed on major holidays. Phone: (707) 963-7211.*

HOW TO GET HERE: *From San Francisco, follow the directions to St.Helena or Calistoga. The Freemark Abbey complex is clearly marked on the east side of Route 29, north of St. Helena.*

Up in the hills to the east of the Napa Valley, you are a world away from the tourist-oriented towns below. If you take Deer Park Road to Angwin, you will come to one of the few towns in the nation populated almost exclusively by Seventh-day Adventists. It is a quiet town, where much of the activity centers around Pacific Union College, a religious school whose students are quite different from those you might find at, say, Berkeley. For example, tune your car radio to the campus station, KCDS ("Christ Died for Our Sins"), and you will hear "The Inspirational Top 40." It's the only FM station that will come in loud and clear in Angwin.

The supermarket in the center of town is worth browsing, if only to notice the absence of items like meat, alcoholic beverages, cigarettes, and other items forbidden by the faith.

Another point of interest is Elmshaven, the Victorian estate of Ellen G. White, one of the founders of the Seventh-day Adventist religion. She is said to have had 2000 visions and nine prophetic dreams, upon which the teachings of the church are built. Ellen White lived in this house, ironically situated in one of the best wine-growing regions of the world, from 1900 to 1915. Today it is a must stop for Adventist pilgrims on their way to Angwin, but the Victorian home and bucolic estate are also of interest to many people regardless of faith.

Whatever your religious inclinations, there is a peaceful, refreshing quality to Elmshaven and Angwin, sort of like stepping onto the set of a Frank Capra movie, a small town where everybody knows everybody, tips their hats, and tries to do good. Just don't look for a pub to hang out in.

ELMSHAVEN, *125 Glass Mountain Lane, St. Helena. Open 10 A.M. to 5 P.M. Sunday through Thursday; 10 A.M. to 1 P.M. Friday; 2 to 6 P.M. Saturday. Admission: Free, though donations are requested. Phone: (707) 963-9039.*

HOW TO GET TO ELMSHAVEN: *Take Highway 29 through St. Helena. One mile past town, turn right on Deer Park Road; there will be a sign pointing to Angwin.*

ELMSHAVEN AND ANGWIN

Pass the flashing red light, then bear left at the Y in the road (the sign will point to the hospital). Turn left on Glass Mountain Road. Elmshaven will be on the right at the white bridge.

HOW TO GET TO ANGWIN: *Take Highway 29 through St. Helena, but instead of bearing left on Glass Mountain Road, keep to the right and go up the hill, following the signs to Angwin.*

HUBCAP HEAVEN

Outside of Angwin and over the hill, you will enter the rural and picturesque Pope Valley. In such a serene setting, it is a jolt to be greeted by the sight of one of the greatest folk art collections in the world.

At first it looks like a giant glare in the distance. As you get closer, you realize you are seeing hubcaps, thousands and thousands of hubcaps displayed in an endless variety of patterns. This is Litto's Hubcap Ranch. Name the car or a year, and the hubcap is there somewhere.

The collection belonged to Litto Diamonte, an Italian immigrant who settled in this valley to farm. When he started collecting hubcaps and arranging them in an artful manner, his family was at first amused, then amazed, then embarrassed, and finally accepting. The patriarch passed on in 1983 at age 93, but the Diamonte family has come to appreciate the folk art treasure they have on their hands and is doing everything possible to preserve it.

Although the family is not in the tourist attraction business, they maintain the property, keep those hubcaps shining, and welcome the curious who want to stop by and have a look. You can either stare from the road or get out of your car and wander around to have a closer look at the hubcaps, plus Litto's collection of birdhouses, which are placed around the property.

This collection simply sits in the yard and driveway of the family house. Though visitors are welcome, this is not an amusement park. There are no official greeters. No admission is charged, and last time I checked there were no souvenirs. It's simply there for all to see and to marvel at one man's dedication and ingenuity. Litto's has been established as a registered California landmark.

HOW TO GET HERE: *From San Francisco, the direct route is to follow the directions to St. Helena. On Route 29, north of St. Helena, turn right on Deer Park Road and follow the signs up the hill to Howell Mountain Road. Take Howell Mountain Road until it intersects with Pope Valley Road and turn right. You can't miss Litto's. This is about a 30-minute drive from St. Helena. A more scenic route is to exit Route 29 earlier at Rutherford, turning right onto Route 128. Take Route 128 to the Chiles–Pope Valley Road, turn left, and follow it all the way until you are blinded by the hubcaps. Litto's is from 45 minutes to an hour from the Rutherford turnoff.*

Just down the road from Litto's is a small family-run winery that is well worth a stop. The Pope Valley Winery is run by the Peddy family, a typical nuclear contingent of two parents, one teenage daughter, and one preteenage son. One of them will show you around, depending on who has some spare time at the moment.

Obviously, this tour is a far cry from the organized jaunts you will encounter when you visit the bigger wineries. There will be no slide presentation, no fancy descriptions of the wine's bouquet or legs. I was shown around by 14-year-old Elisa, who told me that she just pours, then listens; the customers love to tell her all about the wine.

Elisa did know a lot about the history of the place. It was originally built in 1909 by a fellow named Ed Haus. He and his brothers came to the Pope Valley when there was even less around there than there is today. They built some of the buildings in town, including the old blacksmith shop, which is now owned by the County Historical Society but as of this writing is not open for tours. Old Ed was something of a futurist in his day. He said that someday cars would replace horses, there would be airplanes in the sky, and people would take pleasure boats onto a nearby lake. Everybody thought he was crazy, of course; there were no lakes for miles around. Since then, many lakes have been created in the area, including Lake Berryessa.

Anyway, Ed apparently foresaw the wine industry boom, too, so he built this winery. He did well with it until Prohibition. The winery stopped production for quite a long time, and now the Peddys are trying to make a go of it. They are also restoring the wonderful historic buildings on the property, which also makes the place worth a visit.

POPE VALLEY WINERY, *6613 Pope Valley Road, Pope Valley. Open 8:30 A.M. to 4:30 P.M. Monday through Friday; weekends by appointment. Phone: (707) 965-9463.*

HOW TO GET HERE: *From San Francisco, follow the same directions as to Litto's. Continue down Pope Valley Road to the south; the entrance is on the other side of the street. Another route is to take the Bay Bridge to Route 37 to Napa. Get on Route 29 to Rutherford and follow the signs to Lake Berryessa. Take the Lawson-Chiles Road to the Pope Valley Road and continue past the little village of Pope Valley. Go for about a mile; the winery will be on your left.*

Calistoga is one town in the Napa Valley famous for something other than wine. Its claim to fame is mineral water and mud baths. Tourists come in droves to visit the various spots offering rest, relaxation, and various "cures." They also come to see a very attractive little town that has a special place in the history of the development of Napa County, which brings us to the Sharpsteen Museum.

From the outside it looks like a small house, hiding the fact that this is a very large and well-designed museum worthy of your attention. As you enter, you might think you've walked into the wrong place. A room full of drawings of Mickey Mouse and Donald Duck? That's right, because this is the room honoring Ben Sharpsteen, founder of this museum, who was also one of the original Walt Disney animators. For many years Sharpsteen vacationed in the area and later retired to Calistoga. He wanted to help preserve the rich history of the area, so he personally paid for the museum project. One thing he had learned from Disney is that audiences want to be entertained, so he set up the museum accordingly.

One of the highlights of the visit is the glass-enclosed diorama showing in great detail the master plan of the original town. Calistoga was intended to be a grand spa, similar to New York's Saratoga. The man behind the plan was a fascinating figure named Sam Brannan, reputed to be California's first millionaire. He also performed the first American marriage ceremony in California, published the state's first American newspaper, and was the man credited with starting the Gold Rush. As the legend goes, he ran up Montgomery Street in San Francisco with a vial of gold in his hand, shouting that gold had been discovered in the foothills of the Sierras (of course, he did this only after cornering the market on supplies to miners, hence Sam Brannan's millions).

To kick off his grand resort scheme, Brannan threw a large party. He may have had too much to drink, for during the ground-breaking ceremony for Saratoga, California, he proclaimed the founding of "Calistoga, Sarafornia." The name stuck.

Brannan's resort never really captured the loyalties of the very rich, but it did lead to the development of the town and the valley. Part of the museum is one of the cottages from the original spa. It is lavishly decorated with the original piano, Oriental rugs, and decorative Victorian furniture. In 1882 the cottage rented for $10 a week. This was too expensive for a newlywed writer named Robert Louis Stevenson, who had to go further up to Mount St. Helena for his honeymoon (see item 6, Silverado Museum).

You can be your own tour guide at the Sharpsteen Museum, although there are docents on hand to answer questions. Plan to spend at least an hour here enjoying the diorama, Wild West displays, stagecoaches, firearms, costumes, and artifacts of Messrs. Sharpsteen and Brannan.

SHARPSTEEN MUSEUM AND SAM BRANNAN COTTAGE, *1311 Washington Street, Calistoga. Open noon to 4 P.M. daily. Phone: (707) 942-5911. Wheelchair accessible.*

HOW TO GET HERE: *From San Francisco, take the Golden Gate Bridge to Highway 101 North. Exit to the right (east) at Route 37, heading for Vallejo. Turn left on Route 29 and follow it all the way into the town of Calistoga. You will be on the main street, which is Lincoln. When you come to Washington Street, turn left and you will come to the museum.*

Remember back in school learning about Old Faithful, the geyser in Yellowstone National Park? Well, for some reason the textbooks and teachers didn't seem to know about the Old Faithful geyser outside of Calistoga, California. This Old Faithful is, well, different from the famous one. For one thing, it's smaller and less crowded.

After following the several road signs pointing to the geyser, you see what looks like a national park entrance arch. But behind it is a little ticket booth, not far from a modest frame home. You buy your ticket and park the car. You walk around a fence and some trees until you come to a few picnic benches overlooking a pond that is sort of bubbling. Then a voice on the loudspeaker announces when the next eruption is expected (usually it's every 20 minutes). While you're waiting, you can read the yellowed magazine articles that are posted on a wooden fence leading to the rest rooms. In December 1948 *National Geographic* published an article about this place. And *Life* magazine did a spread in the 1950s; various newspaper headlines proclaim that this phenomenon you are awaiting is indeed "stranger than fiction."

Then you turn your attention to the bubbling pond. By George, it starts spouting, just like they promised. A huge stream of water shoots 60 feet or so for a few minutes. Then the eruption dies down, and the pond gurgles until the next eruption.

That's about all there is to it, but there is a very compelling charm about the place, as if stepping back to a more innocent time. Part of that is due to the operators, Harry and Olga Cream. They live in the house near the ticket booth; they retired to this 26-acre property in the early 1970s. They love it, and their enthusiasm is infectious. The Creams even heat their hot tub with steam from the mysterious underground waters. Harry and Olga keep running records on eruptions and will gladly tell you everything they know about geysers. And, according to Harry, Olga still gets a kick every time the darned thing goes off.

OLD FAITHFUL GEYSER, *1299 Tubbs Lane, Calistoga. Open 365 days a year, 9 A.M. to 5 P.M. during the winter months, 9 A.M. to 6 P.M. during the summer. Phone: (707) 942-6463. Admission: $2 for adults, $1 for children, under 12 free. Wheelchair accessible.*

HOW TO GET HERE: *From San Francisco, take the Golden Gate Bridge to Route 101 North. Follow Route 101 to Route 37 and turn right toward Vallejo. When you come to Route 29, turn left and go all the way through the Napa Valley to Calistoga. Go through town, and after leaving the main part of Calistoga, look for Tubbs Lane on the left. Turn left and you will soon come to the entrance for the geyser.*

PETRIFIED FOREST

If you are overwhelmed by the excitement of Old Faithful, you can calm yourself at another natural wonder of the world just down the road. The Petrified Forest is also another example of private enterprise at its best, a roadside attraction that is such a throwback to 1930s Americana that it doesn't even matter that not much happens here.

As you might expect from the name, the Petrified Forest is a collection of tree logs that have fossilized over the eons. Frankly, one tree that has turned into a rock doesn't look all that much different from the next tree that has also turned into a rock, but there's still something appealing about wandering through the well-marked paths that meander through the forest.

This has been a tourist attraction much longer than the wineries peddling their chardonnays (Robert Louis Stevenson wrote about it in 1883), and it is apparently an item in tourist guidebooks for Europeans because you will see people from all over the world strolling around, knocking on petrified wood.

The place was discovered by a Swedish seaman who retired and was looking for a field for his cow, so the legend goes. Six million years before that, Mount St. Helena had erupted, belching ash that engulfed the forest, which in turn seeped all the water from the trees and turned them into stone. Today in the gift shop you can purchase key rings and other souvenirs of this phenomenon.

By the way, if your image of a petrified forest is the classic Humphrey Bogart film, forget it. That was another part of the forest. . . .

PETRIFIED FOREST, *4100 Petrified Forest Road, Calistoga. Open 9 A.M. to 5 P.M. 365 days a year. Admission: $3 per person; under 10 free. Phone: (707) 942-6667. Wheelchair accessible.*

HOW TO GET HERE: *From San Francisco, follow the directions to the town of Calistoga. In town, Route 29 and Route 128 separate. Take Route 128 to the left until you come to Petrified Forest Road. Turn left and you will come to the forest, approximately 6 miles outside Calistoga.*

LILLIE LANGTRY SLEPT HERE

Driving north of the Pope Valley, you will cross over into Lake County, with Clear Lake as a major attraction. This is the largest lake entirely in California. Tahoe is larger, but part of it is in Nevada. Lake County also boasts a growing new wine industry, with one winery offering an unequaled bit of history. It's the house where Lillie Langtry lived, her hideaway when she needed a quiet place to be by herself. In case you don't know about Lillie, she was a turn-of-the-century entertainer as big in her day as, say, Barbra Streisand is today. Nicknamed the "Jersey Lily" (after her home island off the English coast), she was said to be the most beautiful woman in the world. Oscar Wilde said he would have rather discovered Lillie than America; the legendary Judge Roy Bean named a town in Texas for her, even though they never met. She was mistress to King Edward VII.

Lillie spent her weekends in this house from 1888 to 1908; she even started a winery here. A few years ago the property was purchased by a family that made a fortune farming in California and Hawaii. Son Orville Magoon lives in Lillie's house and runs things. He has lovingly restored the home to give it the look and feel of the Langtry era. Orville can tell you more about Lillie and her times than Lillie herself probably would have remembered.

He has also put her picture on the label that graces the wine made here. The winery is called Guenoc, named for the valley in which it rests, and it produces a very fine chardonnay and other varietals.

The house is used for special occasions, which includes open houses for the neighbors and whoever else happens to be on hand. Even if you can't be there for the big party, it's worth a trip to visit Guenoc. The setting is quite beautiful, with a shaded picnic area outside the tasting room, overlooking a pond and the hillside. You will want to linger and get the feeling of being out in the middle of nowhere, much as Lillie was when she sought her refuge from hordes of fans and suitors. Someday the Lake County region may be as popular as Napa and Sonoma counties, so you might as well see the area while it is still comparatively pristine. For now, there are no traffic jams, no souvenir shops or boutiques, and no restaurants, just quiet and wonderful scenery.

LILLIE LANGTRY HOUSE AND GUENOC WINERY, *21000 Butts Canyon Road, Middletown. Open house is held just twice a year. Call to find out when it is; admission is free. The winery is open 10 A.M. to 4:30 P.M. Thursday through Sunday; closed major holidays. Phone: (707) 987-2385.*

HOW TO GET HERE: *From San Francisco, take the Golden Gate Bridge to Highway 101 North. Exit onto Route 37 toward Vallejo and Napa. At Route 29, turn left and continue through the Napa Valley, past Calistoga to Middletown. Just past town, turn right at the Guenoc Valley sign onto Butts Canyon Road. Go 6 miles to the winery. The trip from Calistoga can take close to an hour if there is any traffic.*

From the Pope Valley, continue on Pope Valley Road all the way to the Guenoc winery.

South Bay

During commuting hours, the roads going south from San Francisco resemble one big parking lot. But if you avoid the crush of commuters along the industrial corridors from San Francisco International Airport down to San Jose, you can find much to see and do on a back-roads trip south.

If the northern Bay Area offers a chance to visit small farms and stay in touch with old-fashioned California, the southern Bay Area is a jolt into the present—and the future. This area has been more developed than preserved, and development often centers around one high-tech industry or another.

Still, it is an area rich in tradition, with a beauty and a character of its own. Here you will experience more of a Southern California—type of atmosphere in history, style, and climate. Just remember, don't judge the area by what you see from Highway 101. Many surprises await on the back roads.

CHAPTER **4** South Inland

So far in this book we have arranged our chapters by county, since Marin, Sonoma, and Napa are usually classified as specific destinations. However, as we head south the classifications change. People in the area don't talk about going to San Mateo County or San Benito County; they talk about going to the Peninsula or the Coast.

AREA OVERVIEW

83

If we wanted to get technical about it, San Francisco is the beginning of the peninsula that stretches from the city down almost to San Jose, encompassing the counties of San Francisco, San Mateo, and Santa Clara. For our purposes, we will call this general area South Bay Inland.

There are two main routes through this area, Highways 101 and 280, which interconnect in San Jose. U.S. 280 is one of the most scenic highways in America; U.S. 101 is the more industrial route.

From San Francisco, the nearest destinations, such as South San Francisco and Colma, are only a few minutes' drive from the southern city limits. The more distant destinations, such as Fremont Peak and Pinnacles National Monument, involve drives of 2 to 2½ hours. Most of the stops fall somewhere in between, in the 1- to 1½-hour range.

The major tourist attractions in the inland South Bay are the giant Great America amusement park in Santa Clara, the Winchester Mystery House in San Jose, and the Rosicrucian Museum, also in San Jose. This part of the world is also famous as the home of Silicon Valley, where the semiconductor and computer chip replaced the prune and apricot as the area's major products. Stanford University, the beautiful century-old campus of sandstone buildings sometimes called the "Harvard of the West," is a major attraction in Palo Alto.

But beyond the university, the suburban and industrial sprawl, and the freeways are less well publicized places with wonderful characters to meet. Here are some of them.

ACRES OF ORCHIDS

Just a few minutes outside the city of San Francisco is a place I can wholeheartedly recommend for anyone who loves flowers. Rod McLellan's Acres of Orchids is in a rather unlikely location, in an industrial section of the town of South San Francisco. But once you drive into the parking lot, you are in another world.

The name Acres of Orchids is no exaggeration. McLellan is the largest supplier of orchids in the world. Every kind of orchid imaginable is here, in an area that includes over a million square feet of greenhouses. There are other flowers on display, too, including a fragrant gardenia section (in fact, Rod's father, who started the family floral business in the late 1890s, takes credit for developing the gardenia corsage) and roses in a greenhouse three times the size of a football field. The big attraction, though, is the orchids, and a public tour is offered that will teach you not only about the incredible variety of the exotic flora but also how they are cloned to produce perfect new plants.

Do you need some orchid facts to entice you to take the one-hour tour? OK, did you know that orchids grow in almost every environment, from deserts to mountains to icelands like Iceland? Did you know they can live to be 40 to 50 years old and that despite their reputation, they are neither fragile nor tempera-

South Bay
(Inland)

South
San Francisco

280

Palo Alto

San Jose

Saratoga

Santa Clara Co.

101

Watsonville

Salinas

85

mental? Did you know that orchids are the largest flowering group in the plant kingdom, with more than 30,000 species?

Amazing facts aside, the tour of the greenhouses is a visual treat, as you see fascinating plants of all shapes and colors. I was particularly intrigued by a cloning process, whereby a tiny seed is placed in a solution in a bottle. As the seed sprouts, the bottles are rotated to give each plant uniform growing conditions. Eventually the plant is moved to a larger bottle, then to a pot and soil. All this is done in a laboratory-like situation, easy to see as the guide takes you through the operation.

While you're here, the McLellans would not be displeased if you stopped in their sales room. That's where you can buy plants to take home or just browse in what feels like a lush tropical garden. Acres of Orchids also offers a plant-sitting service for taking care of people's plants while they travel and frequent orchid-growing classes.

ACRES OF ORCHIDS, *1459 El Camino Real, South San Francisco. Gift shop open 8 A.M. to 5 P.M. every day, except major holidays. Tours are offered twice daily, at 10:30 A.M. and 1:30 P.M. Admission: Free. Phone: (415) 871-5655. Wheelchair accessible.*

HOW TO GET HERE: *From San Francisco, take Highway 101 South to Route 280. Exit on Hickey Boulevard and proceed east to El Camino Real. Turn right and one block later, start looking for the entrance. It's just 15 minutes south of San Francisco.*

COLMA, DEAD OR ALIVE ②

There is no town anywhere like Colma. Population 731 above ground, 1,500,000 underground and still growing.

Colma is certainly the cemetery capital of the world. If a certain deceased had any part of the making of San Francisco history, chances are he or she is buried in Colma.

The reason for this is that in the 1920s, the City of San Francisco declared that city real estate was too precious a commodity to be used as burial ground. So a law was passed not only forbidding new graves within the city limits but ordering the removal of existing ones. The lone exception was the military cemetery in the Presidio, which is federal property.

So began the great exodus of the deceased to the suburbs. Thousands of memorial monuments and the accompanying remains were transported to a community a few miles south of the city limits, and new industries developed: grave digging, memorial garden care, monument making, and floral offerings.

Even today, when the backhoe has cut back on the need for gravediggers and the weedwhacker has reduced the opportunities for lawn workers, Colma still has an economy dependent on the life of cemeteries. There are 14 memorial gardens in town, including ones for those of Italian, Japanese, Chinese, Serbian, and Jewish descent. Perhaps the most unusual of all is Pet's Rest, where some 11,000 graves mark the memory of dogs with names like Ferocious and Pepi and cats named Sabrina and Marcello. According to cemetery insiders, the pet cemetery gets more floral offerings daily than the final resting places for people.

For a crash course in Bay Area history, you can search the various cemeteries for famous names. At plush Cypress Lawn, which features duck ponds and a spectacular display of stained glass in one of the huge cremation mausoleums, you will find monuments that bear names like Hearst, Crocker, and Matson. At the Jewish Home of Peace, you'll find the group nicknamed the Merchant Princes of the City: Levi Strauss, Zellerbach, Magnin. At another Jewish cemetery, Hills of Eternity, you'll find the grave of the famous lawman Wyatt Earp, which comes as a surprise to many visitors. Marshall Earp lived out his later years in Oakland and is buried next to his wife, who was Jewish.

The revered Emperor Norton, the first in a very long line of famous only–in–San Francisco characters, is at Woodlawn. His final resting place is the site of an annual shindig thrown by the self-appointed guardians of Bay Area history, E Clampus Vitus; this organization of hard-drinking, party-loving men spends its nonparty time placing very authentic-looking metal plaques as historical markers all around the Bay Area. The Emperor, who proclaimed himself King after he lost all his money and part of his mind in the Gold Rush, is the patron saint of the "Clampers."

You can visit the various cemeteries just about any time during daylight hours simply by driving through the gates. Each cemetery has a large parking lot, and you can drive through the grounds of some of them. If you're feeling adventurous and want to hear some old-time stories about the town, drop in to Molloy's Bar, a century-old Irish bar where the locals always seem to be having a wake. It's at 1655 Mission Road; phone (415) 755-9545.

TO GET TO COLMA *from San Francisco: Take Highway 101 South to Route 280. Exit at the Junipero Serra Boulevard exit and head east, which is to the left away from the Serramonte Shopping Center, then down the hill to El Camino Real. This is Colma, and the cemeteries are on both sides of the road.*

FROM ACRES OF ORCHIDS: *Continue south on El Camino Real to the town of Colma.*

COYOTE POINT MUSEUM

Practically in the shadow of San Francisco International Airport, on the Bay side of what is known as the Peninsula, is a large and appealing park at Coyote Point. The 670-acre recreational area offers biking and walking paths, a picnic area, golf, and a marina, all under the shade of fragrant eucalyptus trees.

The highlight of the park is the Museum for Environmental Education, which is one of the best museums of its type I've seen anywhere. The San Mateo County

Park System has done a wonderful job in designing a facility that is entertaining and informative, one that effectively illustrates an important fact: that the earth is very fragile and we need to take care of it. The exhibits are presented in such a way that if this place had been around when I was in school, I think I would have been a more willing participant in field trips.

It is an ambitious presentation, with exhibits on three descending levels, representing the areas of the Peninsula from the mountains to the ocean to the Bay. There is a light and airy quality to the place; you feel like you are outdoors much of the time. Almost everything that lives in the Bay and on the Peninsula is shown here in a way that reveals its connection to our daily life.

The museum is set up for a self-guided stroll through descriptive exhibits. The one that fascinated me most shows the relationship of predators to the ecological balance by displaying what a hawk eats in one year. On a facsimile of a tall tree you see representations of more than 1000 mice plus birds, squirrels, gophers, snakes, weasels, and the rest of the hungry hawk's diet. It's a graphic demonstration that one man's killer is another man's pest control, or vice versa. I'm sure you'll find your own favorites and draw your own conclusions on your quick and entertaining lesson about the environmental balance of the Bay at the Coyote Point Museum.

THE COYOTE POINT MUSEUM FOR ENVIRONMENTAL EDUCATION, *Coyote Point County Park. Open 9 A.M. to 5 P.M. Tuesday through Friday, 1 to 5 P.M. Saturday and Sunday. Admission: Park entrance fee, $2.00 per car, plus museum admission, adults, $1.00; children, 50 cents. Phone: (415) 342-7755. Wheelchair accessible.*

HOW TO GET HERE: *From San Francisco, take Route 101 South to the Poplar Avenue exit. Follow signs to Coyote Point Drive and the park entrance. When you pay the entrance fee, the person at the gate can direct you to the museum.*

DYNASTY HOUSE

The suburban communities of Atherton, Hillsborough, and Woodside are among the wealthiest in the nation. Here you will find estates owned by families like the Hearsts, the Davies of San Francisco Symphony Hall fame, heirs to Levi Strauss, and other names synonymous with Bay Area society. You will also find Blake Carrington's mansion.

Though the exterior of the house is shown every week on television, the *Dynasty* folks don't really hang out here, except to shoot an occasional scene outside. No matter, the history of the house known as Filoli is better than TV writers can come up with.

The name is a combination of the words *FIght, LOve,* and *LIfe.* This was the motto of one William Bourne, a gold-mining millionaire and the original water baron of the Peninsula. He's the one who saw that the expanding San Francisco suburbs would need lots of water, so he figured out a way to bring it down from the melting snows of the Sierra. That's still the way the Bay Area gets its water, often in competition with Southern California for the rights.

In 1916 Bourne commissioned the noted architect Willis Polk to build him the 43-room mansion and 16 acres of gardens that would become known as Filoli. Though he paid $109,000 for it—a very tidy sum in those days—there's no point in trying to guess what it would cost now. This kind of place simply isn't built anymore, not even for the Carringtons. It is spectacular.

Among the many features are 20-foot ceilings, priceless Oriental rugs, rare French furniture, and a bank-style vault for storing the family china and silver. Each room has a distinct character, from the massive book-lined library to the elegant "French Room," all powder blue with white trim and very delicate. The centerpiece of the house is the grand ballroom, complete with a stage, crystal chandeliers, and impressive murals.

The outside is just as impressive, especially on a pretty day. The gardens are extensive and beautifully maintained. The rose garden features at least 250 varieties, including the Bing Crosby, named after the guy who used to live down the road.

Filoli is a big operation, run by the National Trust for Historic Preservation. Tours include a walk through the house and gardens. Special events, including teas and luncheons, are offered on occasion, and there is a large garden and a gift shop featuring plants, gardening books, cookbooks, and potpourri made from the plants grown on the grounds. However, you must have reservations, even if you plan only to visit the gift shop. Saturdays during the summer are particularly busy times, so be sure to call two weeks to a month in advance of your visit.

FILOLI, *Cañada Road, Woodside. Open mid-February through mid-November. Admission: $6 per person; children under 12 not admitted. For tour schedule and reservations, call (415) 364-2880.*

HOW TO GET TO FILOLI: *From San Francisco, take Highway 101 South to Route 280. Exit at Edgewood Road (the exit right after Highway 92); go right (west) on Edgewood a short distance until the road ends. Make a right turn and you will be on Cañada Road. Less than a quarter mile later you will see a sign for Filoli; the gate will be on your left.*

ELECTRONICS MUSEUM

Here in the heart of Silicon Valley is a museum dedicated to the electronic wonders before the computer.

Perhaps you're old enough to remember big console radios, the kind you were never supposed to touch because the dials were set for Grandpa. Well, this type of radio is on display at the Electronics Museum, on the campus of Foothill College in Los Altos. It takes a little work to find the place, but if you are fascinated by anything to do with radio, television, and telephones, it's well worth the effort.

The Electronics Museum is the object of affection for a group of former broadcast and telephone company engineers. Together they managed to collect and build a wonderful exhibit of artifacts from the earliest ham operations to the dawn of the tiny portable. No boom boxes here.

You'll see all sizes and shapes of tube radios, most of them still working, and you'll see the smallest transistor jobs. You'll see early television sets, including the first portable (which, by the way, Arnold Schwarzenegger would have a difficult time lugging around). There are telephones of all vintages, sizes, and shapes, and microphones used by Groucho Marx and Bob Hope, and, for real connoisseurs, an artful display of telephone cable insulator covers—very colorful!

Other displays trace the history of communications and show the technical process by which sound is transmitted. The hero of the place seems to be Lee DeForest, who made radio possible by developing the first electronic tube that would amplify sound. Another treat is meeting the people who run the museum. All are volunteers, and they are here because they truly love equipment and communications and showing people around. They'll operate a ham radio for you or deliver a brief lecture on the comparative contributions of David Sarnoff and Thomas Edison, if requested. The guides are especially turned on when they get to show kids the glories of radio.

FOOTHILL COLLEGE ELECTRONICS MUSEUM, *12345 South El Monte Road, Los Altos Hills. Open 9 A.M. to 4 P.M. Thursday and Friday, 1 to 4:30 P.M. Saturday and Sunday. Admission: Adults, $2; children, 50 cents. Phone: (415) 948-8590.*

HOW TO GET HERE: *From San Francisco, take Route 101 South to Route 280 and take the Foothill exit. You will see the college on the right. That's the easy part. Now enter the campus and ask directions for the museum. If no one can help, wind up the main road as it climbs a hill to the right and look for a building on top of the hill with a radio tower outside. It's not really all that difficult; it's just that at last report, there was no sign in front of the building indicating the museum.*

ALLIED ARTS GUILD
⑥

The suburbs of the South Bay are dotted with symbols of the old and the new California. As you drive through communities like Palo Alto, Los Altos, and San Mateo, you see the old Spanish architecture (white adobe homes with red tile roofs) and the new all-American type shopping mall. At the Allied Arts Guild in Menlo Park, the two influences are combined.

Once a part of the Spanish land grant known as the Rancho de las Pulgas ("Ranch of the Fleas"), the Arts Guild might have been the first shopping center in the state. It certainly is a lovely place to visit and shop. Located in the middle of an attractive tree-lined neighborhood, the Guild is a series of small shops and artists' work spaces. Stone and brick pathways lead you through a beautiful garden and courtyard; murals, statues, and tiles decorate the walkways. It resembles the great crafts guilds of Europe and was built in the 1930s, before grand projects like this became economically prohibitive.

The Guild is operated by volunteer groups to benefit the nearby Children's Hospital at Stanford. The Palo Alto Auxiliary runs a charming tearoom; the Woodside-Atherton Auxiliary runs the Traditional Shop, the largest store in the complex, featuring fine china, silver, antiques, and gifts for the home. In case you're not familiar with the communities of Atherton and Woodside, they are among the wealthiest suburbs in the nation, and the merchandise in this shop reflects a lifestyle of elegant entertaining.

The rest of the shops offer a variety of items for a variety of tastes and budgets. At last check, there was an art gallery, a kitchen shop, a candle shop, a children's store, and shops for weaving and sewing supplies.

In barns at the end of the pathway are large crafts operations: glassblower, carpenter, furniture restorer. These are private businesses that rent space from the auxiliaries, so a portion of the proceeds from any sale goes to the hospital, which serves children from all over the world.

ALLIED ARTS GUILD, *Arbor Road at Creek Drive, Menlo Park. Shops open 10 A.M. to 5 P.M. Monday through Saturday; closed Sunday. Tearoom seatings are at noon, 12:30 P.M., and 1 P.M. Monday through Friday; a buffet lunch is served on Saturday. Reservations are a good idea. Phone: (415) 324-2588.*

HOW TO GET TO ALLIED ARTS: *From San Francisco, take Highway 101 South to the Marsh Road exit in Redwood City. Follow Marsh Road to the right to Middlefield Road and turn left. Continue on Middlefield to Ravenswood Avenue; turn right and continue to El Camino, then turn left. Go a few blocks to Cambridge Street, turn right, and continue about five blocks through a residential area. The street will end in the Allied Arts parking lot. It may sound complicated, but it's actually easy.*

SUNSET MAGAZINE

There have been many attempts to describe the California lifestyle. Those who do not live here often characterize it as trendy, kooky, and glitzy. And though those adjectives all have their basis in truth, if you want to see how Californians see themselves, pick up a copy of *Sunset* magazine. Better yet, visit their headquarters in Menlo Park, just a few minutes away from the Allied Arts Guild.

Sunset magazine is an extremely successful monthly publication that focuses on four aspects of life on the West Coast: food, travel, gardening, and home improvement. A tour of the magazine's spacious facilities follows suit.

Visitors gather in the sprawling lobby of the main building, which is designed to look like the archetypical California ranch house. In the lobby, make sure you look closely at the receptionist's desk; it dates back to the 1600s. The tour begins with a brief history of *Sunset* magazine, which began as a house organ for the

Southern Pacific Railroad. In 1898 the first issues were used to entice people riding the Sunset Limited from New Orleans to Los Angeles to move out West. Later it became a literary magazine, featuring the likes of Jack London, Mark Twain, and Bret Harte. Later still it was sold to the Lane family, which continues to operate the company.

After the history lesson, the guide takes you through three major areas of the building: the editorial offices; the entertainment center, which is a large conference-type room where the magazine holds some of its major social functions and which features the ultimate appliance of the West, a large barbecue grill; and the test kitchens for the recipes that appear in each issue. Unfortunately, tasting is not usually a part of the tour.

But the highlight for most people can be seen with or without the tour: the spectacular *Sunset* magazine garden. It features nearly 300 species of plants and is arranged to show off the plants native to the Pacific states, from Northwest rhododendrons to desert cacti. The plants surround a 1-acre lawn with flat, easy-to-walk paths around the perimeters. As you stroll, keep in mind that until the magazine moved here in the 1950s, this was a barren field. Everything, including the redwood trees, was brought in by gardening experts. The stroll through the garden is enhanced by stopping at the reception desk to pick up a pamphlet that identifies each plant on the path. The best times to visit are spring and fall, but something will be blooming all year round.

SUNSET MAGAZINE LABORATORY OF WESTERN LIVING, *80 Willow Road, Menlo Park. Tours of the building are offered at 10:30 A.M., 11:30 A.M., 1 P.M., 2 P.M., and 3 P.M. Monday through Friday; closed Saturday, Sunday, and holidays. The gardens are open 9 A.M. to 4:30 P.M., Monday through Friday. Admission: Free. Phone: (415) 321-3600. Wheelchair accessible.*

HOW TO GET HERE: *From San Francisco, take Highway 101 South to the Willow Road exit in Menlo Park. Follow Willow Road west to the intersection of Middlefield Road. Sunset's visitor's center is on the southwest corner.*

BARBIE DOLL HALL OF FAME ⑧

From the outside of the Doll Studio in Palo Alto you would think that this is just another store that sells dolls. But no. Inside, you will find the world's largest collection of Barbies. Owner Evelyn Burkhalter says her collection is more complete than that of the manufacturer, Mattel Toys. She has collected 14,000 Barbies and Kens, including the first black Barbie, a hippie Barbie, Barbie as the first woman astronaut, and Barbie as the ultimate yuppie. She says there are only three outfits and one version of the doll that she does not yet have.

When I visited, Evelyn and her husband were making plans to expand the display, but in the meantime it will remain in the back of the Doll Studio. Even in these cramped quarters you get a history of modern America as evidenced by the changes in Barbie's clothes, accessories, and hairstyles. The fact that Evelyn bears a striking resemblance to America's doll sweetheart will not escape you. She says she likes Barbies because they symbolize that women are survivors, capable of anything.

BARBIE HALL OF FAME, *in the Doll Studio, 325 Hamilton, Palo Alto. Open 10:15 A.M. to 5 P.M., Tuesday through Saturday. Admission: Adults, $1; children, 50 cents. Phone: (415) 326-5841.*

HOW TO GET HERE: *From San Francisco, take Highway 101 South to the University Avenue exit. Turn west into Palo Alto. In downtown Palo Alto, turn left at Middlefield Road to Hamilton; turn right on Hamilton to 325.*

PALO ALTO BAYLANDS ⑨

There are several places in the Bay Area that birdwatchers love. Baylands Nature Preserve near Palo Alto is near the top of the list. More than 100 species of birds have been seen on this marsh, including a variety of ducks, hawks, herons, and owls. And even if you are not a bird fan, you can get a sense of what the Bay was like years ago, before development.

Situated at the end of Embarcadero Road, this 120-acre salt marsh is alive with birds and plants. Though it's just a short drive from Route 101, it feels far removed from the noise and pollution of the freeway; possibly due to the influence of plant life and the Bay, the air feels better out here.

The activities are low-key and simple. At the attractive interpretive center you can see what to look for once you go out on the trails. The trails are a system of boardwalks and levees that take you out at water level into the marsh. You can roam on your own with your binoculars or hook up with one of the trained naturalists for a guided walk.

BAYLANDS NATURE PRESERVE, *2775 Embarcadero Road, Palo Alto. The boardwalks are usually open during daylight hours, but the guided tours and the interpretive center are subject to changing schedules; it's best to call ahead. The most recent schedule for the interpretive center was 2 to 5 P.M. Wednesday through Friday and 1 to 5 P.M. Saturday and Sunday. Admission: Free. Phone: (415) 329-2506.*

HOW TO GET HERE: *From San Francisco, take Highway 101 South toward San Jose. Exit onto Embarcadero Road in Palo Alto and go east, which is to the left, until you come to the end of the road. You will be at Baylands.*

RADIO-CONTROLLED AIRPLANE CLUB

There's a terrific free show put on daily for anyone interested in airplanes. It takes place at a small airfield on the grounds of a state hospital, in the shadow of the San Jose Airport. Here, members of the Pioneer Radio Control Club turn out to tinker with their miniature planes, then get in line for their turn at the miniature airstrip.

Here's the scene: You take a long driveway that borders Agnews Hospital.

After passing several buildings, you are in one of the few open fields still untouched by developers. There, a small grandstand overlooks a tiny airstrip with several flagposts on its border. The posts signify the various radio frequencies that can be used by Pioneer Club members to fly their craft; when a flag is up, that frequency is in use.

There are no tickets to buy, no formal program. You can just wander around, talk to the fliers, and watch them show off. Don't be surprised if one of the Pioneers tries to get you to join the club, or to at least take some flying lessons. Though it looks easy, several experienced pilots told me that remote-controlled models are more difficult to operate than a real plane.

As for the aircraft themselves, every model imaginable is on display, from tiny replicas of historic craft to 4-foot planes that will fly at 150 miles per hour. Many of the club members made their planes from scratch and are only too happy to tell you all about them. These treasures sit on patches of carpet in the field as the pilots await their turns to fly. The average plane is 2 to 3 feet long and weighs about 30 pounds.

The air show is spectacular. The models go through a variety of tricks and maneuvers that would challenge any stunt flier. The loop-de-loops, spins, and dives make even the most seasoned club member duck for cover every now and then. There are also occasional midair collisions, especially when seven or eight planes fill the skies at the same time. But even though each plane represents an investment starting at $200, the pilots appear to take "wipeouts" as part of the fun.

By the way, the administrators of the hospital love having the Pioneer Club use their grounds. They feel that having such an activity on their grounds provides therapeutic entertainment for their mentally handicapped patients.

THE PIONEER RADIO CONTROL CLUB, *on the grounds of Agnews State Hospital, east of Mountain View. There are no formal flying times, but at almost any time during the day, every day, someone from the club will be out there; Sundays draw the biggest crowds. For information, call Ken Willard, (415) 967-3828; the number of the pay phone out at the airstrip is (408) 988-9543.*

HOW TO GET HERE: *From San Francisco, take the Bay Bridge to Route 880 South toward San Jose. Exit onto Route 237, following the signs to Mountain View. After a few miles, turn left onto Lafayette Street, which is at a stoplight. Drive 1.8 miles to a traffic signal and the Agnews State Hospital entrance. Turn left and continue past the hospital buildings to Lick Mill Road. You will see the airfield on the left.*

It comes as a surprise to many people to learn that NASA has a major facility in the San Francisco area. While Houston is the center for activities in outer space, the giant NASA-Ames research facility at Moffett Field near Mountain View is a center for studying such issues as commercial aviation flight safety and aircraft design.

The center is open for public tours. They begin in an auditorium with a film that outlines the kind of work done at this facility, followed by a question-and-answer period. It's important to get a lot of the talking out of the way here because the rest of the tour is quite noisy; the human voice is often drowned out by the roar of engines and the hum of wind tunnels.

In fact, the largest wind tunnel in the world is here at Ames, with an interior test space of 80 feet in height and 120 feet in width. The wind is too strong to permit visitors to go inside, but you can look through windows. All in all, there are 20 wind tunnels on the property.

Until recently, hangars and wind tunnels were the main tools used to test aircraft. But now the computer has been introduced for testing aircraft safety—not surprisingly, considering the facility's location in Silicon Valley, one of the major computer development centers in the world. The world's largest computer is used at Ames to simulate aeronautical conditions and is expected to be the most valuable device yet for preventive safety.

The tour makes selected stops throughout the facility, depending on the nature of the work being done at the moment. You might see a flight simulation laboratory, and you will certainly be taken into one of the immense hangars that house experimental aircraft.

There is no charge for the tour, but you will probably not be able to resist the small gift shop back in the visitor's center, which offers space memorabilia and even sells the space snacks astronauts use. The freeze-dried ice cream is really something.

NASA-AMES RESEARCH CENTER, *Moffett Field, Mountain View. For information about visiting, call (415) 966-5976. Wheelchair accessible.*

HOW TO GET HERE: *From San Francisco, take Highway 101 South. After the Palo Alto exits and just before Mountain View you will see the huge hangars from the road. Look for the NASA-Ames exit and follow the signs.*

NASA
⑪

Here's a trivia question that you can use to dazzle your friends. Long before Dionne Warwick sang "Do you know the way to San Jose?" a famous Frenchman asked the same question. Who was he?

Answer: Alexander Eiffel, of tower fame.

Monsieur Eiffel came to this small California town back in the 1880s to get some ideas for the tower he was to build in Paris. He wanted to see the famous San Jose Tower of Light.

SAN JOSE HISTORICAL PARK
⑫

The story of the light goes like this: Two years after Edison perfected the light bulb, electric light was introduced to the town of San Jose. The town fathers had the bright idea to save on the cost of individual street lights by erecting one giant tower to illuminate the entire community. A magnificent tower was built. Unfortunately, it lit the sky more than the streets. It was so intense that nearby farm animals became confused and couldn't sleep. Roosters crowed at the wrong times; cows didn't know when to give milk. The tower stood for several years until it fell over in a storm. Once the beacon hit the dirt, it was decided to leave well enough alone and relegate the memory of the tower to a historical park.

Today, a half-size replica of the infamous tower of light is the centerpiece of a park that commemorates the early days of San Jose. It stands in the midst of a re-created Main Street. Here you can wander inside a full-scale version of the Pacific Hotel, where you could get room and board for $1 a night in 1881. There's the original Banca d'Italia, started by A. P. Giannini, who later built the Bank of America. You can get a soda in O'Brien's Candy Factory, the place that first served ice-cream sodas west of Detroit, and you can visit a firehouse and many other buildings that give you a taste of the olden days. It's done on a small, easily manageable scale, so you are not overwhelmed by induced nostalgia.

The historical park is inside a larger community park of 150 acres of picnic grounds, a miniature train, a children's petting zoo, and room to roam. Kelley Park also includes a very different sort of attraction, the Japanese Friendship Garden. As you might expect, this is a serene, well-manicured, formal Japanese garden, complete with bridges, paths, waterfalls, and streams filled with colorful Japanese goldfish called *koi*. Here you can wander at your own pace or ask one of the guides to explain the various symbols in the garden.

SAN JOSE HISTORICAL PARK, *in Kelley Park, 635 Phelan Avenue, San Jose. Open 10 A.M. to 4:30 P.M. Monday through Friday; noon to 4:30 P.M. Saturday and Sunday. Admission: Adults, $1.00; children, 50 cents. Phone: (408) 277-5351 or (408) 287-2290.*

HOW TO GET HERE: *From San Francisco, take Route 101 South to Route 280 South to San Jose. Exit at Tenth Street and follow it to Senter Road. The entrance to the park is at Senter and Phelan Avenue.*

LICK OBSERVATORY ⑬

One of the most powerful telescopes in the world is located atop Mount Hamilton, above the metropolis of San Jose. Astronomers from all around the globe come here to use the 120-inch reflector telescope. The operation is run by the University of California, Santa Cruz, and tours are available.

The story behind the observatory is almost as fascinating as the place itself. Its benefactor, James Lick, was one of the more eccentric Gold Rush millionaires. He became obsessed with Egyptian culture and had a plan to build a pyramid in the center of San Francisco. The city fathers talked him out of it (though many years later, the Transamerica Corporation built its office building in the shape of a pyramid, and now it is a city landmark).

Lick also became obsessed with astronomy. He was convinced that there was some form of life on the moon. So he decided to build the largest telescope and observatory possible, again in the center of San Francisco. And again the city fathers talked him out of it. Undaunted, Lick found a remote mountaintop for his project.

The task of building the observatory was monumental. To begin with, there was no road, so one had to be built to accommodate all the heavy machinery and supplies for the construction of the place. As a matter of fact, Lick turned out to be a shrewd negotiator. He agreed to provide the $700,000 necessary to build the complex only if the county would build a road to the top. The road was finished in 1876, the same year Lick died. His dream observatory wasn't completed until 12 years later. His remains are buried at the base of the telescope.

Early visitors had to take a five-hour horse-drawn stage ride to the top. No doubt the scientists and tourists found it worth the trip. After all, it was the first attempt at a mountaintop observatory, and at the time, it was the largest telescope in the world.

Today a small community resides atop the mountain to study at the observatory and maintain the property. The road is paved, but the drive up the 4200-foot mountain takes at least an hour. It is not recommended for anyone who tends to get carsick on winding roads. The scenery, however, is spectacular, and the even longer road down the back side takes you into the least developed sections of Santa Clara and Alameda counties.

Atop the mountain, several buildings house telescopes. Visitors have many things to see, determined by the time of year and the various projects in progress. Always there is the visitor's gallery, where you can browse through a large institutional-type building and see photographs of the skies as seen by the telescopes. There is also a gift shop and of course the featured attraction, the giant telescope, which has the power to see stars 10 billion light-years away. If you want to imagine how big this instrument is, imagine a telescope the height of a six-story building. A huge domed ceiling opens to allow the telescope its view of the sky.

On Friday nights from April to October, special programs are conducted at the observatory, such as a lecture by an astronomer and a nighttime peek at the heavens through the big lens.

LICK OBSERVATORY, *Mount Hamilton. Open to the public daily except Thanksgiving, Christmas, and New Year's Day from 10 A.M. to 5 P.M. Programs change often, so it is best to call ahead. Phone: (408) 274-5061.*

HOW TO GET HERE: *From San Francisco, take Highway 101 South to San Jose. Exit at Route 130–Alum Rock Road and continue up the hill until you reach the top. You will see signs marking the way; at some points the road will be called Mount Hamilton Road.*

SASO HERB GARDENS

On a quiet street not far from Saratoga's city hall is a place that attracts visitors from all over the world. Still, many people in the Bay Area have never heard of it, unless they happen to love herbs. But for those who know, the Saso Herb Gardens are truly first-class.

On the acre of land that surrounds their modest home, Louis and Virginia Saso have devoted a quarter of a century to growing herbs and spreading the word about what they can do for us. Their garden, which Louis says he's sure is the most extensive herb collection in the country, is well worth a visit.

First of all, the place is beautiful; 1000 plants are arranged in display areas you can stroll through at your leisure. This is also an educational experience because as you wander around, you can read about the various kinds of herbs. Did you know that basil symbolizes love?

There's a medicinal section, with herbs that resemble organs of the body; the herbs are supposedly good for the part they look like, like lungwort for the lungs. Though Louis is quick to point out that he is not practicing medicine, he will tell you about the latest research. He told me about a healing herb called feverfew that is supposed to be good for headaches, but I haven't gotten around to trying it yet.

Another area of the garden shows home gardeners how to rid themselves of pests without resorting to chemicals. One of the Sasos' favorite devices is to plant garlic chives as a protective ring around plants. This is supposed to be particularly good for discouraging aphids.

There's an astrological garden watched over by the statue of St. Phac, the patron saint of herb gardens. In a circle, the herbs that refer to each sign of the zodiac are neatly arranged.

Organized tours are available, and twice a year, in April and August, the Sasos hold a giant open house. Otherwise, the visitor is pretty much left to wander independently, since Louis and Virginia are busy taking care of the garden. Virginia also makes dried flower arrangements, available for sale in the small gift shop.

SASO HERB GARDENS, *14625 Fruitvale Avenue, Saratoga. Open 9 A.M. to 2:30 P.M. Monday through Saturday; closed Sunday. Admission: Free. Call about guided tours. Phone: (408) 867-0307.*

HOW TO GET HERE: *From San Francisco, take Highway 101 South to Route 280 to Highway 85. Take the Saratoga-Sunnyvale Road through Saratoga, where it becomes Highway 9 at a stoplight. Continue toward Los Gatos. One mile after the light, turn left on Fruitvale Avenue. The Sasos' place is .7 mile on the left, on the corner of Farwell. There is a sign at the driveway.*

Rare and unusual gardens seem to thrive in the town of Saratoga. Just a few minutes away from the Sasos' world-class herb garden is a world of peace and tranquility, the Hakone Gardens. This is a city park, just a few blocks from the downtown area. Once inside, you would swear you are in Japan.

Hakone Gardens was built in the second decade of this century by Isabel Stine, a wealthy San Franciscan. Having once lived in Japan, she wanted to create the unique quality of a Japanese garden on her estate in Saratoga, which was used by her family as a summer retreat. At first the garden was used only by the family, their children swimming in the pond with neighbors such as the young sisters who went on to become known as Joan Fontaine and Olivia de Havilland.

In 1932 the garden was sold to Charles Tilden of Berkeley's Tilden Park fame, and in 1966 it was made a city park to preserve the place for future generations. The 16-acre park is said to be the finest hill and water garden outside Japan.

Named after the national park at the foot of Mount Fuji, Hakone is a living example of a seventeenth-century Zen garden. The hillside creates several levels, with streams and bridges. Typical of traditional Japanese gardens, it is elegantly simple and basically monochromatic; the belief is that too much color calls attention to itself, a dissonant chord in the overall harmony of the place.

The park is not only lovely, but the components have symbolic meaning. The footbridges are arched, and the paths and walkways are curved. This geometry suggests purity; straight lines are avoided due to the belief that evil spirits travel only in straight lines.

A Japanese house built on the property shows how a samurai might have lived 200 years ago. It's apparent that the traditional Japanese home hasn't changed much. You will learn that Japanese homes are measured not in square feet but by the number of tatami mats a room can accommodate. You will also see how Japanese design makes a tiny space function on many levels. All furniture is kept behind screens. When it's time to eat, the proper table is brought out; when it's time to sleep, the futons are brought out; and when guests arrive, the correct number of tatami are put into place. Most of the time, however, the room is bare, save for a few tatami and a floral arrangement.

A visit here requires that you have no expectation other than wanting to tune out the busy world and relax. It is quiet, the only sound being the pleasant rush of the streams over rocks. This is a place to do nothing.

HAKONE JAPANESE GARDENS, *21000 Big Basin Way, Saratoga. Open 10 A.M. to 5 P.M. Monday through Friday; 11 A.M. to 5 P.M. Saturday and Sunday; closed legal holidays. Admission: 25-cent donation. Phone: (408) 867-3438.*

HOW TO GET HERE: *From San Francisco, follow the directions to Saratoga and the Saso Gardens. Once in the center of Saratoga, at the stoplight at the intersec-*

ton of Routes 9 and 85, take Big Basin Way up the hill until you come to the entrance to Hakone Gardens.

VILLA MONTALVO

The town of Saratoga reminds me of Carmel-by-the-Sea without crowds, the beach, or Mayor Clint Eastwood. Main Street is filled with very expensive shops and restaurants, serving for the most part the wealthy residents of this lovely community.

Saratoga is known for its spacious country estates, but none is more impressive than Villa Montalvo. It was one of the last great estates built in California in the days before income taxes made such dream palaces impossible.

It was built for James Phelan, a three-term mayor of San Francisco and a U.S. senator. Phelan befriended artists and writers, and using the fortune he made in banking, he built his estate to fulfill a lifelong dream of being a patron of the arts. He used the Italian Renaissance–style villa to entertain lavishly, and he bequeathed the estate to be used as a special place for musicians, writers, and painters to work. He named it after a Spanish writer, Ordonez de Montalvo, who, in the sixteenth century, used the word *California* in a fantasy novel to describe a place of great beauty and fertile soil.

Villa Montalvo is now a park and cultural center, where artists are given room and board in beautiful surroundings, with nothing to worry about but their work. From the front of the villa, you can look out on a vast expanse of green lawn bordered by rows of trees. Behind the home you will find terraces, courtyards, and a small area for evening concerts. Though picnicking is not allowed, it is lovely to wander around. In addition, immediately behind the house is a 170-acre arboretum and bird sanctuary maintained by the local county parks department, perfect for a stroll on nature trails for a look at a wide variety of plant life.

Inside Villa Montalvo, the first floor has been transformed into an art gallery to display the works of the artists-in-residence. The villa is an active arts center, offering many types of cultural programs. The carriage house has been converted into a theater.

VILLA MONTALVO, *15400 Montalvo Road, Saratoga. Arboretum open 8 A.M. to 5 P.M. Monday through Friday; 9 A.M. to 5 P.M. Saturday and Sunday. Admission: Free. The villa, including the art gallery, bookstore, and gift shop, is open 1 to 4 P.M. Thursday and Friday, 11 A.M. to 4 P.M. Saturday and Sunday. Admission: $1.00. Phone: (408) 741-3421. Wheelchair accessible.*

HOW TO GET HERE: *From San Francisco, follow the directions to Saratoga via Route 280. After the stoplight, continue toward Los Gatos on Saratoga Avenue. About a half mile after the light, look for Montalvo Road on the right. Follow Montalvo Road to the entrance of the villa.*

Alternative route from San Francisco: Take Highway 101 South toward San Jose. Take the exit for Highway 17 South to Santa Cruz. After passing San Jose, exit at Saratoga Avenue. Follow Saratoga Avenue west, past Los Gatos. About half a mile before entering the village of Saratoga, look for Montalvo Road on the left. Follow Montalvo Road to the entrance of the villa.

**FLYING LADY
COLLECTION OF NEARLY
EVERYTHING**

It seems to me that one of the benefits of traveling the back roads is that it offers one a chance to renew one's perspectives. Those of us who spend time in cities can get very jaded. An unusual character becomes just another face in the crowd; a unique building is easily overlooked as you pass through a neighborhood filled with places that can dazzle the eye.

And yet, if you took Irv Perch and his Flying Lady complex and put them in the center of Manhattan, this guy and this place would manage to attract attention. It just so happens they're in the middle of nowhere, on the outskirts of Morgan Hill, which really makes them stand out.

First, Irv. For most of his life he ran a trailer manufacturing company, then made a fortune by selling out to a conglomerate. One day his wife decided she wanted to learn to fly. So Irv built her an airport. Then she wanted a place to play golf. So Irv built her a golf course next to the airport. He's always been a collector, obsessed with buying mementos of the past. Instead of buying one of a kind, he bought entire collections of things and became a one-man Smithsonian. So he decided to open a museum in the airport hangars, and what the heck, he might as well open a restaurant, too.

All this can be found in the Flying Lady complex, about 2 miles off Highway 101. What do you like? Cars? Irv's got a zillion of them: antique cars, buses, and trucks. Planes? There are several, from the Ford trimotor job that Steven Spielberg borrowed for the movie *Raiders of the Lost Ark* to small craft from all over the world. How about license plates? One of Irv's prize possessions is his complete set of the license plates of Canada.

But that's not all. Up the hill from the hangars, the Flying Lady restaurant features—you guessed it—more collections. First of all, the place is big enough to accommodate 1200 diners simultaneously. Irv's large-scale model airplanes fly above the tables on motorized tracks. The restaurant also houses a collection of jukeboxes and telephones. The Wild West Saloon in the basement displays cowboy memorabilia.

The only thing I can't rave about here is the food. But who comes for the food? This is a place to see.

THE FLYING LADY, *15060 Foothill Avenue, Morgan Hill. Museum open 8 A.M. to 5 P.M. Wednesday through Friday; 9 A.M. to 5 P.M. Saturday and Sunday; closed Monday and Tuesday. Admission: Free. Restaurant open Wednesday through Sunday, serving lunch and dinner. Phone: (408) 779-4136. Wheelchair accessible.*

HOW TO GET HERE: *From San Francisco, take Route 101 South past San Jose to Morgan Hill. Exit onto Tennent Avenue, and take Tennent to the left, which is east. Stay on Tennent until you come to Foothill Avenue. Turn right, which is south, on Foothill to the entrance to the Flying Lady.*

ADMAR CHEESE COMPANY

Some of my favorite back-roads discoveries have been "turnarounds." That's something that catches your eye as you drive by, and you have a quick debate with yourself about whether to turn around and see what it is. Well, being employed by a TV show called *Bay Area Backroads* affords me the luxury of checking out as many "turnarounds" as possible.

After spending many hours at the Flying Lady Museum and feeling that I had seen everything, it was a pleasure to turn around and drop into a tiny store that advertised homemade cheese. The Admar Cheese Company, as it turned out, offered even more. It is the province of one Moroni De Bruen, the founder, chief bottle washer, and cheese maker. Moroni is a big, friendly guy who will quickly tell you that his name is spelled like *moron* with an *i* at the end.

After years of teaching school, Moroni decided it would be fun to open his own business. He found himself a niche as the only maker of the exotic cheeses of Central and South America. The day I found him he was making a Nicaraguan cheese called *duro blendido*. He sells to San Francisco restaurants and to drop-in customers in the front of this little cheese factory.

When you walk into the tiny place, you will see a retail counter, a refrigerated case, and probably no one in sight. Peek your head in the back. It's a good bet Moroni will be back there mixing up a fresh batch. This back room is filled with metal tubs and vats; the entire process takes place right there. Unfortunately, due to health code restrictions, Moroni can't offer public tours, but you can get an idea of what goes on by standing in the doorway, and he'll be glad to visit with you out front. You'll be able to buy the freshest cheese in the world. Besides, where else will you find *duro blendido*?

ADMAR CHEESE COMPANY, *1470 East Middle Avenue, San Martin. Open 10 A.M. to 5 P.M. daily. Phone: (408) 683-4110.*

HOW TO GET HERE: *From the Flying Lady, head south on Foothill Avenue, which is a left turn from the Lady, until you come to East Middle Avenue. Turn right, back toward Route 101, and look on the left for a sign advertising "Admar Chee e." One of these days Moroni will find time to put the "s" back in the sign.*

SAN JUAN BAUTISTA

Most of the towns along the Bay Area's back roads feature attractions. In San Juan Bautista, the town *is* the attraction. It is a landmark, preserving California as it was in prestatehood days. Somehow, in this tiny village, you will encounter almost every phenomenon that made California famous: movies, earthquakes, and sunny weather.

There are two main stops on a visit to town. One is the downtown collection of Mexican restaurants, antique stores, and such businesses as the San Juan Bakery, the oldest continuously operating bakery in the West. In fact, the family that now owns the business never lets their huge oven cool; it keeps burning all night, and they keep churning out wonderful breads and pastries, many from Portuguese recipes (many Portuguese came to California to fish, though some moved inland to farm).

Downtown also features the John Cravea clothing store, which has more goods crammed into a tiny space than you would think possible. Outside the store is the Liar's Bench, where locals sit to pass the time and tell stories (don't ask them for directions; you might end up in San Diego).

Not far from the bench is a garden tended by a charming little old man named Chepito. Sometimes he can be seen wandering around town selling his specialty, garlic braids. But most of the time he can be found in his little garden along the main drag behind a homemade sign bearing his name. If you play your cards right, he'll take you to his home, around the corner, where he braids his "stinking roses" and keeps a menagerie of parakeets and a collection of lanterns, pots, and items I can classify only as folk art. According to Chepito, people come from all over the country to buy his garlic braids. He also says ladies find it difficult to resist his charms.

The other destination in town is the old plaza, a state historical park. The park surrounds a beautiful mission, which movie buffs will recognize as the setting for a key scene in the classic Alfred Hitchcock film *Vertigo*. The tower where Jimmy Stewart and Kim Novak played their final scene was grafted onto the mission via Hollywood special effects magic, but there is a belfry tower atop the chapel. Visitors may tour the building, which is the largest of all the 21 California missions.

Unfortunately, when the well-meaning Franciscans chose the San Juan Bautista site, they didn't know that the San Andreas Fault ran through its back yard. Regardless, Catholic services are held regularly, and at Christmas there is a lavish pageant worth making the trip to see. It is presented by the internationally famous theater group El Teatro Campesino, the troupe that grew out of the Farmworkers Union struggle during the heyday of César Chávez. Founder, director, and playwright Luis Valdez has since won acclaim for such productions as *Zoot Suit* (also made into a film directed by Valdez) and *Corridos*. El Teatro still operates out of an old spinach-packing factory in San Juan Bautista. No matter what time of year you may visit, if the Teatro is performing, take advantage of the opportunity.

Behind the mission is an Indian burial ground where thousands of the area's original residents are interred.

Then there's the plaza itself, featuring several Old West re-creations such as a replica of the town's original hotel, jail, and blacksmith shop. The buildings face a large parklike square where you can sit on benches and watch the world go by. At the far end of the square the San Andreas Fault line is marked, and you can see the damage done by several quakes on the terrain and the bleachers of the nearby rodeo stadium. There is also a seismograph and an exhibit about earthquakes.

SAN JUAN BAUTISTA STATE HISTORICAL PARK, *open 10 A.M. to 4:30 P.M. daily. Phone: (408) 623-4881. To inquire about El Teatro Campesino, located at 705 Fourth Street, call (408) 623-2444.*

HOW TO GET TO SAN JUAN BAUTISTA: *From San Francisco, take Highway 101 South, past San Jose and Morgan Hill, and watch for the exit to San Juan Bautista, near Gilroy. The entire town is quite small, so I recommend parking as you enter the main town section. You can walk past the shops and walk to the mission and plaza, which are just a block or two away.*

FREMONT PEAK TELESCOPE ⓴

The Bay Area is a popular site for astronomy buffs. Why? Perhaps there is a feeling that after you go West and can't go any farther on land, the next place to go is up. Whatever the reason, a subculture of people with telescopes has developed. They spend their spare time roaming the hills away from the city lights in hopes of getting a glimpse of the heavens above.

And thanks to the efforts of two such buffs, Kevin and Deborah Medlock, a state park is developing into an astronomer's paradise. Fremont Peak State Park is a remote jewel, only about 200 acres and well removed from the nearest city. It is named for the earth explorer John C. Frémont, who was the first to stab an American flag into California soil. For years amateur astronomers have been lugging their telescopes to this peak because it sits above the Bay Area fog, giving them a clear shot at the stars.

Kevin had the idea to build one giant telescope for everyone to use on the peak. From his Oakland home, he and wife Deborah spent five years scrounging around for junk metal parts and buying the necessary items to build an imposing, 13-foot-long telescope with a 30-inch mirror—to their knowledge the largest telescope ever made available to the public absolutely free, with no institutional connections. Kevin says he invested a total cash outlay of $2600; purchased new, such an instrument would cost about $60,000.

With the help of volunteers and of park ranger Enrique Morales, the astronomers have also built a house with a retractable roof for the telescope and have plans for a visitor's center. Again, all of this has been accomplished with no help from the taxpayers, only volunteer time and money plus some help from corporations that Kevin was able to interest.

It is wonderful to visit here, far removed from the often institutionalized feeling of observatories. Kevin and Deborah remind me of modern-day Mickey Rooney–Judy Garland types: "Hey, we've got the brains and the talent—let's build our own telescope!" They are so involved with astronomy that they were married at an observatory; their big thrill is watching your reaction when you take your first look through their telescope.

What can you see? I saw an extreme close-up of the surface of the moon, which to the naked eye was a small and distant crescent. Kevin says he has been able to see the rings around Saturn quite clearly.

There are a few things to know when planning a visit. Though nights at sea level can be pretty warm, it can get cold on the peak, especially in winter, so bring something warm just in case. Die-hard astronomers like to do their viewing around midnight, so they bring sleeping bags and camp on the peak. But you can see through the telescope pretty well as soon as the sun sets, particularly if the fog rolls in and covers the nearby lights.

FREMONT PEAK STATE PARK, *on San Juan Canyon Road, south of San Juan Bautista. The state park offers overnight camping facilities, so the peak is accessible almost all the time; however, the telescope schedule varies, so be sure to call ahead. Admission: $3 per vehicle (use fee for the entire park). Phone: (408) 623-4255 or (408) 623-4526.*

HOW TO GET TO FREMONT PEAK: *From San Francisco, take Route 101 South to Route 156. Head east on Route 156 and turn right at the entrance of Fremont Peak State Park. The observatory is right behind the ranger's residence, the first building you see when you arrive in the park.*

CASA DE FRUTA

Remember the old Burma Shave billboards, the ones that used to dot the byways back in the days before interstate highways? Well, you might think you're back in the good old days when you're tooling down Highway 101 south of San Jose and you start seeing signs for Casa de Fruta. One by one, they promise you just about everything you could want or need, if you'll just get off the main road and head over the pass to the intersection of Routes 152 and 156.

I should point out that Routes 152 and 156 are not quiet country roads. These are rather busy truck routes leading to and from the Sierras. Because of that built-in traffic flow, many years ago, the Zanger family decided to add to the income of their cherry farm by putting a little fruit stand out by the road. It did pretty well, but then the mother of the family had an idea that would turn the place into a major roadside attraction: bathrooms. "People on the road need a good, clean rest room," Mama told her sons. "Put one in and our business will double."

Mama Zanger was right. Pretty soon the fruit stand and comfort station, known as Casa de Fruta, turned into one of the strangest empires you'll ever hope to see. People on the road want a cup of coffee, so the Zangers added a little coffee shop and called it Casa de Coffee. People on the road want a snack; voilà: Casa de Burger.

Today Casa de Fruta includes 100 acres of attractions, including a trailer park, a miniature zoo, gardens, a train ride, and a Casa de Gifts.

The Zangers have never forgotten that it was the cherries that got them started. Every June, when the cherries are in full bloom, there is a giant Cherry Festival, including a pit-spitting contest. All year there is a 24-hour coffee shop, and you can picnic on the grounds overlooking a duck pond labeled Casa de Cold Duck. The Zangers have a sense of humor as well as a sense of good business.

CASA DE FRUTA ORCHARD RESORT, *6680 Pacheco Pass Highway, Hollister. Open 9 A.M. to 6 P.M. daily. Admission: Free to the grounds; use fee for trailer park. Phone: (408) 637-0051.*

HOW TO GET HERE: *From San Francisco, follow Route 101 South to the Route 152 turnoff. Head east to the intersection of Route 152. Be careful—this is a heavy truck route, and accidents are frequent.*

PINK POODLE FARM

For some 30 years, motorists on Echo Pass Road in Prunedale have done a double take when they pass a bright pink apparition along the road. That's the idea: The huge pink poodle and shocking pink buildings are supposed to attract our attention.

This is part of the plan of a shrewd entrepreneur named Una Buckmaster. She is a successful breeder of toy poodles. I should mention that there is not a pink poodle on the premises; the pink refers to the color of the farm buildings, not the animals.

Una says people come here from all over the world to buy her puppies, and dog lovers are invited to drop in just to see her broods. The puppies are kept inside the farmhouse, nurtured by Una until they are seven to eight weeks old and ready for a new home. They range in price from $200 to $1000. Customers range from San Francisco society ladies to big burly truck drivers looking for a small but affectionate traveling companion. I asked if a toy poodle wasn't a tad wimpy for your average teamster, and Una laughed and said I would be surprised by her macho clientele.

The older members of Una's "family" live outside. These 40 or so poodles who roam the yard are not for sale. Some are breeders; others are the dogs Una loves best and wants to keep around. She knows each one by name and can identify them not only by their looks but by the sound of their barks.

When the Buckmasters first moved to California from Oklahoma, Una had troubles with neighbors because she liked to have a few dogs around. Finally she asked her now late husband to get her a house in the country with no rugs, no expensive furniture, and no neighbors so she could keep as many dogs as she liked. (By the way, for Una, *dog* is synonymous with *poodle*.) She started breeding them as a hobby and later turned it into a career.

When they first moved to this farm, Route 101 was just a quiet, two-lane road through farmland. Today the highway is four lanes and loaded with traffic. But once you enter Una's yard and hear those poodles barking, you wouldn't know there's a truck for miles.

THE PINK POODLE FARM, *19000 Morrow Road, Prunedale. This is a drop-in business, and visitors are always welcome. Phone: (408) 663-3709.*

HOW TO GET HERE: *From San Francisco, take Route 101 South past Gilroy and look for a huge flea market on the left side of the highway. Then start looking for Echo Valley Road. Exit onto Echo Valley and turn right immediately onto Morrow Road. Then turn left into the poodle farm entrance. It's right off the highway.*

FORTINO WINERY

As you head west on Route 152, also called Hecker Pass Road, you pass through the outskirts of the town of Gilroy. Most times of the year, Gilroy is a quiet farming community. But one weekend every autumn it is jammed with people from all over who adore garlic. Gilroy is the garlic capital of the world; the annual garlic festival celebrates the fact that most of the nation's garlic used to be grown here. Recently, most of the "stinking rose" farms have moved south, but most of the processing continues to be headquartered in Gilroy.

As you leave Gilroy and head for the Monterey Peninsula, you are soon in rolling hillside country. And just about anywhere in the Bay Area that you see beautiful countryside, you can be sure wineries can't be far.

Indeed, the wineries of the South Santa Clara Valley are not nearly as well known as their neighbors to the north, but that means that these small, family-run wineries fall more in the category of special finds. A good example is the Fortino Winery, run by Ernest Fortino, who is also likely to be your tour guide. Ernest is a charming middle-aged man who speaks with the accent of his homeland. He and his family run the place like a family farm. This "little old" winemaker learned his trade from generations of winemakers in Italy. He operates by instinct as he walks through his vineyard, picking a grape here and there to see if it is yet ready to be made into wine. He does not use fancy wine-tasting vocabulary words like *bouquet* or *nose* to describe his product; either it tastes good or it doesn't.

According to Ernest, whom you'll be calling Ernie by now, wine to the Italians is like milk to Americans—an important part of family life that everybody can enjoy. The setting is in keeping with the Fortino philosophy. A visit here is like dropping in on a small winery in Italy. This is a working farm, with just enough buildings on the property to get the job done. There are no fancy tasting rooms or special visitor's centers. The tasting often takes place at one of the picnic tables that border the vineyard.

Ernest is also a driving force in the community of winemakers in the Santa Clara Valley. They often get together and stage public events, such as the annual harvest celebration in the fall. At this function, you're invited to take off your shoes and participate in an old-fashioned barefoot grape crush. This is only for fun, though; state health codes forbid making wine the really old-fashioned way.

FORTINO WINERY, *4525 Hecker Pass Road, Gilroy. Open 9 A.M. to 5 P.M. daily. Phone: (408) 842-3305.*

HOW TO GET HERE: *From San Francisco, take Route 101 South to Gilroy and then Route 152. Turn right, which is west, and stay on Route 152. You will pass several small wineries on the way. Fortino's is well marked, right on Route 152, which is also called the Hecker Pass Road.*

PINNACLES NATIONAL MONUMENT
(24)

Though there are several national parks and forests in the Bay Area, there are only two national monuments. What's the difference, you might ask? A national park is created by an act of Congress; a national monument is created by a presidential order. The Bay Area's monuments are Muir Woods (see Chapter 1) and the Pinnacles. Both were declared national treasures by Theodore Roosevelt in 1908.

The Pinnacles is about a three-hour drive south from San Francisco. It is a truly unique spot, with remarkable spirelike formations that have names like Machete Ridge and the Balconies. This place feels as far removed from the rest of civilization as you can get in the heart of California, and I should let you know right off the bat that this is *not* a place for a casual drop-in visit. This is a hiker's and rock climber's paradise; very little can be seen without parking the car and traversing some of the 26 miles of trails.

The monument is run by the National Park Service and is separated into east and west sides. Most visitors go to the east entrance, where you'll find park headquarters and the Bear Valley Visitor's Center, complete with a mini-museum, picnic areas, and rest rooms. The west entrance offers a more spectacular view. This is the backside of the monument, and you see the actual pinnacles— huge, ragged peaks rising dramatically from the hills. They stand where the American plate of the earth's crust meets the Pacific plate, along the San Andreas Fault. In other words, this is a spot with a whole lot of shakin' goin' on.

One of the easiest and most interesting hikes takes about an hour and a half. It begins at park headquarters on the east side, takes you through caves at Bear Gulch (be sure to bring a flashlight), and brings you out on Moses Spring Trail back to park HQ. A more spectacular view on the east side is offered from Condor Gulch Trail, a four-hour journey through the high peaks and along the monument's reservoir. On the west side (where there is a ranger station, campgrounds, picnic tables, and rest rooms) you'll find a variety of trails overlooking the awe-inspiring view of Machete Ridge and a multihued rock formation known as the Balconies.

Spring and fall are the recommended times to visit; the wildflowers are in bloom, and the often desertlike climate is neither broiling hot nor deathly cold. No matter where you go, you'll be surrounded by the quiet wonders of nature. If you're lucky, you'll meet up with Cecilia Bjornerus, a retired schoolteacher known as the Flower Lady. Cecilia lives in a trailer in the park and is making a list of all the plants that grow there, including the digger pines, blue oaks, and other flora. She leads groups on nature walks. If Cecilia isn't available, the park rangers occasionally offer guided tours.

Campers can settle down in a privately run campground just outside the east entrance, and 24 walk-in sites within the Pinnacles National Monument on the west side are available on a first-come, first-served basis. If camping is not your style, the park offers a list of nearby motels and hotels and places for recreational vehicles.

Again, let me emphasize that this is not a place to visit casually. Plan your trip, bring lots of water, and prepare to walk.

PINNACLES NATIONAL MONUMENT, *Paicines. Admission: Free for walk-ins, $1 fee per car.*

EAST SIDE ENTRANCE, *phone (408) 389-4578; Pinnacles Campground, phone (408) 385-4462.*

HOW TO GET HERE: *From San Francisco, take Route 101 South past Gilroy to Route 25 toward Hollister. Follow Route 25 all the way south to the Route 146 turnoff, which is marked as the entrance to the monument.*

WEST SIDE ENTRANCE, *phone (408) 389-4425.*

HOW TO GET HERE: *From San Francisco, take Route 101 South to Soledad and turn east on Route 146 through town. Follow Route 146 all the way to the Pinnacles entrance.*

CORRALITOS SMOKEHOUSE

Of all the stories that have appeared on the *Bay Area Backroads* television program, none has received as many inquiries for directions as the Corralitos Market and Sausage Company. I don't know what to make of this. Maybe people in the Bay Area are addicted to sausage; perhaps they're simply fascinated by the idea of a small town where the main attraction is a combination grocery store and smokehouse.

The Corralitos Market is tucked away in a small town called Corralitos in the Santa Cruz Mountains. It is a family-run business, an all-purpose community store with bread and milk in front and a terrific smokehouse in back. The owner, Joe Cutler, wiped his hands on his white apron and took a break to show me around. I saw the slabs of curing bacon and sausages smoking slowly over applewood from Joe's own orchard. In another room were chickens being prepared for the smokehouse. Not an artificial ingredient or shortcut in the place, just the sweet smell of burning applewood mingling with smoking meats.

After a tour of the place, we stepped outside and talked about the rest of the town, which seems to be slowly dissolving into an extension of nearby Watsonville. Pointing in all directions, Joe talked about the many farms that used to surround the few buildings of downtown Corralitos and observed that the apple trees are being replaced by TV antennas.

All this seems to make Joe even more determined to hold out. He says there will be no TV antennas atop the Corralitos Market in his lifetime.

CORRALITOS MARKET AND SAUSAGE COMPANY, *569 Corralitos Road, Corralitos. Open 9 A.M. to 6 P.M. Monday through Friday, 9 A.M. to 5 P.M. Saturday and Sunday. Phone: (408) 722-2633.*

HOW TO GET HERE: *From San Francisco, take the Bay Bridge to Highway 880 South toward San Jose. After a while, the freeway reverts to its original name, Highway 17. Follow Route 17 to Route 1 at Santa Cruz and continue south to the Freedom Boulevard exit. You will cross over the freeway and continue down Freedom for about 5 miles to Corralitos Road. Turn left and continue to the end of the road (about 2 miles); you will see the market on your left. Corralitos is about a 30-minute drive inland from Santa Cruz.*

PICK-YOUR-OWN FRUIT

Your image of Santa Cruz may well be that of the boardwalk, surfers, and beach boys, but if you go just a few miles in almost any direction you will soon see that this is farm country. On just about every hillside you see something growing for the dinner table. There are more artichokes in this region than anywhere else in the country. The combination of sunny days and cool, foggy nights is also perfect for brussels sprouts, lettuce, kiwis, and pumpkins. And if you travel inland to the area around Watsonville, there are many farms specializing in fruits.

If you'd like to visit a working farm and enjoy its bounty, Gizdich Farms is a worthwhile destination. If you choose, you can pick your own apples off a tree or berries off a bush. The people who run the place will send you off on your own with a bucket, after making sure you know how to pick fruit without destroying the rest of the plant. Picking fruit may sound simple, but even a guy like me who grew up in Indiana was surprised to find that there's a right way and a wrong way to pick an apple. You don't yank; it takes the finesse of an upward flick of the wrist.

Even those not inclined to pick fruit enjoy visiting with Nita Gizdich. She runs the place and her sons are her top hands. Nita is a charming hostess who loves to show people around her very attractive farm. In addition to orchards, there are barns with the latest equipment. Nita showed me her coring machine, which can core 58 apples in a minute. The apples are not cored in vain; they get turned into some of the best apple cider and apple pie you've ever tasted.

Gizdich Farms also offers special events to celebrate each crop. Fall is apple time; springtime is for the berries: strawberries, olallies, and raspberries. Again, you can pick them yourself or buy already picked fruits or jellies. And if you visit when the farm is not too busy, there are carriage rides for the kids.

GIZDICH FARMS, *55 Peckham Road, Watsonville. Open for the spring berry harvest from 8 A.M. to 5 P.M. every day, May through June; open for the fall apple harvest from 9 A.M. to 5 P.M. every day from September through January. Closed Christmas afternoon and from February through April. The seasonal schedule may vary by a week or so, depending on when the crop is ready, so it is a good idea to call ahead. Phone: (408) 722-1056.*

HOW TO GET HERE: *From San Francisco, take Highway 101 South to Gilroy. Take the Route 152 West exit and go over the Hecker Pass toward Watsonville. This is well past Fortino's and the other wineries of the South Santa Clara Valley. Continue to Carlton Road and turn left. Soon you will see signs directing you to Gizdich Farms (the entrance you use depends on which crop is in season).*

STEINBECK ARCHIVES

The great writer John Steinbeck is usually associated with the Monterey Coast and the Cannery Row that he made famous. His home, however, was in Salinas, about an hour inland. Today Steinbeck is honored by the town public library, which is named for him. His statue stands on the lawn outside the library, as if beckoning visitors to come see the rare collection of Steinbeck memorabilia inside.

On the main floor is a room entirely devoted to the American author. Here you will find most of his books, plus photos, magazine stories about him, awards, newspaper clippings, and correspondence. All this reminds you of the major role he played in our literary history.

The real treasures, however, are downstairs, locked away behind a steel gate in the Steinbeck Archives, a destination for Steinbeck scholars from all over the world. This basement room, about the size of a junior executive's office, is accessible to the general public with advance notice.

Here you will see his family photos, personal mementos, and first editions and autographed copies of his books. Perhaps the real treasures are the original handwritten manuscripts. Steinbeck didn't use a typewriter; what he wrote every morning on lined notepads would be typed by a secretary in the afternoon. In this day of word processors, it is remarkable to pore over the meticulous pages and imagine the author at work.

The archives also has oral histories of the man, told by folks who knew him during various stages in his life. One tape features Steinbeck himself, reflecting on his life and the endless battles he fought because he was committed to writing what he had to say about the human condition.

Try to meet library director John Gross. He is a charming scholar who can offer additional insights into Steinbeck and his community. He told me that Steinbeck was hated in the area during his lifetime. After he published *Cannery Row,* the Monterey town council threatened to tar and feather him if he ever showed his face in town. In Salinas, where he exposed the dark and sad sides of life in this quiet farming area, he was considered an enemy of his class. But as Gross pointed out, "All prophets are unpopular in their own town because they write the truth and don't care who they might hurt to tell it."

Today Steinbeck is not only forgiven but is a figure of pride in the area. Even his former home, a lovely Victorian just off Main Street, has been carefully restored and is operated by a women's guild as a popular luncheon spot.

THE STEINBECK LIBRARY, *110 West San Luis Street, Salinas. Open 10 A.M. to 9 P.M. Monday through Thursday, 10 A.M. to 6 P.M. Friday and Saturday. An appointment is required to see the archives. Phone: (408) 758-7311.*

JOHN STEINBECK HOUSE *is just a few blocks from the library at 132 Central. Open for lunch with seatings at 11:45 A.M. and 1:15 P.M. Monday through Friday. Reservations requested. Phone: (408) 424-2735.*

HOW TO GET TO THE STEINBECK LIBRARY AND ARCHIVES: *From San Francisco, take Highway 101 South to Salinas. Take the North Main Street exit and continue to San Luis Street. Turn right and go one block to Lincoln; the library is on the corner of San Luis and Lincoln.*

CHAPTER **5** South Coast

AREA OVERVIEW   Taking the coastal route from San Francisco to Santa Cruz and beyond requires the willingness to take it easy and drive slowly. Route 1 is the main road here, except in places where the pavement has been washed away by a rainstorm. Detours are only temporary, and the road always gets patched back together so you can continue your two-lane jaunt down the coastline.

Most travelers who take the coastal route to Southern California bypass the area between San Francisco and the Monterey Peninsula and begin their trip to points south from Carmel. They save some time, but they miss out on some terrific sights and characters.

From San Francisco, you can arrive at the nearest stops in this chapter in less than an hour. The attractions around Santa Cruz are approximately 90 minutes away, and the farthest destination, Elkhorn Slough, is approximately two hours from San Francisco. These places can be reached by using Route 1 all the way, or you can take faster north-south roads, Highway 101 or 280 to Route 17, which

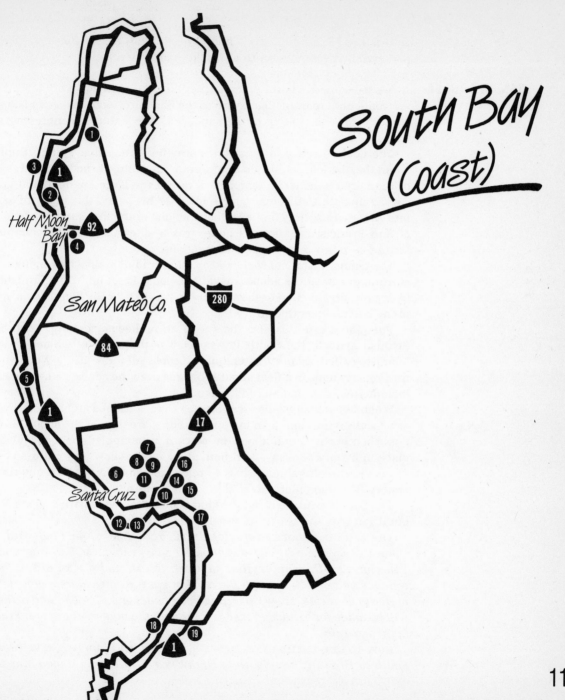

South Bay
(Coast)

Half Moon Bay

San Mateo Co.

280

Santa Cruz

113

goes directly to Santa Cruz. A midway solution is to take Route 92 to Half Moon Bay and then continue south along the coast.

SANCHEZ ADOBE

If you tell someone to meet you at the Ramada in the town of Pacifica, chances are you'll end up in the back yard of the Sanchez Adobe. *Ramada* is Spanish for "arbor," and the grounds of the Sanchez estate feature an impressive shelter of trees.

The adobe itself is a noteworthy architectural achievement. Built in 1846 when the Mexicans still ruled California, the whitewashed abode was the home of Francisco Sanchez, a recipient of one of the large Spanish land grants that carved up Alta California. Unlike many of his peers, this landlord assimilated into American society and even became one of the first supervisors for the City of San Francisco. Sanchez's home was a showplace for the community, the setting for many festivals and celebrations.

The county historical society keeps that tradition alive by staging fiestas and cultural events at the adobe. Inside, the house is set up with a furnished parlor, bedrooms, and kitchen to show what life was like for the Peninsula's upper crust in the late nineteenth century.

The 5-acre estate is also the site of an archaeological dig. Long before the Spanish arrived, the South Bay coast was the home of Ohlone Indians. The Spanish called them "Costonians—"people of the coast." What you see on the property now, in a field about 100 yards from the adobe, is the ramada, which includes an arbor and an Indian roundhouse.

When I visited, my guide was Shirley Dyre, a trained archaeologist who works at a local savings and loan but spends her spare time at the adobe. She recently published her research about the place in a pamphlet about the adobe and its place in history. She says her motivation was to show how cultured and industrious the early inhabitants of the area were and to fix the land and the adobe in history. The pamphlet is available on the premises.

The Sanchez Adobe is not the kind of place you would drive a long way to see, but if you're in the area it's a worthwhile diversion.

THE SANCHEZ ADOBE HISTORICAL SITE, *1000 Linda Mar Boulevard, Pacifica. Open 10 A.M. to 4 P.M. Tuesday and Thursday, 1 to 5 P.M. Saturday and Sunday. You can visit the site anytime between 8 A.M. and 5 P.M. to see the Ohlone remains and to look through the windows at the downstairs rooms; but if you'd prefer to go inside, show up during open hours or call ahead and arrangements will be made for a guide to take you through the home. Admission: Free. Phone: (415) 359-1462.*

HOW TO GET TO THE SANCHEZ ADOBE: *From San Francisco, take Highway 101 South to Highway 280 South to Highway 1 South to the Linda Mar Boulevard exit. Turn left (east) and go about a mile.*

Just 20 minutes south of the Sanchez Adobe is a small, uncrowded county park that features some of the best tidepooling you'll find anywhere. The James V. Fitzgerald Marine Reserve is in the town of Moss Beach, right off the main road.

In the parking lot there's a small visitor's center with descriptive information, displays about the various kinds of marine life to be found at the reserve, and current information about tides. The best time to visit is at low tide, and you can call ahead to check when that will be. Bob Breen is the chief naturalist at the reserve, and he is a storehouse of information. He's also a delightful guide; jokes about "clamming up" and "mussel beach" are not beneath his dignity.

It's a very short walk to the beach itself. There you'll find a series of unusual reef formations that make perfect subdivisions for crabs, sponges, sea anemones, mollusks, starfish, rockfish, abalone, eel, and a seemingly endless variety of seaweed. It's a veritable marine laboratory. In fact, in the 75 years that scientists have been studying the reserve, at least 25 new species of marine life have been discovered here. You can wander around on your own or tag along on a group hike led by one of the naturalists on duty. I suggest the latter because the guides invariably point out things that are dismissed by the untrained eye. Speaking of eyes, Bob suggests you keep one of them on the ocean at all times when tidepooling because a wave can sneak up on you suddenly; his tip for the day: *never* turn your back on the ocean.

Even though this is a quiet, small, low-key park, there is much to see. You might find yourself spending several hours here without realizing the time has gone by. Plan ahead and pack a lunch—a picnic area is provided.

JAMES V. FITZGERALD MARINE RESERVE, *Moss Beach. Open sunrise to sunset daily, but the best time to visit is at low tide. Call ahead for information. Phone: (415) 728-3584. Admission: Free.*

HOW TO GET HERE: *From San Francisco, take Highway 101 South to Highway 280 to Route 1. The Marine Reserve is right off Route 1 in the town of Moss Beach. Just look for the sign on the right side of the road as you head south from Pacifica. Turn right and follow the driveway to the parking lot and visitor's center.*

Within an hour of San Francisco you can have oceanfront accommodations in historic settings for just a few dollars a night. All you have to do is pitch in a bit and suspend any desire for room service and privacy.

I'm talking about staying in places run by the American Youth Hostel Service. Don't let the name put you off; people of all ages are welcome. The goal of AYH is to make hosteling as popular in this country as it is in Europe.

Along the South Bay coast, the AYH accommodations are the Montara Lighthouse Hostel, about 25 miles south of San Francisco, and the Pigeon Point Lighthouse Hostel, about 50 miles south of the City. Both establishments are clean, friendly places. If you're not familiar with the hostel setup, these are cooperative overnight accommodations. The hostel provides shelter, a bed, and kitchen facilities; the visitors provide their own food and pick up after themselves. These lighthouse hostels offer wonderful settings for the experience.

Montara Lighthouse is set in a restored 1875 lighthouse and fog signal station. The seven-bedroom duplex can accommodate 35 guests, with two fully equipped dining rooms, a common living room, and a laundry. There's also a volleyball court, a private beach, and an outdoor hot tub. Not bad for roughing it. You can rent a bicycle and head to the Fitzgerald Marine Reserve at Moss Beach, just a few miles away.

At Pigeon Point, the setting is a former Coast Guard residence—three bungalows, each with its own kitchen, accommodating a total of 50 persons. The lighthouse there is a beauty, one of the tallest in the United States. It's open for tours and a 150-step climb to the top on Sundays. The former fog signal building has been converted into a communal recreational lounge. Pigeon Point is only a few miles from Año Nuevo Beach (see entry 5).

Space at either facility goes for $5 or $6 a person and is available on a first-come, first-served basis. Reservations can be made by sending the first night's fees in advance. Remember, these are minimal accommodations, an experience that is not enjoyed by everyone.

For information and reservations for either facility, call the American Youth Hostel office in San Francisco: (415) 771-4646. You can also call the Montara Lighthouse at (415) 728-7177 and the Pigeon Point Lighthouse at (415) 879-0633.

HOW TO GET TO THE MONTARA LIGHTHOUSE: *From San Francisco, take Highway 101 South to Highway 280 to the Route 1 exit and follow it south on the coast. The hostel is in the town of Montara right off Highway 1 at Sixteenth Street.*

HOW TO GET TO THE PIGEON POINT LIGHTHOUSE: *From San Francisco, follow the directions to Montara and continue down Route 1 past Half Moon Bay. After the town of Pescadero, look on the right for the lighthouse.*

HALF MOON BAY
④

The town of Half Moon Bay is famous for one thing: pumpkins. This is the pumpkin capital of the state, maybe even the world, and it is a destination for thousands of families each year around Halloween. In fact, the annual Pumpkin Festival each October draws so many tourists that the usual one-hour drive from San Francisco takes three hours.

Other annual events bring people to town. The Portuguese community celebrates its heritage with the Chamarita Festival each May, and in July the Coastside Country Fair celebrates the summer fruit harvest. However, most visitors never make it past the farms on Route 92, the main road that takes you to the coast; they don't realize that the town itself is a wonderful destination all year round.

It was originally called Spanishtown by the Mexican settlers, a name that lasted into the twentieth century even after other residents referred to the place as San Benito. Eventually the name Half Moon Bay stuck, and the area all around became an abundant farming area, attracting immigrants from Portugal and Italy. The town's proximity to San Francisco and its secure harbor made it a popular rum- and whisky-running site during Prohibition.

A walk through the lovely little downtown area of Half Moon Bay will give you an idea of what Carmel and Mendocino used to be like before they became major tourist attractions. The town is not only picturesque, compact, and easy to walk around, but it also feels more like a warm community than a commercial tourist attraction.

The local historical society has recently prepared a map for a self-guided walking tour. In just a few blocks you can see interesting buildings and several good inns and restaurants. The tour begins by crossing a white concrete bridge that leads you onto Main Street. At 326 Main you will see the town's grand old lady, the Zaballa House. Built in 1859, it is the oldest building in town. It is currently used for offices. The Zaballa House is next door to a wonderful place to eat or spend the night. The San Benito House (at 356 Main Street) is a recently restored hotel decorated with antique furnishings that features 12 rooms for overnight guests, lunches and dinners prepared from local produce and seafood, and a lovely flower garden next door. Another point of interest farther down the street is the Half Moon Bay Bakery (at 514 Main), which still uses a brick oven from the nineteenth century. A copy of the walking tour map can be picked up at almost any business downtown.

On your way in or out of town, you might notice an abundance of flower fields. That's because this is one of the largest flower-growing centers in the nation. In fact, flower sales here outgross vegetable income. As one flower farmer poetically said to me, "Flowers are food for the soul." Unfortunately, due in part to insurance problems, most flower farms are not set up for public tours. But you can see many of them from the side of the road off Route 1.

HALF MOON BAY, *Route 92 at Route 1. You can pick up a copy of the Historic Half Moon Bay Walking Tour Map at almost any shop along Main Street or at the Chamber of Commerce, located in a red railroad caboose at the Shoreline Station Shopping Center; Chamber phone: (415) 726-5202.*

HOW TO GET HERE: *From San Francisco, take Highway 101 South to Highway 280. Continue on Route 280 South to Route 92 to Half Moon Bay. Main Street is the last street before you hit Route 1 and the coast. Turn left onto Main to get to the shopping and restaurant district.*

HOME OF THE ELEPHANT SEALS

⑤

One of the Bay Area's most popular shows featuring sex, violence, and larger-than-life characters is to be found at Año Nuevo State Beach. It is under the auspices of the state park service, and tickets are so much in demand you must make reservations weeks, if not months, in advance.

The stars of the show are the elephant seals that have adopted this beautiful stretch of land as their winter home. Some loll around here all year, but the prime time to see them is mating season, from December to April. Perhaps the idea of watching elephant seals mate isn't your idea of a good time, but I've never heard of anyone regretting the trip, even those who have been caught in one of the area's frequent rainstorms during showtime.

The audience checks in at the visitor's center. Then the group walks about a mile and a half to the ocean. Just about the time you begin to wonder if you really want to be doing this, you catch a sight of the first elephant seal, a 6000-pound blob with a prehistoric-looking face. He'll probably be asleep, but he'll wake up every 20 minutes. You see, elephant seals don't breathe while sleeping; when it's time for some air, they'll awaken, take a whiff, then catch some more zzz's until it's time to breathe again.

Soon you will reach a point where everywhere you look there are elephant seals. Though it may look like nothing but a random assortment of bodies, there is a definite order to the living arrangements. The dominant males, led by one king bull, live in one area; they brawl occasionally to establish the power structure. Another section has been nicknamed the "Bachelors' Pad"; this is where the males who do not get to mate this year must hang out. They too will occasionally start a brawl, in the hope of proving themselves worthy of membership in the dominant club next year.

Actually, the "bachelors" were the first residents of this beach. Elephant seals have always bred off this shore. The frustrated losers would inhabit this beach while a mating party went on on a nearby island. Then for reasons no one has yet figured out, females started showing up in 1975. The dominant bulls followed, and Año Nuevo became the only mainland breeding colony for elephant seals north of the equator.

Though you will see a lot of bodies lying around on the beach, these elephant seals are not being lazy. The males don't want to go in the water because they might lose a chance to mate. The females don't want to leave their babies. So they stay on shore and fast for the several months of this particular part of the life cycle.

This once endangered species is protected by laws, to the point that their rights come before tourists'. Today visitors must remain at least 20 feet away from the seals, and if one comes your way, it's your obligation to move. Anyway, the rule makes sense; who wants to argue with a 6000-pound animal? Elephant seals have no desire to attack humans but can inadvertently trample one when angry. And they are much faster than they look, so be careful.

Again, let me emphasize that this is a popular attraction, and buying tickets in advance is a must.

AÑO NUEVO BEACH. *Tickets are sold through Ticketron; to find the location of the most convenient outlet, call (415) 392-7469 or (408) 247-7469. Tickets cost $4.*

Since parking space is at a premium, public transportation is available on weekends. The San Mateo County Transit District picks up passengers in San Mateo and Half Moon Bay. The cost is $8 per person and includes the round-trip ride and the tour. For reservations and information, phone (415) 348-SEAL. During the nonmating season, from May through November, visitors are free to roam around on their own.

HOW TO GET TO AÑO NUEVO BEACH: *From San Francisco, follow the directions to Half Moon Bay and continue on Route 1 until you come to Año Nuevo, which is well marked, on your right.*

BONNY DOON WINERY

Ever heard of Flying Cigar Wine? How about Clos des Gilroy? These are the creations of one of the more unusual and entertaining wine producers in California. He's Randall Grahm, and he's headquartered, appropriately, in the attractive and eccentric Santa Cruz hills in the town of Bonny Doon.

You find the place by driving about five minutes inland from the ocean until you come to a sign that says "Welcome to Bonny Doon." Then, after you pass the winery tasting room across the street, you will see another sign that says, "You are leaving Bonny Doon." That will give you some idea of the nature of the place.

The tasting room used to be the Lost Weekend Saloon, a notorious hangout for the bikers who zoom around these hills. Randall says that every so often a big, burly guy on a Harley will stagger into the place, look around bewildered, and then roar away. Once in a while, though, the biggest, meanest biker will wander in, sample a glass of white wine, and carry on a connoisseur's discussion about the relative merits of the vintage.

Most of the visitors, however, are your average back-roads adventurers out to explore the countryside. The winery itself is on a hill above the tasting room, where you will probably encounter Randall's assistant, Michel. The two of them comprise the entire winemaking staff and can give you a brief tour that is so folksy that you can imagine yourself opening your own little winery. A tour of the grounds, where you will see some old barrels, some storage equipment, and a basketball court, is rounded out by the sight and sound of the neighbor's turkey ranch.

You'll probably want to end up back in the tasting room or at one of the picnic tables in this lovely and remote wooded area. If the opportunity presents itself, engage Randall in a conversation. He's an original: a long-haired, disarming former Los Angeleno who once considered becoming an alchemist but instead has won a national reputation for his Bordeaux-style claret, his Burgundy-style chardonnay, and his white table wine called Le Sophiste—Cuvée Philosophique. Though he makes serious and not inexpensive wine (he is one of the few American winemakers who closely follows the traditional Bordeaux way of growing grapes and making wine), he likes to give them funny names. He has been known to barge into fancy New York restaurants with bottles in a milk delivery basket, offering tastes to owners and chefs. His top salesperson is his mother, whom he calls "the terror of the L.A. wine market."

BONNY DOON WINERY, *10 Pine Flat Road, Bonny Doon. Open noon to 6 P.M. Tuesday through Sunday from June 15 to October 1; open the rest of the year on weekends noon to 6 P.M., or by appointment. Phone: (408) 425-3625.*

HOW TO GET HERE: *From San Francisco, follow the directions to Año Nuevo Beach and continue down Route 1 past the town of Davenport to Bonny Doon Road. Turn left and the winery is 3.7 miles away on the right-hand side of the road.*

TYROLEAN INN

The town of Ben Lomond has an unusual international flavor. Within a few blocks, you can see a Scottish castle, a Hylton hotel (built by a man named Hylton and run by a family from India), and a Tyrolean inn. For some reason, this little town tucked away in the Santa Cruz Mountains reminds all of these people of their homelands.

The Scottish castle, which is now a private home and not open for tours, is worth looking at from the side of the road. It is the stuff of local legend. Built by a Scottish gent years ago, the place was sold to a lady who ran tours through it. Locals say she used to collar people on the street and convince them that they would never again have the opportunity to see a home like hers. After charging them $2.50 each, the lady would make up stories about the various antiques and goings-on in the house. She would hold them for four hours, insisting they not leave until they got the entire tour.

Without even needing a passport, you can travel to the Austrian Alps by simply traveling a block from the Scottish castle to the Tyrolean Inn, which is a pleasant place not only to stop for a *mittel*-European meal or to have a beer but also to spend the night.

The Tyrolean Inn is run by Tony Wolf, a native of the Austrian Alps, and his Scottish-born wife Joyce. In the early 1970s Tony took over a dilapidated motel and turned it into a place that would remind him of home—a European-style inn with a restaurant serving German-Austrian food and nine moderately priced cabins in back.

If you can forget for a moment that Ben Lomond is some 4000 feet lower in altitude than Tony's native village of Neustift and that you are surrounded by native Californian flora and fauna, you can experience a little bit of alpine atmosphere. Tony and Joyce have painted the cabins a nice Tyrolean brown and added some Austrian-style balconies to the roadhouse. The wood-paneled dining room is decorated with a collection of beer steins, and it is not unusual to find Tony decked out in lederhosen behind the bar. The food is good, featuring wursts and red cabbage and hot potato salad, all made from fresh ingredients selected by Tony himself. On a warm day you can sit out in the biergarten, tapes of German music wafting in the background.

THE TYROLEAN INN, *9600 Highway 9, Ben Lomond. Restaurant open 11 A.M. to 9 P.M. Sunday through Thursday, 11 A.M. to 9:30 P.M. Friday and Saturday. Cabin rates are modest, about $40 a night, which includes cable TV and a kitchenette. Phone: (408) 336-5108.*

HOW TO GET TO BEN LOMOND: *From San Francisco, take Route 101 South to Highway 280. Exit onto Highway 17 South to Santa Cruz. Take Route 17 to Scott's Valley, before Santa Cruz, and turn west onto Mount Hermon Road. Follow Mount Hermon into the town of Felton, where it intersects with Highway 9, and turn right through Felton to Ben Lomond. The inn and the castle are on Route 9, which is the main street of town.*

The most scenic route in these parts is to be seen by rail, and a very old-fashioned railroad at that. Lumberjacks rode these narrow-gauge rails in the 1880s on their way to and from work; so did Teddy Roosevelt, on a whistlestop campaign tour. Until 1941, families on an outing could pack a picnic lunch, ride these rails on the "Suntan Special" to the beach at Santa Cruz, and return home by nightfall. Then passenger service stopped; for years this scenic railway service simply traveled a 5-mile loop past the Big Trees, the first grove of redwoods to be preserved as a tourist attraction.

But in 1986 the necessary negotiations and paperwork were completed, and the Santa Cruz, Big Trees, and Pacific Railway Company was again in the business of taking visitors all the way to the beach at Santa Cruz and back. The trip begins at Roaring Camp, a re-created 1880s Western village just outside the town of Felton. You enter by walking across the oldest covered bridge in California; then you'll find a snack bar, the obligatory souvenir shop, a general store, and a lovely picnic area with lots of lawn, tables, and a duck pond.

But the real reason to come here is to see and ride the steam trains, all of them built around the turn of the century. The main ride, up 6½ miles of narrow-gauge track, takes about an hour and 15 minutes, round trip, and offers a chance to stop and picnic in the woods. The round trip to Santa Cruz takes two hours, if you stay on board and head right back. You can also disembark for a day at the

ROARING CAMP AND BIG TREES RAILWAY
⑧

beach and return to Roaring Camp and your car later. Both rides take you through a virgin forest of coastal redwoods, and you'll see the generations-old tourist attraction of the Big Trees, purchased in 1867 by a San Francisco businessman who wanted to be sure these natural monuments would not fall prey to the lumber industry. As the train chugs up the steepest narrow-gauge railroad grade in North America, you can sit inside the railroad cars or, if the weather is pleasant, head out to one of the open flatbed cars to breathe some of the freshest air in this part of the world. Tour guides will fill you in on the history of the place and identify the passing trees and plant life.

ROARING CAMP AND BIG TREES NARROW-GAUGE RAILROAD, *Felton. Trains run every day of the year except Christmas. Round-trip fare: Adults, $8.75; children, $5.75; under 3 free. Schedules vary, according to time of year, so call ahead. Phone: (408) 335-4400.*

HOW TO GET HERE: *From San Francisco, take Highway 101 South to Highway 280 to Highway 17 toward Santa Cruz. Exit at Mount Hermon Road and follow it into Felton. Turn south, left, on Graham Hill Road to the entrance, which will be on your right.*

THE NONALCOHOLIC WINERY (9)

At last, a lovely winery where nondrinkers don't have to feel left out. Along with producing award-winning white rieslings and gewürztraminers, Felton-Empire Vineyards produces nonalcoholic varietal grape juices. These are tasty and are much better than the grape juices you'll find in supermarkets. This small winery was the first in the area to produce nonalcoholic wines.

If you bring a picnic basket loaded with goodies, you can take advantage of the setting. Felton-Empire Vineyards is nestled in a redwood forest, on 15 acres of beautiful mountainous vineyard land. As you enjoy the surroundings, you can drink all the grape juice you want and not worry about getting behind the wheel.

FELTON-EMPIRE VINEYARDS, *379 Felton-Empire Road, Felton. Open 11 A.M. to 4:30 P.M. Saturday and Sunday. Phone: (408) 335-3939.*

HOW TO GET HERE: *From San Francisco, follow the directions to Felton, but at Graham Hill Road, turn right, north. Soon after joining Graham Hill Road, turn left onto Felton-Empire Road. The winery is a short distance up the hill on the left.*

SANTA CRUZ BOARDWALK (10)

The city of Santa Cruz is one of the great playlands of the West Coast. Originally developed as a blue-collar resort by the rail barons who foresaw a big business in day trips from San Francisco, Santa Cruz has grown to a bustling beach town. Today the city hosts a major university, a revitalized beachfront, beautiful homes, and scads of motels and restaurants. Perhaps because of the original design, there is no grand hotel here, and most visitors just come for the day.

A visit to Santa Cruz wouldn't be complete without a stop at the fabled boardwalk. This is one of the last great amusement strips in the West, perhaps in the nation. Here you will find the opulent Coconut Grove, where the great big bands played and where dancing has been restored. There are the rides, including the breath-stopping Big Dipper roller coaster, the bumper cars, and the historic carousel. There are corn dog stands and salt water taffy shops. Incidentally, Joe Marini, who has sold taffy here since the 1920s, assured me there was no salt water in the taffy. The name came from Coney Island, where a taffy stand caught fire and water had to be pumped from the Atlantic to put out the blaze. The clever entrepreneur put up a sign advertising "salt water taffy," and the name stuck.

A great deal of money and effort has been spent to make the boardwalk modern and clean. It's a pleasure to visit.

SANTA CRUZ BOARDWALK, *at the beach, Santa Cruz. Open daily during the summer and during Easter vacation. Phone: (408) 426-7433.*

HOW TO GET HERE: *From San Francisco, take Highway 101 South to Highway 280. Follow Route 280 to Route 17 South to Santa Cruz. Exit for the municipal center and the beaches. You will be on Ocean Avenue. Follow Ocean to the end; then turn right. At the first stoplight, turn left on Riverside. At the first stop sign, turn right. Then at the next stop sign, turn left again. (There is a series of one-way streets to deal with.) You will now be heading directly toward the Coconut Grove. Turn left on Beach Street and park in the lot on the left.*

The University of California at Santa Cruz has one of the most beautiful campuses I have ever seen. With its various buildings hidden from the road by redwood trees and surrounded by hillside meadows, it's like going to school in a national park. Tours are offered all year round, but if you only have enough time to see one thing, make it the Arboretum, which takes up 150 acres on the west side of campus.

UCSC ARBORETUM

Even if you don't have a green thumb, this is a beautiful place to enjoy nature, a getaway from the bustle down the hill at the beach and in downtown Santa Cruz. The climate here is perfect for growing the nation's largest collection of plants native to the Mediterranean, South Africa, New Zealand, and Australia. This arboretum is blessed with an incredible range of soil conditions and temperatures, some areas filled with warm sun, other valley sections dipping to temperatures as low as 18 degrees in winter. As a university project, the main function of the Arboretum is to experiment with new kinds of plants for this region and to pass this newfound knowledge on to those who make a living in the plant and flower industry. The Arboretum staff has introduced more than 200 new plants to the United States.

The protea garden alone is worth the trip. These spectacular plants, which sell for as much as $20 apiece in some flower shops, grow in an unimaginable variety of sizes, shapes, and colors. The Arboretum's output of proteas is outranked only by South Africa's.

The Australian gardens have the feeling of the Outback, with a thick growth of exotic plants, bushes, and trees that you will find nowhere else but Down Under and at UCSC. This includes some 70 species of eucalyptus trees.

The staff—a few paid employees and many volunteers—consists mostly of folks who either are associated with the university or are local residents who want to spend their spare time in gardens. My guide was a gentleman with the wonderful name Linton von Beroldingen, who turned out to be the retired editor of the *San Francisco Examiner*. He told me that the daily grind of newspaper life can't hold a candle to the excitement he has found learning about life in the Arboretum.

If you do have any questions about gardening or want to learn how to introduce new life into your garden, Linton or any other member of the staff will be glad to help you. Staff members are also available for tours and advice on Saturday, Sunday, and Wednesday afternoons.

UCSC ARBORETUM, *on the campus of the University of California, Santa Cruz. Open to the public 2 to 4 P.M. Wednesday, Saturday, and Sunday. Admission: Free. Phone: (408) 427-1305 or (408) 426-8750. The university admissions office conducts two-hour tours of the entire campus twice each weekday throughout the year; for a reservation, call (408) 429-4008.*

HOW TO GET TO THE ARBORETUM: *From San Francisco, take Highway 101 South to Route 280 to Route 17 to Santa Cruz. Exit on Route 1 North, which is Mission Street. Follow Mission to Bay Street and turn right. Take Bay to the main campus gate. Turn left on High Street, which changes its name to Empire Grade Road. It's a short ride to the Arboretum, which will be on your right.*

LONG MARINE LAB

One of the great tourist attractions in the South Bay is the Monterey Bay Aquarium in Monterey. What most people don't know, however, is that there's another marine wonderland at the north end of the same bay, in Santa Cruz. Though it's on a smaller scale than its counterpart to the south, the Joseph M. Long Marine Laboratory is rarely, if ever, crowded, needs no reservations, and is free.

Situated right on the beach on a 40-acre site of sand, wetlands, and marine terraces, this facility is run by the Center for Marine Studies at the University of California, Santa Cruz. This is a study center for marine ecology and marine mammal behavior. Trainers and scientists work with dolphins and sea lions daily, learning more and more about such things as communication and survival. It is a highly sophisticated research center; it's also one of the few marine labs on the West Coast that allows visitors to watch undergraduate and postgraduate trainers and researchers in action. Visitors can get very close to this free show.

The tour is led by one of more than 80 docent volunteers. The day I went, my docent was probably the youngest guide in history, an 11-year-old named Sierra. She had visited the research center so often that she asked if she could lead tours. As an illustration of how open and friendly the place is, they didn't brush her off and tell her to come back in 10 years; they put her to work. And Sierra rose to the task. She was a friendly and informative guide.

The tour begins in a small indoor aquarium that highlights the marine creatures that live in Monterey Bay. First stop is an open touching tank. Adults usually shudder and squirm, while kids immediately plunge their arms in to pick up a crab or a starfish. The tour continues past 20 or so other tanks filled with interesting critters. Magnifying glasses are available for close-up views.

After the aquarium section comes a visit to the outdoor tanks. The day I was there I was able to watch the sea lions go through the paces of a communications experiment with their trainer. Next door was a tank of rare Alaskan fur seals, about to be sent back home to the Pribiloff Islands after the completion of a round of experiments. The stars of the show, the dolphins, were viewed from a platform overlooking their tanks.

The tour ends up in a small museum featuring whale and shark bones and teeth, plus a gift shop. Visitors are encouraged to come to the lab. This is a comparatively new facility, only about 10 years old and still growing. Plans call for a large visitor's center with even more exhibits and an auditorium for lectures and movies. Tours last about an hour.

The lab is located next to Natural Bridges State Park, a place I also recommend, especially around October, when this becomes a favorite spot for monarch butterflies. On a cool day they will be everywhere.

JOSEPH M. LONG MARINE LABORATORY, *100 Shaffer Road, Santa Cruz. Open for tours 1 to 4 P.M. Tuesday through Saturday; closed holidays. Appointments necessary only for groups of 10 or more. Admission: Free. Phone: (408) 429-4308.*

HOW TO GET HERE: *From San Francisco, take Route 101 South to Route 280, then Route 17 South to Santa Cruz. Exit onto Route 1, heading north toward Half Moon Bay. This is also called Mission Boulevard. Turn left at Swift Street to Delaware Avenue. Turn right on Delaware and continue to the entrance to the lab.*

An alternate route is to take Route 1 from San Francisco all the way down the coast into Santa Cruz. At Swift, turn right and follow to Delaware.

SURFING MUSEUM

Thirty years before the Beach Boys ever heard the word *surfboard*, a group of die-hard surfing enthusiasts caught the waves on the beach at Santa Cruz. Today they are among the volunteers at what is probably the only museum in the continental United States devoted to the sport of surfing.

In this brick lighthouse high on a bluff above a surfing beach below, you're likely to meet Dave "Buster" Stewart, Harry Mayo, and Bill Grace. They're all pushing 70 now and are full of stories about the days on the beach before fiberglass and wetsuits. In the 1930s, with the music of Glenn Miller in their heads, they lugged 100-pound boards around; to keep warm, they wore old-fashioned wool-knit bathing suits they found at the Goodwill. There's a picture of their club on the wall, taken about 1941, not long before they all went to fight in World War II. Some of the boys in the picture didn't come back.

Harry, the museum's unofficial historian, says the parents thought their sons were crazy and were certain these pioneer beach boys wouldn't amount to anything in life. Bill's father expressed his opinion of his son's surfing buddies when he said, "When you sleep with dogs, you get fleas."

Well, today the gang is less muscled, less hairy, and more bifocaled than they were in the photograph, but at least they can laugh and say they all turned out OK. One's a retired fireman; the other two were businessmen. They still talk with a gleam in their eyes about the joy only catching a wave can bring, even though most gave up surfing years ago. When I asked if they ever wish they could get back on their boards just once more, sweet sad smiles of longing accompanied their affirmative answers.

You'll bump into surfers of all ages at the museum. But if you want to get the story from the real pioneers, just look for the old-timers with the wistful looks. The museum itself is small, but chock full of photographs, newspaper and magazine clippings, surfboards of every age and size, all housed in a lighthouse on the ocean. And when the weather is right, the new breed will be surfing right below the museum.

THE SURF MUSEUM, *Lighthouse Point, Santa Cruz. Open hours are iffy, since staffing is solely by volunteers and sometimes someone has to miss a shift, but general hours are noon to 5 P.M. daily. Admission: Free. Phone: (408) 429-3429.*

HOW TO GET HERE: *From San Francisco, take Highway 101 South to Route 280, then head south on Route 17 to Santa Cruz. Take the downtown Santa Cruz exit onto Ocean Street. Follow Ocean to Water Street and turn right. Take Water to Front Street and turn left toward the ocean; keep to the right for the ramp up to West Cliff Road. This is where the large Dream Inn Hotel is. Take West Cliff to the right until you arrive at the lighthouse.*

SALZ LEATHER GOODS (14)

From the courtyard entrance you might think you are about to visit a quaint art gallery. There's a huge fountain in the garden, and the red frame buildings look like an old New England home. If you explore inside, you will find the oldest leather tannery in the West.

Salz has been operating in Santa Cruz since 1861, which is recent history by

New England standards but ancient history in California time. Like so many California institutions, the tannery started because of the Gold Rush; the tannery made saddles, leather clothing, and other products for the flood of new residents. There wasn't much around Santa Cruz in those days, but there were 10 tanneries in the town by 1870. Salz is the only one that remains.

So what's so interesting about a tannery? For one thing, I found the process fascinating, from the cutting and dyeing to washing, shrinking, and drying; it gave me a new appreciation for my favorite jacket.

But more important, my tour guide, Susan McNight, was a delight. She was bubbly and excited and really made the process come alive. She also manages the gift shop, which sells brand-name products such as Florsheim and Adidas that are made from Salz leather.

In case you are concerned, this is not a slaughterhouse. Hides are purchased from beef processors and arrive here in huge sides.

SALZ LEATHER, *1040 River Road, Santa Cruz. Gift shop open 10 A.M. to 6 P.M. Monday through Friday, 10 A.M. to 5 P.M. Saturday; closed Sunday. Phone: (408) 423-1480.*

HOW TO GET HERE: *From San Francisco, take Highway 101 South to Route 280 to Route 17 South to Santa Cruz. Exit on Route 1 toward Half Moon Bay. Continue north to Route 9, which is River Street, and turn right. Salz is three blocks ahead, on the right. There are plenty of signs.*

"THE LAST SUPPER" IN WAX

Santa Cruz is probably the last place in the world you would expect to find a tribute to the work of Leonardo da Vinci, yet here it is, as big as life. This version of "The Last Supper" is in the gallery of the Art League of Santa Cruz, an organization run by very nice elderly ladies. These ladies would look totally out of place on the boardwalk or nearby beaches, but they have a tourist destination of their own to occupy their time: a life-size wax replica of the Leonardo masterpiece.

All of the figures from the famous meal are there, seated around a table loaded with wax food. Jesus sits wondering who has betrayed him, Judas with his moneybags looks the other way, just like in the original in Milan. The figures are very lifelike, down to details like the hair, reportedly put into place strand by strand.

When this Last Supper was unveiled in Santa Cruz in 1951, it was national news; more than a million pilgrims from around the world have come to see it. Though the idea may sound a bit bizarre, it is presented quite tastefully. A friend who went to the University of California at Santa Cruz says he always wanted to sneak in one day and put a bottle of ketchup on the table, but so far the waxwork has escaped vandalism and pranks.

THE LAST SUPPER, *in the Santa Cruz Art League Galleries, 526 Broadway, Santa Cruz. Open 11 A.M. to 4 P.M. Tuesday through Sunday; closed Monday. Admission: Free, but donations are requested. Phone: (408) 426-5787.*

HOW TO GET HERE: *Follow the directions to Santa Cruz, but take the exit to the municipal center and beaches (not Highway 1 North). You will be on Ocean Avenue. Continue on Ocean to Broadway and turn left. There will be a sign pointing to the Last Supper.*

MYSTERY SPOT

I'm a sucker for hokey places, and there is nothing hokier in Northern California than the Santa Cruz Mystery Spot. It's a tourist attraction that should be approached with a sense of humor and a sense of affection for the times when we were more easily entertained. This pre–high tech amusement (it opened in the 1940s) is designed to give you your money's worth.

The tour starts at a painted white line marking the spot where the mystery begins. Stand on one side of the line and you are shorter than your guide; stand on the other side and you are taller. Intrigued?

Next you start the long hike up a paved path to the mystery house. As you turn a corner, it suddenly gets harder and harder to walk, as if some something is pushing you back down the hill. It's just "the Force," your guide will tell you knowingly.

At the top of the hill you come to a little cabinlike house that looks like it is about to slide down the hill—just held up by the Force, the guide will explain. Inside, everything is on a slant, and it is difficult to walk upright and keep your balance. Like a carnival fun house, the place is designed to make your perceptions go haywire. Hold a purse by its shoulder strap and it appears to rise; roll a golf ball down a slanted board and it will stop and, seeming to defy gravity, roll back up.

Personally, I have a weak stomach and found it hard to keep my lunch inside the place, so I waited outside while the others in my group frolicked inside. A busload of Japanese tourists were having the time of their lives. They couldn't figure it out any more than I could, but so what? I don't want to know how it works. Mysteries are more fun when they stay mysteries.

THE SANTA CRUZ MYSTERY SPOT, *4 miles north of Santa Cruz, on Branciforte Road. Open 9:30 A.M. to 5 P.M. daily. Admission: Adults, $3.00; children under 11, $1.50. Phone: (408) 426-1282.*

HOW TO GET HERE: *From San Francisco, take Highway 101 South to Highway 280, then Route 17 South toward Santa Cruz. Before entering Santa Cruz, at Scotts Valley, exit onto Glen Canyon Road and head east, to the left of the freeway. Follow Glen Canyon Road to Branciforte Drive and turn left. Then watch for the signs for the Mystery Spot.*

Just 3 miles south of Santa Cruz is a completely different kind of beach town. Capitola was built as a resort community in the late 1800s. Whereas almost every nineteenth-century California community had a major fire or flood, Capitola escaped such a fate. As a result, there was never any need for urban renewal. Today you will see the town dotted with the original summer cottages and Victorian homes and, most significant for tourists, very narrow streets, which were built for horse-drawn wagon traffic; hence, on a warm day, especially during the summer, there are immense traffic jams.

I was taken around town by Sandy Lydon, a historian who teaches at nearby Cabrillo College. As he teaches in his local history lectures, Capitola was originally a haven for people from the steaming inland cities of Fresno, Modesto, and Madera who came to the beach to escape the sun. Trains would bring folks in from the valleys to sit on the foggy beach and cool off. Even when the sun would burn through the coastline fog, visitors would sit on the beach fully clothed. That's because in those days pale skin was a sign of luxury; tan skin meant you were a humble farmworker.

After Coco Chanel and Douglas Fairbanks popularized the suntan as a symbol of prosperity and health, bathing suits appeared on the beach. Nowadays during foggy times visitors to the area hang out in one of the many restaurants or boutiques in town, most of which are right on the beach.

Sandy took me up on one of the many hills above Capitola for what he considers the best way to see the town. From above you can see the little town that once had grand plans. Somebody thought the place would be the ideal location for the state capital, hence the name. You can see the remains of the original municipal wharf, much of which was washed away (a section has been restored and is a magnet for fishermen); the original railroad trestle, below which is a small historical museum; and the Esplanade, the elegant name for the walkway along the beach. You can also see what Sandy calls "the first condos in California": a string of Venetian-style court apartments built in 1924; these connecting housing units have been individualized by colorful paint jobs.

In the mid-1980s the yuppies discovered Capitola. According to Sandy, the measure of yuppiedom is the number of espresso machines within a given radius. He claims there are more espresso machines in Capitola than in any village in the South Bay. If his definition is right, I admit that I'm a yuppie after all. Spring and fall are the best times to visit, but no matter when you come, park in the first space you find when you get close to town. Parking is difficult all year round. Capitola is small, and it is easy to walk to the beach and commercial area.

CAPITOLA, *right off Route 1, a short drive south of Santa Cruz.*

HOW TO GET HERE: *From San Francisco, follow the directions to Santa Cruz and continue on Route 1 South until you come to the Capitola exit, about 10 minutes from Santa Cruz.*

MOSS LANDING

The Monterey Peninsula is one of the most popular tourist attractions in the Bay Area. The city of Monterey has a wonderful aquarium, and the town of Carmel-by-the-Sea has cute shops and Clint Eastwood as its mayor. Unfortunately, most visitors whiz past Moss Landing, which is also picturesque and worth a stop.

This is a real fishing village. Only two types of businesses flourish here, those that cater to the fishing industry and, for some reason, antique dealerships.

First, fishing. The town started back in the days when farms covered the surrounding area; Moss Landing was the port for shipping wheat out of the area. Then it became a whaling station and is now an active fishing port. If you ate Monterey Bay squid or prawns in a Bay Area restaurant last night, there's a good chance it came from the waters off Moss Landing. It looks like Monterey's waterfront looked 50 years ago, when John Steinbeck wrote about Cannery Row. Fortunately, it doesn't smell that way.

A land bridge takes you to the waterfront. Just park your car on the side of the road and wander around. You will see an active fisherman's wharf with absolutely no tourist attractions like wax museums or souvenir shops. This is the real thing. If you stay out of their way, and if they have the time, some of the old salts will tell you about their unique town. You also can't miss the giant Pacific Gas and Electric plant, which towers in the foreground, across Route 1. There appears to be a peaceful coexistence between the industrial giant and the small town. The power company employs nearly all residents who aren't in the fishing business.

Aside from the colorful fishing area, the major attraction in Moss Landing is antique stores, 23 of them, all clustered around the main drag in town—truly a browser's paradise.

MOSS LANDING, *just off Route 1 on the road to Monterey.*

HOW TO GET HERE: *From San Francisco, take Highway 101 South to Route 280 to Route 17 South to Santa Cruz. Take Route 1 South from Santa Cruz and look for the huge PG&E towers on the left. Then watch for the sign on the right to Moss Landing. It's about a 30-minute drive from Santa Cruz, in light traffic.*

ELKHORN SLOUGH

Just down the road from Moss Landing is one of the hidden treasures of the South Bay. Elkhorn Slough (pronounced "sloo") is a 7-mile waterway flanked by the largest salt marsh in the state. It all empties into an estuary where salt water mixes with fresh water. This marshland attracts an incredible mix of birds. It is said that more species of birds can be seen here than in any other spot in California—truly a birdwatcher's nirvana.

In addition to our fine feathered friends, there are easy-to-hike nature trails that lead to places that feel far removed from the hectic world (in spite of the constant hum from the nearby PG&E plant).

Before venturing out to the slough, it's a good idea to stop at the visitor's center to find out the best places to visit for the time of year you're there. If it's spring or summer it's likely they'll suggest you head for the shallows, where you'll see schools of leopard sharks and bat rays giving birth. At other times of the year they may suggest a visit to the old barns left over from the days when the area was a dairy farm, where you're likely to spot some birds of prey.

Elkhorn Slough is also an active research facility, so even though you may feel like you're in the middle of nowhere, there is always something going on, and there are enthusiastic people interested in showing you around.

ELKHORN SLOUGH *National Estuarine Sanctuary, 1700 Elkhorn Road, 2 miles from Moss Landing. Open 9 A.M. to 5 P.M. Thursday through Sunday. Admission: Free. Phone: (408) 728-2822.*

HOW TO GET HERE: *From San Francisco, take Route 101 South to Route 152 West to Route 156 to Castroville Boulevard, which you will come to just before entering the town of Castroville. Turn right on Castroville Boulevard. When you come to a yield sign, veer to the right and then take the next left onto Elkhorn Road. Follow it a short distance to the visitor's center.*

From Moss Landing, cross Route 1 and follow the road inland, adjacent to the power plant. That is Dolan Road, and it will take you to Castroville Road. Turn left on Castroville and then follow the signs to Elkhorn Slough.

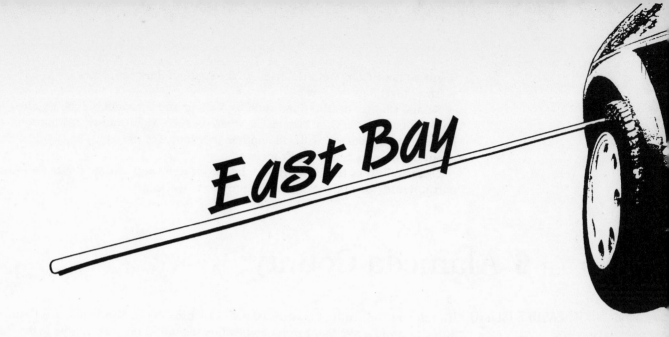

East Bay

Two major bridges connect San Francisco to the rest of the Bay Area. We have already used the Golden Gate Bridge as our link to Marin, Napa, and Sonoma; now we will use the larger, more heavily traveled, and less famous Bay Bridge to take us to the broad area called the East Bay. For our purposes this will include Alameda County with the major cities of Oakland and Berkeley; Contra Costa County, farther east, featuring a vast suburban sprawl reminiscent of the San Fernando Valley; the counties of Solano and Yolo, which have banded together as "Yolano" to offer tourists a Farm Trails guide of places to visit; and last but not least, the Sacramento Delta.

Much of this area is practically ignored by most visitors. People from Chicago or Rome usually don't make it out to Hayward or Walnut Creek or the Delta. But they are missing out on a scenic and cultural diversity that is truly wonderful. Here you will find touches of the Old West, the Deep South, and the American heartland. The spaces are wider open than anywhere else near San Francisco. And in this setting the attractions are surprising.

The closest East Bay destinations are in Alameda County, just over the Bay Bridge. If you avoid the rush hour from 4 to 6 P.M. weekdays, the trip will take you about a half hour from the city to the rolling hills of Tilden Park above Berkeley. Most of Contra Costa County is reached by driving through the Caldecott Tunnel north beyond Berkeley and, again in ideal traffic conditions, can be reached within an hour. Keep in mind that when you come out the other side of the tunnel you will be in another climatic zone; the weather will usually be 10 to 20 degrees warmer than in San Francisco. Hayward and Fremont are also

133

about an hour from San Francisco, to the south of Berkeley. They are also much warmer than San Francisco.

Solano County destinations such as Vallejo and Fairfield can be reached in an hour or so from San Francisco, whereas such Yolo County destinations as Esparto and Woodland will add another 30 minutes to the trip. The Delta begins about 90 minutes from San Francisco.

Once you cross the Bay Bridge, the major highways will be Route 80 to the north, Route 580 to the east, and Route 880 to the south.

CHAPTER **6** Alameda County

TREASURE ISLAND
①

To tell you the truth, Treasure Island is technically in San Francisco County. But when you leave San Francisco heading toward Alameda County via the Bay Bridge, it is your first possible stop, and it feels like you're in the next county. Amazingly, hundreds of thousands of motorists whiz by the Treasure Island exit and have never made the turnoff to visit. They are missing something wonderful.

Most of the island is now a naval base, but at one time it was a world-famous attraction. Treasure Island is one of the largest artificial islands in the world, created from tons of silt from San Francisco Bay and the Sacramento Delta to be the site of the 1939 World's Fair, or Golden Gate Exposition, as it was also called. There was competition from the New York World's Fair of 1939, but in 12 months some 10 million people descended on the island.

Let's set the scene a bit more. In 1939 the country was coming out of the Great Depression; two new bridges had just been constructed (the Bay Bridge and the Golden Gate), connecting the city of San Francisco with land to the east and north; and there were hopes of a new alliance with the nations of the Pacific. The Golden Gate Exposition was to herald a new era of Pan-Pacific partnership. Only two years later, the attack on Pearl Harbor would alter those plans.

In the meantime, optimism hung in the air like the colored lights all over the new island. The fair had everything: rides, fireworks, gardens, industrial exhibits, and entertainment extravaganzas like Billy Rose's Aquacade and Sally Rand's Nude Dude Ranch.

After the fair, the island was supposed to become an airport. The famed China Clipper had landed here, delivering passengers to the fair from the Orient. But the site was soon discovered to be too windy and too close to the Bay Bridge to be safe for regular commercial air traffic, so the city leased the island to the Navy. Now it is federal land.

Almost all of the glitzy, futuristic buildings from the fair have been torn down, and only three original structures remain. Two of them are hangars, which were to be used for the airport. The other is the Fair Administration building, which was to be the airport terminal building. Now it houses a museum open to the public.

The Treasure Island Museum is well worth a visit, if for nothing else than the unparalleled view of San Francisco from its parking lot. But even better, inside the museum are real treasures. Displays show the building of the island (named for Robert Louis Stevenson's book because dirt from the Sacramento Delta was thought to have gold in it), the history of sea services in the Pacific, and, most interesting to me, memorabilia from the fair. I could spend hours combing through the old ads, buttons, postcards, and photos from the ambitious exposition. By prior arrangement, groups of 10 or more can see a film about the fair.

TREASURE ISLAND MUSEUM, *open seven days a week from 10 A.M. to 3:30 P.M.; closed on federal holidays. Admission: Free. Phone: (415) 765-6182. Wheelchair accessible.*

HOW TO GET TO TREASURE ISLAND: *From San Francisco, get on the Bay Bridge; stay in the left-hand lane and midway across look for the Treasure Island exit (it is a left-side exit). Follow the road signs to Building One. If you are stopped by a guard at the gatehouse, simply tell him you're going to the museum.*

SHIP RADAR STATION

Connected to Treasure Island is yet another island, this one made by nature, called Yerba Buena, which was the original name of San Francisco. Even fewer Bay Area residents have been here than to Treasure Island, but this too is a stop worth making.

At the top of this 148-acre island someone is watching everything that goes on in the Bay, 24 hours a day. This is not some Orwellian type of surveillance but a service designed to prevent accidents on the Bay. It is the Vessel Traffic Center, operated by the Coast Guard. The service operates like a control tower of an airport, keeping tabs on who's where and how fast they're going. However, the vessel service does not have the same authority as an air control tower; it's more of a central clearinghouse of information that promotes communications between ships operating in the busy Bay.

Also unlike an air control tower, this center welcomes visitors, 24 hours a day, 365 days a year. The only requirement is you call first, especially if you plan to arrive outside of normal visiting hours (9 to 5-ish).

Inside the center, you will see a high-tech operation with radar screens showing blips throughout the Bay as ships move in and out. The officer in charge will probably have time to explain all the machinery, unless it's a foggy night. Then things get very busy, and you'll have to just stay clear and watch them in action.

A visit to the center illustrates what a challenge San Francisco Bay is to navigators. Listening to the controllers talking with the various ships gives you an idea of how important it is for seamen to know where everybody else is. Even a weekend sailor will learn something valuable about such factors as tricky weather, heavy currents, and the surprisingly shallow depths of the Bay.

VESSEL TRAFFIC CENTER, *Yerba Buena Island. Phone: (415) 556-2760.*

HOW TO GET HERE: *From San Francisco, take the Bay Bridge and stay on the right for the Yerba Buena exit. After the exit, make a quick left under the bridge, and then bear left again. Continue up the hill, bearing left all the way to the top. There are signs pointing to the Vessel Traffic Center.*

From Treasure Island, go back around the bridge and continue up the hill, bearing left until you reach the top.

Two thousand–acre Tilden Park is the closest thing to a wilderness area you can find in the center of the Bay Area. Unlike Golden Gate Park, with its manicured lawns and distinctly urban atmosphere, Tilden offers expanses of wooded hillsides, grassy meadows, and a variety of trails where you can be virtually alone in the hills of Berkeley and Oakland.

If you are not looking for solitude, Tilden Park also features an antique carousel, Anza Lake for swimming and sunbathing, the aptly named Inspiration Point (located on a very popular jogging trail), a golf course, and tennis courts.

There are three additional attractions in Tilden Park that I'd like to highlight. Each one alone is worth a trip over to the East Bay.

✓ Miniature Train Rides. The first is tucked away in the south section of the huge park. Here you'll find two, count 'em, two separate collections of old-fashioned steam trains. The first is the Redwood Valley Railway. It has been in operation for nearly 40 years, taking children and their parents on rides through the trees of Tilden Park. You ride in open cars while the steam engine chugs its way through the woods. The engineers and train operators are dressed in authentic railroad uniforms (just like in the movies), and when they yell "All aboard!" it's a thrill to see the excitement on the faces of the passengers.

Eric Thompson owns and runs the railroad and has been working on this rail long enough to have seen generations of Bay Area kids take their first train ride at Tilden. His daughter is now one of the conductors. Eric charges only a dollar for the ride, but he says even that embarrasses him because he can remember when the ride cost only a nickel.

If you thought video games, space travel, and television were the only things kids are interested in these days, you're in for a pleasant surprise. Business is brisk enough that Eric would like to add more trains.

Downhill, just below the ticket office and platform of the Redwood Valley Line is where you'll find the Golden Gate Steamers, a club of train lovers who build their own miniatures—scale models of actual trains that once traveled in the Wild West. Club members bring their creations from home to tinker and then run them on the club's 1½-mile track.

This place differs greatly from the professional operation up the hill. The Redwood Valley Line trains are large enough to accommodate 40 to 50 passengers per car, kids and full-sized adults. With the Steamers, part of the fun is watching them work over their homemade miniatures at individual work stations inside the track. Every member is a combination of engine builder, engineer, maintenance person, and conductor.

Every Sunday the club offers free rides on the one miniature train that is strong enough to carry a load of maybe 60 visitors. Most of the engines can pull only 450 pounds, and it's not uncommon to see two elderly gents in greasy overalls riding along the track with their knees up against their chest. The trains vary in size, but most cars are 2 to 10 feet long and only a few feet off the ground. They are short enough to make the men running them look like adults on kids' bikes. It's wonderful to watch these club members—retirees, history buffs, amateur mechanics—working away on their creations and using toy-sized shovels to put tiny pieces of coal into their engines.

Although the rides are free, donations are gratefully accepted; the money goes to keep up the facility, which involves quite a lot of track plus an intricate series of connecting portable tracks that can be rolled around the inside of the main track to act as work stations. I should mention that the intricate engines are perfect in detail, the result of exacting, painstaking, and time-consuming work. The members have every reason to be proud of their trains.

✔ **Native California Plant Garden.** The next stop, by car, will be the Botanical Gardens, about 10 minutes away from the train area. Here you'll find 6½ acres of land on which you can see the entire state of California, horticulturally speaking. The garden represents every plant that grows naturally in the state.

Pick up a brochure at the visitor's center and it's easy to give yourself a tour. One path takes you to the desert area, where you'll find a variety of cacti and succulents. Then maybe you'll want to visit the redwoods, the Shasta Cascades, or the sea bluff regions. Remember, you'll find the plants native to the regions, not all those trees and shrubs brought into California by people who moved here from back East.

The Botanical Gardens also serve an important function of preserving endangered plants. For example, there is more of the once prominent manzanita in the garden than remains elsewhere in the entire state. The garden paths are easy to walk, and each plant is clearly labeled.

It takes four visits to really see the garden, one visit each season. In fact, the Tilden Botanical Gardens is one of the few places in the Bay Area where you can see a dramatic change from season to season. All year round there is something to see: a solid wall of flowers at the sea bluff in spring, coastal plants in bloom all summer, and colors in fall. Steve Edwards, the director of the gardens, says his favorite time is in winter right after a rainstorm; the creek suddenly becomes 6 to 8 feet deep, and an area that is dry and warm in the summer is suddenly filled with the rushing sounds of high water.

✓ **The Little Farm.** As for the third stop within Tilden Park, drive to the north end of the park for a visit to the Tilden Little Farm. Everyone who lives in the Bay Area has heard the commercial for a local milk company that ends with a slogan, "Farms, in Berkeley?" Well, even though the farms that used to dot the university town are long gone, there is one very lovely working farm within Berkeley's city limits. Luckily for us, this farm is set up for visitors, complete with park rangers and naturalists who work with the animals and give tours for people.

The Little Farm is a good name. The place is, well, little, and quite manageable. It is also spotlessly clean and reasonably devoid of the odors that can discourage city slickers from breathing deeply. The place was built in the 1950s by a Berkeley High School woodshop class, constructed to half scale so the barns aren't as cavernous (and therefore hard to manage) as the ones you'll find out in the country. It's like Old MacDonald's place had come to life, with chick-chicks here and quack-quacks there, running freely. Don't be alarmed if they charge up to you; they just think you might have something to feed them. In addition you'll find cows, goats, sheep, rabbits, and a donkey who's called the Boss. It has nothing to do with Bruce Springsteen; it's simply that the donkey has been there longer than most of the other animals and knows how to get its own way. My favorite Little Farm animals are two pigs named Broccoli and Tofu. They were named by a visiting schoolboy who thought those names would ensure that the pigs would never be eaten.

The best time to visit is in the morning, between 7 and 10 A.M., when the animals are frisky and eager to be fed. You'll probably also want to stop in next door to the interpretive center. Along with many farm and wilderness exhibits, you'll find a 10-foot stuffed lizard called a Komodo dragon; it's a very popular display.

TILDEN PARK, *Berkeley. General information number: (415) 531-9300.*

TILDEN PARK REDWOOD VALLEY RAILWAY *runs from 11 A.M. to dusk on weekends and holidays all year and from 1 to 6 P.M. on weekdays during Easter week and all summer. A ride costs $1 per person. Phone: (415) 548-6100. The Golden Gate Steamers set up their own tracks every Sunday, from about noon to 3 P.M., weather permitting. Phone: (415) 540-9264.*

HOW TO GET TO THE TRAINS OF TILDEN: *From San Francisco, take the Bay Bridge to Highway 24, following the signs to Walnut Creek. Take the Claremont Avenue exit. At the stoplight at the bottom of the exit ramp, turn left. Follow Claremont all the way to the top of the hill until you come to Grizzly Peak Boulevard. Turn left and after 10 minutes or so look for the sign on the right for the Tilden Park steam trains.*

TILDEN BOTANICAL GARDENS *are open every day of the year during daylight hours. Admission: Free.*

HOW TO GET HERE: From the steam trains, take the South Park Drive and you will end up at the gardens. There is a small parking lot across the road from the entrance. From San Francisco, follow the directions to the steam trains, but instead of turning off at the train entrance continue on Grizzly Peak Boulevard until you come to the Shasta Road entrance to the park. Turn right and follow the signs to the gardens.

TILDEN LITTLE FARM is open from dawn to 10 P.M. every day; the interpretive center is open from 10 A.M. to 5 P.M. Tuesday through Sunday. Admission: Free. Phone: (415) 525-2233.

HOW TO GET HERE: From the Botanical Gardens, go back to Grizzly Peak Boulevard and follow all the way to the intersection of Spruce. Turn right and then immediately bear left at a 45-degree angle and follow Canyon Road until you enter the Tilden Nature Area. Technically, this is separate from Tilden Park, but there is no practical difference for the visitor. Park your car at the first lot and walk up to the farm and interpretive center.

LAWRENCE HALL OF SCIENCE (4)

One of the best sunset-viewing spots in the Bay Area is from the parking lot of the Lawrence Hall of Science. Facing west, you have a hilltop view of the Bay, Alcatraz Island, Marin County, San Francisco, and both the Bay and Golden Gate bridges, all backlit by the setting sun.

But it's worth arriving early to take advantage of the inside of the building serviced by the parking lot. From the outside, the Lawrence Hall of Science looks like a concrete airline bunker. But once you're through the door you'll be in an inviting, open wonderland for the kid in all of us.

The Lawrence Hall of Science is a hands-on science museum. Most of the exhibits are designed for touch and interaction. Computer games illustrate everything from your reaction time to what is in the food you ate for lunch. Two telescopes are open to the public for viewing the heavens, and there's a prehistoric animal exhibit featuring moving, bellowing dinosaurs. In addition, the Hall of Science offers special seasonal programs on a variety of topics.

For me, the most remarkable exhibit came about by chance. It is a life-size replica of the *Challenger* space shuttle. It sits just outside the main building, poised as if ready to take off any second.

This shuttle model began as a class project at UC Berkeley. A teacher and former NASA scientist, Larry Kuznetz, was so moved by the shuttle tragedy of 1986 that he wanted to create a tribute to the *Challenger* crew. So as a class project his "Life in Space" students designed and built a shuttle replica.

At first the plan was simply to build a papier-mâché and cardboard model on the grass outside the museum. But then the project took on a life of its own. A contractor heard about it and offered to donate some concrete, establishing a solid and permanent foundation. Then a tilemaker came by with some gleaming black and white tiles to decorate the exterior. Suddenly the temporary structure became a permanent structure. This caused a conflict with the museum folks, who had not planned or budgeted for a space shuttle on the premises, but there it was. And the craftsmanship was so good that it only made sense to make it part of the Hall of Science.

The most impressive work was done inside. Every button, every switch, every detail of the *Challenger* has been re-created. There's even a computer program that simulates the navigational function of the craft. You can get an idea of what space pioneers must endure. Clearly, space travel is not for the claustrophobic. First stop on the visit is a chamber where space walkers must stand for several hours until the nitrogen in their bodies is removed before venturing into space. The next door takes you into the main living quarters, a room about the size of a large closet containing sleeping compartments that resemble built-in dresser drawers. When the replica was first built, Larry Kuznetz had to sleep in one of the bunks to protect the shuttle project from nighttime vandals.

Upstairs is the cockpit, with seats for a pilot and copilot and room for one or two standing crew members. Again the most remarkable thing is the detail. Looking from the pilot's seat out the front windows, there is a remarkable effect of soaring above the Bay Area, especially at night.

LAWRENCE HALL OF SCIENCE, *University of California, Berkeley. Open 10 A.M. to 4:30 P.M. daily; open 10 A.M. to 9 P.M. Thursday. Admission: Adults, $3.50; young people 7 to 18 and seniors, $2.50; children 2 to 6, $1.50. Special rates are available for groups of 12 or more; reservations must be made at least two weeks in advance. Phone: (415) 642-5134. Wheelchair accessible.*

HOW TO GET HERE: *From San Francisco, take the Bay Bridge and continue on Route 580 West to the University Avenue exit. Follow University several miles until it ends at the edge of the UC Berkeley campus. Turn left, go one block, then turn right on Hearst. Follow Hearst up the hill to Gayley Road and turn right. At the Strawberry Canyon left turn you will see a sign to the Lawrence Hall of Science. Follow the signs up the hill.*

Though most people in the Bay Area know there is a county called Alameda, surprisingly few know there is a town by the same name. This old city, which can be reached only by tunnel or bridge, remains a bit of a mystery.

Alameda is an interesting amalgam of old-time sea resort, naval air station, and new condo developments. It also happens to have a fine beach—a narrow, 2-mile strip where you can sun, swim, toss a Frisbee, and picnic. And at the western end of the beach you'll find one of the Bay Area's hidden treasures, a small shoreline park officially named Robert Crown Park but more commonly known as Crab Cove.

Run by the East Bay Regional Park District, Crab Cove is the site of what was

CRAB COVE

once a huge amusement park. At the turn of the century this was Neptune Beach, sort of a West Coast Coney Island, a place to ride a carousel, have a clambake, take a romantic promenade. But time was not kind to Neptune Beach, and after the Depression the place was torn down. After years of abuse, the park district took over the land and established the first marine reserve in the state.

The visitor's center is a good place to start a visit to Crab Cove. Here you'll find a large saltwater aquarium so you can see what lives out there in the Bay without having to don scuba equipment. You'll also find exhibits about the marine environment and the history of Alameda, including pictures of long-gone Neptune Beach.

Once you are acquainted with the region, park rangers will take you out to the mud flats to show you firsthand what you saw in the exhibits. On the rocky shore, the crabs are the main attraction. Turn over almost any rock and you will find one of the little creatures. As I learned during my visit, the crab is a fine example of one of nature's wonders. If it loses a leg, it will grow another, a phenomenon scientists are trying to understand in the hope that it will lead to eventual human limb regeneration.

Out in the mud flats, boots are a necessity (bring your own; they don't have any to loan you). While sloshing around out there it is difficult to imagine that any kind of life resides at the water's edge. But as the exhibits inside illustrate, this area contains the highest concentration of life of any habitat. Marine algae abound, as do many forms of sea lettuce. You can look but not take souvenirs; this is an environmentally protected area, and everything must stay where it is.

This is not the sort of place I would recommend to adults who are traveling on a tight schedule. But it is a wonderful destination for a family outing.

CRAB COVE MARINE RESERVE AND VISITOR CENTER, *Crown Memorial State Beach, 1252 McKay, Alameda. Visitor's center open 10 A.M. to 4:30 P.M. Wednesday through Sunday; closed Monday and Tuesday. Robert Crown Park and Memorial Beach has showers, a snack bar, picnic tables, and a 10 P.M. curfew. Admission: Free. Phone: (415) 521-6887.*

HOW TO GET HERE: *From San Francisco, take the Bay Bridge to Route 880 South toward San Jose. Exit at Broadway–Alameda and proceed on the service road parallel to the freeway. Watch for a 45-degree turn left to Alameda. Go through the tunnel. You will be on Webster Street. Take it to the end where it intersects with Central. Turn right on Central and go half a block to McKay; turn left and follow the Crab Cove signs.*

There are wonderful Victorian houses throughout the Bay Area, but I didn't expect to find any in Hayward, a city synonymous with suburban housing. But right there on busy Hesperian Boulevard, across from a McDonald's, is the McConaghy Estate, a nineteenth-century 12-room farmhouse furnished in the style of 1886 and open to the public.

This was the home of the town's original "Big Mac," John McConaghy, who lived in it from age 15 to his death at 101 in the late 1970s. Concerned citizens with an interest in preserving the community's history convinced the city to buy the house.

Today volunteers keep the house open for tours. They dress in clothing of the period to set the proper mood. Every room has been restored and furnished with pieces from the period, even down to the hairbrushes and nail files that sit on dresser tops. In the children's room you'll find antique dolls and other toys; in Papa's office you'll find a deer-head rifle rack, a footstool made of antlers, and a roll-top desk stuffed with bills yet to be paid. Downstairs you'll see such up-to-the-minute conveniences as a working icebox and an original washing machine, the tub with a hand crank. Also on display is some wonderful vintage clothing, including Victorian gentlemen's underwear and ladies' bustles. (I had always wondered how women could sit down while wearing one of those things. I learned at the McConaghy House that it was easy: The bustle was wooden and collapsed like a fan.)

The McConaghy House is different from the Victorians open to the public in San Francisco. The Haas-Lillenthal House and the Spreckels Mansion in the big city are examples of homes of the very rich; the McConaghy House is set up to show how a middle-class farm family lived. It will strike you as pretty opulent anyway, certainly compared to the typical modern middle-class home in the rest of town.

Special events are staged throughout the year, including a Victorian Christmas during the month of December when the entire house is decorated for the holiday with a Christmas tree in every room. There are also special displays at Easter, the Fourth of July, and, in late July, an outdoor antique sale with dealers throughout the East Bay offering their wares.

In back of the home is a carriage house with wagons and buggies. You will also find a boutique on the second floor of the main house selling country-style gifts, books, and items for children.

MCCONAGHY ESTATE, *18701 Hesperian Boulevard, Hayward. Open 1 to 4 P.M. Thursday through Sunday. Donation: Adults, $2.00; seniors, $1.50; children, 50 cents. Special rates of $5 for classes and youth groups. Phone: (415) 581-0223.*

HOW TO GET HERE: *From San Francisco, take the Bay Bridge to Route 880 South to the Hacienda exit in Hayward. Go right on Hacienda to Hesperian Boulevard and turn left. The house is well marked and will be on your right.*

Hayward is about 45 minutes from San Francisco, 30 minutes from Oakland and Berkeley.

BUFFALO BILL'S BEER

There's a new trend in beermaking called the "brewery pub," places that serve beer made right on the premises. One of the first of these is Buffalo Bill's in Hayward. The owner is Bill Owens, who gained national attention as a photojournalist in the 1960s for his book *Suburbia,* a collection of affectionate and revealing portraits of life in the suburbs.

Well, here he is in the 1980s living in the heart of the suburbs and making the best beer I've ever tasted. I'm hardly a beer connoisseur, but friends who are rave about Bill's brew. It certainly doesn't taste like anything you'll get in a bottle.

Bill, who oversees the making of the beer and usually dispenses it himself from behind the bar, is a man with a mission. As he'll be sure to tell you, the beer is made on the premises and travels by pipeline just 62 feet from the brewery in the back room to the bar—no kegs, no bottles. And he'll tell you that unlike most American beermakers, who use bland corn or rice in the brewing process, he uses only the more flavorful barley and hops. The entire process of fermentation, brewing, and injecting carbonation takes about a week.

The pub itself is fashioned after the British concept of a neighborhood place where you can go and feel at home. Food is served, and moderation is urged. Bill closes early and frowns on "happy hours" and other gimmicks that encourage people to "get loaded." His concept is to have the pub act as an extension of the family living room, a place to relax and converse. Bill also makes a point of keeping everything clean and approachable, down to the rest rooms. Since Buffalo Bill's opened, several brewery pubs have followed, in Berkeley, Santa Cruz, and San Francisco.

BUFFALO BILL'S, *1082 B Street, Hayward. Open 11:30 A.M. to 10:30 P.M. Monday through Thursday; Friday open to 1 A.M.; Saturday open to 12:30 A.M.; Sunday open 1 to 7 P.M. Phone: (415) 886-9823.*

HOW TO GET HERE: *From San Francisco, take the Bay Bridge to Route 880 South toward San Jose. At Hayward, exit on A Street. Turn left and follow A Street toward downtown. At Foothill, turn right for one block, then right again on B Street. The pub is right off the intersection of Foothill and B Street.*

A GHOST TOWN CALLED DRAWBRIDGE
Our next stop in this area involves a ghost story of sorts. Let me set the scene.

Back in 1876 two characters named Hog Davis and Slippery Jim Farr decided to build a train from Santa Cruz to Fremont. To do this they needed to provide a drawbridge for the wetlands around the community of Newark. This drawbridge needed an operator, so Hog and Slippery built a shack for the bridge keeper. As the legend goes, he noticed that the area was full of ducks, birds, and fish, and he told a few friends. Before long the area around the drawbridge became a hunter's paradise; more shacks were built, and a duck club was established. Soon there was a community called Drawbridge. One could get there only by boat or train. There was no police department, no government; everybody simply agreed on proper rules of behavior and got along just fine.

Today Drawbridge is a ghost town. It was a victim of the development of the wetlands. Office complexes, housing developments, and industry crept in from all sides. In addition, airports were built, and it wasn't long before the ducks and other wildlife that had attracted people to Drawbridge were gone from the area.

Where there were once two hotels and lots of vacation cabins there are abandoned shacks sinking in the mud flats on both sides of the railroad track, now an active Amtrak line.

I was shown around by a docent for the San Francisco Wildlife Refuge Center, an amateur historian named Monty Dewey. Monty thinks Drawbridge is a symbol for the Bay Area. As we stood out in the mud flats he observed that once the entire area, as far as we could see, was bay. Now only one-eighth of the wetlands remain. The rest has been lost to so-called progress. He says Drawbridge is a vivid reminder of what can happen when land and wildlife are not protected.

This is not to say that a visit to Drawbridge is grim. There are still birds to see and the nearby salt ponds, in addition to the curious appeal of strolling through a ghost town. To see Drawbridge and understand its role in our present life, you must first check into the San Francisco Wildlife Refuge Center, and a guide will escort you.

As long as you're here, by all means take a look around the Refuge Center. It is filled with interesting displays about the Bay and its environment as well as photographs of the original town. Also, many well-marked nature trails lead from the center through protected marshland abuzz with wildlife.

SAN FRANCISCO BAY WILDLIFE REFUGE CENTER, *Newark. Open all year, except on major holidays. Tours begin at 10 A.M. and end around 1:30 P.M. Saturday and Sunday, May to September. Admission: Free. Reservations are a must. Phone: (415) 792-0222.*

HOW TO GET TO THE REFUGE CENTER: *From San Francisco, take Highway 101 South to the Dumbarton Bridge (Highway 84); once across, look for signs to the San Francisco Wildlife Refuge Center on your right. It is located very near to the junction of Highway 84 and Thornton Road.*

ARDENWOOD

Just across from the huge auto plant that marked the first cooperative venture between General Motors and Toyota, tucked away in a clump of eucalyptus trees, past Ardenwood Industrial Park, you can find a *real* park that offers not only a place to rest and enjoy nature but also the chance to see what life was like around here 150 years ago.

This is Ardenwood Historical Farm, a faithful re-creation of life on the farm in the old days. This is the original home of a golddigger and sharecropper named George Patterson. His small farm stayed active until the last of the family died out. Then the house was simply abandoned and hidden from view by the eucalyptus grove.

A few years ago an East Bay Regional Parks District employee named David Luden noticed the old house as he was taking a back road to work. He notified the city of Fremont that the abandoned mansion, which sits on city property, was going to waste. The city then asked Luden and his wife to move in as caretakers; they could live there free in return for fixing up the place. David had been waiting for a chance like this all his years as a Parks naturalist.

Luden enlisted the help of volunteers, and before long the Victorian farmhouse sparkled and the farm was back in operation. Farmers from around the state donated antique farm equipment left by their parents; others donated cows, pigs, sheep, goats, rabbits, and chickens. Eventually the East Bay Parks District took over, and Luden and his wife moved on to restore another crumbling mansion elsewhere in the East Bay.

So today visitors can enjoy the fruits of the labors of Luden and his hundreds of volunteers. Ardenwood is a living history center. Grains are grown on the grounds of the 205-acre preserve and processed like the Pattersons did for generations. You can churn butter, or watch somebody else do it, and visit a working blacksmith shop on the premises. On weekends you can go on a tour of the house and ride a hay wagon and horse-drawn railcar. School groups book for months in advance for this firsthand hands-on experience of nineteenth-century farm life.

ARDENWOOD HISTORICAL FARM, *Fremont. Open 10 A.M. to 6 P.M. Thursday through Sunday (the gate closes at 4 P.M.; visitors who enter before then are welcome to stay until 6). Admission: Thursday and Friday, adults $1.50; children under age 14, $1; under age 2, free; Saturday and Sunday, adults $3; children under age 14, $2, under age 2, free. Phone: (415) 796-0663. Wheelchair accessible.*

HOW TO GET HERE: *From San Francisco, take the Bay Bridge to Highway 880 South toward San Jose. After you pass the Hayward exits, look for State Highway 84 to the Dumbarton Bridge. Exit to the right toward Newark until you come to Newark Boulevard. Turn right and watch for the sign on the right for Ardenwood Historical Farm. Don't be confused by all the signs to the Ardenwood Industrial Park. The sign to the farm is clearly visible shortly after you turn onto Newark Boulevard.*

You may have noticed that most historic places I've recommended so far attempt to re-create California life of the Gold Rush days or the Victorian era. Well, here's a place that looks back even further, to the original inhabitants of this area, the Ohlone Indians.

The Ohlones were a remarkable people, a tribe that lived here in complete harmony with their environment. These people lived on this land for 5000 years; Ohlones were born, lived, and died on the same land as their parents and grandparents, century after century. They lived in a supportive environment that provided a kind of stability that allowed them to remain in a place that offered abundance and variety. If the acorns failed one year, there were buckeyes; if salmon didn't run one year, there were shellfish or deer. Their myths assured them that they lived at the center of the universe and that the gods meant well.

The Ohlones may have been perfectly integrated with their environment, but tragically for them, their lives changed when the Spanish arrived. By the 1790s the Spanish had cleared the East Bay of Indians, moving them to Mission Dolores in San Francisco. There many Indians died from the epidemics of the time: smallpox, measles, and cholera. The survivors eventually drifted south. Some married into the Mexican-American population around Monterey, and others moved back to the East Bay and assimilated into the white man's culture.

You can visit the remains of an Ohlone village in Coyote Hills Park near the sprawling suburb of Fremont. This was one of several Ohlone villages in the area, each with a community of about 100 people. When I visited I couldn't help but wonder about the arrogance of the present inhabitants of this state. We've made more changes around here in the past five years than the Ohlones made in 5000.

A trip to the Ohlone shell mounds begins at the visitor's center. There you will find a guide to escort you (you must have a guide to enter the re-created village). First you will see three or four structures, a home, a sweat house, and a dance hall. Then you will notice several shell mounds, the Ohlone version of a dump. All this may not seem like much at first until your guide starts telling you stories about the Ohlone way of life. You learn that such mounds hold the key to the day-to-day life of the people. The Indians created layers and layers of clam, oyster, and mussel shells, plus other discarded organic material. When a mound reached a certain height, they would simply move a little farther away and start over. The homes were built to last only a season or two anyway, so it was easy to keep moving. There used to be over 400 such archaeological treasures in the Bay Area; most have been destroyed by development.

The ingenuity of the Ohlone Indians is demonstrated further inside the visitor center. Naturalists will show you how fires were started (the old rubbing-two-sticks-together method), acorns were ground, and boats and baskets were made.

On special occasions a surprisingly seaworthy longboat made of tule strands is taken out into the Bay. And there are numerous exhibits and photos.

The rest of the park is also of interest, 1200 acres of wildlife sanctuary set up for environmental education and recreation. You'll find grassy hills, freshwater marshes, and willow runs. In winter and during migrations thousands of birds can be seen in the park. Trails will take you through all major habitat areas, with a convenient boardwalk crossing the marsh. Serious hikers may want to take advantage of the 11-mile Alameda Creek Trail, leading to the mouth of Niles Canyon. Picnic areas with tables and braziers for grilling are provided, as are bicycle trails, day-camping sites, and nature study programs.

COYOTE HILLS REGIONAL PARK, *8000 Patterson Ranch Road, Fremont. Park open 8 A.M. to sunset daily; visitor center open 9 A.M. to 5:30 P.M. daily. Ohlone Village and shell mound is open only at certain times with a guided tour, so call ahead. Admission: $1.50 parking fee. Phone: (415) 795-9385. Visitor center is wheelchair accessible.*

HOW TO GET HERE: *From San Francisco, take the Bay Bridge and follow Route 880 South to the Route 84–Dumbarton Bridge exit. Go west on Route 84 to Newark Boulevard; turn right and continue to Patterson Ranch Road. There will be signs directing you to the park entrance. It's just a few minutes down the road from the Ardenwood Farm. Again, don't be misled by the huge industrial park; there is a "real" park in there.*

THE ORIGINAL HOLLYWOOD ⑪

Once upon a time, before Hollywood became established as the American movie capital, the little town of Niles was one of the major centers for moviemaking. Niles was the West Coast headquarters of the Chicago-based movie company Essanay Studios. Between 1911 and 1916 over 450 Essanay one-reelers were filmed and edited in Niles, including the hit westerns that featured Bronco Billy Anderson. Such stars as Ben Turpin, Wallace Beery, Zazu Pitts, and Marie Dressler worked in Niles. And at the end of the silent classic *The Tramp,* when Charlie Chaplin waddles down a country lane to a brighter tomorrow, he's walking on a tree-shaded avenue somewhere in Niles. Chaplin made several films here, commuting from San Francisco, until Mack Sennett offered him a fortune to come to Hollywood.

In its day, Essanay was one of the most modern and complete film studios on the West Coast. The main section of the studio was a sprawling two-story facility, mostly devoted to a large stage for shooting interior scenes; other areas were taken up by costume storage, editing suites, and props. Nearby weather-perfect Niles Canyon became the setting for Bronco Billy's adventures. And Niles itself, with its quaint hotels, storefronts, and saloons, was a perfect set for town scenes.

Niles still looks like a perfect set for small-town scenes. It is a quiet little community that is remarkably untouched by its moviemaking past; the citizenry was unimpressed with the movie crowd back then and it still is. Old-timers love to tell stories of how the cowboy extras would get drunk every night and do things much wilder than anything that ever made it onto film. There's very little left of the original studio, and the town offers no organized tours of the hotels, saloons, or other locations used in the movies. The one concession to the past is the town merchants' association's small collection of films made in Niles; once a year they'll dust off a couple and hold a little festival.

But anyone remotely interested in silent movies might get a kick out of visiting the site of a once lively moviemaking center. The main part of the studio stretched out between Niles Boulevard and Second Street between G and F. Today the spot is marked by the presence of a gas station. The only part of the original studio left standing is a row of cottages on Second Street between G and F. These were inhabited by the stars when they came to town to work on a picture. Around the row at 153–155 G Street are the cottages used by Bronco Billy as his office and dressing room (in addition to starring in over 200 films, Bronco Billy Anderson also ran the studio).

On I Street you will see the former train depot that made its way into a forgotten film or two. It now functions as the office of the Chamber of Commerce and is a good place to stop for directions.

The other reminder of the days when Niles was California's first movie capital is the town's version of the Hollywood sign. High on a hill overlooking the rail depot you can see the giant letters NILES. Folks around town seem very pleased that the movie affair never went further than it did.

HOW TO GET TO NILES: *From San Francisco, take the Bay Bridge to the Nimitz Freeway (Route 177). Follow the Alvarado-Niles off ramp east. It becomes Niles Boulevard as it approaches the railroad tracks. Continue to F Street; turn right and you will see the remaining cottages left from Essanay's heyday.*

MISSION SAN JOSE

As every student in a California public school is taught, Catholic missionaries established a well-designed system of missions in the state, 21 in all, each within a day's walk of the next. Some of the missions, like the Mission Dolores in San Francisco, wound up in heavily populated areas; others, like the Mission San Jose de Guadalupe in Fremont, are more removed from major centers.

Perhaps that's what makes this mission stand out. The city of Fremont is a sprawling suburb, with housing developments, industries, and shopping centers built around the major highway, Route 880. Far to the east of the main town is an area called the Mission District, and that's where you'll find this gleaming white adobe structure, an unexpected sight out in the suburbs.

Mission San Jose is the most recently restored of California's 21 missions. Originally built in 1797, the mission had fallen victim to traditional enemies of

California buildings, earthquakes and fires. The major restoration was completed in 1986. Now Mission San Jose is considered to be a jewel.

From the outside the mission, the grounds, and adjoining museum are very inviting. Every effort was made to maintain the look of the original adobe, down to the adobe refuse cans.

Inside, the 295-seat chapel shows the painstaking six years of work by art restorers and architects. Every wall is adorned with beautiful paintings; elaborate chandeliers hang from the high, wood-beamed cathedral ceiling. The centerpiece of the project, the altar, was reconstructed from 180 ornate pieces highlighted with gold leaf and evoking the spirit of high mass.

Father Michael Norkett can tell you about each piece, such as the candelabras fashioned as exact replicas of the ones in the original mission. Father Michael is a sight as unexpected as the mission itself. During the summer months, when the temperature often hovers in the 90s, it is not unusual to see this hip, young fellow roaming around the mission in a polo shirt and shorts. That's Father Michael, who came to the Fremont mission after spending years in the rougher sections of San Francisco. Since Mission San Jose is the working church of his parish, he is a key figure in the neighborhood. He's also great fun and brings a good sense of humor to his role. He says his mother once asked him if he even owns a clerical collar and cassock (he does, but prefers to avoid wearing black when the temperature pushes 100 degrees).

MISSION SAN JOSE DE GUADALUPE, *corner of Mission and Washington boulevards, Fremont. Open 10 A.M. to 5 P.M. daily. Phone: (415) 657-1797.*

HOW TO GET TO THE MISSION SAN JOSE: *From San Francisco, take the Bay Bridge to Route 880 South to Fremont. Exit at Route 84 and follow the road east toward the Niles junction. At Mission Boulevard, turn right (south) and continue to the mission.*

ELLISTON WINERY
(13)

Before Prohibition, the Livermore Valley was one of the original centers for winemaking in the Bay Area. Once there were 37 wineries there; today there are only six. The valley is now better known for the famous, or infamous, Livermore Labs, home of sophisticated weapons research programs, than for its chardonnays.

But wineries are making a comeback in this lovely, little-traveled valley, a valley that feels remarkably untouched by time. One of the most appealing wineries is Elliston, located on a road that once was lined with the country estates of super-rich residents of the Bay Area, citizens with names like Hearst. One grand home was owned by Henry Hiram Ellis, a successful forty-niner (Gold Rush panner, not football player). He was also a sea captain and a chief of the San Francisco Police Department.

Several years after the last of the Ellises moved on, the house was discovered by a schoolteacher named Ray Awtrey. He and his wife Amy moved in to restore the house and opened a winery on the premises to help support the place.

It's a beautiful place that is as noncommercial and ungimmicky as a winery could possibly be. Even if you don't drink wine, the place is worth seeing. The 17-room mansion has been furnished with antiques from the 1860–1900 period and is open for tours and wine tastings in the drawing room by appointment. Once a month dinner is served in the mansion, and the grounds are available for weddings and receptions. The winery and tasting room are in the old carriage house. If you are so inclined, it is worth picking up a few bottles of their white zinfandel or cabernet sauvignon while you're there, since Elliston wines are made in small quantities and are hard to find outside the Livermore Valley.

Ray loves showing off the house and telling tales of the Ellis family as much as he enjoys showing off his wine, so when you go, plan to stay a while.

ELLISTON VINEYARDS, *463 Kilkare Road, Sunol. Tasting room open 9 A.M. to 4 P.M. Monday through Friday; noon to 4 P.M. Saturday and Sunday; or by appointment. Admission: Free. Tours of the house are for groups of 15 or more and must be arranged in advance. The charge is $10 per person, including wine and hors d'oeuvres. Phone: (415) 862-2377.*

HOW TO GET HERE: *From San Francisco, take the Bay Bridge to Route 580 toward Stockton. When you reach the Livermore area, exit onto Route 84 West. Follow Route 84 to the town of Sunol. Turn right on Main Street, then right again in Kilkare. Elliston Vineyards is about a half mile up the road on the right side.*

HINDU TEMPLE

Like most towns and cities in the Bay Area, Livermore is growing by leaps and bounds. Suburban tract developments sprout up at nearly every turn, pushing small ranches out in favor of houses and endless rows of cul-de-sacs.

Near the area of town called Springtown, not too far from a new housing tract called California Cabernet, is the most unusual new development in the entire East Bay. It's the Shiva-Vishnu Temple, an authentic place of worship for Hindus.

As you might expect, Livermore is not exactly the Hindu hotbed of the West Coast. First the sect tried to build a temple in nearby Pleasanton (which seems just as unusual), but the town turned it down; apparently there were fears that a new Jonestown might be created.

The good townspeople of Livermore either didn't mind or didn't pay attention, for a permit was granted without much ado. Now, in the shadow of split-levels, is an ornate temple handcrafted by artisans from India.

Visitors are welcome, though there is no formal, organized tour. Instead you may roam peacefully on your own, speak to any priests who know English, and simply marvel at the architecture. You will see shrines to Vishnu, Shiva, Krishna, Rama, and other deities. You are asked to remove your shoes before entering the temple area.

So far, only phase 1 of the project is complete. Eventually there will be a large study center, a tower, and other buildings designed to bring together various Hindu communities of Northern California. Chances are you will be visiting during some phase of construction, since the building plans will take years to complete.

SHIVA-VISHNU TEMPLE, *Arrowhead Avenue, Livermore. For information or an appointment, call (415) 449-6255.*

HOW TO GET HERE: *From San Francisco, cross the Bay Bridge and take Route 580 East from Oakland toward Stockton. At Livermore, look for the Springtown Boulevard exit; then cross the bridge back over the freeway. At the first light, turn right onto Bluebell Drive. After you see a church, turn right onto Wisteria Way, then left on Arrowhead Avenue. Suddenly you are there.*

LAWRENCE LIVERMORE LABS ⑮

In the late 1930s Robert Lawrence, one of the founding fathers of nuclear science, assembled a distinguished coterie of scientists (including Robert Oppenheimer and Edward Teller) at the University of California, Berkeley. Much privacy was needed for research and development of sophisticated nuclear weapons, so two remote sites were chosen. One was Los Alamos in New Mexico. The other was the little town of Livermore, about 30 miles from Berkeley.

Today Livermore has grown to a busy town with more than 50,000 residents, and the Lawrence Livermore Laboratory has expanded to employ 8500 people, who work in more than 700 buildings squeezed into 1 square acre of land. Although run by the university and funded by the U.S. Department of Energy, the primary purpose of Livermore Labs is the nation's defense. No weapons are built here. This is a center for research, design, and development for various projects ranging from the creation of new fusion devices to "Star Wars" weaponry.

Not surprisingly, Lawrence Livermore Laboratory is often the scene of antinuclear demonstrations. And perhaps since that's the kind of coverage the labs usually get in the media, the persons in charge have decided to try to drum up some positive PR by encouraging visitors to come and see what their research is all about.

At the east gate, off Greenville Road, there is a visitor's center open seven days a week featuring interesting exhibits, including many of the "touchy-feely" variety that let you play while you learn. The public can also take a tour of some of the other inside facilities, by advance appointment. The only rules for tours of inside facilities are that tourists must be at least 18 years old and that groups have a minimum of 15 and a maximum of 30 people.

In the visitor's center, you can begin your tour with an 11-minute multimedia slide show telling the story of the place. It's very well done. As for the exhibits, I must confess that I barely passed high school chemistry (didn't even attempt physics), so a lot of it was beyond me. But there is a wonderful globelike sculpture with a colorful light shooting out from the center; the energy of your hand moves the light toward you. Other popular attractions include computers that talk, a hologram of Robert Lawrence, and a model train that travels through a model of the laboratory and teaches . . . well, I'm not quite sure what it teaches, but it's a nifty train.

If you go beyond the visitor's center, you are bound for some really heavy science. In the laser room I was told about how they are creating tiny stars by combining deuterium and tritium nuclei to form a helium nucleus and neutron, the point of which is to illustrate that Lawrence Livermore scientists are hoping to create a safe, renewable resource for energy.

As you might expect, the most frequently asked question is how the people who work here feel about working on the design and development of weapons that can destroy the world. The most frequent answer is that they feel just fine, proud in fact, for they believe they are helping prevent destruction of the planet by developing deterrents.

Whatever you believe, it's worth the trip, even if for no other reason than to see your tax dollars at work.

LAWRENCE LIVERMORE NATIONAL LABORATORY, *Livermore. Visitor's center open 9 A.M. to 5:30 P.M. Monday through Friday; noon to 5 P.M. Saturday and Sunday; closed holidays. Admission: Free (your tax dollars at work). Tours of some of the other areas of the laboratory are offered to groups of 15 or more and must be arranged at least two weeks in advance. Phone: (415) 422-9797. Wheelchair accessible.*

HOW TO GET TO LAWRENCE LIVERMORE LABS: *From San Francisco, take the Bay Bridge to Route 580 toward Stockton. Stay on Route 580 until you come to the Livermore area. Exit on Greenville Road to the right and drive 2 miles to the south until you come to the entrance to the center. It's clearly marked.*

WENTE BROTHERS SPARKLING WINE CELLARS

As I mentioned before, the Livermore Valley has a rich history as a wine-producing region. Nowhere is that history more in evidence than at the Wente Brothers Cellars. The Wentes have been operating as a family business since 1883, and the site for their sparkling wine operation is a state historical landmark that once housed the old Cresta Blanca winery. If you're old enough, you might remember Cresta Blanca as the first wine to advertise on the radio. (I can still hear the jingle, "C-R-E-S-T-A B-L-A-N-C-A, Cresta Blanca.")

Back to the Wentes. They run the oldest continuously operating family-owned winery in California (and thus, presumably, the United States). Founder C. H.

Wente chose the gravelly soils of the Livermore Valley well before anyone ever knew the chic places would be well to the north in Sonoma and Napa. In the 1930s Wente Brothers became the first American winery to use varietal labels rather than generic names. In other words, they produced sauvignon blanc rather than white wine, a practice that most certainly paved the way for today's boutique wineries and their specialty wines. The Wentes' sauvignon blanc won the Grand Prix in Paris in 1937, the first international recognition of an American wine.

For years the Wentes ran their winery in Livermore while Sonoma and Napa became tourist attractions. Finally, in 1986 they began competing as a destination when they finished building new sparkling wine cellars. To do this, they bought the old Cresta Blanca winery, about 8 miles from their main operation. They spent five years restoring the place and adding new buildings. They have also built a conference center and a beautiful restaurant (see our section on restaurants).

The result is one of the most attractive winery complexes you'll find anywhere. The buildings are old California style, done in white stucco with red tile roofs, sets on more than 100 acres of vineyards, gardens, and lawns. It could be the setting of a luxury resort.

Tours are given hourly. You will be taken through the *méthode champenoise* process, from the vineyards to the winery, and will end up back in the visitor's center for a tasting. The highlight for me was the original sandstone caves, built into the hillside by Cresta Blanca. Even though the temperature can reach the 100-degree mark in the Livermore Valley in the summer, the caves keep the wines cool, between 50 and 55 degrees, all year round. Even if you visit on a warm day, you might want to have a sweater with you for the walk through the caves.

A word or two about the contemporary Wente Brothers operation. The name may soon have to be changed since one of the three key executives is a Wente sister, Carolyn Wente. She heads up marketing and public relations. She and her coexecutives, her brothers Eric and Philip, continue to operate Wentes' as a family business and take pains to make visitors feel at home. The Wentes grew up in the valley, and despite their success, they try to maintain a homey quality that is sometimes missing in the large operations in Sonoma and Napa. In other words, don't look for a glamorous spread on the Wentes in *Vanity Fair* or *GQ*. Carolyn says she is still a "Livermoron," a term only locals are advised to use.

WENTE BROTHERS SPARKLING WINE CELLARS, *5050 Arroyo Road, Livermore. Open 11 A.M. to 6:30 P.M. daily. Admission: Free. Phone: (415) 447-3023. Wheelchair accessible.*

HOW TO GET HERE: *From San Francisco, take the Bay Bridge to Route 580 East to Livermore, about a 45-minute drive from the City. Exit at Portola Avenue.*

Turn right (south) and follow Portola to North L Street. Turn right and L will eventually become Arroyo Road. If you get lost and have to ask directions, be sure you specify that you want to go to the Sparkling Wine Cellars and not the original Wente operation.

From Livermore Labs, take East Avenue, heading west, to the center of town. At Fourth Street turn left and then left again on South L, which will eventually become Arroyo Road. Follow it all the way to the Sparkling Wine Cellars.

WIND FARM

When driving on Route 580 near the Altamont Pass, most people are stunned by the presence of hundreds of windmills on the hillsides. It is a remarkable sight, one that often prompts the question, "What in the world are they doing here?"

As it turns out, this is California's premier wind farm. These windmills generate power that is sold to PG&E, which in turn sells the power to its customers. In fact, power is the first crop anybody has been able to raise on this land.

For years farmers tried everything, but nothing would grow because of the ceaseless winds. Finally, the family at the Jess Ranch decided to use the land for cattle grazing. They applied to PG&E to install electricity in their ranch house, but the cost of bringing power to the place was astronomical. So the family decided to put up some windmills and generate their own power. It worked, and by law the electric company had to buy it. The Jess family sends a bill to PG&E, rather than the other way around.

Although no organized tours are offered, Connie Jess told me that people are always stopping by just to gawk or to listen to the metallic whir of the windmills. Sometimes she'll look off her front porch and see 10 to 15 photographers clicking away; the major "photo opportunity" is the unusual sight of cows grazing next to a field of windmills.

In case you've never seen one of these modern, high-tech windmills, they look like airplane propellers in giant Erector Set stands. On a clear day the effect is dazzling. They appear to dance together in different patterns with one set of windmills on one hill moving clockwise, the next set on the next hill moving counterclockwise, and still another set on another hill moving in another pattern.

THE ALTAMONT WINDMILLS *are on both sides of Highway 580 between Livermore and Tracy. It's at least an hour from San Francisco. You can't miss them.*

HOW TO GET HERE: *From San Francisco, take the Bay Bridge to Route 580 East and follow it all the way past Livermore until you see the windmills on both sides of the highway.*

HOTELS OF PLEASANTON

The city of Pleasanton looks like a hundred other American pleasant towns. There's a tree-shaded Main Street and a welcoming sign on an archway crossing the heart of the downtown district. The Alameda County Fair is held here every year, and the annual high school soccer tournament is big stuff. But nothing else of note happens here except business as usual.

But what business! As you drive around the newer parts of town, you will be astounded to discover that Pleasanton is also the new home of the corporate world. Its gigantic business parks are sprinkled with names from the *Fortune* 500, and many companies have moved their headquarters here.

With all these corporations and the huge Lawrence Livermore Laboratory not far away, lots of business travelers come to the area. And with all those expense accounts, could Sheraton, Marriott, and Hilton be far behind?

The fact is the city of Pleasanton has plenty of huge hotels that are filled with business people during the week. But the travelers go home on weekends, and that's good news for us. You see, Pleasanton is a place that enjoys good weather; when it's cool and foggy in San Francisco, chances are it's warm and sunny in Pleasanton. And since all these hotels are equipped with such amenities as exercise rooms, pools, saunas, and the like, these hotels make for a nice get-away, less than an hour from San Francisco and close to the Livermore Valley wine country.

But even better, the hotels want to entice you to take advantage of them, so most of them offer weekend deals. The specials will vary from month to month, but let me cite one example from one hotel to give you an idea of what you can get: Thirty-nine dollars for a deluxe room for two, children under 12 free, which includes local calls, cable TV with remote control, use of the pool and exercise facilities, a cooked-to-order breakfast, cocktails, and a late-night snack.

This example is from the Compri Hotel, though by the time this book is published prices may have gone up. Call around and see what's available at the various places on the weekend you plan to visit.

HOTELS OF PLEASANTON: *Compri, 5990 Stoneridge Road, (415) 463-3330; Hilton, 7050 Johnson Drive, (415) 463-8000; Holiday Inn, 11950 Dublin Canyon, (415) 847-6000; Marriott, 5059 Hopyard Road, (415) 463-1414; Sheraton, 5155 Hopyard Road, (415) 460-8880.*

HOW TO GET TO PLEASANTON: *From San Francisco, take the Bay Bridge to Route 580 and continue until you see the hotels facing the highway in Pleasanton.*

CHAPTER 7 Contra Costa County

As mountains go, Mount Diablo is a real shrimp, only 3849 feet high. But its claim to fame is that you can usually see more from its peak than from any other place in the United States. So even if you think Mount Diablo doesn't have the best view, it at least offers the most view.

It is, however, a spectacular view. From the observation deck at the mountain's peak, directly north you look out on the rich farmland of Yolo and Solano counties; if the skies are crystal clear you can see Mount Lassen, some 163 miles away. To the northeast the Delta unfolds and leads to Sacramento. To the east and a bit to the south you may see Yosemite Valley and Half Dome, and directly to the south you see San Jose and Mount Hamilton and its Lick Observatory. The Sonoma and Napa valleys are to the northwest, and directly west are Mount Tamalpais, San Francisco, and the Bay.

But there's more to the mountain than the view. There are trails to hike, many rare species of flora and fauna to explore (as Euell Gibbons could probably have told you, this is one of the few places in the world you can find digger pine trees, with their huge cones and delicious pine nuts), and special areas to visit. One of my favorites is Rock City, a unique formation of huge stones arranged by nature to form lookouts, caves, and tunnels. This area is said to have been a spiritual place for the Indians who lived on this mountain. On hunting trips the stone tunnels and caves were used for shelter, contemplation, and observation of prey.

The best way to get the most out of Mount Diablo is to pick up a map at the ranger station (you have to stop there anyway to pay your $2 day-use fee). Then pick out one or two areas to explore, making sure you save time for the drive to the peak for the view. Don't forget the binoculars.

As for the name, there are many stories about why this mountain was named after the devil. I have yet to hear the definitive legend, but there are many people who believe that spirits roam the mountain. Apparently sober people have told me about hearing strange sounds and seeing strange lights at night on the mountain. All I can say is that if I were looking for a movie location to stage a UFO landing, Mount Diablo would be perfect.

MOUNT DIABLO STATE PARK. *Open 8 A.M. to dusk every day. $2 per car use fee. Phone: (415) 837-2525.*

HOW TO GET HERE: *From San Francisco, take the Bay Bridge to Route 24 toward Walnut Creek. Exit at Ygnacio Valley Road to the right. Follow Ygnacio Valley Road to Walnut Avenue. Turn right; Walnut runs into North Gate Road, which leads into the north gate of the park.*

BLACK DIAMOND MINES ②

Gold was not the only treasure in them thar hills in the 1850s. Coal was discovered in the shadow of Mount Diablo, and people came from all over the world to work in the mines. This became the largest coal-producing region in the state. Three boomtowns for the miners and their families were created.

The towns were Nortonville, Stewartsville, and Somersville. Most of their residents came from Wales and Ireland. They came to California hoping to find the American dream; instead, they discovered a very difficult existence, in an area riddled with epidemics of smallpox and scarlet fever. By the turn of the century much of the population had been wiped out and the mines closed.

Today the area around the mines and the now extinct towns has become the Black Diamond Mines State Preserve. It's a lovely park with a sad history. The main attraction is an underground mine that is open as a museum. With advance reservations, guides will take you through the huge tunnels. This was a sandstone mine; inside you will see the enormous excavations and even a few signs of mishaps. The park provides a hard hat and a flashlight, though you may bring your own if you wish.

Outside you can walk through the hills where the towns once existed. Rose Hill cemetery tells the story of the hard lives of the immigrants. Reading the epitaphs on the gravestones, it is easy to imagine their dreams of what life would be like in the New World.

If you happen to be in the area during the last week of April, you may want to attend Black Diamond Days, the annual gathering of descendants of former residents of Nortonville, Stewartsville, and Somersville. It is a celebration at the mines, with music, dance, an oral history forum, and food.

In addition, the park offers 20 miles of hiking trails; one 12-mile trail leads to Mount Diablo.

BLACK DIAMOND MINES REGIONAL PRESERVE, *Antioch. Park open 8 A.M. to dusk seven days a week; mines open on Saturday and Sunday only, by reservation. Mine tours at 10 A.M., 11 A.M., 1:30 P.M., and 2:30 P.M. Admission: Adults, $2; children 7 to 11 and seniors, $1; children under age 7 not permitted in the mines. Phone: (415) 757-2620.*

HOW TO GET HERE: *From San Francisco, take the Bay Bridge to Highway 24 toward Walnut Creek. Stay on Route 24 to Route 4 toward Pittsburgh and Antioch. Turn right onto Route 4 and follow it to the Somersville Road. Turn right and go straight to the entrance.*

EUGENE O'NEILL'S HOUSE ③

When America's greatest playwright, Eugene O'Neill, and his wife Carlotta were looking for "a final home and harbor," they decided to live in Northern California. They looked in Marin, the South Bay, everywhere, in fact, until the day O'Neill saw this special parcel of 158 acres in Contra Costa County overlooking the Las Trampas wilderness and said, "This is it."

Contra Costa

Using funds from the Nobel Prize O'Neill won in 1936, he and Carlotta built a beautiful home with gardens, a swimming pool, and plenty of peace and quiet so that O'Neill could write. They named their home Tao House, from the Chinese, meaning "the right way of life"—a simple, unencumbered existence. Recently, the National Parks Service opened Tao House to the public.

Situated on a hill high above the town of Danville, this is a must stop for anyone interested in the American theater. O'Neill wrote some of his major works in this house, including *The Iceman Cometh, A Moon for the Misbegotten,* and the autobiographical *Long Day's Journey into Night* (for which he would, posthumously, win his fourth Pulitzer Prize).

The home has been restored to look and feel as it did in the 1940s when Eugene, Carlotta, and their beloved dog Blemie lived here. I mention the dog because O'Neill was exceptionally attached to Blemie; you will see a replica of the dalmatian's crib with a silk pillow that was custom-made at Gump's, the fine San Francisco specialty store and, in the pasture south of the house, her tombstone. You will also see Rosie's Room, the playwright's favorite place in the house, the room where he had his morning coffee. Rosie is O'Neill's beloved player piano; neighbors claimed that on warm days, with the windows of Tao House open, they could hear Eugene O'Neill's player piano.

EUGENE O'NEILL NATIONAL HISTORIC SITE, *Danville. Open seven days a week, but by reservation only; closed on major holidays. No private cars are allowed on the site (you have to go through a private residential development to get there, and the neighbors didn't want a flow of traffic through the neighborhood, so you must go by tour bus). Buses run up the hill twice each day, once in the morning and again in the afternoon. Though the tour of the house is free, there is a charge for the bus service. For a reservation, call the National Park Service in Martinez at (415) 228-8860. Since your first destination will be dependent on your arrangement with the bus company, please ask them for directions.*

EDIBLE LANDSCAPING

Right in the center of the suburban sprawl in the community of San Ramon is an oasis of lush flowers and vegetables. Better yet, it's located behind a very attractive restaurant that prepares the food with the bounty from this garden.

The restaurant is a commercial enterprise called Mudd's; the gardens are the project of a nonprofit organization called the Crow Canyon Institute. Its purpose is to develop new ways to grow edible landscapes, to provide classes on gardening and food preparation, and to make nature available to schools and other groups.

On less than an acre of land you will see fruits, vegetables, and edible flowers (yes! primroses, nasturtiums, and marigolds, to name but a few), all flourishing naturally without the aids of chemicals. Abundance is their form of pest control; enough is grown for everybody, including the bugs.

Since this is hot, dry territory, the institute's gardeners specialize in drought-resistant plants. For them, trying to grow a lush, English-style garden would be downright irresponsible. If they had their way, the neighboring corporations would develop their own edible landscapes and "pocket orchards" instead of planting thirsty lawns and manicured flower gardens.

In addition to the garden and restaurant, there is a greenhouse and a shop selling seeds and gardening tools. Part of the institute's land includes a serene park in the actual Crow Canyon, which runs along San Ramon Creek. This is a very restful, shady spot for a picnic, hidden away from the rest of the world. It also happens to be a popular spot for weddings.

CROW CANYON INSTITUTE, *10 Boardwalk, San Ramon. Gardens and nature park are open sunrise to sunset daily; guided tours by appointment. Admission:*

Free. Restaurant is open for lunch and dinner every day, plus Sunday brunch. Phone: Gardens, (415) 820-3634; restaurant, (415) 837-9387.

HOW TO GET HERE: *From San Francisco, take the Bay Bridge to Route 24 toward Walnut Creek. Turn right onto Route 680 South. Exit at Crow Canyon Road, turning right onto Crow Canyon. Turn left at Park Place and you will see the sign for Mudd's restaurant. The gardens are in back.*

JOHN MUIR HOUSE

After native son Joe DiMaggio, John Muir was the most famous citizen of the town of Martinez. It was here that the famous naturalist and conservationist lived the final 25 years of his life, in a house built by his in-laws.

There is irony here. In Muir's day, around the turn of the century, Martinez was a quiet little town, a community in harmony with the principles Muir stood for. But today Martinez is a booming suburban community. Though many citizens are trying to preserve what's left of the town's past, Muir the environmentalist would shudder at today's view from the hillside house—a confluence of highways below, an occasional helicopter above. The irony is that such recent developments as the John Muir Motel, the John Muir Shopping Center, and the John Muir Parkway have been named for the environmentalist. Certainly Muir Woods and Muir Beach in Marin are more fitting honors for the father of the conservation movement! More about Muir's life when we get to Yosemite (in "Beyond the Bay").

His home is certainly worth a visit. It was here that Muir wrote the numerous letters and magazine articles that would establish the National Park Service and give birth to the Sierra Club. Upstairs in the modest but spacious Victorian house is Muir's study, on display in creative disarray, with papers spread about, correspondence to be answered, and bill receipts. You can stroll the grounds, which are lovely and restful—8 acres of orchard trees and grapevines, with a creek running by. Appropriately, the National Park Service operates the house and garden of one of its founding fathers and offers tours to visitors.

JOHN MUIR NATIONAL HISTORIC SITE, *4202 Alhambra Avenue, Martinez. Open 10 A.M. to 4:30 P.M. seven days a week; closed major holidays. Admission: Adults, $1; seniors and children 11 and under, free. Phone: (415) 228-8860.*

HOW TO GET HERE: *From San Francisco, take the Bay Bridge and follow the signs to Highway 24 to Walnut Creek. In Walnut Creek follow the signs to Route 680 North and continue for several miles until you see signs for Highway 4 toward Richmond–Vallejo. Five miles farther, you will see a sign for Alhambra Avenue–John Muir Home; turn right and follow the signs up the hill to the house.*

ADOPT-A-PIONEER

You can learn a lot about any town by visiting its cemeteries, but the one in Martinez is truly special.

In the 1970s the historic Alhambra Cemetery was a mess. Vandals had desecrated the gravesites, weeds had taken over, and the growing community of newcomers had very little connection to the history buried on the hill. Then a group of concerned citizens started the Adopt-a-Pioneer Gravesite program. Volunteers came two days a week to care for a selected gravesite, pulling weeds, planting flowers, sweeping. They also researched the occupant of each plot and uncovered a treasure trove of history.

Today volunteers still help maintain the place. Many have family ties; for example, the chairman's grandfather was county sheriff in 1888; others care for the sites of their grandmothers and great-aunts.

Even though this is a lovely spot on its own, overlooking the Bay, the best time to visit is when the volunteers are in action. They are an extremely lively and likable group that will change your preconceptions about cemeteries. They will also entertain you with stories about their families and their love for their community. As one of the volunteers said to me, "We are all so transient. I'm taking care of someone's grave in the hope that someone will come along years from now and take care of mine."

ALHAMBRA CEMETERY, *on Carquinez Scenic Drive, Martinez. Open Sundays; other days you must get a key from the police station in the heart of town, at 525 Henrietta Street. For more information, you can call Charlene Perry, (415) 228-2364.*

HOW TO GET HERE: *From San Francisco, take the Bay Bridge and follow the signs to Route 24 toward Walnut Creek. Continue on 24 to Pleasant Hill Road. Turn left on Pleasant Hill Road and continue until you reach Alhambra Avenue. The police station where you will pick up a key for the cemetery is at the corner of Alhambra and Henrietta. Key in hand, continue on Alhambra Avenue north to Escobar Street, turn left to Talbart Street, and follow Talbart to Carquinez Scenic Drive. The cemetery is about a fourth of a mile up the hill on the right.*

VIANO WINE AND GOOSE EGGS ⑦

There is no shortage of wineries in the Bay Area. Go to just about any rural road, look for a beautiful setting, and chances are you'll find one.

However, it is unusual to find a winery in a densely populated suburban environment, which makes the Viano Winery a special treat. Just a few minutes from a busy intersection in Martinez you will see a handwritten sign advertising wine, goose eggs, and lemons. Follow that sign.

Three generations of Vianos live and work here. It looks like the average working farm with a couple of barns, several other small buildings, and lots of equipment scattered about. There is no attempt to put on a show for visitors. The tasting room is in the basement of Papa Viano's house, where you will be served in good, solid drinking glasses, like water glasses—not chic goblets. Instead of fancy talk about the wine's bouquet, the Vianos are more likely to show you pictures of the family or talk about how their area used to be filled with farmers growing apricots, walnuts, and grapes. They are the lone holdouts against the developers now, and the Vianos say they are determined not to join the trend.

You can purchase not only the Vianos' homemade wines but also eggs, walnuts, lemons, and whatever else happens to be on hand. The wine is very good, but the best part of the experience is a visit with the Vianos to catch their enthusiasm and determination.

VIANO WINERY, *150 Morello Avenue, Martinez. Open 9 A.M. to noon and 1 to 5 P.M. seven days a week. Phone: (415) 228-6465.*

HOW TO GET HERE: *From San Francisco, take the Bay Bridge and stay on Highway 80 toward Sacramento. Go past Pinole and Rodeo to Highway 4. Take Highway 4 East and wind through the canyon about 10 miles. One mile past Martinez, exit at Morello Avenue and turn left at the bottom of the ramp. The Vianos' place will be about another mile down the road on the right.*

Maybe it's just me, but I have a great time whenever I visit a place intended for kids. For example, I was hooked by the Alexander Lindsay Junior Museum, which is in Larkey Park in Walnut Creek.

JUNIOR MUSEUM

The building used to be an East Bay Utility District pumping station. Now it's an indoor wildlife sanctuary, where you can come nose-to-nose with some of the strangest-looking creatures you've ever imagined. For example, you'll encounter Lord Bradley, a turkey vulture, sitting on a perch. Though he is chained down, he is not in a cage. And when he spreads his giant wings, it is a simply awesome sight. His roommates include a Swenson's hawk, a yellow-billed magpie, a giant owl, and other birds all native to Contra Costa County. Some of the birds that live here were raised from chicks by the volunteer staff; others were psychological or physical misfits, unable to survive in the wild, and were given a new lease on life, uncaged, in the museum.

Next there's a reptile room. Thankfully, these guys are behind glass, aquarium-style. Here you'll encounter snakes of every variety.

Another room has exhibits intended to teach kids about the wonders of nature. The highlight here is the feely boxes. You're supposed to stick your hand inside, feel what's there, and guess what it is. To find out if you're right, you lift a flap and see what's inside. When I tried it, I felt something small, round, and hard, rather nondescript. Imagine my thrill to discover I was fondling owl pellets. Sandy Fender, the museum's wildlife supervisor, explained to me that when an owl eats, it regurgitates its food and makes these pellets. (I think the experience of the feely box works better for kids.)

Another popular spot is the museum's medical center, where baby animals are nursed back to health. Almost every day someone walks in with a wounded bird or a damaged wild animal. You can watch the dedicated volunteers with eyedroppers full of medicine lovingly saving lives—a St. Elsewhere for the animal kingdom.

Finally, the Alexander Lindsay Junior Museum offers an unusual service to locals. It lends rabbits, rats, hamsters, and guinea pigs to families to have the experience of having a pet around. Like lending libraries of books, the family must give the animal back in a week or so, but then they will know if they are suited for a full-time pet.

ALEXANDER LINDSAY JUNIOR MUSEUM, *in Larkey Park at 1901 First Avenue, Walnut Creek. Open 11 A.M. to 5 P.M. Wednesday through Sunday, June to September; 1 to 5 P.M. Wednesday through Friday, noon to 4 P.M. Saturday and Sunday, September to June. Admission: Free. Phone: (415) 935-1978.*

HOW TO GET HERE: *From San Francisco, take the Bay Bridge to Route 24 toward Walnut Creek. Route 24 joins Route 680 North. Continue on the freeway to the Geary Road exit. Turn left at the exit and go 1 mile to Buena Vista. Turn left and continue to First Street; Larkey Park on the right. There is a parking lot in the park, and the museum is well marked.*

MUSEUM OF VINTAGE FASHION ⑨

I thought I had gone to the wrong address when I pulled up the hill to Patti McLean's place. It looked more like a typical suburban house—the sort of nice, normal place where Steven Spielberg likes to set his movies—than the home of the country's largest museum of vintage clothing.

Once inside, I was still confused. Where does the museum end and the house begin? Even Patti isn't always sure. In her son's bedroom, for example, next to the photos of friends and sports heroes, is a display of Victorian high-button boots and ladies' hats. In his closet, next to the jeans and sweatshirts, are velvet dresses from the 1800s and lace nightgowns from France.

In the master bedroom Patti and her insurance executive husband share the space with mannequins, ancient Chinese ceremonial robes, and Coco Chanel originals. It's a collection that antique clothing dealers would sell their grandmothers for.

Since this is a nonprofit foundation, none of the items is for sale. Patti probably wouldn't part with any of them anyway. As founder and curator of the Museum of Vintage Fashion, she is obsessed by her collection and has dedicated her life to preserving clothes as a history of past generations. She also teaches classes in clothing restoration.

Patti hopes that someday her son can have a closet of his own. She's trying to raise money for a permanent home for the museum outside her home. In the meantime, she often has fund-raising parties on the patio and fashion shows out back by the pool.

Anyone interested in clothing and accessories from 1720 to 1970 is welcome to see the collection. Many visitors are students of design and fashion; theatrical costume designers travel from all over the country to examine the pieces Patti has in her collection. She prefers to give tours to groups of five or more and can handle busloads at once. Be prepared to spend several hours; your tour guide knows her subject and is a very entertaining storyteller.

MUSEUM OF VINTAGE FASHION, *1712 Chapparal Lane, Lafayette. Open by appointment. Admission: Donations to build a permanent home for the museum are requested. Phone: (415) 944-1896.*

HOW TO GET HERE: *From San Francisco, take the Bay Bridge to Highway 24. Continue to Pleasant Hill Road; head north, which is to the left on Pleasant Hill until you come to a Y in the road; follow the left fork (Taylor Street), continue to Greenhills Road, and turn left; you will enter the Lafayette Hills subdivision. Turn right on Chapparal Lane and continue up to the top of the hill and 1712 Chapparal.*

MURIEL'S DOLLHOUSE

Port Costa is a rarity in a county filled with town after town of unrelieved suburbia. Enclosed by farmland and forest, this waterfront town is situated at the end of a country lane, which makes getting there half the fun. Port Costa's weathered storefronts and warehouses (left over from the days when the town was a bustling grain-shipping port) have been turned into artist's studios, antique shops, and restaurants. The town has a lot of charm and character.

Port Costa also has a lot of charming characters. Perhaps the best known of them is a sweet little old lady named Muriel Whitmore. She is the curator, owner, and sole employee of an amazing museum of dolls.

Even if you're a guy like me who has never had the slightest interest in dolls, Muriel makes the place worth a visit. As you enter the door of the little house she has converted into the museum, you know you're in for something different. On my last visit, Muriel, who stands about 4 feet 10 inches tall, was wearing a babushka around her hair, a checkered shirt, bobby sox, a rock 'n' roll T-shirt, and a cardigan sweater. I would guess her to be in her seventies, and she is a bundle of energy, sharp as a tack.

Several years ago Muriel moved to Port Costa with her lifelong collection of dolls and decided to open a museum. Crammed into three rooms are hundreds of dolls, all of them antiques. Her dolls are made of china, wood, wax, apple, tin, and papier-mâché and are arranged in thematic displays. This setup allows Muriel to tell you stories about her brood. She claims to know each one personally and has given them all names and life stories. In the schoolroom display, for example, she will point out that the little girl with her hand in the air and tears in her eyes has been trying to get permission to go to the bathroom for 15 years. She can't be excused because the room is quarantined due to the case of mumps in another doll. And Muriel will point out that the teacher is pregnant, which was scandalous in the old days. As you can see, Muriel does not lack for humor or imagination.

There are other items of interest. One is an elaborate dollhouse with each room completely outfitted. This is a model of the Ohio farmhouse where Muriel grew up and where she began her lifelong love of dolls. She also has a reproduction of "The Last Supper" on the head of a pin. I know that sounds impossible, but Muriel has a good magnifying glass handy, and you can make out a crude copy of Leonardo's masterpiece. It was painted by a 75-year-old Ecuadorian who, according to Muriel, uses a hair from his arm as a brush and paints rhythmically between his heartbeats. (If you're not yet impressed, Muriel will add that he doesn't wear glasses.)

Muriel takes her congregation seriously. She makes a distinction between being a doll collector and running a museum. She says that if she were merely a collector, she would only choose her favorites, which are French dolls. But as a museum operator she has searched for variety, and many of her dolls are one-of-a-kind, just like their mistress.

MURIEL'S DOLLHOUSE MUSEUM, *33 Canyon Lake Drive, Port Costa. Open 10 A.M. to 5 P.M. Tuesday through Sunday; closed Monday. Admission: Adults, $1; children, 25 cents. Phone: (415) 787-2820.*

HOW TO GET HERE: *From San Francisco, take the Bay Bridge and continue on Route 80 toward Sacramento. Exit at the Crockett–Port Costa exit. Continue past Crockett for 3 twisty miles until you come to the main street of Port Costa, which is Canyon Lake Drive. Muriel's is on the right-hand side.*

CROCKETT ⑪

As you drive north to the wine country on Route 80, you cross the first bridge built to span the Bay, the Carquinez Bridge. If you look to the right and you see the giant C & H sugar manufacturing plant, you know you've reached the town of Crockett. This is a touch of small-town America that is often lost so close to our major freeways.

The town of Crockett is a middle-class hillside community, on the shores of the Carquinez Strait. The unofficial community center is Pedrotti's hardware store, located at the corner of Pomona and Second streets, also the site of the town's only stoplight. Here's where you can find out what's going on in town. If you're there in the morning, you will probably see a bunch of the local men huddled around a stove, drinking coffee and exchanging gossip. Maybe this is the major appeal of Crockett. It's an old-fashioned small town, the kind of community you don't see much anymore, where everyone knows everyone by name. You can just stand in the store and be amazed by the familiarity people have with every person from town who walks through the door.

If there is an attraction specifically geared for tourists, it is the row of antique stores along Pomona Street. Each store appears to have its own specialty, whether it's furniture, knickknacks, or, as in the case of Another Time Antiques, neon. This place is run by "Pink" Floyd Wyrick, who keeps his personal collection of antique neon all over his shop—incredible old signs advertising everything from cleaners to dentists. It's like a very funky museum of neon; in fact, most of the items are not for sale, just for show.

If you are a movie buff, you might like to know that Crockett gave the screen world Aldo Ray. In fact, the world headquarters of the Aldo Ray Fan Club is in town. The muscular, raspy-throated character actor (who appeared in such classics as *The Naked and the Dead, Pat and Mike,* and *God's Little Acre*) is a hometown boy. His mom still lives here, and so does Aldo, when he's not out on location.

There is even a small Aldo Ray exhibit at the town museum. This a volunteer-run place that is well worth a visit. Set up in a former train station, right across the street from the C & H sugar plant, the town's history is set out in a very informal fashion. Three wonderful characters, Tony, Joe, and Skipper, all retired employees of C & H, take care of the museum and give history as Damon Runyon might have written it.

Crockett used to be a company town; C & H provided the housing, parks, and other services for years, until the plant was unionized. Then the workers and the town's government were on their own. Today most of the town is still employed by C & H.

What makes the museum so special is the personal feel to the place. It's like browsing in an entire community's attic. Along with the expected historical artifacts and sugar company memorabilia, there are objects from people's homes: a giant stuffed sturgeon (the largest caught in the area), a poster from the movie *Yes, Giorgio* (Tony's cousin Dave played accordion in the movie). Items are piled up in every corner and plastered on the walls and ceilings.

One thing Crockett is proud of is the fact that it was the last town in California to give up the old manual telephone switchboard on which an operator would personally connect callers. That last switchboard and the chair Operator Myrt sat in are on display inside the museum.

This is a town filled with characters, and the reason may be that the Wild West has always been alive and kicking here. That's because there's no police force. Law enforcement has always been left up to the highway patrol and the county sheriff's department. The town was once characterized by fierce feuding between the Italians on one side of town and the Portuguese on the other. Ethnic peace was finally reached in the 1950s, but soon there was a new element in town—the hippies, who knew they could grow and smoke whatever they liked here; "rooms for rent" ads placed by Crockett landlords in the *Berkeley Barb* used to advertise "cheap rent, no cops." By the 1980s the yuppies had started to move in, finding Crockett to be an affordable suburb.

Today all factions seem to get along well enough to make Crockett an inviting place for visitors.

HOW TO GET TO CROCKETT: *From San Francisco, take the Bay Bridge to Route 80 toward Sacramento. Cross the Carquinez Bridge, but exit just before paying the toll. The town of Crockett is directly below the Carquinez Bridge. The Historical Museum is in the old railroad station across from the huge C & H plant. You can't miss it.*

POINT RICHMOND

As I travel around, I am endlessly amazed by the hidden towns and villages that offer charm and history just a few minutes from a crowded freeway or heavily industrialized zone. Point Richmond is a case in point. Just down the road from a huge Chevron plant, surrounded by a rather ugly road, and often hidden from view by huge tractor-trailers and road construction crews, Point Richmond is a little oasis, as quaint as a New England village.

Point Richmond is part of the industrial city of Richmond. During World War II this was the home of Kaiser shipyards and Richmond was a 24-hour town. Today the main part of Richmond is modern and industrial, but the Point remains isolated, a throwback to a quieter, more gracious time.

In Point Richmond there are only a few streets to roam, past nicely restored buildings, inviting restaurants, an old hotel, an old theater still used for live performances, and a restored jail that now houses lawyers' offices (there must be a message there somewhere). The best way to see the town is to park your car and stroll.

All roads seem to lead to the most unique building in Point Richmond, the Natatorium. From the outside it looks like a huge museum, but inside you'll find a busy community swimming pool that also functions as the town's community center. The beautiful façade of the Natatorium is a bit misleading. Instead of finding an art deco treasure inside, you might think you have gone back to your high school or Y swimming pool. The first memory flashback for me was the smell of heated chlorine. At the entrance there is a small gray industrial lobby with posters advertising the swimming schedule and other local events. Behind the doors is the huge pool with its high glass ceiling. The pool itself is well designed, with a horseshoe-shaped balcony for viewing.

Visitors are welcome to drop by and see the Natatorium, learn more about its history from an exhibit near the entrance, and swim or watch. (The infants' swimming lessons are a great show.)

This large facility might strike you as out of proportion to a community this small, but it is for the entire city of Richmond. It ended up here because of a quirk of fate. What happened was that the land was originally owned by a family who thought there was oil underneath. After drilling, all they came up with was water. So in the 1920s the family gave the land to the city with one stipulation: that it build a community swimming pool. As long as the pool remains, the city owns it. If the pool is removed, the land goes back to the heirs of the original owners.

The pool remains and offers an elaborate schedule of classes, social events, and lap-swimming times. You don't have to be a town resident to swim there. If you ever meet anyone who grew up in Richmond, chances are he or she learned to swim in the Richmond Natatorium, nicknamed "The Plunge."

Immediately behind the Natatorium, a drive through a tunnel takes you to a lovely town park and a beach on the Bay, a nice place for a picnic or simply to get some peace, quiet, and sunshine.

POINT RICHMOND NATATORIUM, *1 Gerrard Avenue, Point Richmond. Open 7 A.M. to 10 P.M. Admission to the building is free. To swim: Adults, $1.75; youngsters aged 7 to 17, $1.25; children 6 and under, $1. Richmond residents get a 25-cent discount. Phone: (415) 620-6820.*

HOW TO GET TO POINT RICHMOND: *From San Francisco, take the Bay Bridge to Route 80 North toward Sacramento. After the Berkeley exits, look for the exit on the left to Route 580 and the San Rafael Bridge. After you make a left turn onto Cutting Boulevard, which is still Route 580, get to the left side of the road and watch for the left turn into Point Richmond. Do not follow the traffic turning right to the San Rafael Bridge. The Natatorium is behind the business section of town, within easy walking distance of the cafés and restaurants.*

BED-AND-BREAKFAST ISLAND

Even natives are often surprised to learn how many islands there are in the Bay Area. Most know about Alcatraz and Treasure Island, and many are familiar with the artificial Forbes Island, a private playland floating (for the time being) off the shore of Sausalito.

But few know about East Brother Island, the site for a unique one-day getaway and a one-of-a-kind bed-and-breakfast inn. At one time the lighthouse on the tiny island was considered the architectural gem of the many lighthouses that dotted the Bay. In 1873 a beautiful Victorian home was constructed to accommodate two lighthouse keepers (one for the day shift, another for the night) and their families. But with the coming of automation, lighthouse keepers became a thing of the past. The Coast Guard was left with a beautiful but deserted Victorian mansion on an island hardly anyone knew about.

In 1976 along came a group of concerned citizens from the nearby mainland town of Richmond. The citizens offered the Coast Guard a deal: They'd restore and maintain the historic home by running it as a bed-and-breakfast inn at no cost to the government. The Coast Guard agreed, with the stipulation that the inn be run as a nonprofit operation and that the island be made available to the public for day use.

So today we can all enjoy an island excursion that is less than an hour from San Francisco but feels like hundreds of miles from the cares of civilization. On a fog-free day the temperature on the island is usually about 15 degrees warmer than in San Francisco. You can spend the day just strolling around, picnicking, sitting in the sun, watching sea lions. Phil Hurleigh, the caretaker of the inn and island, will pick you up at a small dock in Richmond and take you to the island in a small motorboat. Be sure to wear something warm for the crossing.

Those who care to spend the night are greeted right off the boat with wine and champagne. Overnight guests arrive at 4 P.M. and leave around 11 the next morning. Dinner is a gourmet affair, cooked by Phil's wife, Linda, and includes several courses and appropriate wines with each course, served on china and crystal. The inn has four rooms and is open for visitors Thursday through Sunday all year. There's no TV or radio. But after that meal, you'll probably be ready for bed and so tired that you won't even notice the foghorn that goes off every half hour or so. In the morning, a full breakfast is also served.

This is not an inexpensive visit. The price for an overnight is $250 for two, which does include the meal, all you can drink, and your breakfast. The day-use program, which begins by being picked up at 11 A.M. and ends with returning to the mainland at 4 P.M., is $10 a person and includes a tour of the island.

EAST BROTHER LIGHTHOUSE, *on East Brother Island, north of Point Richmond. For information on how you can visit the island or make reservations for the bed-and-breakfast inn, contact Linda Hurleigh at (415) 233-2385. She or Phil will give you directions for the boat pickup. By the way, if you are curious as to the whereabouts of East Brother Island, next time you're crossing the Richmond–San Rafael Bridge, look to the north when you are just a mile or so off Richmond. You can see the lighthouse from there.*

CHAPTER **8** "Yolano"

MARINE WORLD
①

This is a major tourist attraction that would usually not qualify as a back-roads-type destination. But lo and behold, we found a back-roads-type way to see the place.

First, a little background on the operation. Marine World/Africa USA was forced to leave its home in Redwood City and moved to the comparatively wider open space of Vallejo in 1985. At the time of the move, the operation changed

Yolano
(Yolo & Solano)

from a strictly commercial attraction to a nonprofit foundation, emphasizing education and research. You will still find souvenir stands and fast food, but the place is many cuts above the average amusement park in quality.

About the back-roads way to see the place: It turns out that guided behind-the-scenes tours are offered during the fall and winter months on days when the amusement park is closed. This is a marvelous opportunity to mingle with the animals and their trainers.

To take the tour, all you have to do is show up at the front gate at 10:15 A.M. Monday through Wednesday during the spring and fall, Monday through Friday during the winter. You will pay half the usual admission price; then a member of the education staff will greet you and take you on a two-hour walk. If nobody else shows up, you'll get a private tour; if 50 people show up, so much the merrier.

The tour I took started with the bird areas. I hung out with the flamingos and learned that they are pink because they subsist on shrimp and the vitamin A colors their feathers. I got to stand next to a trainer who was working with vultures and hawks in the birds-of-prey section. You can get as close as you want, although I can tell you that when the vulture spreads his wings to enjoy the sun, you don't want to be too close.

A reassuring side note: Most of the birds have been sent here by the state fish and game department; they have been rescued after being abused or illegally kept and have been given a new lease on life in this park.

After the birds we went to the marine theater, where the trainers were working with whales. Depending on the day of the visit, you might also see dolphins or sea lions in action. This is almost the same as seeing a complete show, but without the crowds around. You can get a front-row seat as new routines are being learned. It's great watching the trainers and the affectionate killer whales in action; to them, practice is playtime.

Also included on the tour are the trained African animals, be they camels, elephants, or tigers. The handlers keep a tight rein on them, though I did have an amusing brush with an orangutan who was being exercised without a leash.

The added bonus of this tour is being able to visit the research center, which is closed to weekend visitors. Otters and seals are kept here for mating. It's like a zoo, with pens created to look and feel like their natural environment (presumably to get them "in the mood").

All this takes place on very attractive grounds, which are easily manageable in a wheelchair. The tour moves at an easy pace, with plenty of opportunity for questions and answers.

MARINE WORLD/AFRICA USA, *1000 Fairgrounds Avenue, Vallejo. "Back-stage" tours begin at 10:15 A.M. Monday through Friday in the winter, Monday through Wednesday in the fall and spring. Admission: Half the regular fee. Phone: (707) 644-4000.*

HOW TO GET HERE: *From San Francisco, take the Bay Bridge to Highway 80 North toward Sacramento. A few miles after crossing the Carquinez Bridge, look for the Route 37 Napa–Vallejo exit. You will exit onto Marine World Parkway. The entrance is about a mile after you leave the freeway.*

Before the bridges that connect the various communities of the Bay Area were built, ferryboats were the only source of mass transportation across the water. The oldest continuously operating ferry service in the western United States is the Mare Island Ferry, which was founded along with the first U.S. Navy station in the Pacific in 1854. For more than 130 years the Mare Island Ferry has carried workers from the Vallejo waterfront across the channel to the naval facility on Mare Island and back again.

In the early part of the century these ferryboats were also used to give scenic harbor tours to visitors; that operation ended in 1936. During World War II the Vallejo waterfront buzzed with activity, then slowed down into quiet decay over the years.

Recently there has been a civic effort made to bring the waterfront back to life. It got its real boost with the Marine World/Africa USA move to Vallejo. The influx of visitors brought by that attraction triggered a major renewal on the waterfront and in the town itself. New restaurants have opened, Victorian homes have been spruced up, and the operators of the Mare Island Ferry have decided to resume scenic tour service.

For $5 you can take a ride on a 70-seat ferry that will take you along the Carquinez Strait and under the Carquinez Bridge. Along the way you will see many points of interest, including the Mare Island Naval Base, the Maritime Academy, and the town of Crockett. The deck has lots of room for sunning and getting the full effect of the sea breezes. Although the view is not as spectacular as the one you can get on San Francisco Bay, you will see some beautiful scenery, and you'll probably be able to enjoy it in shirtsleeves (on San Francisco Bay you usually need a parka).

MARE ISLAND FERRY TOURS, *Georgia Street Wharf, Vallejo. Fare: Adults, $5; seniors and children 13 and under, $4.50. Schedules change often, so it's a good idea to call for the latest information. Phone: (707) 643-7542. Charter tours of the Napa River and wine country are also offered.*

HOW TO GET TO THE FERRY: *From San Francisco, take the Bay Bridge to Route 80 North toward Sacramento. After you cross the Carquinez Bridge, look for the Tennessee Street–Mare Island exit in Vallejo. Follow Tennessee Street west through town all the way to the wharf.*

MARE ISLAND FERRY

MARITIME ACADEMY

When driving across the Carquinez Bridge, I would often see a large ship docked on the northern side of the Bay. After passing it enough times I concluded there must be a story there.

As it turns out, the ship is the *Golden Bear*, and it's a floating classroom for the California Maritime Academy, a training college for the merchant marines.

The campus is tucked away from view in the grove of trees between the Bay and the freeway. It's a lovely campus that could be the setting for any small college. This one just happens to have classrooms filled with computerized simulators and has a merchant marine ship parked outside. The students, 410 men and women, can earn a bachelor of science degree and be prepared for jobs as deck officers or engineers on merchant ships.

The *Golden Bear* is the major attraction for most visitors. Built in 1939 as a first-class passenger ship, this 8500-ton four-decker now carries midshipmen to the Pacific for four months of training each year. Much of the ship has been redesigned to suit this purpose, but there are still some vestiges of the ship's glory days when it made its luxury run from New Orleans to Rio de Janeiro. While walking through the wood-paneled lounge rooms, you can imagine the parties that went on here.

Tourists are very welcome and are usually shown around by senior-year students at the academy. They feel that most people in the Bay Area don't know they exist, so they are glad to show off the place. If your image of the seafaring type runs to *McHale's Navy* and *Mister Roberts*, you might be surprised to see so many women in uniform. My guide was proud to tell me that the first female to be appointed chief engineer of a ship in U.S. history was a graduate of the Maritime Academy.

CALIFORNIA MARITIME ACADEMY, *1 Maritime Drive, Vallejo. Tours by reservation only. Admission: Free. Phone: (707) 648-4200.*

HOW TO GET HERE: *From San Francisco, take the Bay Bridge to Route 80 toward Sacramento. After crossing the Carquinez Bridge, exit onto Sonoma Boulevard and look for signs to the Maritime Academy.*

From downtown Vallejo and the Mare Island Ferry, take Sonoma Boulevard toward San Francisco. Take the last right turn before entering the bridge and follow the signs.

BENICIA
④

There were once big plans for the town of Benicia. It was going to be an international port, a major military outpost, and the California state capital. Luckily for those who like small, charming towns, none of the plans worked out.

√ **Camel Barn Museum.** A good place to begin your visit is in the Camel Barn, a small museum that is in the original Benicia Arsenal. This building played a role in an unsuccessful and rather humorous experiment by the U.S. Army back in the 1850s. Jefferson Davis, then secretary of war and soon to become president of the Confederate States, had the bright idea to import a bunch of camels to the United States for military use in the American southwestern deserts. Although the camels did travel easily, carrying heavy loads across the desert, nobody knew how to take care of them, nor were they prepared for the adverse reaction other animals had toward them. The experiment was an expensive failure, and when the Civil War broke out, the camels of the U.S. Camel Corps were driven to the Benicia Arsenal to get them out of the way. They were auctioned off in 1864, but Building 9 of the Benicia Arsenal became known forever more as the Camel Barn.

It was an interesting building to begin with. Craftsmen from Europe had been hired by the military to design and build a series of buildings that would be used for storage. The Camel Barn, built in 1853, was made of sandstone quarried from nearby hills and featured hand-hewn pine planking on the floors and a series of arched windows. Recently renovated, it is an ideal setting for the community museum that chronicles the unusual history of the town.

For example, it was here that I learned why the town is called Benicia. The town fathers—probably the same guys who wanted the place to be a major port, military arsenal, and state capital—wanted to name the town Francisca, after the wife of the ubiquitous General Vallejo, whose land grant extended to this area. But the big power brokers in San Francisco thought that would be confusing and insisted the little town up north choose another name. The town fathers settled for Benicia, General Vallejo's wife's middle name.

The barn is divided into two large floors. On the ground floor you can see some of the stalls provided for displaced camels, plus huge meeting rooms. Upstairs you'll find the very spacious museum with nicely planned displays. It is in many ways like the historical museums you will find in most small towns, but I find that each town tends to have its own special history.

Not far from the Camel Barn and the old military arsenal is the old industrial section of Benicia, which is now a modern artist's colony. Many of the artists and craftspeople moved up from Berkeley because they could get large warehouse spaces at affordable rents. A stroll through the huge old warehouse buildings will take you to studios and workshops of glassblowers, neon makers, potters, and painters. Some of the town's artists, such as Judy Chicago, have national reputations. During the week, visiting artists is a hit-and-miss proposition, but on weekends, many of them open their areas to the public and sell their works, including seconds at a discount rate.

✔ **Old State Capitol.** In the main business section of town, you can get another sense of Benicia's history by visiting the Old State Capitol Building, now a state historic park. Actually, this was California's third capital, from February 1853 to February 1854. (The transfer of the capital to its permanent home in Sacramento was considered treasonous by the townspeople, and they never forgave the instigator, Governor John Bigler; perhaps that is why Lake Bigler's name was later changed to Lake Tahoe.) Outside, the former capitol building is very small, about half the size of an average county courthouse these days. Inside you can walk through the old senate chambers, committee rooms, and assembly halls, decorated with such artifacts as newspapers from 1853, the editions probably read by the legislators when they assembled here.

The capitol building is located near the Old Town shopping district, which, of course, features an antique row, plus some very inviting restaurants and an appealing waterfront where you can stroll or just watch the ships go by.

✔ **Mothball Fleet.** One more curiosity you might happen to notice just outside of town is called the Mothball Fleet. Out on Suisun Bay, you will see some 85 warships, just sitting there. Actually, the name Mothball Fleet is a misnomer because scores of workers are out there every day, keeping the vessels shipshape for action, in case their country calls. The public is not allowed to go on board, but you can see the ships from the shore.

CAMEL BARN MUSEUM, *2024 Camel Road, Benicia. Open 1 to 4 P.M. Friday, Saturday, and Sunday in the summer, Saturday and Sunday only the rest of the year. Admission: Donations requested. Phone: (707) 745-5435. Wheelchair accessible.*

BENICIA CAPITOL STATE HISTORIC PARK, *115 West G Street, Benicia. Open 10 A.M. to 5 P.M. seven days a week. Admission: Adults, $1; children, 50 cents. Phone: (707) 745-3385. Wheelchair accessible.*

TO GET TO BENICIA: *From San Francisco, take the Bay Bridge to Highway 80 North. After crossing the Carquinez Bridge, take Route 780 into town. Take the Second Street exit and turn right onto Second. Continue several blocks to Military.*

FOR THE CAMEL BARN, *turn left and follow the road until you see the military arsenal and signs to the Camel Barn Museum.*

FOR THE OLD STATE CAPITOL *and the Old Town shopping section, turn right on Military. Go one block to First Street and turn left. The Capitol is on the corner of First and G streets; the shops are farther down on First Street.*

FOR THE MOTHBALL FLEET, *take Route 780 East to Route 680 North to the Lake Herman Road exit; there is a vista point next to the highway.*

BUDWEISER TOUR ⑤

My head turns every time I drive past the huge Anheuser-Busch plant off Route 80 near Fairfield. It's not located on a back road by any stretch of the imagination, but it's one of those places I just had to see from the inside.

As it turns out, public tours are available, and it's a good way to spend a couple of hours, especially during the rainy season. Bobbie Pearson is in charge of the tours. She is a charming lady, ready to answer any questions you might have about how beer is manufactured and bottled. Bobbie says most people ask about the Clydesdale horses, which do come to the plant for an occasional visit.

The plant sits on 550 acres, though only about 100 are used now. This must mean that someday a theme park will follow, à la Busch Gardens in Southern California. As for now, this plant produces about 1 million bottles of beer a day (what a song that would be!). The plant operates 24 hours a day, seven days a week.

The tour begins with a brief videotape about the brewing process. Then Bobbie or one of her aides takes you through the plant, a model of industrialization, with huge machines handling the bottle washing, pasteurizing, pouring, labeling, and capping. You must wear protective goggles because a bottle will break now and then. Also be prepared for an intense level of noise. Still, if you're a fan of "industry on parade"–type assembly lines, you won't be disappointed by the Bud tour. You wind up back in the reception area for a taste of Bud—if you're of age, of course—and a question-and-answer session. Cleverly, the tour ends up in the gift shop, where you can buy a zillion doodads advertising Anheuser-Busch products. I went for the red, white, and blue Bud Light ashtray.

ANHEUSER-BUSCH BREWERY, *located off the Abernathy exit from Route 80— you can't miss it. Be sure to bring warm clothing; temperatures can get down to the 40s during certain parts of the tour. Call ahead; tours are by appointment only. Phone: (707) 429-2000.*

HOW TO GET HERE: *From San Francisco, take the Bay Bridge to Highway 80 North toward Sacramento. Exit at Abernathy Road near Fairfield and head for the sign of the Clydesdales.*

JELLY BELLY

Another all-weather tour is available just down the road from Budweiser. It's the Herman Goelitz Candy Factory, which has played an important role in diplomacy in the 1980s.

This is the home of Jelly Belly, the jelly bean that has for years been the favorite snack of one Ronald Reagan. His obsession with the candy started years ago, even before he was governor of California. When the future president gave up smoking, he started popping jelly beans whenever he got the urge to light up. Someone introduced him to Jelly Belly, and he was hooked.

When he moved into the White House, Reagan brought his jelly beans with him. He served them at cabinet meetings and left commemorative jars for foreign dignitaries when they arrived for state visits (and they probably thought they'd get champagne and a fruit basket!).

All this publicity did wonders for the Goelitz company, which had been in business for 62 years in the industrial section of Oakland. Sales tripled, and the company moved into an industrial park on a back road in Solano County. With the new plant came a new policy of offering tours to the public.

The original founder's great-granddaughter, Becky Joffer, is in charge of the tour operation. Walking you through racks and racks of candy in their football-field-size factory, Becky will proudly show you how her family's beans are cooked, molded, flavored, coated, and packaged. Be prepared for some intense aromas as you pass vats of cinnamon, mint, or peanut butter (yep, peanut butter jelly beans).

You will also see some of their newer products, including those lovable, squishy Gummi Bears, Gummi Worms, and even the new Gummi Rat, which is 9 inches long and is sold complete with pet adoption papers.

HERMAN GOELITZ CANDY FACTORY, *2400 North Watney Way, Fairfield. Retail shop open 11 A.M. to 5 P.M. weekdays; tours of the factory Monday through Friday by appointment only. Tours are free, with sweet samples at the end. Phone: (707) 428-2800. Wheelchair accessible.*

HOW TO GET HERE: *From San Francisco, take the Bay Bridge to Highway 80 North toward Sacramento. At Fairfield, exit at Abernathy Road. Then go left on Busch, right on Chadbourne, left on Courage, and left again on Watney Way. The directions may sound involved, but it's really very simple, just a few minutes off the freeway.*

IS MR. WRIGHT RIGHT?
⑦

There is a lot more to Fairfield than roaming through factories. On a quiet, suburban street a few blocks from the main drag—which for some reason is called Texas Street—you will find the world's only Museum of Space Action. It's in the home of Walter Wright, whose major aim in life is to prove that Isaac Newton's theory of gravity was wrong. In Walter's theory, the apple that fell on poor Ike's head wasn't pulled down by gravity; it was pushed.

The museum is scattered over a few rooms in the back of the house, off a back yard that is worth the trip itself. A devoted father, Walter built a series of play areas for his young sons, including a train area and several other interesting designs. It looks like a playground designed by Mr. Wizard and a collection of folk artists.

Walter is a trained electrical engineer and a teacher at heart. His tour lasts for two hours, giving him time to explain many of his theories and answer all your questions. There are over 100 exhibits to see, but the tour doesn't take in every one, unless you are really interested. Basically, each exhibit is another graphic example of the Wright theory of magnetism and how everything is pushed rather than pulled. Some of the displays are more elaborate than others, but all are colorful and fun, whether or not you choose to believe Wright.

So far, the scientific community sticks with Isaac, and Walter is quick to tell you that all he wants is for "them"—meaning the scientific establishment—to just come and look at what he has. He says he may not be right, but so far no one has proved him wrong, so they should take him seriously. For now, he remains the Rodney ("Can't get no respect") Dangerfield of the world of science, but he is sure "they" will catch on someday.

Frankly, I couldn't make heads or tails out of the displays or the theory or even figure out why it makes a difference if gravity is a push or a pull, but I was fascinated by the place and found Walter to be a very sweet, entertaining man. He is very serious and excited about his findings, but also has a sense of humor about them and about life in general. Also, there is something very appealing about a person who takes a stand against all odds and sticks with it, despite the establishment.

THE WRIGHT MUSEUM OF SPACE ACTION, *732 Ohio Street, Fairfield. Admission: Free. Call for an appointment. Phone: (707) 429-0598.*

HOW TO GET HERE: *From San Francisco, take the Bay Bridge to Highway 80 North toward Sacramento. Take the first Fairfield exit, which is West Texas Street. Take West Texas to the courthouse, which is on Union Street. Turn right on Union. Go four blocks to Ohio Street and turn right again. The museum is two blocks down the road.*

MUSEUM OF AVIATION

The Wright brothers may have picked Kitty Hawk, North Carolina, as the place to fly an airplane for the first time, but California has been an important place for the next steps of aerospace development. That is the theme of the air museum, which is open to the public daily at Travis Air Force Base.

According to Lt. Colonel Lou Tobin, who helped start the museum in 1986 and runs it when he is not flying huge C5 transport planes, there are only a few such museums in the United States. His hopes are for an eventual rival to the main Air Force facility at Wright-Patterson in Dayton, Ohio.

This museum has a definite California slant. One of the prize possessions in the indoor part of the facility is an original Gonzales biplane, built in 1910 by the Gonzales brothers of San Francisco. It was a one-of-a-kind airplane; the brothers would pack it up in boxes, take it on a train to the wide open spaces up north, fly it for a week or so, and then pack it up again and flag down the train for the ride back home. The biplane remained in the family until nephew Bob gave it to the museum with the understanding that it never leave Travis.

There are many other things to see as well, including planes from both world wars, space capsules, training simulators, and a huge transport plane outside that is big enough to drive trucks into. This jumbo is opened on weekends for visitors to climb up and roam around. Another interesting area is the maintenance shop, where the continual process of renovation and repair takes place.

One of my favorite planes at the museum is the old presidential support plane that was used to fly President Roosevelt from his historic meeting in Yalta to a nearby aircraft carrier. This plane really has a checkered past. After the Roosevelt years it was sold to a Brazilian airline for short flights and then was purchased by a private pilot from nearby Rio Vista, who converted it to a restaurant at the small California airport. I'm happy to say that I had lunch once at the

Flying Down to Rio Café. I'm sorry to say I may have been one of the few because they went out of business and turned the plane over to Travis Air Force Base.

You can spend several hours or just a short time at the museum, but chances are if you have any interest in anything to do with flying or space, you will find something here for you.

THE TRAVIS AIR FORCE MUSEUM, *Building 80, Travis Air Force Base. Open 9 A.M. to 4 P.M. seven days a week. Admission: Free. Phone: (707) 438-5605. Wheelchair accessible.*

HOW TO GET HERE: *From San Francisco, take the Bay Bridge to Highway 80 North toward Sacramento. Exit at the Travis Air Base exit and take Travis Parkway to the entrance. The road ends at the gate. At the visitor's entrance, just tell the guards you are going to the museum, and they'll give you directions.*

ANTIQUE TRAINS AND STREETCARS ⑨

Tucked away in the countryside between Fairfield and Rio Vista is a museum devoted to a different America, the one in which the railroad was the key to the future. It's a history rich with romance, style, and technology, when streetcars and trolleys provided mass transit and steam locomotives moved people and goods around the nation. Many rail buffs feel that in this day of automotive gridlock and air pollution, we may once again return to the rail.

At the Western Railway Museum trains and streetcars are kept at the ready. Situated on a 25-acre site, with practically nothing else around, the museum offers a great opportunity to see 85 pieces of operating vintage railcars and to ride on one of them. It might be a wooden electric car from the Midwest or an early California trolley. Trains run every 10 minutes or so on a half-mile track that will carry you past a duck pond, around a good number of scenic curves, and by the barn where cars are being stored and restored. The price of admission pays for as many rides as you care to take. There are also picnic tables strategically placed with views of the rolling stock. Once you get here you will probably want to stay awhile, so it's a good idea to bring some food.

Inside the barn almost all the cars are open for visitors to climb aboard and roam around. One prize possession is the 1931 *Scenic Limited,* which ran from Oakland to Chicago. It was once used by Franklin D. Roosevelt on a whistle-stop campaign tour, and it appeared in the film *Harold and Maude.* It is locked up for protection, but you can see from the outside the still-working radio and Victrola and the kind of luxury afforded by such transportation.

The museum is run entirely by volunteers, who are constantly searching the country for more cars to add to their collection. They've picked up a car for a few dollars, then spent thousands getting it to run again. One treasure had been used as a sewing room for a home in Palo Alto, if you can imagine that. All restoration is done faithfully, down to matching the original nails, wood, trim, and glass.

Keep in mind as you roam the grounds that this was nothing but an open field when the organization first bought it in 1960. Every building, every foot of track, even the grass and landscaping, was the result of volunteer efforts.

WESTERN RAILWAY MUSEUM, *Highway 12, at the Rio Vista Junction. Open noon to 5 P.M. Saturday, Sunday, and holidays. Admission: Adults, $3; ages 12 to 17, $2; children 11 and under, $1. Phone: (707) 374-2978.*

HOW TO GET HERE: *From San Francisco, take the Bay Bridge to Route 80 North toward Sacramento. At Fairfield, exit on Route 12 East and continue for several miles to the museum, on the right side of the road.*

You'll see all kinds of animals tooling around on the back roads, but nothing will turn your head so quickly as the menagerie at the Trotter Ranch outside of Esparto.

CAMELS OF ESPARTO

Imagine this: You are driving through real farm country, the flatlands north of the Sacramento Delta, miles from anything resembling an urban environment. As you pass the Trotter place, suddenly you see two or three camels peeking their faces over the fence. Then you see dozens of camels ambling about the fields. You have arrived at the ranch of the American Camel Association, a group devoted to one goal: that there be camels in the United States.

Why camels? Ask Catherine Arlett, who is the most fervent spokesperson for an organization that you will ever want to meet. Boy, does she love camels. She knows all about them, too. Catherine will tell you that camels have this bad reputation of being mean, nasty animals that spit and snap at humans. Then she'll go up to a towering camel and hug and kiss it, like it was a cuddly kitten. Soon you are both surrounded by camels, being showered with affection from these 1800-pound specimens.

Believe me, before I visited the ranch I had no interest in hanging out with camels. But Catherine convinced me they are lovely, bright, cooperative creatures who have been mistreated and misunderstood. These guys will get down on their knees for you, let you pet them until you are exhausted, and let you feed them carrots. They'll let you know that they think you're OK, even if you do smell like a human.

What does the American Camel Association want? They want you to adopt a camel—not to take home with you but to help pay the cost of the association's care for the animals, which are often sickly or abused when they are brought to the ranch.

CAMELS OF ESPARTO, *at the Trotter Ranch at the intersection of County Roads 23 and 85B, Esparto. To phone the American Camel Association, call (916) 662-6591.*

HOW TO GET TO THE CAMELS OF ESPARTO: *From San Francisco, take the Bay Bridge to Highway 80 North toward Sacramento. Take the Highway 505 exit and continue until the exit for Esparto. Head west into town until you come to*

County Road 85B. Turn left and continue to the intersection of County Road 23.
Believe me, you will notice the camels right away.

A. W. HAYS TRUCK MUSEUM

The town of Woodland, north of Highway 80, is one of wealthiest agricultural towns of Northern California. Its rich history has been preserved in a beautifully restored opera house and a wonderful museum (more about those later), and most important, at least for lovers of trucks, the A. W. Hays Antique Truck Museum.

A. W. has amassed what is believed to be the largest collection of antique trucks in the world. He houses them on the same property where he once ran his trucking business. As you pull up to the site, you might think you're in for a disappointment. It certainly doesn't look like an interesting museum as you drive through the gate and park near one of the aluminum storage buildings.

But once inside you will see at least 100 trucks, representing 60 different manufacturers. There is a remarkable variety in the painstakingly restored collection, encompassing not only the bodies but transmissions, tires, and ornamentation. They date from a beauty from 1901 (the year A. W. was born) to some of the more recent Peterbilt monsters that now rule the highways.

Chances are your guide will be A. W. himself, a gentleman who spends his days since retirement caring for this unique collection. A. W. can still replace a fender and fabricate a wooden steering wheel with the best of them, and he is filled with stories about each of his prized possessions. (A. W. is also full of homespun humor. He told me his associates call him "Aw," his friends call him Pop, and his wife calls him to dinner.)

He started in the trucking business by driving for other truck owners, delivering produce from the farms around Woodland to the San Francisco markets. During the Depression he scraped up enough money to buy his own truck. His business was so good that soon he had several trucks and the desire to start a collection.

According to Aw, the most unusual truck in his collection is a made–in–San Francisco model with a hauling platform only 14 inches above the ground. This was made before hydraulic lifts to make it easier to load the truck. I'm sure it worked just fine, but one pothole would surely cause the bottom to scrape the road.

Even if Aw isn't on hand for a tour, you'll do just fine on your own. Each exhibit is set up with a card with all the vital information. As you walk down the line of vehicles, a history of transportation in America unfolds, and you begin to see how the demand for moving goods created our highway system. You'll also see some great-looking machines.

THE A. W. HAYS ANTIQUE TRUCK MUSEUM, *2000 East Main Street, Woodland.*
Open 10 A.M. to 4 P.M. Monday through Friday, and sometimes on weekends if

A.W. feels like being there. Call first, as this is a very informal operation. Admission: Adults, $3; teens and younger, $1. Phone: (916) 666-1044. Wheelchair accessible.

HOW TO GET HERE: *From San Francisco, take the Bay Bridge and stay on Route 80 heading for Sacramento. About an hour after the bridge, assuming you're in normal traffic, you will come to the Route 113 exit for Woodland. Take Route 113 North to Main Street in the town of Woodland. Turn right (east) and go to the corner of Route 102, where it intersects with Main. The museum is on your right.*

While you're in Woodland, you ought to see some of the town itself, and that simply involves a short ride down Main Street from the truck museum. As you move into the town's center, you can see this is a lively community. Thirty thousand people live here, and the modern Yolo County Courthouse is a focal point of activity. But Woodlanders have a keen sense of history, too, and they have preserved some of the town's most precious buildings.

On Main Street at Second you will find one of the finest of these, the Woodland Opera House, a beautifully restored brick building that is now open for shows and for tours.

This was a very busy theater back in the late 1800s. All the shows on the circuit from Seattle to San Francisco stopped here. Not much in the way of grand opera was performed, but every traveling melodrama and dog-and-pony show packed 'em in. Young actors like Walter Huston and Sidney Greenstreet honed their craft here before moving on to more illustrious careers.

The place was boarded up in 1913 after someone fell in the theater and sued the owner. It stood as a decaying relic of the past until the 1960s, when a group of citizens raised enough money to restore it. Now it is a state historic site.

When the concerned citizens went inside to fix the place up, it was as if they had entered a time capsule. Costumes still hung in the downstairs dressing rooms; yellowed advertising posters adorned the walls. The gas stage-lighting panel was found in the wings.

There were also tons of dust. After years of work, much of it volunteer, the Opera House reopened and is now a must stop for anyone interested in theater or architecture. It's a jewel of a house, with a rounded balcony, high ceilings, perfect acoustics, and the proverbial "not a bad seat in the house."

WOODLAND OPERA HOUSE, *Second and Main streets, Woodland. Open for tours 2 to 4 P.M. Saturday and Sunday, 10 A.M. to 2 P.M. Monday and Tuesday. It's a good idea to call ahead. Phone: (916) 666-9617.*

HOW TO GET HERE: *From San Francisco, follow the directions for the truck museum. From there, follow Main Street past Route 113 to Second Street. The theater is on the northwest corner.*

WOODLAND OPERA HOUSE
⑫

GIBSON HOUSE

Nearly every county has a historical museum these days, and after a while they start to blend together. This is not the case in Yolo County at the Gibson House Museum.

This county museum stands out from the rest for two reasons. First, the building looks like it belongs in the Old South. That's because William Gibson, the original occupant, was from Virginia, and to feel at home in the Wild West he embellished his 10-room house with impressive white columns, à la Tara in *Gone with the Wind*.

The museum's other distinction is its director, Monica Stengert, whose background is unique indeed. Before moving to Northern California in 1975 Monica worked at the largest museum in her native Warsaw, Poland. She brings to her current job not only a world view of history but also a great appreciation for the immigrants who settled and built the town of Woodland. A visit with Monica is worth the trip, but the museum is an added treat.

The Gibson House is arranged to show the various periods during which the Gibson family lived here, from 1850 to 1940. Each room represents a different era and a different generation of Gibsons.

One of my favorite displays is the collection of barbershop glass. This includes two display cases of beautiful bottles used for lotions and shampoos by the town barber, back in the days when the barbershop was an unofficial gentlemen's club. Some of the bottles were made in Venice and Murano, others were made locally; they are all spectacular.

Outside you'll find three smaller buildings, which housed the dairy, the root cellar, and the washroom. Each of these is operational, so you can have a hands-on experience churning butter or turning a hand-cranked washing machine.

There is also a small display of antique farm equipment, an herb garden, and a park for picnicking. It can get very hot in the summer in Woodland, but the shade provided by a 200-year-old oak and other trees makes for a comfortable parklike setting on the property's 5 acres.

The Gibson House has been in operation only since 1982. It's another example of community volunteers getting together to enrich their town. For many years the home had been abandoned; local legend said it was haunted. Then a historical society was formed and the county was convinced to buy the house. Volunteers spent nearly 10 years fixing it up and acquiring donations for the exhibits. Today it's a county treasure.

GIBSON HOUSE MUSEUM, *512 Gibson Road, Woodland. Open noon to 4 P.M. Saturday and Sunday, 10 A.M. to 4 P.M. Monday and Tuesday. Admission: Free. Phone: (916) 666-1045.*

HOW TO GET HERE: *From San Francisco, follow the directions to the truck museum, but when you reach the shopping center at Gibson Road, turn left.*

From the opera house: go back to Route 113 at Main Street. Turn right, heading south. After several blocks, you will come to a stoplight at Gibson Road, with a shopping center entrance on the left. Turn right and continue for a few blocks. The Gibson House is on the left side of the road.

CHAPTER **9** Delta

AREA OVERVIEW

California epitomizes America's love affair with the automobile. But the Sacramento Delta is one place in the state where the car loses out to the boat. The Delta is truly a marvel: 1000 miles of waterways connecting some 55 islands. More about how to use those waterways later.

In this boater's paradise there is still much to see by taking a drive. This is an agricultural area, with levees along the roadside, built to control the flow of the Sacramento and San Joaquin rivers. These levees were the work of Chinese laborers who had come to the United States for the Gold Rush and stayed to work on the continental railroad.

There are few towns. What you see on a drive on the main road, Route 160, is scenery and history. Even though you're only an hour or so away from the Bay Bridge, you're a long way from the "California chic" of the Bay Area. Restaurants are not called "Chez" or "Casa de"; they are called Sid's, Doc's, and Al's. Beer outsells white wine by a wide margin.

The roads are mainly two-lane, and they meander. The best plan for a drive is to pick just one or two destinations and simply wander, taking a turn to see where it will lead you. Sooner or later the maze will always get you back to Route 160. If there is one "must see" town in the Delta, it is Locke (see entry 5).

If you have some time, the absolute best way to see the Delta is by water. Boats are available for rent at several locations. You can rent a small boat by the hour and simply putt around, or you can rent a houseboat for several days or weeks and live on the Delta. Marinas with waterfront services such as grocery stores and restaurants are easy to find.

Portions of the Sacramento Delta are reminiscent of the Mississippi Delta, with channels that take you through narrow aisles of moss-covered willow trees. In fact, movie producer Samuel Goldwyn remarked when looking for a place to shoot *The Adventures of Huckleberry Finn,* "It looks more like the Mississippi than the real thing." Don't worry; there are no alligators here.

A word to the wise: This is a popular place in the heat of the summer, and I do mean heat. A beautiful slough can lose some of its glamour when you are trying to navigate your way past a houseboat full of amateur sailors. The best time for a trip on the Delta is in the late spring or early fall.

HOW TO GET TO THE DELTA: *From San Francisco, the most direct route is to take the Bay Bridge to Route 80 North to Fairfield. Turn right on Route 12 and follow it into the town of Rio Vista (see Yolano map). Once you cross the bridge onto route 160, you are at the beginning of the Delta. This is the spot where Humphrey the Whale made his world-famous visit in 1985.*

Another route, which will take you past the scenic town of Benicia, is to take the Bay Bridge to Route 24 toward Walnut Creek. Route 24 eventually joins Route 680. Follow 680 North to Route 4 toward Antioch until it meets Route 160. Take Route 160 all the way through as much of the Delta as you wish to visit.

For information about houseboat rentals, write or call the Rio Vista Chamber of Commerce for a list of agencies. The address is 60 Main Street, Rio Vista, CA 94571. Phone: (707) 374-2700.

FOSTER'S BIG HORN

The town of Rio Vista, the gateway to the Sacramento Delta, spent year after year relatively unnoticed by the rest of the world until fall 1985. Then the world took notice due to an unexplained yet magical visit by a huge whale named Humphrey.

But as impressive a specimen of mammal life as was Humphrey, he was small potatoes compared to the big game to be found in Foster's Big Horn Saloon.

The name Big Horn ought to give a clue to the kind of place this is. The walls of the barroom and back dining room are covered with every kind of animal head you can imagine. Lions and tigers and bears, oh my! And elephants, too. In fact, the best seat in the house is right under an enormous elephant's head with huge tusks. Groucho Marx fans love to sit under it and say that in Alabama the tusks are looser.

If Bill Foster were alive today, he would be the target of every animals' rights and environmental group in the world. But his hunting was done back in Hemingway's time, when the great white hunter was a hero and shooting game was accepted as a sport.

This collection is even more incredible in light of the fact that every specimen was shot by Foster himself. It is heralded as the world's largest one-man collection of big horns and heads in the world. Foster apparently zipped off to Africa quite regularly; in its heyday, Foster's Rio Vista joint was a gambling parlor successful enough to fund frequent safaris. Foster would return with yet another prize to decorate his saloon.

Before Foster retired in 1950, his Big Horn Saloon had everything: gambling, hooch, big spenders from the city on their way to do some pleasure cruising on the Delta. Today the place is much quieter. It is owned by the son of the woman who bought the place from Foster. It is a hangout for locals who drop by for a drink or a bite to eat and an attraction for tourists who drop by to see if what they've heard about the place could possibly be true; they are seldom disappointed.

FOSTER'S BIG HORN, *Main Street between Front and Second, Rio Vista. Open 10 A.M. to 2 A.M. daily. Phone: (707) 374-2511.*

HOW TO GET TO FOSTER'S BIG HORN: *From San Francisco, take the Bay Bridge to Highway 80 toward Sacramento. At Fairfield, exit onto Route 12 and follow it all the way to Rio Vista. On entering town, bear right at the sign for the business district. Foster's will be on your right on Main Street.*

RIO VISTA MUSEUM

We have the 1976 Bicentennial celebration to thank for the plethora of town historical museums that can be found throughout the United States. In the Bay Area, in the Delta town of Rio Vista, a group of citizens decided they should do something to celebrate the nation's 200th anniversary, so they turned an old blacksmith shop in the middle of town into a museum. Therein lies the beauty and the problem of these new museums.

Since history had not formally been organized, categorized, and cataloged for the town until 1976, creative methods had to be devised. The call went out for all locals to bring in anything they thought might be of interest. Practically nothing was refused. Then W. H. K. Dunbar, a 50-year resident of Rio Vista and a retired electrical engineer, set about the task of creating a showplace.

When I visited, Mr. Dunbar was well into his eighties but still full of energy and still trying to organize the place. He calls the collection "mostly junk," but I found it a fascinating representation of the town—of the entire nation, as a matter of fact.

People brought in newspapers from hometowns across America, and Dunbar framed the front page of each one. The result is a wall of nationwide headline history, from the turn of the century through world wars, assassinations, depressions, and space voyages. Below the newspapers an ever changing display of artifacts is arranged: old typewriters, early radios, personal pictures, even an amusing assortment of beverage containers including jars of sarsaparilla, a can of Billy Beer, and tiny airplane-service-size whisky bottles.

There are several rooms, each filled to the ceiling with what I can only call stuff. The original part of the building, the blacksmith's shop, is filled with farm equipment from the area's earliest agricultural days. This is a very charming place, and I hope you'll get a chance to meet W. H. K. Dunbar, too.

RIO VISTA MUSEUM, *16 North Front Street, Rio Vista. Open 1:30 to 4:30 P.M. Saturday and Sunday only. Admission: Free, but a donation of $1 is greatly appreciated. Phone: (707) 374-5169.*

HOW TO GET HERE: *From San Francisco, follow the directions to Foster's Big Horn. From there, simply walk around the corner to the left to Front Street.*

MUSEUM OF DREDGING

I have been to the town of Rio Vista several times in the past few years. For reasons that may seem obvious, I always avoided visiting a place called the Museum of Dredging. Really, what could sound more drab and boring?

Well, I'm happy to report I was wrong. This place is neither drab nor boring, and it is a stop I can heartily recommend.

The Dutra Museum of Dredging happens to be set up in a beautiful old house in a residential section of this picturesque town. It's the kind of house every boy or girl in the 1940s wished were home: a stone structure with a beautiful garden and a porch that goes from the front all the way around the side to the back of the house. You can imagine sitting on a swing or glider on a hot day, waiting for the ice-cream truck to come by.

This has been the Dutra home for years, and Mrs. Linda Dutra has opened the place to tourists to show the private collection of memorabilia and models and to tell the story of the Dutras' involvement with developing the Delta region. Linda begins the tour at a huge mural that shows how the Dutra family first came to the United States, then headed west by wagon train to California. Several generations ago the Dutras developed what is called the clamshell style of dredging. Using huge cranes that look like giant clams, they cut the intricate series of canals that now make up the Delta. Of course their work never ends, as the flow of the rivers brings new silt that must be continually dredged to maintain a navigable depth. Every room in the house is decorated with memorabilia from the exploits of the clan.

You wouldn't believe that there could be so many fascinating pieces of machinery to see; there are scale models of early dredges and a working hydraulic model to show you the latest in equipment.

But for me, the personal stories were the most fascinating. In seeing the history of this one Portuguese-American family, complete with personal photographs and mementos, you see a dramatic illustration of the American dream through their eyes. This is a family that made it, accumulated a lot of money, and is still working to keep the Delta open.

There are several bittersweet elements to a visit here, too. Edward Dutra, the patriarch of the family, suffered a crippling stroke a few years ago and sits in a corner watching his wife give the tours. He is unable to speak. There is also a twinge of bewilderment from Mrs. Dutra that some environmentalists oppose the kind of work they do and have made the Dutras a symbol for rallying supporters to their cause.

Linda says that most people expect to stop in for just a few minutes but end up staying a long time. She says the men get fascinated by all the equipment and the women fall in love with the house.

DUTRA MUSEUM OF DREDGING, *345 St. Gertrude's Avenue, Rio Vista. Open by appointment. Admission: Free. Phone: (707) 374-5015.*

HOW TO GET HERE: *From San Francisco, follow the directions to Foster's Big Horn and the Rio Vista business section. From Main Street, turn right on Fourth Street and follow it to the corner of St. Gertrude's Avenue. The house is directly across from the high school.*

RIDE THE J-MAC

Do you love boat rides but don't have the time for a long trip? Maybe you like the idea of the high seas but are subject to *mal de mer*? Do I have a ride for you!

Because there are so many inland waterways to cross in the Sacramento Delta, the state provides free ferryboat service from island to island. The quickest, shortest ride is on the J-Mac, which connects Grand Island and Ryer Island, crossing the Steamboat Slough.

You drive your car right onto the ferry, which looks like a glorified barge. In less than two minutes you are on land again, on the other side. The smooth sailing comes courtesy of such pilots as Earl Whiteley, who makes the trip back and forth, back and forth every day. This is a guy who spent years on a sailboat in the Pacific, and he says the river is so fascinating that he always sees new things.

The J-Mac ferry crosses 160 times a day, and there are lots of other ferries at other crossings all along Route 160. It's the only way to get between the many islands of this unique region.

For more information call Caltrans. Phone: (415) 923-4444.

LOCKE: THE TOWN THAT TIME FORGOT

Of the few towns in the Delta, none is more interesting or unusual than Locke. This was one of California's original Chinatowns, constructed for the Chinese laborers who built the intricate systems of levees that control the flow of water in the Delta. There isn't much left of the town, and every now and then somebody comes up with a grand scheme to buy the place and turn it into a commercial enterprise. One such plan was to build a theme park to compete with Disneyland. But for now this is a one-block village with a past. In 1915 discriminatory laws did not allow the Chinese to own land. A white farmer named George Locke leased a parcel of his land to the Chinese to build a town; by 1920 Locke was an active community with a school, church, and population of around 2000.

During the Depression, since Locke was really out in the sticks, it became a place to which city slickers could come for a night of gambling; the Star Theater, which had once hosted operas every week, became the town brothel.

Today the Chinese population has dwindled to 45. Their fate has been a sad one. The younger generation has moved on to the cities, and most of the old businesses that served the once thriving community have closed.

There is some concern about the longevity of the ramshackle wooden buildings that line the town's one street; they tend to lean a bit, and these structures may not last long, so a visit to this little town should not be put off. It represents a slice of history that doesn't exist anywhere else. A stroll through Locke will probably include a visit to the old Star Theater, the Chinese schoolhouse, and the Dai Loy Gambling Museum.

The only real action is at Al's, an old-time bar in the front where regulars pass the time of day and night. But Al's main claim to fame is the culinary offerings in the rear dining room.

People come from all over for the house specialty at Al's: steak and peanut butter. You order a grilled rib steak that comes with a side of toasted, buttered French bread. On each table there is a big jar of peanut butter and a companion jar of jelly. Some put the condiments on the bread, others on the steak. Some make a sandwich of the whole thing. But everyone in the place seems to get a kick out of the fact they are eating such a weird lunch.

I should mention that the new food consciousness has even caught up with Al's. Recently they added an alternative for those cutting down on the consumption of red meat: chicken. So now you have your choice of steak or chicken with peanut butter. By the way, they only offer the smooth kind. No chunky.

LOCKE, *right off Route 160, the main road through the Delta. Park your car and then walk in. The street is very narrow, and no parking is available on Main.*

AL'S DINER, *on Main Street in Locke. Open for lunch and dinner. Phone: (916) 776-1800.*

DAI LOY GAMBLING HOUSE MUSEUM, *13951 Main Street. Phone: (916) 776-1246.*

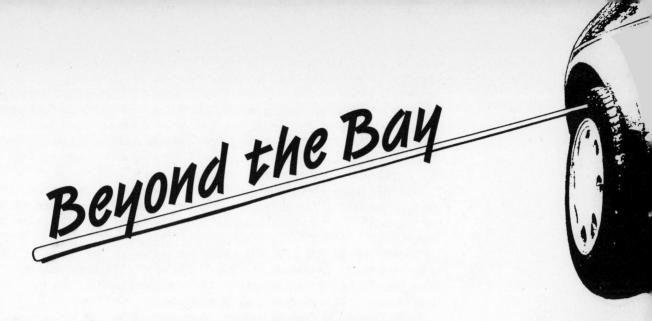

Beyond the Bay

Several destinations four and five hours from San Francisco are still considered to be part of the Bay Area. These places add to the pleasure of visiting or living in this part of the world, offering access to snow and skiing in the winter, crystal-clear lakes and water sports in the summer, and forests and wilderness activities all year round.

The destinations in this broad chapter require more planning than the places in the other chapters. Overnight accommodations will be necessary, and during peak seasons reservations are a must.

The Gold Country is the Beyond the Bay destination closest to San Francisco; sections of it can be reached in about 2 hours. Mendocino and Carmel are 2½ to 3 hours away, and Yosemite, Lake Tahoe, and the Redwood Empire are at least 4 hours away. These are average driving times, which are to be used only as a point of reference. I recommend taking your time and stopping to see the sights along the way.

CHAPTER **10** Gold Country

Imagine California before the Gold Rush in 1848. Hollywood didn't exist. San Francisco was only a tiny waterfront village. Monterey was the capital city of this Spanish-American outpost of farmland and cattle.

AREA OVERVIEW

191

Then word went out around the world that fortunes were to be found in them thar foothills of the Sierra, and people have flocked to the Golden State ever since.

For a few short years the action was in the area known as the Gold Country. Boomtowns housed thousands upon thousands of people; saloons, hotels, and other businesses sprang up overnight to provide services. In fact, many who found fortunes during the Gold Rush were suppliers to the miners, companies like Levi Strauss, Studebaker, Armour, and Ghirardelli.

But Gold Rush fever cooled rapidly, and most of the people who had arrived from points all over the globe headed to San Francisco or Sacramento to build new lives. Only a few stayed behind. The Gold Country was more or less abandoned.

Today there is still gold in the hills, but it's simply too expensive and too damaging to the environment to mine it. The new gold is the tourist trade. The nine counties in the mother lode area have banded together to try to strike it rich. Every effort is made to make the area a year-round attraction. The most popular time for tourists is between May and October, when the weather is warmest and the counties hold fairs. The most famous of these is the Calaveras County Fair, site of the annual jumping frog contest, an event first made famous years ago by a local newspaper writer named Mark Twain.

The weather for the region is more like the Bay Area than the neighboring mountains of the Sierra. Most of the Gold Country is below the snow line, and roads are passable throughout the year. The days get very hot during the summer, but the nights tend to cool off.

The main road connecting the counties of the mother lode is appropriately named Route 49 (gold miners seeking their fortune were called forty-niners, just like San Francisco's professional football team). Route 49 leads you 317 miles from the southern tip of the Gold Country at Oakhurst to the northernmost town of Downieville.

No one should try to take it all in on one trip. The best plan is to select one section and concentrate on it. No matter where you go you will find beautiful scenery, often corny remnants of the Gold Rush days, and towns with wonderful names like Fiddletown, Grub Gulch, Bootjack, and Humbug.

I recommend that you concentrate on one of three general areas: the Southern Mines, centered around Columbia; the Central Mother Lode, centered around Jackson; or the Northern Mines, centered around Nevada City. Each area has its own local historical museum and its own particular flavor.

To get to the Southern Mines, take Highway 580 out of Oakland to Highway 205 to Route 120 to Oakdale; then take Route 108 to Route 49, which you pick up a bit south of Jamestown. You might recognize Jamestown as the site for the movies *High Noon* and *Butch Cassidy and the Sundance Kid*. Continue on

Route 49 to Sonora, which boasts the county's only stoplight, then on to Columbia. The entire town is a state historic park, faithfully restored like Williamsburg, Virginia, but on a much smaller scale.

To get to the Central Mother Lode, follow Interstate 80 from the Bay Bridge to Route 50 in Sacramento; then take Route 16, following the signs to Jackson. Here, visit the towns of Sutter Creek, Volcano, and the wine region in the Shenandoah Valley. If you have time, you might want to take a look at the town of Ione, which used to be called Bedbug. In fact, the town's one hotel was actually called the Bedbug Hotel. A very impressive castle overlooks the town; it was formerly used as a boys' reform school, but now it's left empty and the school is in a new building.

To get to the Northern Mines, take Interstate 80 from the Bay Bridge to Route 49 North at Auburn and continue to the towns of Grass Valley and Nevada City. In Nevada County, the Chamber of Commerce is located in the house once occupied by the legendary actress Lola Montez; the flower planter out front is her bathtub ("It was the only clean thing about her," one of the Chamber of Commerce people remarked). It's located at 248 Mill Street, Grass Valley. Phone: (916) 273-4667.

Also of note, just south of town, is the Empire Mine State Historic Park. This was the largest and richest of all the hard-rock gold mines in the state and operated for more than 100 years. A tour of the mine and its many buildings and passages is offered by park personnel. A highlight is a visit to the home of the owner of the mine, William Bourne, whom we met earlier as the owner of Filoli in Woodside.

In terms of distance from San Francisco, most areas of the Gold Country can be reached in 2½ to 3 hours. The roads that take you there are all good and fast. Route 49 is slow and requires that you take your time.

Keep in mind that night life is close to nonexistent in the Gold Country, and great restaurants are few and far between. Columbia in the south is one exception. The old hotel is run as a culinary school, and the dining room produces wonderful meals. Nevada City also has good restaurants, as well as many attractive homes and neighborhoods.

I'm sure you will find your own special places simply by driving around the back roads off Route 49. To get you started, here are some spots of special interest, arranged south to north along Route 49.

For general information about traveling in the Gold Country, contact the Golden Chain Council of the Mother Lode, P.O. Box 1246, Auburn, CA 95603. Phone: (916) 885-5616.

MERCER CAVERNS

About a mile north of the town of Murphys is a tourist attraction that is corny, predictable, and too good to pass up. Mercer Caverns has been a tourist attraction since 1885, after a gold prospector, Walter J. Mercer, discovered the place. The legend is that after a long, fruitless day of searching for gold, Mercer stumbled across these caverns while looking for some water (and considering that he was nearly 40 years behind everybody else, it's not surprising he was tired and thirsty). He noticed some bay bushes growing near a bluff of limestone; upon further investigation he found an entrance leading to the caverns. Since then, thousands have paid admission for the experience of visiting the wonders inside Mother Earth.

Today you will be led through the caverns by tour guides who have preset speeches yet manage to seem fascinated by the material. They will tell you how Mercer probed in the darkness, risking life and limb to see what was there. They will tell you of his discovery of an ancient Indian burial ground. They will explain stalagmites and stalactites, and, as a climax to the tour, they will turn off the flashlights to show you what it is like to really be in the dark.

Before the lights go out, what you will see is truly spectacular. It's a constantly changing show of underground rock formations, illuminated by colored lights and seemingly reaching to endless depths. I liked the weird formations named for items they resemble. For example, the area named "Chinese Meat Market" features shapes hanging from the ceiling that look like the objects to be found hanging in a butcher's shop (sort of). The "Organ Loft" is to be found in a section with a vaulted chamber, and with a little imagination it does remind one of a giant church organ. Other formations with names like "Angel Wings" and "Rapunzel" are self-explanatory. (Look, you paid for the tour. Does it hurt to let your imagination go for a while?)

This is a place to visit in the summer, when the temperature outside hovers around 100 degrees. It's always about 55 degrees inside the caverns, and it feels wonderful. You will want to wear good walking shoes, and the tour is not recommended for anyone who might have trouble climbing back up the steep stone steps.

MERCER CAVERNS, *Murphys. Open 9 A.M. to 5 P.M. daily Memorial Day through September; 11 A.M. to 4 P.M. Saturday, Sunday, and school holidays October through May. Admission: Adults, $4; children 11 and under, $2. Phone: (209) 728-2101. The tour takes about a half hour.*

HOW TO GET HERE: *From San Francisco, take the Bay Bridge to Highway 580 East, which becomes Route 205. Follow Route 205 to Route 120 to Oakdale; then take Route 108 to Route 49. Continue north on Route 49 until you come to Route 4 at Angels Camp. Take Route 4 into Murphys. Mercer Caverns is 1 mile north of Murphys, off Highway 4, on the Ebbetts Pass Highway.*

Not far from the Mercer Caverns is a less commercial but equally spectacular destination. Long before Walter Mercer or any other white man even dreamed of settling in California, this was the home of giant sequoia trees. In fact, not only are these trees thousands of years old, but they are the largest living things in the world. When they named this park Big Trees, they weren't kidding.

How big are the trees? Well, when the grove was discovered in the 1850s a group of businessmen cut down one of the trees to take it on the road as a traveling exhibition. The remaining stump was large enough to be used as a dance floor. For many a Saturday night, an orchestra, dancers, and the crowd of onlookers would gather on this 27-foot-diameter tree stump. Fortunately, after the parks service was established, further abuses of the forest were prohibited. Today visitors may walk on the stump while enjoying the majesty of the trees towering over the site of their fallen relative. This park is practically devoid of gimmicks; other than the stump and a tree with a hole that you can walk through, every effort has been made to preserve the natural beauty of the area.

Guided tours by park rangers are available and recommended. In places such as this, the rangers are thrilled to be where they are and love to share their enthusiasm. My guide was Kurt Craft. He calls his outpost "the jewel of the state park system." And no wonder. His territory includes 6000 acres of mountainous terrain, deep canyons, riverside beaches, two groves of giant sequoias, and mountain meadows. He says people come here for hiking, peace, and a chance to lose themselves in the woods for a while. The park features more than 40 miles of hiking trails, most of them easy to navigate. Highly recommended is the Three Senses Trail, an area that encourages the use of sight, smell, and hearing —not only fascinating but therapeutic.

CALAVERAS BIG TREES STATE PARK, *Highway 4, near the town of Arnold. Open all year. For information about camping, swimming, and fishing, phone (209) 296-7488.*

HOW TO GET HERE: *Follow the directions to Mercer Caverns, but continue on Ebbetts Pass Highway until you come to the park. It's about a half hour from the caverns.*

THE JEWEL OF THE STATE PARK SYSTEM

Did you ever see the Will Rogers movie *Boys Will Be Boys*? How about the television series *Petticoat Junction*? Both have a connection to the Amador County Museum, a former residence that sits high on a hill overlooking the town of Jackson. Rogers used the house as the setting for his 1920 epic, and the train from the TV series sits outside, with a paint job designed to remind visitors of the Gold Rush days.

These examples will give you some idea of the flavor of the museum, an eclectic, show-bizzy collection of items that tell the story of the Central Mother Lode.

AMADOR COUNTY MUSEUM

The main house is a lovely two-story brick building, filled with furniture from the period. The place is arranged as if the family still lived there and had stepped out for the afternoon. The kitchen is ready for a meal to be prepared; the parlor has been tidied up for guests.

Then there are the show-biz touches. In the parlor you'll see a 1920s vintage radio on display, and you'll hear the crooning sounds of Russ Columbo and young Bing Crosby (but if you peek behind the radio you'll find a modern tape recorder). Out back in the old livery stable you'll find a working scale model of one of the largest mines in the area, the Kennedy Gold Mine. You will first be ushered into the stable, probably under the guidance of museum curator Cedric Clute. Then he will turn out the lights, rush over to yet another tape recorder, and begin a 10-minute multimedia presentation about the mine and how it operated. It is great fun, and the miniature mine actually works.

After viewing the model, it is recommended that you drive up to the top of the hill on Route 49 to overlook the remains of the original mine. Much of it is still underground, but you can still see the huge wheels and other gizmos used in the process of gold mining.

Back at the museum, you can ask Cedric about the infamous heart-shaped plaque that is no longer on display in town. It was a tribute to the ladies of the Gold Rush who came to work in the brothels. Replicas of the original are available on a key chain in almost every trinket shop in the area.

As for the *Petticoat Junction* train, a resident heard that the *Hooterville Cannonball* was sitting around on an empty lot in Hollywood. So he bought it and contributed it to the museum. It doesn't go anywhere, but it's interesting to find it here.

AMADOR COUNTY MUSEUM, *at the top of Church Street, Jackson. Open 11 A.M. to 4 P.M. Wednesday through Friday; 10 A.M. to 5 P.M. Saturday and Sunday. Admission to the museum is free, but the mine program costs $1.00. Phone: (209) 223-3230.*

HOW TO GET HERE: *From San Francisco, take the Bay Bridge to Interstate 80 toward Sacramento. In Sacramento, exit to Route 50 East toward Lake Tahoe. Take Route 16 off Route 50 toward Jackson. Follow Route 16 to Route 49, the main road of the Gold Country. Turn right (south) on Route 49 and follow the signs to the town of Jackson. You will be on Main Street. Turn left onto Church and follow it up the hill to the museum.*

VOLCANO

This is one of the prettiest towns in all the Gold Country. It is a very small place with a very large sense of community pride. A visitor isn't in town long before being reminded that Volcano is the home of many "firsts" in the state, including the first circulating library, theater group, private law school, and solar still.

When you drive into town, the first thing you will see in this one-street town is the quaint though obligatory National Hotel (in the Gold Country, restored National Hotels are like wineries in the rest of the state—they are everywhere). You will also see shops and lovely historic buildings, all surrounding an inviting parklike town center. There's a park bench out in front of the general store, facing a large grassy knoll. In front of the knoll there are a few exteriors of old buildings being held up like stage sets, offering a flavor of the old town.

Also on display is the town cannon, set up to deter a possible Confederate uprising during the Civil War. It has never been fired, so apparently it was effective against the rebels.

Then you will see the town's sore thumb, the modern, ranch-style post office. If you want to start a conversation with anybody, just ask about the post office. You'll hear all about the town's battle with the U.S. government.

It seems that the post office used to be in a beautiful old building across the street from the hotel. That was fine, but the residents didn't get along with the postmaster. You must understand how important the post office is to a community like this. People come down from the hills and mingle with the townsfolk as they all pick up their mail; it's as important a community center as the neighborhood pub is in England. The good folks around Volcano complained loud and long to the powers that be in Washington, D.C., and eventually they got their way, sort of.

To make a long story short, according to the residents' version of the story, they were able to get rid of the postmaster, but as punishment the government took away their nice post office building, claiming it was no longer suitable. Stuck with an ugly old trailer, the citizens battled long and hard to get a more suitable building, possibly restoring the old historic one and bringing it up to code. No luck; the government finally got rid of the trailer but put up a modern building that looks like it might be a dry cleaner's.

If you are really lucky, you might run into a fascinating man named George Oxford. He looks a lot like Walter Cronkite. In fact, George did spend his career in broadcasting, but not as a newsman. To Bay Area listeners of the 1950s he was Jumpin' George. He says that as a native Southerner, he had an affinity for black rhythm and blues music. He introduced the sounds of the Penguins, the Moonglows, and the Orioles to radio listeners while affecting a jargony delivery that made most people assume he was black, too. Jumpin' George was a smash, and he has wonderful stories to tell about people's reactions when they would discover he was a white man. Now retired, this distinguished-looking gentleman loves to tell stories about the old days of radio. His wife runs the county Chamber of Commerce.

If you visit in the spring, George, or anyone else in town, will surely direct you to a favorite spot around here, Daffodil Hill. Each April the 300,000 bulbs that have been planted on this hillside will be in bloom. It is a dazzling show.

VOLCANO, *about 20 minutes from the larger town of Sutter Creek. The county Chamber of Commerce can tell you if Daffodil Hill is in bloom. Phone: (209) 223-0350.*

HOW TO GET TO VOLCANO: *From Jackson, take Route 88 to the Pine Grove Road until you reach Volcano Road. Turn left and follow for a few miles into Volcano.*

HOW TO GET TO DAFFODIL HILL: *It's 3 miles beyond Volcano, still on the Pine Grove–Volcano Road. There are signs to the hill.*

INDIAN GRINDING ROCK STATE PARK

Several places in Northern California are dedicated to preserving the lifestyle of the original Indian inhabitants of the state. In my opinion, the most impressive of these is outside the town of Volcano at the Indian Grinding Rock State Historical Park.

There is much to see and do here, but it is best to start at the park's namesake rock. Until the turn of the century Miwok Indians of the High Sierra would travel to this meadow to gather food. The rock was used for grinding acorns from the surrounding oak trees into meal, a staple of the Indian diet. This giant slab of limestone, 173 feet by 82 feet, was the social center for Miwok women; while the men hunted, the women would gather the acorns and other seeds and pulverize them while swapping stories and tending their children.

The rock is the largest of its kind in California and is fenced off with a platform for public viewing.

There's another part to the story. After the Indians left, the property was in the hands of a family that passed the land down from generation to generation. The family knew the rock had significance but wasn't sure how to protect it for the future. In the 1950s the family enlisted the support of Muriel Thebaut, the county's unofficial historian and a wonderful lady. She took it upon herself to convince the authorities that something should be done to preserve the rock.

She went to the county supervisors, suggesting that a park be established, but they weren't interested. She went to some local Indian families, who said they were sure no one cared about their heritage. Finally, she went to the state parks department, who became interested. After years of lobbying, a park was finally established. Muriel remains a park docent and an active board member.

The park features 21 campsites with tables and stoves, a picnic area, many hiking trails, several re-created Indian dwellings, and a wonderful cultural center with displays from several tribes and occasional demonstrations of Native American crafts. The center is built in the style of an Indian roundhouse and is quite beautiful.

INDIAN GRINDING ROCK STATE HISTORICAL PARK, *14881 Pine Grove–Volcano Road, about 15 minutes outside the town of Jackson. Open 8:30 A.M. to 4:30 P.M. Wednesday through Friday, 9:30 A.M. to 5:30 P.M. Saturday, Sunday, and holidays. A nominal fee is charged for parking. Phone: (209) 296-4440.*

HOW TO GET HERE: *From Jackson, take Route 88 to Pine Grove, then bear left and follow the Volcano Road to the park.*

RED MULE RANCH

Although the Gold Country is beautiful and fun, there is a movie-set quality to the place; much of what you see looks as though it was put there to attract tourists. But if you want to feel like you're stepping back in time to the Old West, visit the Red Mule Ranch. This is the genuine article.

As a working ranch, Red Mule is not open as a drop-in spot for visitors, but Ron Scoffield, who created the place, is happy to share his ranch and his lifestyle with those who call for an appointment.

Even though I am spreading the word about this place, it is not likely to get swamped. First of all, getting there is not easy. Ron likes to live as though it is the 1880s, and the first proof is the long dirt road leading up the hill to the property. Ron keeps it rough, dusty, and filled with holes.

If you brave the road, you will wind into what looks like a frontier town, with a blacksmithing and wagon repair shop and a charming Victorian-style house. Ron built it all. He and his family arrived before electric lines came to this region, so he built the house with hand tools. His most recent structure is a log cabin, which serves as a guest house for his kids and grandchildren.

You will see little here that represents contemporary life. Ron does admit to owning a truck, but it's hidden behind a barn so he doesn't have to look at it. He makes his living repairing covered wagons and wagon wheels. Even Ron is surprised that business is brisk and that owners are able to find him. Ron owns several wagons himself, and a family outing usually means a wagon ride, pulled by a team of mules.

One wagon has a special claim to fame. In 1976 the Scoffields celebrated the Bicentennial by riding in a wagon train across the United States. They were the only Californians on the team. Ron and his wife sold everything, including the ranch, to go on this journey. Their plan was to settle anywhere in the United States that looked good to them. After making the entire trip (at 3 miles an hour), they decided Amador County was the best place for them. They came home and bought back their ranch. It is worth a trip out here just to hear Ron's stories about this remarkable journey.

I have to admit that after working in television, it's easy to become skeptical; somebody is always trying to sell something. But as we spent time at the Red Mule Ranch we realized that Ron isn't selling anything. He created this scene for his own enjoyment and that of his family. Besides that, Ron is a charming and philosophical host.

I cannot give directions to the ranch; you'll have to get them from Ron, as visits are by appointment only. Phone: (209) 296-4519. He does not charge admission.

VICTORIANS OF THE GOLD RUSH

Most people are surprised to learn that Nevada City is in California. This Gold Country town is full of surprises.

First of all, the town itself is a gem. Its historical buildings, including a number of Victorian homes, are beautifully restored. And considering its location, Nevada City is quite cosmopolitan; several shops downtown sell everything from chic clothing to Gold Rush memorabilia, and there are good places to eat and stay. Nevada City is also one of the few places in California where you can find fall foliage as lovely as that in the East, thanks to the many trees brought in by transplanted Easterners.

Nevada City also has the obligatory National Hotel, this one famous for the fact that the papers that led to the creation of the Pacific Gas and Electric Company were signed in one of its suites. Herbert Hoover was a regular guest here when he was a young mining engineer.

The most impressive place in town is a huge building a block south of Main Street that houses a theater, a radio station, a restaurant, and a museum dedicated to the Victorian era. This former miners' foundry functions as the civic and cultural center for Nevada City, under the banner of the American Victorian Museum.

When you enter the building, you find yourself in the lobby of KVMR, which, of course, stands for Victorian Museum Radio. To their knowledge, this is the only radio station owned and operated by a museum. The programming is suitably eclectic, with a mixture of contemporary rock, classical, theater music, opera, and community discussion. The station originated in the belief that a modern-day museum must develop modern methods of communication.

As you descend a grand staircase, you enter the museum proper. Like so many other aspects of Nevada City, it is a surprise. The museum is devoted to collecting, preserving, and exhibiting the art and artifacts of the Victorian period, 1840–1900. The collection is impressive, but one might ask, why is it here in Nevada City? Charles Woods, the cofounder of the museum, has a sensible answer. He points out that many of the early settlers of this part of the Gold Country were from England. When they immigrated, they brought their best worldly possessions with them. When they went broke and moved on, they left behind countless toys, furniture, jewelry, and various and sundry items of everyday life. Here they are in the museum, on display as a tribute to the early settlers of the community.

After browsing through the museum, you walk into a large theater with a fully equipped stage. This is where the community's many dramatic and musical productions are presented, often augmented by the concert-sized pipe organ, built in 1871 and rescued from an abandoned synagogue in San Francisco. Many of the concerts are also broadcast on KVMR. Community events are also held in the theater, including the annual Teddy Bear Convention each April, Fright

Night each October, and Robert Burns Night each January (celebrating the Scottish poet's birthday).

In yet another large room downstairs is the restaurant, which serves Sunday brunch, weekend dinners, and holiday feasts.

THE AMERICAN VICTORIAN MUSEUM, *325 Spring Street, Nevada City. Open 11 A.M. to 5 P.M. Monday through Saturday, 10:30 A.M. to 2 P.M. Sunday. Admission: Free. Reservations for the restaurant are advised. Phone: (916) 265-5804.*

HOW TO GET HERE: *From San Francisco, take the Bay Bridge to Route 80 toward Sacramento. Exit onto Route 49 at Auburn and follow Route 49 into Nevada City.*

MALAKOFF DIGGINS

Almost everything in the Gold Country is what I would call "cute." Everywhere you see icons of grizzled old prospectors, Wild West saloons, and mementos of the good old days of the forty-niners. It's all done in a fun, corny way.

But the Malakoff Diggins illustrates the dark side of gold fever.

Malakoff Diggins is a huge pit cut out of what was once a beautiful flat ravine. During the Gold Rush, this was the largest hydraulic mining operation in the world. In a literal rush to get at the gold in the hills, huge hoses attached to powerful pumps were brought in to blast away indiscriminately at the landscape. As the hillside gave way, the gold would be extracted and the rest allowed to wash away down the Yuba River. The gold fever was so intense that in the mining town of Relief, residents stood on the banks of the river with nozzles and washed away the foundations of their own homes.

The environmental impact was felt well beyond the Gold Country. Silt-filled rivers caused flooding 40 miles away in the towns of Yuba City and Marysville and even clogged San Francisco Bay, inhibiting the shipping industry. A lawsuit was brought to stop hydraulic mining. The result was the first major court decision in favor of the environment. The abusive practice was stopped, and much gold still remains in the area. But before packing your prospecting gear, you should know that the gold is protected by law and too scattered to be worth the effort to extract.

Now operated as a state historic park, Malakoff Diggins has several good vantage points where you can walk out to the edge and view the valley cut by greed. In the past century some vegetation has had the opportunity to grow, but you can imagine what a desolate wasteland the area must have been in 1884.

A visitor's center has been set up within the park in the town of North Bloomfield. During the Gold Rush the town had 1500 residents; today there are 16. They operate the town's restored general store, livery stable, and the museum that tells the story of the area.

MALAKOFF DIGGINS STATE HISTORIC PARK, *16 miles northeast of Nevada City on North Bloomfield Road. The 2600-acre park is open year round and has prim-*

itive campsites and accommodations for motor homes (but no hookups). The restored historic town of North Bloomfield is open 10 A.M. to 4:30 P.M. daily from April to October, 10 A.M. to 5 P.M. weekends November to March. If you are in North Bloomfield at 2 P.M. on the weekends, you will see a demonstration of the hydraulic mining monitor. Phone: (916) 265-2740.

HOW TO GET TO MALAKOFF DIGGINS: *Take Route 49 out of Nevada City and turn right onto the North Bloomfield Road. Follow the North Bloomfield Road into the park. It's about a half hour from Nevada City.*

ROUGH AND READY WEDDING CHAPEL

Colorful town names abound in the Gold Country. There's Fiddletown, Grub Gulch, and Humbug, for example. The origin of most has been lost, but no matter; they add to the unsophisticated, fun-loving atmosphere of the place.

One of the most interesting of these towns is Rough and Ready. In 1850, when the U.S. government imposed a tax on mining claims, this northern Gold Country burg seceded from the Union. The citizens of this new republic elected their own president and signed a constitution similar to that of the United States. The new republic didn't last more than a few months; by the time the Fourth of July rolled around, Old Glory was hoisted up the flagpole, and the short-lived Republic of Rough and Ready became a minor footnote in history.

Today the place looks neither rough nor ready for anything in particular. Visitors come to town to see the historic buildings that show what town life must have been like in the Gold Rush days—the remains of a one-room school built in 1868, a blacksmith shop the Chamber of Commerce opens for public viewing once in a while, and the Old Post Office, now operated as a little store.

However, the main tourist attraction in town is rather new, built in 1959. It is the Little Wedding Chapel, and it looks like the sort of place you'd find in a fairy tale. This incredibly cute, one-room chapel is run by Jackie Kelley, whose mother founded the place. Kelley says the wedding chapel is the result of a shipwreck. Her parents were on a voyage from Portland, Oregon, to San Francisco when the ship sank. Her mother promised God she would dedicate her life to providing a memorable service to humanity in return for her survival. She lived, and followed up on her promise.

Today brides and grooms come from all over the world to be married in this chapel. The unusual thing is that most people who travel a great distance to get married continue a bit farther across the state line into Nevada, where they can get a quickie ceremony with no prerequisite tests or licensing hassles. But because this chapel is in California, a valid marriage requires advance planning.

Yet this chapel thrives. Weddings take place every weekend, booked well in advance. In fact, some children who are the product of weddings performed here have made reservations for their nuptials.

The chapel can provide just about anything you might need: a minister or justice of the peace, an organist, caterers, flowers, candles, even witnesses who can't help crying at weddings. And no matter where you are in town, you'll know the bride has been kissed when you hear the ringing of the carillon bells.

LITTLE WEDDING CHAPEL, *on Highway 20, a few miles west of Grass Valley in the town of Rough and Ready. The chapel is also available for baptisms. To make arrangements, phone (916) 273-6678. For more information about the town, call the Chamber of Commerce at (916) 273-8897.*

HOW TO GET HERE: *From Nevada City, take Route 20 West. Rough and Ready is about 20 minues away.*

CHAPTER **11** Yosemite National Park

It's a four- to five-hour drive from San Francisco to one of the most beautiful spots in the world. As early as 1864 its value was recognized by President Abraham Lincoln, who declared the Yosemite Valley and Mariposa Grove to be public parks. In 1890, thanks to the efforts of the Scottish-born naturalist John Muir, the nearly 800,000 acres of wilderness area became our first national park.

AREA OVERVIEW

Since entire guidebooks have been published about this area, I need not go on forever in this section; plus, once you arrive in the park you will be bombarded with maps, printed schedules of events, and lists of services. But I can offer a few tips.

First, the bad news. Today there is one aspect of Yosemite that can make the trip unpleasant: crowds. This is one of the most popular of all national parks, and sometimes it's hard to see the trees for the tourists.

The good news is that there are ways to find solitude in this grand wilderness paradise. The way to avoid the crowds is to stay away from the valley in summer. If you visit on weekdays during any other time of year, chances are there will be no lines of traffic, no wait at the food concessions, and easy access to the cross-country and downhill skiing areas. Winter, though cold up in the mountains, is moderate in the valley. Fall offers a changing of the leaves and quite often warm, clear weather. Spring offers pleasant temperatures, spectacular waterfalls, and probably a lot of mud.

If you are a camper, just about any time of year you can find hundreds of places to hike and set up camp without seeing another soul. But if you are less physical or more accustomed, as I am, to such things as beds, toilets, and restaurants, the Yosemite Valley is probably the best place for you.

In the valley there is a wide choice of accommodations, from the luxurious

Ahwanhee Hotel to the middle-range motel-like Yosemite Lodge. Another alternative is to stay in the tiny village of Wawona, near the southern entrance to the park, via Route 41. Here you'll find the gracious Wawona Hotel, founded in 1856, complete with pool, tennis courts, golf course, and riding stables. It's much quieter here than in the valley.

Even more isolated options for spending the night indoors are the Tuolumne Meadows Lodge, which offers tent cabins and a dining hall about 60 miles from the valley near the park's eastern entrance, or the White Wolf Lodge, offering both cabins and tents, about 30 miles from the valley; however, these are open only during the summer months.

All are owned and operated by the Yosemite Village and Curry Company, a division of MCA, the show-biz giant. The Curry Company has the concession on just about every service in the park except the post office. It even runs the free shuttle buses that will take you on any road in the valley and up to the ski areas at Badger Pass.

Once you get here, there's no shortage of things to do. In the valley, you can walk, rest, look around, and breathe the fresh air. In Yosemite Village you'll find an art gallery dedicated to the work of the great photographer Ansel Adams, who masterfully captured the unique qualities of the national park. Next door, at the art center, free watercolor classes are offered at various times of the year; the classes are taught by artists who spend a week at the park and take their students to a favorite place to paint.

The Pioneer Yosemite History Center, located near the Wawona Hotel, which you reach by covered bridge, is a small historical museum. And you can catch a free tram that will take you through the Mariposa Grove of giant sequoias while park rangers tell the stories of these trees, some of the largest in the world.

For an overview of the park, check into the visitor's center in Yosemite Village, where there are displays of the history of the park and of all the activities available at the time of your visit.

If you're lucky, you'll be there to catch Lee Stetson, an actor who portrays John Muir on stage at the Yosemite Theater. This one-man show, called *Conversation with a Tramp,* is based on Muir's ideas about the environment and mankind's duty to preserve it. On weekends Stetson, still in character, leads tours to some of Muir's favorite spots in the valley. Either way, it is an unforgettable theatrical experience that offers new appreciation for the wilderness.

YOSEMITE NATIONAL PARK. *For general park information, phone (209) 372-0264. All accommodations can be reserved through the Yosemite Park and Curry Company. Phone: (209) 373-4171. For camping reservations, sites can be reserved through Ticketron or by writing the National Park Service, Western Regional Office, 450 Golden Gate Avenue, San Francisco, CA 94102.*

HOW TO GET TO YOSEMITE: *From San Francisco, the most direct route is to take the Bay Bridge to Route 580 East to Route 205 to Route 120 all the way in to the park.*

HOW TO GET TO WAWONA: *Follow the same route but leave Route 120 onto Route 99 South to Route 140 East at Madera. Follow Route 140 until it connects with Route 41, and take Route 41 into the park.*

If you want a real back-roads experience and you are not in a hurry, you can follow Route 580 to Route 205 to Route 120 to Route 99 South. Exit onto Route 132 at Modesto and follow Route 132 into the park. This is the old Yosemite Road, which follows the Tuolumne River past the Old West town of Coulterville; it eventually connects with Route 120 for the entrance to the park.

There are some worthwhile stops along the way or coming back from Yosemite. One is in Modesto, and the other is less than a half hour away in the town of Oakdale.

THE ROAD BACK

✓ **UFO Museum.** The UFO Museum in Modesto is the first museum dedicated to unidentified flying objects. The owner is a soft-spoken real estate agent named Marv Taylor, and he has quite a collection. He's been fascinated by the subject since his youth in Oakland, and he has decided to share his collection and knowledge with anyone who is interested.

Marv has "scientific" displays—over 100 photographs, plus newspaper clippings, videotapes, and exhibits, all supporting the theory that we have been visited often by extraterrestrials. He also has giant photographs of space creatures, a huge plastic likeness of E.T., and a magazine and comic book collection that on its own is worth the trip to see.

Apparently, UFO believers are a tightly knit circle, and anybody who is anybody in this group has made a pilgrimage to Marv's collection or has been in touch with him. The list includes scientists from around the world and people involved with the motion picture *E.T.*

Will this collection change your mind about whether to believe or not believe? I doubt it. If you're already inclined to think it's a bunch of baloney, you'll probably have a good chuckle, but if you are inclined to believe in extraterrestrial visitations, you'll leave the museum feeling vindicated.

I'm afraid I can't give you the exact address for the UFO Museum, since at the time of publication, Marv was in the process of moving his collection from Sonora to Modesto. By the time this book is on the bookstore shelves, you will be able to get it from Modesto information, (209) 555-1212, or the Chamber of Commerce. Phone: (209) 577-5757.

✓ Hershey Chocolate Factory.   The other destination may come as a surprise to you. Did you know there was a Hershey's chocolate plant in the town of Oakdale? Well, there is, and it features tours Monday through Friday from 8:15 A.M. until 3:00 P.M., except on holidays. The tour takes about a half hour. This is the only Hershey plant that offers public tours. If you go to the Pennsylvania town named after the company, you get an amusement park and a simulated factory.

This is nirvana for chocoholics. As soon as you step inside the door of the huge plant, the aroma of roasting cacao beans gets you. Then there's the sight of hundreds of huge vats of melted chocolate being mixed by giant granite mixers. As you walk through, your guide will point out the drums of peanut butter on their way to the Reese's Peanut Butter Cup line, the molds for the various bars, the Kiss inspector, and just about everything else you fantasize a Hershey factory to be. And after the tour, everyone gets a complimentary chocolate bar. I should also warn you that you end the tour in the gift shop, so you will probably walk out with a few more items, too.

This is a major operation, making all the Hershey's products for 11 Western states and the Far East. I even learned something that came as a major jolt to a man who is prone to Mr. Goodbars: Guess what the biggest seller for Hershey is. Reese's Peanut Butter Cups. Hmmm . . .

HERSHEY'S CHOCOLATE PLANT, *Albers Road, Oakdale. Phone: (209) 847-0381. No appointment necessary for tours, unless your group has 15 or more people.*

HOW TO GET HERE: *From San Francisco, take the Bay Bridge to Route 580 and stay on it when it becomes Route 205. Follow Route 205 to Route 120 past Manteca all the way into the town of Oakdale. In Oakdale, turn right onto County Road J-14 (also called Albers Road) and continue a mile south of town until you see the large Hershey's plant on the right.*

From Yosemite, simply follow Route 120 to Oakdale.

CHAPTER **12** Lake Tahoe

AREA OVERVIEW   Lake Tahoe is a spectacular natural attraction, one of the most beautiful mountain lakes in all the world. That alone would be enough to make it an irresistible destination. But there's more. For skiers, the Lake Tahoe area is a winter wonderland a mere four hours from downtown San Francisco. For sun worshipers, the area offers a marvelous blend of hot summers, clean mountain air, and crystal-clear water for swimming and waterskiing. Last but not least, for gamblers, the Nevada side of the lake is Las Vegas North, with fortunes to be won and lost in the 24-hour casinos.

Some quick facts: The lake itself is 22.5 miles long and 12 miles wide. It covers some 70 miles of shoreline in California and Nevada. It's the second deepest lake in the country, after Crater Lake in Oregon; Tahoe's maximum depth is 1645 feet. In the summer the lake's temperature averages 68 degrees. In the winter, despite the huge snows above, the lake never freezes, cooling only to about 50 degrees. Finally, if you want an idea of how much water is in the lake, Tahoe could supply everyone in the United States with 50 gallons of water a day for five years.

Archaeologists tell us that ancient civilizations lived here. The Washoe Indians gave the lake its name; *Tahoe* means "big water in a high place." The lake was first mapped by John C. Frémont's expedition in 1844, not long before the great Gold Rush nearby; water from the lake was used to flush out the gold. In the 1870s lumber barons decided to turn the lake into a fashionable resort. One can still find very fashionable digs, as well as many reasonably priced accommodations.

Make no mistake about it: Lake Tahoe is a major tourist attraction, and a lively tourist-oriented industry has been set up to cater to just about every whim. You don't have to worry about investing a lot of money when trying out a new sport; every kind of equipment imaginable is for rent. In addition to hedonistic temptations, there are 9 museums, 10 state parks, 30 campgrounds, and thousands of acres of national forest in the area.

Most of the action is on the south shore of the lake. If you do not wish to be alone, this is the spot for you. This is where you'll find plenty of franchised restaurants and souvenir shops. The town of Stateline is the home of most of the casinos, and the main road on the south side can get very crowded.

The north shore and the Nevada side of the lake above Stateline offer more seclusion and a less hectic scene. If this interests you, look for accommodations in the communities of Tahoe City or Carnelian Bay. Compared to the south side they are low-key, and it's an easy drive in any direction to a wilderness trail or state park.

Personally, I prefer to rent a cabin in the woods or a condo on the shore and catch up on my reading. It's relatively easy to get a cabin or a condo that comes complete with a modern kitchen and comfortable furnishings. Some of the condo complexes even offer maid service, pools, and hot tubs. Plus there are plenty of motels around.

If you visit in the summer, you might want to take a drive out to Emerald Bay State Park to visit Vikingsholm, a 38-room mansion open for tours July through Labor Day. Built in 1929 and patterned after a ninth-century Norse fortress, it's the kind of place that simply couldn't be built today. It is said to be the finest example of Scandinavian architecture in this country and is filled with Norwegian furnishings and weavings. Emerald Bay and Vikingsholm are located on the southwestern side of the lake, 17 miles south of Tahoe City. Emerald Bay is a pleasant destination any time of year.

There's a very interesting ski museum at Boreal Ridge near Donner Memorial Park. Here you can trace the history of the sport and see the skis of former Olympic champions.

For those interested in gambling, all the casinos are on the Nevada side of the lake, and they range from opulent (like Harrah's and Caesar's Tahoe) to funky (the parlors you'll find along the road on the North Shore).

There are several ways to get here. You can fly into Reno or South Lake Tahoe. At the airports you can rent a car or take a bus or a train (some hotels offer transportation).

But if you want to experience the area back-roads style, that's possible, too. Just stay in the outlying areas, like the town of Truckee to the north or even farther away in the Donner Lake area. Then you can drive to the lake, trek in the woods, or visit some of the smaller yet lovely mountain lakes that surround Tahoe.

For toll-free information on accommodations available, phone the Tahoe North Visitors and Convention Bureau, (800) 822-5959 from California or (800) 824-8557 from out of state; or the Tahoe South Visitors Bureau, (800) 822-5922 from California or (800) 824-5150 from out of state. For information on Emerald Bay, phone (916) 525-7277.

SKI MUSEUM, *Boreal Ridge. Open every day. Admission: Free. Phone: (916) 426-3313.*

HOW TO GET TO THE NORTH SHORE OF LAKE TAHOE: *From San Francisco, take the Bay Bridge to Route 80 North and take it all the way to the Truckee exit. You can stop at Truckee or you can take Route 89 South to Tahoe City.*

TO GET TO THE SOUTH SHORE OF LAKE TAHOE: *Take the Bay Bridge to Route 80 but exit near Sacramento onto Route 50. Then take Route 50 all the way into South Lake Tahoe.*

CHAPTER **13** Mendocino County

As you drive north from Sonoma County into Mendocino County, the change is immediate. If you're inland on Route 101, the four-lane highway becomes a country road that takes you through—not around—the town of Hopland. If you're on the coastal route, Route 1, the road takes even more twists and turns, and the sandy beaches give way to a rocky shoreline.

For the most part, Mendocino County is an unspoiled beauty. It's where San Franciscans go to feel like they're far from home. In this sprawling county of inland farms and rugged beaches, the largest town, Ukiah, would be considered a small town in just about any other part of the world. The major destination in the area is Mendocino. Thousands of tourists flock here each year, yet this village is so small that it isn't even incorporated.

There are three ways to get to the village of Mendocino.

One is to drive straight up the coast. This is not only the longest route but also the most trying for those who tend to get carsick when driving on constantly curvy narrow roads while hugging the ocean's edge. However, this shoreline road does take you to some lovely areas, including Sea Ranch and the old coastal town of Gualala. Sea Ranch is the famous private community of modern homes designed to blend in with the landscape. The homes are architecturally significant, and many of them are available for weekend rentals. There are also a lodge that offers overnight accommodations and a restaurant. Around Gualala the main features are the old Gualala Hotel, which still looks like it did when it was new in 1903, and, a bit north of town, St. Orre's, an inn and restaurant that looks like a small Russian palace.

I prefer to get to Mendocino by going north on Route 101 to the intersection of Route 128 in Cloverdale, then taking Route 128 through the Anderson Valley to the coastline. This joins Route 1 near the town of Albion for the short ride up to Mendocino. (I'll save the third route as the way to get back to San Francisco.)

I suggest taking Route 128 because it will take you through the very interesting little town of Boonville. If you read the gourmet writers, you've probably heard of the New Boonville Hotel, an extraordinary restaurant that transformed this little town into a tourist attraction. It was an ambitious project, which included a lavish garden to raise the food to be served in the restaurant. Well, due to financial difficulties, the restaurant folded, and now the question is what will happen to the bed-and-breakfast inns and other businesses that opened to cater to the flow of traffic generated by the defunct world-class restaurant.

Whatever does happen, Boonville is definitely worth knowing about. It is the only town in California, maybe even the United States, that has its own language. The citizens speak English, but they also speak Boontling. It's a funny version of pig latin that the locals started years ago. The town coffeeshop is called the Horn of Zeese, which is Boontling for "cup of coffee." Outside you can use the Buckey Walter, which is the telephone. Almost anywhere in town you can pick up a booklet with the most important phrases.

Boonville also happens to be in the center of the beautiful Anderson Valley, a worthy destination on its own or a pleasant stop on the road from San Francisco to Mendocino. There are several places to stay, some fine wineries (including Edmeades and Navarro), and some good places to eat. The nearby town of Philo offers some interesting places, including a combined craft gallery and inn fashioned out of a stagecoach stop originally built in 1888 (Philo Pottery Inn, 8550 Route 128, 707-895-3069).

The most valuable information resource around here is the *Anderson Valley Register,* a wonderful weekly newspaper run by a big, bearish fellow named Bruce Anderson. Bruce is a throwback to the old small-town newspaper editor who takes it upon himself to tell it like he sees it. His paper is opinionated, funny, and enterprising. He challenges the establishment, provokes the pompous, and raises hell on every issue. All this has made Bruce a controversial figure in the community, but he's also responsible for keeping people on their toes. Pick up his paper and see what you are missing in your own hometown daily.

MENDOCINO: CALIFORNIA'S NEW ENGLAND TOWN

Continuing north on Route 128 from Boonville, after the tiny towns of Philo and Navarro, you'll drive through a redwood grove and rejoin Route 1 at Albion. In about a half hour you will make your approach to Mendocino. As you enter on this southern route and you get your first glimpse of this town in the distance, you will understand immediately why this is a popular destination. The entire village sits high on a bluff overlooking the ocean. In the foreground, the blue Pacific rushes up to a cove. In the background, red, yellow, and blue Victorian homes dot the landscape, as do seasonal wildflowers. It is a spectacular entrance.

Everything in town is designed to bear the look and charm of a nineteenth-century New England town. In fact, Mendocino looks so much like a New England village that it has been used as the set in such movies as *The Russians Are Coming! The Russians Are Coming!* which was supposed to be taking place in Gloucester, Massachusetts.

Critics say the town is too precious and that too many of the shops and inns cater to the tourist trade instead of the locals. But I think there is also a genuine quality to the place, especially when you get away from the main shopping area. Mendocino first gained fame as an artist's colony, and that tradition is still alive.

Art galleries are found throughout the village, and artists are still attracted to the area. One of my favorites is Larry Fuentes, whose "trash art" sculptures have been featured on the cover of *National Geographic*. He told me he likes living in Mendocino because it's just like high school. Everybody knows everybody, and there is a protected, predictable quality to the place.

Another local artist is Byrd Baker, whose enormous sculptures of whales are to be found all over town (there's one downtown in front of MacCallum House, a bed-and-breakfast inn at 45020 Albion Street, for example). He is a large, Hemingway-like figure who wears an eye patch and has helped lead the fight for the protection of the gray whale, which can be seen swimming offshore at various times of the year. Byrd sees the whale as a symbol of life in Mendocino; he says that by saving the whale, the citizens are saving the traditions of small village life.

PYGMY FOREST

What's there to do here? Walk around on the headlands, calm down, breathe the wonderfully fresh air, shop and dine in town if you like, then head out to one of the many parks in the area. I like Van Damme State Park, which is the home of the Pygmy Forest. This is a grove of trees that have been dwarfed by a twist of fate, not to mention geological and climatic conditions (the ranger on duty can give you a more thorough explanation). These are full-grown evergreens that are about knee-high. The kick for me is to be able to walk through a forest and look down on the trees. Van Damme State Park is 3 miles south of Mendocino on Route 1; it's well marked. Phone: (707) 937-0851.

FORT BRAGG AND ITS SKUNK TRAIN

About 20 minutes north of Mendocino on Route 1 is the larger town of Fort Bragg, which is the center of the lumber industry in these parts. Fort Bragg doesn't have the architectural charm of Mendocino, but there are other attractions. Georgia-Pacific, the town's largest employer, runs a lumber museum that's open to the public; it's located on Main Street and is open Wednesday through Sunday (phone 707-964-5651). There's also a pleasant 47-acre botanical garden (18220 North Highway 1, 2 miles south of Fort Bragg, 707-964-4352) and in Noyo Harbor you'll find a busy fishing port with several good family-style fresh seafood restaurants.

But the main attraction in Fort Bragg is a working railroad called the Skunk Train. The train got its name from the days when steam locomotives ran on these tracks; you could smell one coming from miles away. Today the aroma is gone (they have switched to diesel engines), but the atmosphere and scenic ride through redwood forests are the same as in the old days. The trip is 40 miles each way, with a running commentary over a public address system pointing out significant sights along the way. You can sit inside railroad cars or stand outside in open-air cars. During the summer months it's not unusual to find a guitar-playing troubadour hired by the train company to roam the trains singing old American traveling songs.

You can spend the day on the train, taking the 80-mile round trip through the redwoods to the town of Willits. A shorter alternative is to ride the train for 20 miles to the redwood grove, where there are rest rooms, refreshment stands, and souvenir shops, and catch the next train back to Fort Bragg. This is a half-day excursion. You'll find the Skunk Train depot at the foot of Laurel Street. Just take Main Street, which is Route 1, through downtown and watch for the signs. Laurel is one block to the west, or left, of Main. Reservations are advised, especially during the summer. Phone: (707) 964-6371.

Now for that third route: For the trip back to San Francisco I suggest picking up State Route 20 south of Fort Bragg and following it east to Route 101 at Willits. Take Route 101 South all the way back to the Golden Gate Bridge and San Francisco. On this route you will see a very different kind of countryside, and you can stop in the town of Hopland (see entry 1 in the next chapter).

CHAPTER **14** Redwood Empire

AREA OVERVIEW
The giant redwoods of Northern California are legendary. The largest, most impressive concentration of these awesome trees is called the Redwood Empire, a stretch of forest that begins inland around the town of Leggett and continues north to the coastal city of Eureka. This is an area with many worthwhile destinations. The trip on Route 101 from San Francisco will take four to five hours, but it is an easy drive, and there are many diversions along the way.

About two hours from San Francisco, after you cross the Sonoma County line into Mendocino County, you'll come to the town of Hopland, a good place to stop.

HOPLAND
As the name might suggest, the town of Hopland is a place where hops were grown. In fact, this town was once a major supplier of hops to the American brewery industry. This claim to fame ended in the late 1940s when giant breweries stopped using hops in mass-produced beer. Hopland became a quiet farming community that travelers zipped past on the road to the Redwood Empire.

But today Hopland is experiencing a new lease on life, and if you stop to look around, there's a good chance you'll want to stay awhile.

One must stop is the Mendocino Brewing Company, aka the Hopland Brewery, Tavern, Beer Garden, and Restaurant, a thriving business that has brought beer back to Hopland. This is the place that started the latest California craze of brewery pubs, places that make beer in the back and sell it in front (see Buffalo Bill's, Chapter 6, entry 7). Housed in what was 100 years ago the Hop Vine Saloon, this family-style pub is a very inviting brick building, with inside walls covered with original ornamental stamped tin. In one room there is a handsome, handcrafted oak bar, reminiscent of pioneer California. The pub also includes a stage for performers on weekends and a darts area, where employees will buy you a beer if you can beat them. On a warm day you can rest a spell in the beer garden, shaded by a grape arbor, while the kids play in a sandbox.

Good pub food is available, too, including giant hamburgers, sausages, vegetarian dishes, and various daily specials, all inexpensive. As for the main attraction, the homemade beer, the pub offers four different beverages, ranging from pale ale to dark, thick stout. For the person who prefers not to drink alcohol, the pub also offers their own Hopland Seltzer, made from the same local H_2O that makes the beer so delicious.

But what if your taste runs to sweet things? Well, next door to the pub is a place called the Cheesecake Lady. This is a giant bakery and wholesale operation serving the Bay Area and Sacramento, with many types of luscious desserts available for consumption on the premises. This huge operation at first seems out of place in this neck of the woods, but the owners were able to get a lot of space for low rent in Hopland, so low that it is worth the effort to truck their goodies long distances. To accommodate visitors, there are tables and an espresso machine. After consuming a cappuccino and a slice of their chocolate mousse cake, I could have driven straight to Canada, no problem.

There are more places to visit in Hopland, right on the main road, including Country Christmas, a store featuring holiday decorations and a 9-foot teddy bear; Mendocino Woolens, where they make and sell lovely warm things; and last but not least, the California Yurt Company. In case you don't have the faintest idea what a yurt is (I didn't), it is a type of housing developed in Afghanistan, most often used as a one-room home or a giant sauna. There's a small complex of yurts sitting off the highway just south of town.

And lest we forget, the town of Hopland has a new wine industry. The Milano Winery was first, opening in 1975 in an old hop kiln just a mile south of town. A few years later Fetzer bought the old high school and turned it into a visitor's complex called Hopland Station, complete with a wine-tasting room, a crafts gallery, a gift shop, a good restaurant called Joel's (there's also a Joel's Deli in the complex), and a picnic area (where you can eat what you pick up at Joel's Deli). And just a few miles east of town on Route 175, McDowell Valley Vineyards is proud of being the nation's first solar-integrated winery. Basically that means they collect solar energy for some of their power needs.

HOPLAND BREWERY, TAVERN, BEER GARDEN, AND RESTAURANT, *13351 South Highway 101, Hopland. Hours vary each day. Tours of the brewery are possible by prior arrangement. Phone: (707) 744-1015 or (707) 744-1361.*

HOW TO GET TO HOPLAND: *From San Francisco, cross the Golden Gate Bridge and take Highway 101 about 90 miles north to the place where Route 101 changes from a four-lane highway into a busy country road. A note of caution: Logging trucks seem to appear from nowhere on this curvy stretch of road; be careful whenever entering the highway.*

LITTLE LAMBS

If this section were on television instead of in a book, it would be easy to convince you to visit this place. I would start by showing you a shot of a baby lamb staring into the camera, then racing off to its mother. Then the camera would pull back and show you hundreds of little baby lambs, all adorable and fuzzy, wobbling around on unsure legs.

We all have the image of California as the place where movies are made, high-tech industries are born, and going to the beach is a way of life. But the fact is that agriculture is the main business of the state. It's no wonder, then, that the University of California runs nine different research facilities around the state to study land use, animal behavior, and ecology.

The Hopland Field Station is one of these university-run experimental farms. Here the specialty is sheep, thousands of them. And while researchers are studying breeding, nutrition, grazing management, and wool production, visitors get a rare opportunity to mingle with some of the most entertaining and lovable creatures on earth.

Hopland is the largest of the university's field stations. More than 5300 acres encompass low valleys and brush-covered hills. You can wander around at your leisure or schedule a tour at the range office. A small community of full-time workers lives down by the barns, and they love to have visitors. You can drive down to the visitor's center and not worry about great distances, if you are not a hiker.

What you will see depends on what time of year you visit. From mid-January through March is ramming time, when the ewes give birth. If you miss the actual event, you will certainly see lambs just a day or two old. In spring the hills are awash with wildflowers, and it's shearing time. At all times of the year the daily routines are interesting to watch. It's not every day we get to see a sheepdog and shepherd in a pasture rounding up 50 sheep, the dog moving them exactly where the master wants them to go.

When I was there, I simply sat alone on a hillside, away from all the barns and experimental activity, just watching and listening. There were no cars, no airplanes, just a symphony of baas.

HOPLAND FIELD STATION, *4070 University Road, Hopland. Phone: (707) 744-1424.*

HOW TO GET HERE: *From Hopland, take Route 175 East toward Lakeport. When you come to Valley Oaks Ranch, turn left at the fork and follow the signs to the Hopland Field Station.*

The coastal redwoods of Northern California are worth the trip. Nowhere in the world are there more majestic trees or more beautiful forests. I also doubt if anywhere in the world you can find so many roadside attractions, ranging from truly tacky to just plain funny.

You will see the signs as you near the town of Leggett. There's the Drive-Thru Tree Park, a 240-acre operation with a picnic area, a store, many trails, and, yes, a tree with a road going through it. It costs $2 to enter the park, and you can stay as long as you like, driving through the tree as many times as you like. A quick tree fact: The drive-thru tree is alive, which is proof that the nutrients for the giant redwoods are located on the outside, not the inside, of the trunk.

Farther up the road, the attractions seem to appear with every curve in the highway. There's the store in a tree, the train ride through a tree, and shops selling redwood burl in every grotesque design imaginable. Soon Route 101 again becomes a four-lane highway, and that's where you should look for the turnoff for the Avenue of the Giants. This is a 33-mile stretch of road that parallels the freeway. Actually it's the old Route 101, a two-lane, tree-lined drive through a majestic redwood forest.

From the avenue you can take a back road that leads to the best of the redwood groves, called the Rockefeller Forest. Many of the trees to be found here are virgin growth, meaning they have never been cut. These trees are believed to be at least 3000 years old. You can stay in your car and drive around, or you can park and then walk into areas where you will be virtually alone with nature.

This grove contains what is said to be the tallest tree in the West. In case you're wondering how anybody figures out this sort of thing, park rangers used to measure by floating balloons connected to a kind of measuring tape to the top; but since it's difficult to see the tops of the trees from underneath, it was a less than accurate technique. Today they use elaborate laser beam technology, but even so it's still a matter of estimates.

The Rockefeller Forest is part of Humboldt Redwoods State Park. If you have the time, stop in at park headquarters, which is located right on the Avenue of the Giants, just 2 miles south of Weott. This is the largest of California's state parks. A sawmill for public viewing is in operation in the Rockefeller Forest. They only saw trees that have fallen down naturally, and the wood is then used to build facilities for other park centers. If you are on a tight schedule, the rangers recommend that you at least visit Founder's Grove. This is right off the Avenue of the Giants north of Weott and features a scenic, easy-to-walk, self-guided nature trail. The grove is dedicated to the founders of the Save the Redwoods League, the group responsible for stopping the wholesale logging of the area in the 1920s.

HUMBOLDT REDWOODS STATE PARK. *Phone: (707) 946-2311.*

SCOTIA: A COMPANY TOWN

Scotia is a must stop on a trip to the redwoods. It is one of the few official company towns left in the United States. By "official company town" I mean that the entire town is owned by one business, in this case the Pacific Lumber Company. The only other one I know of is in the coal-mining region of West Virginia, which is hardly as attractive a setting for visitors as Scotia.

Located about 30 miles south of Eureka off Route 101, Scotia is smack in the middle of the Redwood Empire, surrounded by forests, rolling hills, and the Eel River. You know you're in a lumber town right away when you see two of the more imposing buildings in the center of town. They are made entirely of redwood, including the doric columns, which would be made of marble or cement anywhere else.

One of these buildings is City Hall, which is really the main office of Pacific Lumber. Here you'll be greeted and given a glossy visitor's guide that tells you the history of the firm and all about forest management. I should point out that Pacific Lumber was always regarded by environmentalists as one of the most enlightened lumber companies. In fact, even as far back as the 1920s they held off logging what is now Humboldt State Park until the Save the Redwoods League could buy the land for the state park system. However, in 1986 the company changed owners in a hostile takeover, and the jury is still out on how the company will operate in the future.

The visitor's guide includes a small piece of redwood on which is printed the directions for a self-guided tour through the mill. Do it, by all means. You can see the entire process, from the unloading of newly cut trees to the final cutting of boards. Most people spend an hour or two, mesmerized by the sight of huge logs being tossed around by even bigger machines. Two of the highlights are the hydraulic barker (which strips bark off the tree with giant bursts of water) and the edgerman (an area where giant saws are maneuvered by remote control to shape the logs into specific sizes). Everything on the tour is bigger than life, just like the redwood trees. It is also very loud.

As for the town itself, take the time to drive around and visit with the residents. Many are second- and third-generation Scotians. They live in company-owned houses, go to company-run schools, and begin and end life in the company-owned hospital. Scotia has some 300 homes of varying sizes. A typical three-bedroom unit rents for about $200 a month, deducted from the worker's paycheck.

Another thing about life in a company town: You never have to set an alarm. The whistle blows at 6:30 A.M. to wake everyone up and again at 7:25 A.M. to let people know they have five minutes to get to work.

Scotia has a downtown of sorts, with a grocery, a hardware store, a clothing store, and even a diner—all owned by the company but leased to private operators. The diner, by the way, is remarkably good, especially considering it's the only eatery in town that's open for lunch. At the counter you'll see the names of Pacific workers at each setting. They are apparently born into their own counter seat. Visitors should ask where they may sit. The booths are fair game.

The Scotia Inn is a nice place to stay, with fairly luxurious rooms and a formal dining room. In the olden days this grand hotel was for guests only and workers were discouraged from entering. Nowadays locals are encouraged to use the hotel facilities. Many community events take place here, so this is another good place to get to know the town. Overnight guests will also get the 6:30 A.M. wake-up call; there's no way to avoid it.

Much to the chagrin of many of the ladies in town, the company also runs a men's club, meaning for gentlemen only. Inside there's a color TV and pool table —the sort of things one would expect to find in a den of males. One of the wives described it to me as "just a place where men can go to get away from their wives." (It makes me wonder where the women go to get away from their husbands.) Visitors must be accompanied by a member.

SCOTIA. *Tours of the town are offered without appointment, unless you have a group of 10 or more, weekdays from 7:30 to 10:30 A.M. and 12:30 to 2:30 P.M. A logging museum is open to visitors in the summer. For visitor's information, call (707) 764-2222.*

SCOTIA INN. *For reservations and information, call (707) 764-5683.*

HOW TO GET TO SCOTIA: *From San Francisco, cross the Golden Gate Bridge and take Route 101 North about four hours. Follow the signs to Scotia.*

HISTORIC FERNDALE

The town of Ferndale, or "Historic Ferndale," as the road signs on Route 101 call it, is almost too cute to be real. It is an almost perfect Victorian village, filled with color and colorful characters. This small town of 1100 residents features such things as a repertory theater, a rare-book store, a blacksmith shop, two bed-and-breakfast inns, and clean public rest rooms with a Victorian exterior. There's a pool hall called Becker's where the locals gather for lunch, cards, reading, and conversation—everything except pool because Becker's has no pool table.

The characters, who are only too willing to put on a show for you, include Carlos the bookstore owner, who won his place in a poker game, he says with a wink. Maybe he did, maybe he didn't, but it doesn't really matter; it's the story that counts. Carlos is one of the town spokesmen, a world traveler who settled in Ferndale about 20 years ago. He points to the fact that Ferndale looks the way it does because it never suffered a major fire or other catastrophe, so it never needed to be rebuilt.

Joe the Blacksmith has another way of looking at the authenticity of the town. He calls Ferndale "the old town that other cities are trying to create." As you walk down Main Street, the point becomes clear. The stores and services are not just for tourists. You'll find a full range of community services: pharmacy, hardware store, butcher shop, jeweler, bank, bakery, dry cleaner's, and so on, with a few boutiques and candy shops tossed in for the visitors.

What's there to do? The Chamber of Commerce schedules several events throughout the year that draw attention from all over the world. One is the Foggy Bottoms Milk Run, a race through three of the area's dairy farms, held each March. Another is the Arcata-to-Ferndale Cross-Country Kinetic Sculpture Race, a three-day affair held each Memorial Day weekend. This race is the brainchild of Hobart Brown, who runs the local art gallery. He's also a sculptor, and he collects crazy-looking vehicles that look like soapbox racers on drugs. Participants in the race build these exotic machines, powered by the individual's own energy, usually by pedaling. The contraptions are truly amazing, and the race eventually turns into one big party.

If there has ever been a town where you can simply take off your watch and forget about the rest of the world, Ferndale is it. It is a place for doing nothing but hanging out and talking to people. It will stay that way, too; the state has declared it a historic landmark, giving it protection from wholesale development or other major changes.

FERNDALE. *A walking tour guide is available from the Ferndale Chamber of Commerce, 428 Francis Street. Phone: (707) 786-4477. You can also write for a brochure of events scheduled throughout the year: Ferndale Chamber of Commerce, P.O. Box 525, Ferndale, CA 95536.*

HOW TO GET TO FERNDALE: *Just look for the signs along Route 101, approximately 30 minutes south of Eureka.*

EUREKA "Eureka" is the motto of California, the exclamation shouted by the Greek scientist Archimedes when he discovered a way to determine the purity of gold. In the town of Eureka, some real treasures are to be found.

Treasure Number One: Here you'll find the most elaborate, unbelievable, astonishing Victorian home in the world. The Carson House overlooks the old town from the foot of Second Street. From a distance it looks unreal and becomes no less fantastic as you stand outside the gate. Unfortunately, that's as close as you'll get, since it is now used as a private club and no tours are offered.

But that hardly diminishes the spectacle. Built in 1884 by a lumber baron named William Carson, the home features a 68-foot tower, eight gables, balconies, porches, pillars, intricate moldings, stained-glass windows, and gingerbread trim. It sits alone surrounded by lush lawns and colorful gardens. Legend has it that more than 100 craftsmen worked on the mansion. It apparently inspired other homeowners and builders, as the city features many Victorian gems. The Chamber of Commerce offers a pamphlet with the location of more than 30 homes worth seeing. The Carson House is located at Second and M streets. The Chamber of Commerce is located at 2112 Broadway; its phone number is (707) 442-3738.

Treasure Number Two: Down the street from the Carson House, in the center of the newly restored Old Town, is the Romano Gabriel Sculpture Garden. The story of this rare work of folk art tells you a lot about this city and its priorities.

Romano was a reclusive old gent who lived alone in a quiet section of town. Over the course of several years he built an elaborate sculpture garden in front of his little house, fashioning brightly colored figures and flowers and trees out of old orange crates; eventually the entire house was blocked from view. Locals believe that his "art" was his way of communicating with the town.

When Romano died in the late 1970s no one knew what to do with the sculpture garden. The new owners of the house didn't want it, so finally some art-loving citizens intervened, the historical society bought the sculptures, and the city provided a permanent display area.

This is primitive art. Like much of modern art, it is what you think it is, and you could spend hours admiring the intricate details. The sculpture garden is on display at 315 Second Street between D and E streets.

Also of interest: Fort Humboldt State Historic Park, a small redwoods park just outside of town. This is where Ulysses S. Grant was stationed in the 1850s and early 1860s. There was little to do, and apparently he was drunk most of the time. He got wind that he was to be court-martialed, so, to avoid the inevitable, Grant turned in his resignation only to be informed he would be needed for the Civil War. The rest, as they say, is history. He went on to become a general in the Union Army, then president of the United States, but apparently never did stop drinking. Today the pre–Civil War outpost has been partially restored, and there are displays of pioneer logging methods. The view of Humboldt Bay makes this a nice spot for a picnic. The park is located at 3431 Fort Avenue, above Route 101 at the south end of town; the phone number is (707) 443-7952.

I should note that Eureka is a town in transition. It has been hit hard by a bad fishing economy and a changing lumber industry. There is a move to establish tourism as a major industry, but there are not a lot of attractions or services yet.

Still, the city offers great hospitality and can be used as your headquarters for a visit to the Redwood Empire. There is one grand old inn in the Old Town section, the Eureka Inn, which offers comfortable rooms for much less than you would pay for the same room in a larger city. It is located on the corner of Seventh and F streets, phone (707) 442-6441.

I should also point out that the weather is often cloudy or rainy. Count on summers to be foggy, with only occasional periods of sunshine. As in San Francisco, your best bet for sunny and warm weather is either spring or fall.

EUREKA *Chamber of Commerce, 2112 Broadway. Phone: (707) 442-3738.*

HOW TO GET TO EUREKA: *From San Francisco, cross the Golden Gate Bridge and take Route 101 North 235 miles.*

CHAPTER **15** Monterey Peninsula

AREA OVERVIEW

The beach resort of Santa Cruz sits on the northern tip of Monterey Bay. On the other side is the Monterey Peninsula, which you can reach by continuing south on Route 1. Here you will find the famous tourist destinations of Monterey and Carmel.

An Italian friend once prepared me for a visit to Venice by saying that it was Italy's version of Disneyland. I think the same holds true for Monterey and Carmel. They are Northern California's Disneyland. Not only does everything appear to have been arranged for tourists, but there is also a fantasy quality to these places; the countryside and coastline are almost too beautiful to be real, and the shops and restaurants (especially in Carmel) look like stage sets.

Still, these are wonderful places to visit. Since the idea of this book is to offer alternatives to the crowded tourist scenes, I will concentrate here on places you might overlook.

OLD MONTEREY

Monterey is the big city in the area. It used to be the center of activity in Northern California, until the Gold Rush turned San Francisco into a boomtown. Today most of the action is around the Fisherman's Wharf area and Cannery Row. Both places are collections of touristy shops and attractions, the kind you'll find at San Francisco's Fisherman's Wharf. However, the wonderful Monterey Aquarium is there and should not be missed. Get a reservation and go, but don't waste a lot of time hanging around the wharf or Cannery Row. The aquarium is located at 886 Cannery Row. It is open every day from 10 A.M. to 6 P.M.; closed

Christmas. Admission for adults is $7; students and seniors, $5; children 12 and under, $3. Phone: (408) 375-3333.

You can visit a real working wharf at the foot of Figueroa Street, where commercial fishing boats unload the catch of the day into huge processing plants. No organized tours are offered, but you can stroll around and watch the operation on your own.

If you are interested in Mexican and early California history, several well-preserved buildings are in the Monterey State Historic Park, near the downtown area on Olivier Street. These include the Custom House, the oldest government building on the West Coast; California's first theater; and the Pacific House, which is a museum of California history. You can pick up a map of the historic buildings at the Custom House, located at 1 Custom Plaza. The museums are open from 9 A.M. to 5 P.M. Phone: (408) 649-2836.

PACIFIC GROVE: HOME OF THE BUTTERFLIES

If the crowds in Monterey get to you, head south to Pacific Grove. This is a more relaxed and quaint waterfront community, filled with Victorian homes, inviting parks, and nice restaurants and inns. Pacific Grove's claim to fame is that it is the monarch butterfly capital. Like the swallows that return to Capistrano each year, millions of monarch butterflies arrive in Pacific Grove every October to lay their eggs. You're likely to find them in the trees adjacent to the Butterfly Grove Inn, 1073 Lighthouse Avenue; another winter home is Washington Park, which is bordered by Sinex, Short, Alder, and Melrose streets. If you time it right, you'll also see the annual October festival to welcome the monarchs, a celebration that includes a parade of marching bands and children dressed as butterflies.

Another attraction in Pacific Grove is the less costly alternative to the 17-Mile Drive, which most guide books list as a must-see. This is a beautiful, privately owned stretch of oceanfront property that takes you through the Del Monte Forest (owned by the giant canning company) and past luxurious homes, pristine beaches, and the famous Pebble Beach Golf Course.

The only problem is it costs $5 per car to take the drive. Since it irks me even to pay bridge tolls, I can't get myself to plunk down five bucks to drive on the Del Monte company's road. Instead, I take the free 4-mile drive along Ocean View Beach in Pacific Grove and spend the extra five bucks on lunch. Along the way are beautiful Victorian homes, a terrific view of the ocean, tidepools, and the Point Pinos Lighthouse. Built in 1855, it is the oldest continuously operating lighthouse on the Pacific Coast. It stands at the entrance to Monterey Harbor, at the end of Ocean View Boulevard. The lighthouse is open to the public Saturday and Sunday 1 to 4 P.M., with tours given by the Coast Guard. Phone: (408) 373-3304.

Near the lighthouse along the ocean you will come to the often empty beach at Asilomar, a name that means "refuge by the sea." This is a state-run park and conference center, which includes 103 acres of pine forest. Business groups and others may rent the facilities, which include a lodge, several housing units, meetings rooms, and a dining area. Individuals and couples may rent inexpensive accommodations, when available. Phone: (408) 372-8016.

CLINT EASTWOOD'S CARMEL

If you want crowds, you'll find them in Carmel or, as the Chamber of Commerce likes it to be called, Carmel-by-the-Sea. This is a picture-postcard little village, and it ought to be seen at least once. Carmel's success seems to be due to its original intended charm, a simple coastal town and colony for artists and writers. The buildings have no address numbers, billboards and large commercial signs are prohibited, and there is very little in the way of street lighting.

Yet this very quaintness, not to mention the spectacular beach at the end of town, draws more and more visitors each year. And ever since the town's most famous resident, Clint Eastwood, was elected mayor in 1986, even more tourists are flocking in.

My advice is to see Carmel's downtown briefly, then head to two of the area's historical attractions, Tor House and the Carmel Mission.

ROBINSON JEFFERS'S CARMEL

Tor House was the home of the late poet Robinson Jeffers. Though it is only a few miles from the center of town, it feels like another world entirely. The home is a symbol of the original Carmel, before it became a tourist mecca.

Jeffers was a man of nature. He was also an outspoken man of letters, and he was a constant thorn in the sides of those who wanted to turn Carmel into a tourist paradise. He hated them, and they hated him.

At his home you will see Jeffers's vision of how the coast should be treated. He personally built the house of rough rock so that it is in harmony with the natural landscape. He also built a stone tower that affords a magnificent view of the ocean, if you're willing to climb to the top.

Inside, the home is just as it was when the poet was living and writing here. Many of his manuscripts remain, as do the personal artifacts of his life. His widow still occupies the home in front of Tor House. The house is maintained by a group of local residents who want to perpetuate Jeffers's memory and to keep the original artist colony spirit alive in Carmel. They charge a small admission for touring the home and also hold readings and other fund-raising events throughout the year to pay for the upkeep.

Tours of Tor House are given on Friday and Saturday; admission is $5. For reservations and more information, you can contact the Tor House Foundation at P.O. Box 1887, Carmel, CA 93921, or by phone at (408) 624-1813. They will give you directions to the house.

The Carmel Mission is located at the south of Rio Road. This is where Father Junipero Serra established headquarters for the Northern California mission system. It was his residence and headquarters until his death in 1784. Father Serra's remains are buried here, in front of the altar in the faithfully restored basilica. The mission will probably be crowded with tourists (even Pope John Paul II visited in 1987), but there are quiet places on the grounds to rest and reflect, particularly in the courtyards that link the various parish buildings. The mission also includes a museum with some of the original artifacts from Father Serra's day.

CARMEL MISSION, *3080 Rio Road, Carmel. Phone: (408) 624-3600.*

HOW TO GET HERE: *From downtown Carmel, get back on Route 1 and head south until you come to Rio Road, which is a major intersection. Turn right on Rio Road, and the mission is just a few blocks away on the left.*

CARMEL MISSION

It's about an hour's drive from Carmel down the coast to Big Sur, and I heartily recommend it. In fact, this is one of the most scenic drives in the world.

Many visitors come to the area looking for a town called Big Sur. Well, to paraphrase Gertrude Stein, there is no Big Sur in Big Sur. It is 70 miles, more or less, of craggy peaks, beautiful forests, and breathtaking coastline that does not have any official boundaries. The residents, many of them artists and writers, like it that way.

Route 1 is the main road through Big Sur, and almost any attraction you would like to see is right along it.

One way to explore the area is to pull into one of the several state parks and start walking. Pfeiffer State Park, for example, features a self-guided nature hike. Along the way you're likely to see coastal redwoods, sycamores, and cotton-woods, raccoons, wild boars, and unusual birds like water ousels and belted kingfishers. This park is located about 37 miles south of Carmel. For more information about state parks in the area, call (408) 667-2315.

Big Sur is also the home of the famous Esalen Institute, where many of the innovative psychotherapists of the 1960s first explored the human potential movement. It is still a center for healing and experimentation, closed to the public except during the middle of the night, when they open their hot springs for a fee. Phone ahead first for the current schedule and directions: (408) 667-2335.

The major literary figure in Big Sur was Henry Miller, who lived here from the late 1940s to the mid-1960s. His former home is now a memorial library, containing many original manuscripts and mementos from Miller's life. The library is run by the late author's old friend, painter Emile White, and is open by appointment only from 9 A.M. to noon daily. Phone: (408) 667-2574.

If there is one must stop in Big Sur, it is Nepenthe, located on the right side

BIG SUR

of the road (going south) a few miles past a series of small resorts on the Big Sur River. It is well marked. Even though you are likely to run into a lot of other tourists, you'll also be able to rub elbows with the locals. It's the unofficial community center of the area. The name comes from a mythical Egyptian drug meaning "no sorrow."

Nepenthe is definitely a place to see. Sitting 800 feet above the ocean, with a remarkable view of the coast, Nepenthe is a restaurant, a gift shop, or just a place to sit in the sun with a drink in your hand. A protégé of Frank Lloyd Wright designed the main restaurant; following the teachings of the master, the buildings look as though they have always been a part of the landscape. The design is spectacular in its simplicity, and whether you are outside on the huge deck or inside the dining pavilion, you always have the sense you are nowhere else but Big Sur.

The place has a romantic history. The original main house was spotted in the 1940s by Orson Welles and Rita Hayworth as they were driving from Carmel to Los Angeles. They decided it would be a perfect honeymoon cottage and bought the place. According to the present owners, Orson and Rita spent about eight hours on the site, arguing about the drapes and this and that, and never came back.

The food is decent, ranging from standard burgers to vegetarian specials. If you are hungry and the wait is too long in the restaurant, down below there's a smaller café, the Café Amphora, adjacent to the combination art gallery and gift shop (which is called the Phoenix). At the Amphora you'll find light fare like sandwiches, good coffee, and wonderful desserts you can enjoy outdoors on the lower terrace. Nepenthe opens at noon daily. Phone: (408) 667-2345.

HOW TO GET TO BIG SUR: *Simply continue south on Route 1 from Carmel for about an hour.*

Restaurants

Each week on the *Bay Area Backroads* television program I recommend a few places to eat. In this section of the book, you will find a listing of some of my favorite spots.

First of all, I believe that the Bay Area features some of the best restaurants in the world. Several culinary trends began here, most significantly California cuisine. This cooking is based on the fact that Bay Area restaurants have access to the region's rich bounty of land and sea—the freshest produce, fish, and dairy products imaginable.

There are famous and influential restaurants here: Chez Panisse in Berkeley, Masa's in San Francisco, and many more. Such places are well publicized in other publications. So, just like the criteria for the back-roads stories, I look for places you might not hear about otherwise that offer good food and good value. And I will not mention franchised or fast-food operations. I look for personal places that offer fresh ingredients, interesting atmosphere, and fair prices. Please keep in mind also that I am not a restaurant critic, just someone with a healthy appetite who loves good food.

It is difficult to report specific hours and menu prices since they change so often. Instead of hours I will state which meals the place serves, unless the hours of operation are unusual. Instead of fixed dollar amounts I will use the categories "inexpensive," "moderate," and "expensive." I realize these are relative terms, determined by one's own wallet. For the purpose of this book, "inexpensive" will mean that there are currently (1987) many lunch items $5 and under, sandwiches are $3.50 to $4, and desserts cost $2 or less. It means a cup of coffee is 50 or 60 cents. For dinners, "inexpensive" means there are entrees in the $6 and

$7 category and that two people can feel satisfied and still get out of the place with a $10 to $15 tab.

"Moderate" means that there are many lunch items for $8 to $10. It means that sandwiches are offered for around $5 and that desserts are in the $2.50 to $3 range. A cup of coffee is usually under $1. For dinner, "moderate" means that entrees average in the $10 to $12 range and that two people can dine for $30 to $40, exclusive of wine.

"Expensive" is anything above the moderate category.

Keep in mind that since there are so many restaurants in the area, competition is intense, and changes are frequent. Chefs move on to new jobs, quality can vary, and yesterday's hit can be history by the time you get there. Please call ahead to check current hours and prices.

Marin County

BOLINAS ✔ **Bolinas Bay Bakery.** If you're in Bolinas and you find yourself hungry and in need of hospitality, head to the Bolinas Bay Bakery. The people are genuinely friendly and helpful, and they really know how to bake. The New York cheesecake reminded me of the heyday of Lindy's, the pecan pie is filled with nuts instead of syrupy glop, and the more health-conscious items are good, too. You can also get lunch to take outside and eat on the steps; you can act like a local, watching the tourists go by.

BOLINAS BAY BAKERY, *15 Wharf Road. (415) 868-0211. Open 7 A.M. to 6 P.M. weekdays, 8 A.M. to 6 P.M. weekends; open Monday to 8 P.M. for Pizza Night. Inexpensive.*

CORTE MADERA ✔ **Savannah Grill.** For years Marin was considered to be a wasteland as far as restaurants go. But in the mid-1980s the culinary trends that began in Berkeley and San Francisco finally moved across the Golden Gate Bridge. Now there are several fine places to eat in Marin, and perhaps the most popular is the Savannah Grill.

This is yet another restaurant run by the same people who run Mustard's in Napa Valley, the Fog City Diner in San Francisco, and the Rio Café in Carmel. Though each place has its own unique flavor, the formula is the same: the finest ingredients put together in interesting combinations, minimal decor with lots of fresh flowers (Fog City Diner is an exception), and a menu that offers complete meals or light snacks. In this health-conscious area, it is not unusual for customers to have just an appetizer and salad or a small plate of pasta instead of an entree. No matter what, everything they make at Savannah's is very good. Reservations are advised.

SAVANNAH GRILL, *55 Tamal Vista. (415) 924-6774. Lunch Monday through Friday, dinner daily, brunch Saturday and Sunday. Moderate.*

✔ **Barnaby's.** This is the restaurant connected to the Golden Hinde Motel, right on Tomales Bay in Inverness. You can eat inside in an airy dining room with floor-to-ceiling windows overlooking the water, or you can be served outside on the deck.

The menu features fresh fish and seafood, salads, and barbecued items like chicken and ribs. There's also a selection of appetizers like stuffed potato skins filled with enough stuff to make an entire lunch.

BARNABY'S, *in the Golden Hinde Motel, right on Sir Francis Drake Boulevard as you travel from Inverness to the Point Reyes Lighthouse, just a few minutes from the center of town. (415) 669-1114. Lunch and dinner Thursday through Tuesday; closed Wednesday. Moderate.*

✔ **Chez Madeleine.** This is a very nice country French restaurant, serving unpretentious dinners. Madeleine herself will probably greet you, then run back to check things in the kitchen. The menu offers items you find on most French menus in the United States, all of them well prepared. It's a very informal place, bustling with locals and tourists.

CHEZ MADELEINE, *Inverness Junction on Highway 1. (415) 663-9177. Dinner only, Wednesday through Sunday. Moderate.*

✔ **Vladimir's.** This Czech restaurant is right in the center of town, such as it is, and is decorated like a café in the mountains of Central Europe. The outdoor patio overlooks the traffic of Sir Francis Drake Boulevard and Tomales Bay.

The food and the owner are definitely authentic Czech. You'll get dumplings with everything, including such specials as roast duck and schnitzel. Be in the mood for a substantial and tasty meal. And Vladimir is a charming host.

VLADIMIR'S, *Sir Francis Drake Boulevard and Inverness Way. (415) 669-1021. Lunch Tuesday, Wednesday, Friday, and Saturday; dinner Tuesday through Sunday. Moderate.*

✔ **La Lanterna.** This is a very popular neighborhood Italian restaurant, and for good reason. La Lanterna serves very authentic Italian cuisine at modest prices. In addition to the regular menu, there is a fine buffet lunch offered for about $7, which gives you an opportunity to taste the many talents of the chef. The marinated vegetable dishes are a highlight, and there are always at least two hot meat dishes. The regular menu features a large selection of well-made pasta dishes, plus chicken, veal, and fish.

INVERNESS

KENTFIELD

LA LANTERNA *is at 799 College Avenue, in a small shopping center. (415) 258-0144. Open daily for lunch and dinner. Reservations are advised. Moderate.*

LARKSPUR √ **Marvin Gardens.** If you have ever played Monopoly, you will probably be tempted to try a place that calls itself Marvin Gardens. You won't be sorry. Tucked away off the street in a little shopping center, Marvin's is a comfortable neighborhood café offering an unusual selection of dishes.

Daily specials always feature an Indian curry, a Mexican dish or two, and an Italian frittata in addition to the regular fare of burgers, omelets, soups, and salads. All the food is well prepared. Try the desserts, especially the chocolate mousse cake.

MARVIN GARDENS, *1000 Magnolia. (415) 461-2241. Lunch Monday through Saturday, dinner Thursday, Friday, and Saturday; closed Sunday. Inexpensive to moderate.*

MARSHALL √ **Tony's.** One of the favorite outings for people in the Bay Area is to head to Point Reyes for a day at the beach and then drive up the coast to the town of Marshall for barbecued oysters. Tony's is a charming place offering this specialty for you oyster lovers.

Overlooking Tomales Bay, Tony's also offers fresh seafood and Italian specialties to go along with the main attraction. The atmosphere is very informal, with red-checkered tablecloths, big outdoor grills, and mounds of empty oyster shells lying around.

TONY'S SEAFOOD, *Highway 1, just south of the town of Marshall. (415) 663-1107. Lunch and dinner Friday, Saturday, and Sunday; open Monday in summer. Moderate.*

MILL VALLEY √ **Avenue Grill.** From the decor you might think the Avenue Grill is a bit fancy and pricey, but no; despite the cushy surroundings it's a very informal place with prices in the moderate-plus range.

The food is California cuisine, meaning they specialize in whatever is freshest that day. They even tell you where they get their vegetables and naturally fed beef. There are also touches of the diner revival with such items as meatloaf and burgers.

AVENUE GRILL, *44 East Blithedale Avenue. (415) 388-6003. Dinner daily. Moderate to expensive.*

√ **Café Renoir.** It takes a bit to find Café Renoir, at the end of Shoreline Highway north of Sausalito, but it's worth the search. This tiny café, situated in the rear of an office complex, offers the best salads I have ever had, in addition to other light fare. By all means, try the chicken salad, which is lightly curried, and light fare. By all means, try the chicken salad, which is lightly curried, and served on a variety of wonderfully fresh lettuces, inside an avocado. Coffees and pastries are also top-notch, and you can sit on the patio on a warm day.

CAFÉ RENOIR, *100 Shoreline Highway, near Route 101. (415) 332-8668. Open from 7:30 A.M. to 7 P.M. Inexpensive to moderate.*

✔ **Depot Books and Café.** For years, the semi-seedy Book Depot in the center of town was the place where the literati and filmmakers of southern Marin hung out. Then in 1987, the place was purchased, spruced up, and turned into the new, improved Depot Books and Café. You can still get a good cappuccino and pastry while rubbing elbows with writers and filmmakers, but you can also have a nice lunch and a light dinner. As the name implies, this coffeehouse was fashioned from the town's old train depot and is an excellent bookstore. It's a very pleasant place to sit and read.

DEPOT BOOKS AND CAFÉ, *87 Throckmorton Avenue. (415) 383-2665. Breakfast, lunch, and light dinners daily. Inexpensive to moderate.*

✔ **Santa Fe Mary's.** You wouldn't expect to find a New Mexico–style restaurant in the center of the suburban town of Novato, but that's exactly what Santa Fe Mary's is. I say "New Mexico–style," because the food is not as spicy as the authentic food of the Southwest, but the food is good, and it is an attractive place. You will find everything from typical Mexican specialties to mesquite-grilled items. Some customers settle for Coronas and nachos or other appetizers. Santa Fe Mary's can be jammed in the evenings, as it's probably the liveliest spot in town. Lunchtimes are usually less crowded.

SANTA FE MARY'S, *1200 Grant Avenue. (415) 898-2234. Lunch Monday through Friday, dinner daily. Moderate.*

NOVATO

✔ **Drake's Beach Café.** When you're out at Point Reyes National Seashore, you are a long way from a restaurant. Fortunately, the café adjoining one of the Seashore's visitor's centers is surprisingly good. The Drake's Beach Café ought to be the model for luncheonettes and snack bars at every beach in the United States.

It's a small place with a few tables inside and lots of tables outside overlooking the ocean. Just like every other snack bar in the world, they have burgers and hot dogs, except these are thick, hand-pressed real beef burgers served on great whole-wheat buns from a local bakery and juicy, well-seasoned franks. I tasted both the New England clam chowder and the split pea soup and they were definitely homemade. Also featured are local oysters, vegetarian specials, really good coffee from Graffeo's in San Francisco, and great desserts.

Prices are inexpensive, and the only disadvantage is that the café can be crowded when the weather is good at Drake's Beach.

POINT REYES NATIONAL SEASHORE

DRAKE'S BEACH CAFÉ, *at the end of Sir Francis Drake Boulevard at the ocean's edge, adjoining the visitor's center. (415) 669-1297. Open 11:30 A.M. to 6 P.M. weekdays, 10 A.M. to 6 P.M. weekends; closed on stormy days. Inexpensive.*

POINT REYES STATION

✓ **Station House Café.** If I had only one mealtime to spend in the Inverness-Point Reyes area, I would eat at the Station House Café. This is an informal place in the center of Point Reyes Station, famous for its mooing town clock (see Chapter 1, destination 13). The food here is terrific. You can get everything from egg dishes to great hamburgers on homemade buns to pasta to grilled fresh fish, and it's all prepared perfectly. Be sure to save room for one of their desserts and a cappuccino.

STATION HOUSE CAFE, *Main Street. (415) 663-1470. Breakfast, lunch, and dinner Wednesday through Monday; closed Tuesday. Inexpensive to moderate.*

SAN ANSELMO

✓ **Bubba's Diner.** This is a wonderful place to have breakfast or lunch and to be coddled. The "Bubba" in the name is not the nickname for a former defensive tackle, it's Yiddish for grandmother. When you come in here, you are almost ordered to eat and eat a lot.

Breakfasts feature a variety of egg dishes with a half plate full of hash browns. You can have muffins or bagels or huge fluffy biscuits, too. At lunch, you might want some homemade soup, a giant salad, or one of their unusual sandwich creations. And then, just try to get out without having dessert, I dare ya.

BUBBA'S DINER, *566 San Anselmo Avenue. (415) 459-6862. Breakfast and lunch Monday through Thursday. Breakfast, lunch and dinner, Friday, Saturday, and Sunday. Inexpensive.*

✓ **Comforts.** San Anselmo may have taken the lead in tiny restaurants and cafés per capita, especially those that feature an espresso machine.

One of the nicest is called Comforts. On the lunch menu are several fresh salads, a black bean chili, Thai lemon-lime chicken soup, and pasta primavera, among other items. This international flavor is carried over to dinner, with items like polenta, sashimi, and gado-gado, as well as simply grilled salmon and pasta.

Comforts also offers take-out service, and all the food is nicely prepared.

COMFORTS, *337 San Anselmo Avenue. (415) 454-6790. Open daily for breakfast, lunch, and dinner. Moderate.*

SAN RAFAEL

✓ **Café Pranzo.** Pranzo means lunch or dinner in Italian, which pretty well describes this cozy and contemporary restaurant. Pasta is king here, served in a variety of shapes and sauces. You'll also find fresh fish, veal, chicken, and beef, and the feeling of a trattoria in Italy.

CAFÉ PRANZO, *706 3rd Street. (415) 459-3553. Open for lunch and dinner Monday through Saturday; dinner only on Sunday. Moderate.*

✔ **Café Tango.** Tapas are the main bill of fare at Tango. In case you're not familiar with tapas, they are "little tastes" of food that are served in bars and cafés throughout Spain. The only thing that is not quite authentic, which is fine for me, is that the portions are quite large at Tango. They are also very tasty.

CAFÉ TANGO, *1232 4th Street. (415) 459-2721. Open from 9 A.M. to 11 P.M. Monday through Saturday, 11 A.M. to 5 P.M. Sunday. Inexpensive.*

✔ **Phyllis' Giant Burgers.** This looks like a place you'd find in the Midwest instead of Marvelous Marin. But here it is, with nothing on the menu but hamburgers and accompaniments like grilled onions, fries, cole slaw, and milkshakes. The giant burgers are just that, and you can have them with bacon and/or your choice of four kinds of cheeses. Phyllis' wins the Best Hamburger category every year in a local paper, and I have friends from the city who will drive all the way to Marin to have one. These are not gourmet, fresh-ground sirloin tip; these are old-fashioned, greasy affairs served on a soft white bun. The only concession to gourmet tastes is the optional sourdough roll, with sauteed onions and Dijon mustard. Junior-size burgers are available. Phyllis also has a place in Mill Valley.

PHYLLIS' GIANT BURGERS, *2202 Fourth Street. (415) 456-0866. Open 11 A.M. to 9 P.M. daily. Inexpensive.*

✔ **Royal Thai.** Marin is not generally known for its diversity in restaurants, but some of the best Thai cuisine in the Bay Area can be found in a little shopping center called the French Quarter.

If you have never had Thai food, this is a good place for an initiation. Try the satays, or anything flavored with lemon grass or mint. Be sure to tell them how tolerant you are of hot and spicy foods.

ROYAL THAI RESTAURANT, *in the French Quarter on Third Street, just off Highway 101. (415) 485-1074. Lunch and dinner Monday through Friday, dinner only on Sunday. Inexpensive to moderate.*

✔ **Caffè Trieste.** This is a branch of the famous North Beach institution in San Francisco. The Trieste makes some of the best coffee drinks to be found anywhere. They will also make you a sandwich, and have Italian pastries on hand. The atmosphere is conducive to sitting and reading or having a political discussion with anyone who will listen.

SAUSALITO

CAFFÈ TRIESTE, *1000 Bridgeway. (415) 332-7770. Open from 7 A.M. to 11 P.M. daily, until midnight on Friday and Saturday. Inexpensive.*

✓ Fred's Place. Want to have breakfast where the locals go? There's a good reason they cram into Fred's. Not only is the food good and plentiful, but this is also an informal community center where you can pick up all the gossip, avoid the tourist rush, and read the newspaper with your coffee for as long as you'd like. Payment is on the honor system. Just tell the cashier what you had.

FRED'S PLACE, *1917 Bridgeway Street. (415) 332-4575. Open from 6:30 A.M. until 6 P.M. Monday through Saturday, 6:30 A.M. until 3 P.M. Sunday. Inexpensive.*

✓ Gatsby's. Wandering around the main tourist area of Sausalito, you might wonder where the locals hang out. You'll find them on Caledonia Street, where they can not only go to the drug store or grocery, but also have an informal dinner at Gatsby's. This is a friendly, active place that specializes in Chicago-style pizza. You can also get pasta, a meatball sandwich, salads, and other such fare.

GATSBY'S, *30 Caledonia Street. (415) 332-4500. Lunch and dinner every day. Inexpensive to moderate.*

Sonoma County

ASTI **✓ Asti Store.** In comedian Pat Paulsen's town of Asti, where he has elected himself mayor, he has leased a store to two enterprising women who sell great items for picnics. Located right next door to the Pat Paulsen wine-tasting room, the Asti Store features sandwiches, salads, and just about anything you need to create a fine lunch. If you don't have a picnicking destination in mind, there are tables outside with a beautiful view of the countryside.

ASTI STORE, *26155 Asti Store Road. (707) 894-5266. Open 10 A.M. to 6 P.M. daily. Inexpensive.*

BODEGA BAY **✓ The Tides.** This is a busy tourist complex right on the water. You'll see a gift shop, a tackle and bait store, a fish market—all the trappings of hokeyness that couldn't possibly lead to a decent meal, right? Wrong. The food at The Tides is very good. They know how to cook a fresh fish, and the service is friendly.

THE TIDES, *853 Highway 1. (707) 875-3553. Breakfast, lunch, and dinner daily. Moderate.*

BOYES HOT SPRINGS **✓ Big Three Fountain.** One of the world's most famous spas, the luxurious Sonoma Mission Inn, is here in tiny Boyes Hot Springs. Along with massages and facials and all sorts of treatments for the body, the inn features an excellent restaurant, which is also very expensive.

The back-roads way to visit the Sonoma Mission Inn is to go to the coffeeshop, called the Big Three Fountain, which was the name of this spot long before the inn folks came to town. Located in front of the hotel near the highway, this remodeled glitzy diner serves typical coffeeshop items like hamburgers, shakes, and meatloaf. Most of it is pretty good, and you can tell your friends you ate at the Sonoma Mission Inn.

At breakfast you can make your own toast in the little toaster provided in each booth. I'm not sure why that is so appealing, but it is.

The place is huge, and half of it is a gourmet food section featuring products made locally, and you can order food to take out.

BIG THREE FOUNTAIN, *18140 Highway 12. (707) 938-9000. Breakfast, lunch, and dinner daily. Inexpensive to moderate.*

✔ **40 Karrots Diner.**   The Healdsburg town square is blessed with three good places to eat. The most fun place to go is the hip little diner called 40 Karrots Diner. The design alone is worth the trip, with its black and white floor tile and long lunch counter. The specialty of the house is huge stuffed salads, but you can get all sorts of diner food items. They make a mean milkshake and a decent cappuccino.

40 KARROTS DINER, *109 Plaza Street. (707) 431-8181. Open 7 A.M. daily, serving breakfast and lunch Monday and Tuesday; breakfast, lunch, and dinner Wednesday, Thursday, and Friday; breakfast and lunch only Saturday and Sunday. Inexpensive.*

✔ **Jacob Horner.**   Jacob Horner is the largest of the three good places to eat on the town square. It is probably most attractive to those who have come to Sonoma for the wine. In addition to their extensive wine list, Horner's offers 17 different wines by the glass.

The food is in the California cuisine mode, and it's all prepared very well. The selection of dishes is as extensive and varied as the wine list, featuring such items as fresh fish, pasta, salads, and meat courses.

JACOB HORNER, *106 Matheson Street, on the plaza. (707) 433-3939. Lunch and dinner Tuesday through Saturday, Monday lunch only; closed Sunday. Moderate.*

✔ **Madrona Manor.**   This is Healdsburg's best-known restaurant and its most ambitious. This inn and upscale restaurant was fashioned out of an old mansion. Dinner is served prix fixe or à la carte, blending classic French cuisine with the California tradition of using whatever ingredients are freshest. Since reservations are usually made before you know what will be served, you simply have to put yourself at the chef's mercy. Whatever you end up with should be memorable.

HEALDSBURG

MADRONA MANOR, *1001 Westside Road. (707) 433-4231. Dinner daily, plus Sunday brunch. Expensive.*

✓ **Plaza Grill.**   Right next door to 40 Karrots is a tiny café with an attractive art deco influence. As the name suggests, the emphasis here is on grilled items— chicken, fish, beef—cooked to perfection. The salads are also noteworthy. There is a relaxed, cozy charm about the place that I find very inviting. Since there are so few seats, a reservation is advised. For the money, this is probably the best food in town.

PLAZA GRILL, *109A Plaza Street. (707) 431-8305. Lunch Tuesday through Friday, dinner Tuesday through Sunday. Moderate.*

OCCIDENTAL   ✓ **Howard Station.**   The large and feuding Italian restaurants in town get all the publicity and most of the tourists (see Chapter 2, destination 31). But when I want a less elaborate meal, I head for the other restaurant in town. At Howard Station I can get an omelet and other egg dishes for breakfast and wonderful lunch specialties like polenta with meat sauce. This is home cooking with an Italian flavor and not a lot of fuss.

HOWARD STATION, *95456 Main Street (Bohemian Highway). (707) 874-2838. Breakfast and lunch daily. Inexpensive.*

PETALUMA   ✓ **Lakeville Marina.**   As mentioned in our story (see Chapter 2, entry 1), Phyllis at the Lakeville Marina serves "weird food," meaning that everything is fresh and cooked to order and nonplastic, which in today's world of fast-food franchises is, well, weird. She makes a good hamburger, but also creates imaginative items like stewed pork in green chile sauce, calamari, tripe, and whatever else she's in the mood to whip up. The atmosphere is 1940s roadhouse. You expect to find Ida Lupino sitting in a corner booth, staring wistfully out the window at the Petaluma River flowing by. It's also one of the friendliest joints I've ever known. Phyllis also serves beers from around the world.

LAKEVILLE MARINA *(the sign on the road says Gilardi's), 588 Lakeville Highway. (707) 762-4900. Open 9 A.M. to 9 P.M. daily. Inexpensive.*

✓ **Markey's Café.**   Just a few blocks from downtown is a place where you can have a tasty vegetarian meal or simply a good coffee or tea. Markey's Café is a very informal, hangout type of place serving soups, salads, vegetarian sandwiches, and daily specials like curry, mushroom stroganoff, lasagne, and tofu pot pie. They also feature many kinds of natural juice drinks, as well as an espresso bar. Adding to the pleasure of being there is the classical music playing on the sound system at all times. Take-out service is available.

MARKEY'S CAFÉ, *316 Western Avenue, right next door to the Chamber of Commerce. (707) 763-2429. Open 8:30 A.M. to 9:30 P.M. daily. Inexpensive.*

✔ **Marvin's.** South of the town center is a cozy institution called Marvin's. Here you can get large omelets, sandwiches, salads, and daily specials served by incredibly energetic people. A couple of the waitresses are also aerobics instructors, and the entire staff seems to bounce around the place.

MARVIN'S, *317 Petaluma Boulevard South. (707) 778-8611. Breakfast and lunch daily, dinner Wednesday, Thursday, and Friday. Inexpensive.*

✔ **River Café.** A group of high-powered investors, including Baseball Commissioner Peter Ueberroth, bet that Petaluma could support a big restaurant that caters to locals and visiting yuppies. So far, they seem to be right.

The River Café is located in a big white house overlooking the Petaluma River and across the water from the downtown area. Various rooms on two stories are used as bar and dining areas; one small former bedroom upstairs can be reserved for private dinners. The kitchen offers light fare, full-course meals, and a selection of appetizers that you could turn into a meal. The cuisine is modern American, with an emphasis on grilled and barbecued specialties.

RIVER CAFÉ, *222 Weller. (707) 778-6600. Lunch Monday through Friday, dinner daily. Moderate.*

✔ **Fountain Grove Country Club.** When developers built the elegant Japanese-style Fountain Grove Country Club, the plan was to open the services to members only. However, sales were not as brisk as desired, so the restaurant and a hotel have been opened to the public.

That's good news for us. The setting is lovely, and the food is good and served beautifully. Though the cuisine is not Japanese, the Japanese tradition of treating the eyes as well as the palate is maintained. Menu selections run along the line of chicken dishes, salads, and grilled items.

Better call ahead before venturing out to this place in case their open-to-the-public policy changes.

FOUNTAIN GROVE COUNTRY CLUB, *1525 Fountain Grove Parkway, off Route 101. (707) 544-5100. Lunch daily, dinner Wednesday through Saturday. Moderate.*

✔ **Hemenway and Fleissner.** As is often the case with pioneering restaurants, one success story spawns several spin-offs. Such is the case with Hemenway and Fleissner, which is run by two former employees of John Ash and Company (see next restaurant). In fact, it's only a block or so away, in a newer section of the Montgomery Shopping Center called the Village Court Mall.

SANTA ROSA

Lunch features items from the mesquite grill, including hamburgers, the fresh fish of the day, and daily specials. Savories, such as torta Milanese and brioche stuffed with tarragon chicken, are offered at lunch, as are large main-course salads. At dinner the menu emphasis is on the grill and daily pasta specials. There's also a take-out section called Tote Cuisine.

For those in need of a quick snack you might also want to know about their oyster bar and deli, open all day long, but closed Mondays.

HEMENWAY AND FLEISSNER, *Village Court Mall, near Montgomery Street and Route 12. (707) 526-5111. Lunch Monday through Saturday, dinner Tuesday through Saturday. Moderate to expensive.*

✔ **John Ash and Company.** This is the restaurant that upgraded the quality of food in Santa Rosa. Capitalizing on the interest in fine wines in the region, John Ash sold local vintages in the front room of the establishment, then featured the marriage of fine wine and gourmet food in the restaurant. It worked, and still does.

The food is adventurous, with items like pheasant and squab on the menu, plus interesting selections using fish, chicken, beef, and veal. The food is best described as California French.

JOHN ASH AND COMPANY, *4350 Barnes Road, near Highway 101, at Vintners Inn. (707) 575-7350. Lunch Monday through Friday, dinner Tuesday through Sunday, plus Sunday brunch. Expensive.*

✔ **La Grande's.** On the southern outskirts of town is a restaurant that serves food that I call old-fashioned Italian. In other words, instead of the lighter Northern Italian places that are the rage now, La Grande's serves the Italian food I remember as a kid: spaghetti with meatballs, spaghetti with chicken livers, and ravioli, all loaded with a thick sauce. They also have veal and chicken dishes, beef braciole, and steaks, all served in portions you cannot possibly finish. What's more, it's delicious.

La Grande's is a hangout for the nontrendy, a family place where the kids can play a video game or listen to a live rock band on weekends while the parents eat in peace in another of the restaurant's many rooms or out on the patio. Mangia!

LA GRANDE'S, *corner of Todd and Stony Point Road. (707) 584-8803. Lunch Monday through Friday, dinner daily, plus brunch on Sunday. Inexpensive to moderate.*

✔ **Matisse.** This is another example of California cuisine meets French tradition, and the result is successful. Matisse is a fairly small place, run by a young and eager group of food lovers. The menu changes often, but there is always a fresh fish selection, interesting salads, and a group of imaginative entrees. And as the name suggests, the decor is lovely.

If I had only one meal to eat in the Santa Rosa area, it would be at Matisse.

MATISSE, *620 Fifth Street. (707) 527-9797. Lunch Monday through Friday, dinner Monday through Saturday. Moderate.*

✔ Omelette Express.

Like many other towns with a history, Santa Rosa has re-created its original "old" section, which is called Old Railroad Square. Several restaurants are in the immediate area, many of them trendy and most of them overpriced. A surprising find, however, is the Omelette Express. Nothing tricky or trendy here, just a very large selection of omelets and other light dishes, prepared well and without pretense.

OMELETTE EXPRESS, *112 Fourth Street, in Old Railroad Square. (707) 525-1690. Breakfast and lunch daily. Inexpensive to moderate.*

✔ Ristorante Siena.

The folks who brought us Matisse have also created an Italian café in a shopping center on the outskirts of town. Ristorante Siena is a sprawling space decorated with blond furniture and white walls. The menu features fresh pasta dishes, salads, and grilled items. The accent is on light cooking, free of heavy sauces. As at Matisse, the food is very good. Reservations are recommended.

RISTORANTE SIENA, *1229 North Dutton Avenue. (707) 578-4511. Lunch Monday through Friday, dinner Wednesday through Sunday, plus Sunday brunch. Moderate.*

✔ Chez Peyo.

SEBASTOPOL

This is a French restaurant owned by a Basque named Pierre whose nickname is Peyo. This is also a very popular spot for lunch and dinner. Fresh fish and pasta are featured daily, and the American favorite, the hamburger, is served with a béarnaise sauce. One day for lunch I had a very nice fresh trout in lemon cream sauce, with properly steamed vegetables (still crisp, not soggy).

At dinner the prices jump up a bit but are still in the moderate range. Light and inexpensive suppers are also offered, featuring such things as pumpkin ravioli and broccoli with ricotta wrapped in puff pastry.

The food is not outstanding, but it is a cut above what you might expect in a town this size, and the service is very friendly.

CHEZ PEYO, *2295 Gravenstein Highway South (Route 116). (707) 823-1262. Lunch and dinner Tuesday through Saturday, brunch and dinner Sunday; closed Monday. Inexpensive to moderate.*

✓ **Katie Jean's.**   This is a very congenial little spot, near the main intersection in town. I'm always amazed by the amount of food they serve from their tiny space behind the counter.

As you enter you gaze upon the desserts in the cooler. Then you will see the day's hot specials, which might be a tamale pie, a quiche, and a lasagne, maybe even a vegetarian casserole. You can order any number of sandwiches, including the house specialty, which is turkey, cheese, and cranberry sauce. Whatever you choose will be good.

After you order, take a seat at a table and your food will be brought to you.

KATIE JEAN'S, *6951 Bodega Highway. (707) 823-1324. Breakfast and lunch Monday through Saturday. Inexpensive.*

SONOMA

✓ **L'Espérance.**   Tucked away in a courtyard behind the French Bakery on the town square in Sonoma is a sweet little French restaurant called L'Espérance. Many of the people working here used to be at Sharl's, which used to be the in place to eat in town.

You can have a light lunch or dinner or a full-course meal. Everything will be prepared well and will be made of the freshest ingredients available. Reservations are suggested.

L'ESPÉRANCE, *464 First Street, on the square. (707) 996-2757. Lunch and dinner Tuesday through Saturday, plus Sunday brunch. Moderate to expensive.*

✓ **Sonoma Hotel.**   My favorite spot for lunch in Sonoma is in the courtyard of the old Sonoma Hotel. Even when the temperature is in the 90s, the shaded courtyard is always pleasant. It's a good place to have a salad, light pasta, or a sandwich. Indoor dining is also available.

SONOMA HOTEL, *110 West Spain, on the west side of the square. (707) 996-2996. Lunch and dinner Thursday through Tuesday, plus Sunday brunch. Closed Wednesday. Moderate.*

Napa County

CALISTOGA

✓ **All Seasons Café.**   In what looks like a converted corner grocery store, you can be served a very good lunch or dinner, or you can pick up some food to take out on a picnic. The All Seasons Café is part wine and gourmet shop, part restaurant, and part coffeehouse, and all the parts work very well.

The dessert case is a knockout, the wine selection is as large and diverse as that of many fine restaurants, and the menu offers a surprisingly broad selection to suit many moods and appetites, from salads and sandwiches to grilled meat and fowl.

ALL SEASONS CAFÉ, *1400 Lincoln Avenue. (707) 942-9111. Open 9 A.M. to 6 P.M. weekdays, 9 A.M. to 10 P.M. weekends. Inexpensive to moderate.*

✔ **Bosko's.**   This is an unusual Italian restaurant offering just pasta and large salads. You order cafeteria-style, choosing from a large selection of hot pasta dishes of many shapes, sizes, and colors. One day four of us had linguine with pesto, lasagne with meat sauce, fettucine Alfredo, and tortellini. The pasta was freshly made on the premises, and the sauces were all delicious.

BOSKO'S, *1403 Lincoln Avenue. (707) 942-9088. Lunch and dinner daily. Inexpensive to moderate.*

✔ **Jamee's Restaurant.**   Jamee's is a little jewel box of a restaurant, serving up the kind of home-cooked meals you wish you could cook at home. You can order a light supper or a complete dinner, with entrees like poached salmon or pasta with fresh scallops. The menu changes often, based on what is available and good that week. This is a tiny spot, so reservations are advised.

JAMEE'S RESTAURANT, *1226B Washington Street, off Lincoln. (707) 942-0979. Dinner Wednesday through Sunday. Moderate.*

✔ **Aron's Café.**   As mentioned, downtown Napa has undergone a welcome revival (see Chapter 3, destination 1), particularly on old Main Street. Included in that renaissance is a charming little café called Aron's. Here you will be served good, wholesome, fresh ingredients from the Napa Valley. Salads are creative and filled with all sorts of good things, lunch specials are light and tasty, and dinners are nicely prepared.

Though this is not a health food restaurant per se, the food served at Aron's is geared for people who don't want to feel loaded down after a meal. The atmosphere is low-key, and works by local artists are displayed on the walls.

ARON'S CAFÉ, *823 Main Street. (707) 442-9000. Breakfast and lunch Monday through Friday, dinner Tuesday through Friday. Inexpensive to moderate.*

✔ **Hi-Way 29 Diner.**   This is a real truck stop kind of place, and it's not hard to figure out why. Even truck driver appetites are challenged here, particularly on Mondays, when the house special is two T-bone steaks for $5.00. No kidding, I've seen them, but was never hungry enough to order the special. Customers told me they were great.

The rest of the menu is what you would expect in a highway diner—burgers and meat-and-potatoes items. A place like this may be the norm in many parts of the country, but in the Napa Valley it's downright exotic.

HI-WAY 29 DINER, *on Highway 29 between Vallejo and Napa. (707) 224-6303. Breakfast and lunch daily. Inexpensive.*

NAPA

✔ **Rio Poco.** Back in the center of Napa, just down the street from Aron's, is another low-key spot for a good meal. As the name suggests, Rio Poco serves Mexican food. There's nothing unusual about the menu, but the food is well prepared and inexpensive, and the atmosphere is quite pleasant.

RIO POCO, *807 Main Street. (707) 253-8203. Lunch and dinner Monday through Saturday. Inexpensive.*

ST. HELENA ✔ **Knickerbocker's.** A few miles north of the town of St. Helena in the Freemark Abbey Wine complex is a restaurant popular with the people who live and work in the area. Knickerbocker's opened in late 1986 and became an immediate hit, thanks partly to its array of appetizers available all afternoon. The restaurant itself is in a lovely roadhouse-type building with a deck and garden for drinks and dining.

The food is a mixture of California grill and Asian cooking, a cuisine that is popular on the West Coast.

KNICKERBOCKER'S, *in the Freemark Abbey Wine complex, 3020 St. Helena Highway North (Highway 29). (707) 963-9300. Lunch and dinner, afternoon appetizers Wednesday through Sunday, plus Sunday brunch. Moderate.*

✔ **Spring Street Restaurant.** Did your mother ever take you to lunch at a "ladies'" restaurant? If so, prepare for *déjà vu* when you walk up the stairs of the lovely old home that is now the Spring Street Restaurant. A charming hostess will greet you, then show you a menu that includes salads and light entrees. There's usually a quiche of the day and sandwiches on bread baked on the premises. They also make their own desserts, such as apple pie and lemon cake, accompanied by a selection of teas. Mind your manners!

SPRING STREET RESTAURANT, *1245 Spring Street. (707) 963-5578. Lunch and dinner daily. Inexpensive to moderate.*

✔ **Tra Vigne.** Yet another in the Mustard's/Fog City Diner chain is a Northern Italian restaurant just south of the town of St. Helena. Tra Vigne means among the vines, and this spacious and lovely restaurant is strategically placed to take advantage of the constant stream of visitors to the boutique wineries of the northern Napa Valley.

The menu here is incredibly diverse, offering many pastas, grilled dishes, salads, as well as inventive and unusual combinations. On one visit, four of us had such items as chilled melon and fig soup, grilled, chilled summer vegetables, roast chicken with balsamic vinegar, grapes, and pine nuts, pasta with smoked salmon in a mascarpone cream, and the special sandwich of the day, which was a gourmet hero on homemade Tuscan-style bread for $5.95.

This is a very large place, offering comfortable seating in the dining room or on the patios.

TRA VIGNE, *1050 Charter Oak. (707) 963-4444. Serving lunch and dinner daily. Moderate to expensive, depending on how much you order, as everything is à la carte.*

✔ **The Diner.**   This place is more typical of wine country diners than the Hi-Way 29. Although The Diner is totally unpretentious, the food is closer to cuisine than cookin'. Great culinary skill goes into the hamburgers, sandwiches, and Mexican foods that are featured here. The omelets are stuffed and huge and are accompanied by perfect hash browns; on the weekends, the waffles and berry pancakes can't be beat. Desserts are baked on the premises and are pretty swell, too. This is simply good food. You can sit at the counter or at a booth; at peak meal times, be prepared to wait.

YOUNTVILLE

THE DINER, *6476 Washington Street. (707) 944-2626. Breakfast, lunch, and dinner Tuesday through Sunday; closed Monday. Inexpensive to moderate.*

South Bay Inland

✔ **The Peasant Chef.**   This is a family-run restaurant that serves food that might well be found in middle-class homes throughout Europe. Specializing in stews and casserole dishes, it offers a broad selection of items, including vegetarian dishes. I had something called Russian vegetable pie, while my companions ate French crepes and Greek moussaka. Desserts are given special attention here. The service is very friendly.

LOS GATOS

THE PEASANT CHEF, *368 Village Lane, which is behind the main street in town (Santa Cruz Avenue). (408) 354-8006. Lunch and dinner daily. Inexpensive to moderate.*

✔ **Dal Baffo.**   Some folks who live on the Peninsula swear that Dal Baffo is the best Italian restaurant in the entire Bay Area. You might agree, if your taste runs to classic Northern Italian cuisine, served in an elegant atmosphere. Fresh fish, veal, chicken, and pasta dishes are featured, and great pains are taken to make this a true "dining experience," as opposed to just another fancy meal.

MENLO PARK

DAL BAFFO, *878 Santa Cruz Avenue. (415) 325-1583. Lunch Tuesday through Friday, dinner Tuesday through Saturday. Reservations are a must. Expensive.*

✔ **Flea Street Café.**   Owned by some folks who run Late for the Train, Flea Street Café is a cozier and more stylish place, offering fresh fish, pasta, chicken, and some vegetarian dishes. It is not as large an operation as the Train, so the food is more imaginative. It also tends to get crowded, so reservations are advised.

FLEA STREET CAFÉ, *3607 Alameda de las Pulgas. (415) 854-1226. Breakfast, lunch, and dinner Tuesday through Friday, dinner Saturday; closed Sunday. Moderate.*

✔ **Late for the Train.**   The first thing that endeared me to this place was the sign that said no smoking was allowed on the premises. For a nonsmoker, nothing is worse than having the flavor of cigarette or cigar smoke overwhelm the food. The food here is of the healthy variety, though the menu is quite varied, offering something for every taste. You'll get lots of sprouts on your salad and lots of grain in the homemade bread. The specialty appears to be the omelets, which are thick and fluffy and served with their special tamari-seasoned potatoes (OK, if you count cholesterol and salt, the entire menu is not perfectly virtuous).

The food is good, if not outstanding, the atmosphere is pleasant, and the place is jammed at lunchtime with the *Sunset* magazine crowd from across the street.

LATE FOR THE TRAIN, *150 Middlefield Road. (415) 321-6124. Breakfast, lunch, and dinner Tuesday through Saturday; lunch only on Sunday. Moderate.*

✔ **Webb Ranch Market.**   This is a place to pack your car with snacks for the road or to take home. Webb Ranch grows some of the the best fruits and vegetables in the area and supplies produce to many of the finest restaurants and food shops in the Bay Area. They sell to the public at a stand located a few minutes off Route 280 north of Palo Alto.

Remember tomatoes? Webb Ranch has the real thing. They also have sweet corn that tastes like the kind you can get in the Midwest, plus those tiny green beans the French call *haricots verts*. Everything is seasonal and wonderful. Call ahead to find out what's just been picked.

WEBB RANCH MARKET, *Alpine Road exit off Route 280, on the Bay side of the freeway. (415) 854-5417. Open only during the growing season, which usually means June through October.*

MORGAN HILL   ✔ **Super Taqueria.**   Like so many small towns, Morgan Hill has its share of franchised eateries. Finding a place that serves food of the more homemade variety is not easy. But our friend Moroni the cheesemaker (see Chapter 4, entry 18) told us about the Super Taqueria, and it's a good thing he did. It would have been easy to overlook.

From the outside it doesn't look like much, sort of like a franchised restaurant without the gloss. The decor doesn't improve much inside, but the food is another story. Inside the Taqueria, you get in line to place your order, then you eat it at one of the booths or outside on one of the picnic tables overlooking the town's main drag. You can probably guess the menu selection: tacos, burritos, and so on. But this is no Taco Bell. Meats are nicely cooked, the chicken is very flavorful, and even the beans are delicious. It's all done with top ingredients and good spices.

SUPER TAQUERIA, *16873 Monterey Boulevard. (408) 778-3730. Lunch and dinner daily. Inexpensive.*

✔ **Cowper Corner.**   There is a new version of the fast-food restaurant springing up in the Bay Area, offering good, homemade-style food for the person in a hurry. You stand at the counter and order such items as soup, special salads (such as chicken with cashews and curry mayonnaise), and fresh-baked breads and pastries, which you carry to one of the tables. In other words, this is a good place for a quick breakfast, a light lunch, or an early dinner without a lot of fuss. There's also an espresso machine.

Cowper Corner is also the kind of place you can go and feel right at home if you are eating alone. And the food's good even if you aren't in a rush.

COWPER CORNER, *494 University Avenue at Cowper Street. (415) 322-4242. Breakfast, lunch, and dinner daily. Inexpensive.*

✔ **Crouton's.**   If you are in a rush, there's a very congenial and attractive spot in downtown Palo Alto that specializes in soups and salads. Service is cafeteria-style, featuring a well-stocked salad bar that takes up one entire side of the line. On the other side you'll find four or five soups, including chili. You'll also find a fresh fruit bar and fresh-baked bread. A continental breakfast buffet is offered starting at 7:30 A.M., with cereals, baked goods, and fruit. And, yes, at lunch and dinner there is a very large supply of croutons for your soup or salad or both.

CROUTON'S, *379 University Avenue. (415) 325-2001. Open 7:30 A.M. to 9 P.M. daily. Inexpensive.*

✔ **Fresco.**   Here you will find a touch of contemporary L.A. in Palo Alto. Fresco is a bright, busy, high-tech restaurant offering a little of everything for everyone. The emphasis is on California cuisine, with the freshest ingredients put together in unusual combinations. The menu is extensive, offering many choices, from salads to pasta dishes to grilled items. The only thing that seems to be missing from the genre is an espresso machine, although they do serve good coffee.

Part of the operation is an informal ultramodern diner; the other half is a more subtly decorated dining room featuring the same menu. The food is quite good, and the atmosphere is electric.

FRESCO, *3398 El Camino Real. (415) 493-3470. Breakfast, lunch, and dinner daily. Inexpensive to moderate.*

✔ **The Good Earth.**   There is a chain of Good Earth restaurants, all serving a vegetarian-oriented menu, heavy on the whole grains and sprouts, but also offering chicken and fish dishes. I think the best of these is the original in Palo Alto. It is a terrific place to go when you're in the mood for a huge salad or are willing to stick to the dishes featuring fresh vegetables.

The baked goods are a special feature, and you can buy breads and cookies and other bakery items to go at the front of the restaurant.

THE GOOD EARTH, *corner of University and Emerson. (415) 321-9449. Breakfast, lunch, and dinner until 7:30 P.M. weekdays, 10 P.M. weekends. Inexpensive to moderate.*

✔ **Peninsula Creamery Fountain.**   The Peninsula Creamery is one of the last holdouts, a dairy that delivers milk with the cream on top, and it comes in real glass bottles. This old-fashioned touch carries over to their soda fountain and luncheonette in the heart of Palo Alto. Here you can sit at the counter or at booths and have that authentic grilled cheese or tuna melt sandwich that seems impossible to find anymore, even in this day and age of the diner revival. But no matter what you eat, be sure to have a milkshake. It will be thick and filled with ice cream, and you get the entire stainless steel container to finish off.

PENINSULA CREAMERY FOUNTAIN, *corner of Hamilton and Emerson streets. (415) 323-3131. Open 7:30 A.M. to 5:30 P.M. Monday through Saturday; closed Sunday. Inexpensive.*

✔ **Theo's.**   When I sat down in the very attractive dining room at Theo's, my first thought was that I had not seen so many businessmen in blue suits in years. Obviously this is a favorite lunch spot for Silicon Valley executives.

It's a good choice. The emphasis at Theo's is on fresh fish and seafood, well prepared with a variety of sauces and served with vegetables cooked al dente and rice. Also offered as part of their menu of light meals are chicken and pasta dishes. After a lunch here, you won't need an afternoon siesta.

THEO'S, *546 University Avenue. (415) 322-1272. Lunch Monday through Friday, dinner daily. Moderate to expensive.*

SAN BRUNO   ✔ **Maharajah.**   If you like Indian food, I have a real find for you. Right in the center of the very unchic downtown of San Bruno is a nondescript-looking restaurant serving great Indian food. I don't know what Maharajah is doing here, but they do know their way around a curry and a tandoori oven. The atmosphere is nothing to write home about, but you'll love the food.

MAHARAJAH, *528 San Mateo Avenue. (415) 583-5226. Lunch and dinner weekdays, dinner only weekends. Inexpensive to moderate.*

✓ **Eulipia.** This is a very inviting, airy space that symbolizes the "new" San Jose. Serving continental and California cuisine, Eulipia would be a very good restaurant in any metropolitan area. A very complete menu is offered with many interesting fish and chicken dishes, as well as red meat dishes such as blackened New York steak with Cajun spices. There are also pasta and vegetarian dishes. Service is friendly and efficient.

EULIPIA, *374 South First Street. (408) 280-6161. Lunch Monday through Friday, dinner Monday through Saturday. Moderate to expensive.*

✓ **Gervais.** Just down the street from San Jose's Rosicrucian museum is a charming French restaurant, tucked away in a nondescript shopping center. Gervais and Mary Lou Henric run the operation themselves; he's the chef, she's the friendly greeter, and they serve very good French food. The entrees cover the range of fish, chicken, and meat, but it's the sauces that make each dish stand out.

GERVAIS, *1798 Park Avenue at Naglee. (408) 275-8631. Lunch Tuesday through Friday, dinner Tuesday through Saturday. Moderate to expensive.*

✓ **Original Joe's.** If you've ever been to a "Joe's" in the Bay Area, you know that several claim to be the "original" and that they all offer huge portions of Italian food, plus steaks, chicken, and calves' liver smothered in onions. The food is wholesome and tasty, and there's enough on each plate to feed a family of four.

One of the best Original Joe's is in downtown San Jose. As soon as you walk in the door and take a deep breath, the smell of the food will tell you that you are in for a treat. What's more, the decor is original 1940s, not a re-creation. This is the kind of place your parents may have taken you to for Sunday dinner. And it's one of the few places in the area you can get a full meal after midnight.

ORIGINAL JOE'S, *301 South First Street. (408) 292-7030. Open 11 A.M. to 2 A.M. daily. Moderate.*

✓ **Doña Esther.** My colleague, cameraman Jeff Pierce, has been known to travel an hour out of his way just to eat at Doña Esther. He claims they have the finest enchiladas he's ever eaten (and believe me, Jeff has eaten a lot of enchiladas). Jeff has also been known to have a weakness for their margaritas.

Jeff is not alone in his passion for the place. When he first took me there, we started a conversation with the man at the table next to us who said he had driven from San Francisco for lunch there.

I don't want to oversell the place, but Doña Esther is very good. The menu runs along traditional lines with tacos, flautas, and, of course, enchiladas, and the portions are very large. A nice added touch: the courtyard for eating outdoors on warm days and nights.

DOÑA ESTHER, *25 Franklin Street. (408) 623-2518. Lunch and dinner daily, plus Sunday brunch. Inexpensive to moderate.*

✓ **Felipe's.**   Although this may look like yet another Mexican restaurant, there is a difference. This is a Salvadoran-Mexican restaurant, so in addition to the tacos and so on you can get pork stews and other dishes native to El Salvador. All the food is quite good, and the owner will be thrilled if you experiment with the Salvadoran specialties.

FELIPE'S, *313 Third Street. (408) 623-2161. Lunch and dinner Wednesday through Sunday. Inexpensive.*

✓ **Jardines de San Juan.**   As you can see, you will have no trouble finding Mexican food in San Juan Bautista. One of the most popular spots in town is just down the street from Doña Esther, and the food is quite similar. As suggested by the name Jardines, or gardens, you sit under shade trees in a protected courtyard, and between courses you can wander through their impressive collection of cacti.

JARDINES DE SAN JUAN, *115 Third Street. (408) 623-4466. Lunch and dinner daily. Inexpensive to moderate.*

✓ **Mariposa House.**   If you're in San Juan Bautista and are in the mood for lighter fare than Mexican food, you can get quiche, pastas, salads, and sautés at the Mariposa House. This place really is a house, a block off the main street. The food here is as close as you can get to California cuisine anywhere in town.

MARIPOSA HOUSE, *37 Mariposa Street. (408) 623-4666. Lunch Tuesday through Sunday, dinner Wednesday through Sunday. Moderate.*

SAN MATEO   ✓ **231 Ellsworth.**   One of the newest bastions of fine cuisine is on a quiet street near downtown San Mateo. This is an attractive restaurant, decorated in soft pastels with subdued lighting, and boasting a first-class kitchen. A classically trained chef produces French cuisine, using fresh California ingredients, and the result is wonderful.

A particular bargain is the prix fixe lunch, which as of the fall of 1987, offered soup, appetizer or salad, and entree for $9.50. This may be the best food on the Peninsula.

231 ELLSWORTH, *231 South Ellsworth. (415) 347-7231. Lunch and dinner Monday through Friday, dinner only on Saturday. Moderate to expensive.*

SARATOGA   ✓ **Bella Mia.**   Saratoga has some very fine Italian restaurants. Bella Mia serves fresh pasta dishes, seafood, veal, and other specialties with a nod to Northern Italian cooking, and it's very good. Outside there's a nice little patio in front where you can sit with a cappuccino and watch the shoppers go by. The Sunday brunch is accompanied by live jazz.

BELLA MIA, *14503 Big Basin Way. (408) 941-5115. Lunch and dinner daily. Moderate.*

✔ La Mère Michelle. This is the town's temple of formal French cuisine, and it's very good indeed. The menu is traditional, not nouvelle. Your veal or duck will be richly sauced, and the service will be elegant. This is the place for that special anniversary celebration or somebody else's expense account meal. If you are like me, traveling the back roads wearing jeans, you will want to have a change of clothes along.

LA MÈRE MICHELLE, *14482 Big Basin Way. (408) 867-5272. Lunch and dinner Tuesday through Sunday. Expensive.*

✔ The Trattoria. Whenever I'm in the Saratoga area, I try to get to The Trattoria, which is a touch of Italy in this very chic town. All the pasta is made on the premises and is served in a variety of ways. They also feature chicken, beef, veal, and seafood dishes. My main reason to stop, though, is to get the appetizers called arancini. These are deep-fried rice balls, held together with mozzarella cheese, and they are wonderful.

This is a large, informal place, and if it's crowded you can relax with a drink in the courtyard that separates the restaurant from its take-out pasta shop.

THE TRATTORIA, *14510 Big Basin Way. (408) 741-1802. Lunch Monday through Saturday, dinner daily. Moderate.*

✔ Village Rendezvous. With so many chic continental restaurants in town, you might be in the mood for a good old American hamburger or some scrambled eggs. This place looks like the kind of lunch counter hangout that every town used to have. At breakfast and lunch you can get eggs or burgers, plus items like pancakes and grilled cheese sandwiches served in an informal atmosphere. But for dinner the tablecloths come out and the café competes with the higher-priced neighbors down the street with specialties like chicken sauté, New York pepper steak, and lots of pasta dishes. The food here is good, wholesome, and very American.

VILLAGE RENDEZVOUS, *14420 Big Basin Way. (408) 867-2932. Lunch daily, dinner Tuesday through Saturday. Moderate.*

✔ Max's Fried Chicken Restaurant. If you have never tried Filipino food, Max's will be a good introduction. Located in a small shopping center, Max's is a cafeteria that appears to be quite a hangout for people who have moved here from the Philippines.

SOUTH SAN FRANCISCO

A TV will be blaring, crowds will be chattering, and it may be a bit intimidating to walk up to the cafeteria line to place your order because, despite the name, you might not know anything about the food. The best bet is try anything "adobo." Whether it is the pork or the chicken, it will have a spicy and flavorful sauce that is a staple in Filipino cooking. The fried chicken, as with other deep-fried foods, tends to be on the greasy side.

Put yourself in the hands of the friendly people behind the counter. Tell them what you like and they'll recommend things to try.

MAX'S FRIED CHICKEN, *2239 Gellert Boulevard. (415) 878-0610. Lunch and dinner daily. Inexpensive.*

WOODSIDE √ **Alpine Inn.** Outside Woodside is an institution of sorts. The Alpine Inn is not really an inn but a roadside bar and restaurant that used to be a stagecoach stop. It's rather funky inside, but you can get a large grilled hamburger and take it to one of the picnic benches out back, overlooking the beautiful scenery.

ALPINE INN, *3915 Alpine Road. (415) 854-4004. Opens 11:30 A.M. daily; closes 10 P.M. Monday through Saturday, 5 P.M. Sunday. Inexpensive.*

√ **Nina's Café.** Nina's is *the* place to eat in the gentrified village of Woodside. That means that the place is usually crowded, but it also means that it's worth the wait.

The decor is charming and in keeping with the upscale country look of the town. The menu offers many light dishes like salads and quiche, plus imaginative uses of fresh ingredients to serve with chicken, fish, and meat dishes.

NINA'S CAFÉ, *2991 Woodside Road. (415) 851-4564. Lunch Tuesday through Friday, dinner Tuesday through Saturday, Sunday brunch. Moderate.*

South Bay Coast

CAPITOLA √ **Country Court Tea Room.** The Santa Cruz beach and mountain region is hardly the place one would expect to find a cozy tearoom, but here one is. Nestled in back of a blooming garden in the town of Capitola, this sweet little place looks like it would be right at home in the English countryside.

Breakfast and lunch are served daily, but the treat for me is the very civilized afternoon tea. I love the idea of spending the day at the beach, taking a shower, and at teatime pigging out on little cucumber sandwiches, pastries, and a nice pot of Earl Grey. Lunch is light fare such as salads and quiche.

COUNTRY COURT TEA ROOM, *911 Capitola Avenue. (408) 462-2498. Breakfast, lunch, and afternoon tea daily. Inexpensive to moderate.*

✔ **Trattoria Primizia.** The recent renaissance of Northern Italian cuisine is centered in the Santa Cruz area at Trattoria Primizia. Here you will find fresh pasta enhanced by deliciously light sauces, entrees flavored with porcini mushrooms, superb veal and seafood dishes, and salads using various kinds of lettuces most of us never heard of 10 years ago.

Whoever is in charge really knows how to cook, and even though the place is tucked away in a cute little American shopping center, the restaurant's atmosphere is stylish Italian. The owners also run a deli next door, offering fine Italian food to take out.

TRATTORIA PRIMIZIA, *502 Bay Avenue. (408) 479-1112. Dinner only, Tuesday through Sunday. Moderate.*

✔ **New Davenport Cash Store.** From the highway, the Cash Store looks like an old-fashioned general store, but it's actually a lovely arts and crafts gallery, shop, and restaurant. The food is on the healthy side, with whole-grain breads, chunky soups, big salads, and sandwiches. The emphasis is on the fresh produce grown in the neighborhood, and the style of cooking is both Mexican and Middle American. In other words, you can have a tostada, or you can have a grilled cheese sandwich. Everything is well prepared, and the atmosphere is relaxed and pleasant. You can even see the ocean across the road from the window seats.

You can also pick up a sandwich and take it across the road to the bluffs high above the Pacific. This is a great spot for watching whales when they head south in the summer and fall and return north from December through May.

The Cash Store is a favorite stop of mine because it is a nonsmoking restaurant and because it offers a wonderful assortment of desserts.

NEW DAVENPORT CASH STORE, *right on Highway 1, about 15 minutes north of Santa Cruz. (408) 426-4122. Breakfast and lunch daily, dinner Friday and Saturday. Inexpensive.*

✔ **San Benito House** . The San Benito House offers two entirely different eating experiences. For those in a hurry, try the lunch, which is dished out at a counter. Then you take your food out to a lovely garden. You have a choice of such items as sandwiches on home-baked bread, fresh salads, yogurt, brownies, and other desserts. Dinner there is another matter entirely. This is a leisurely gourmet affair, featuring fresh fish, fowl, and meats served in an elegant manner. Sunday brunch is also an elaborate occasion, and reservations are a good idea. (Also see story about Half Moon Bay, Chapter 5, destination 4.)

SAN BENITO HOUSE , *356 Main Street. (415) 726-3425. Lunch Wednesday through Saturday, dinner daily, plus Sunday brunch. Moderate to expensive.*

DAVENPORT

HALF MOON BAY

MOSS BEACH   ✓ **Dan's Place.**   On a hill overlooking the Fitzgerald Marine Reserve is a somewhat funky Italian restaurant that has been in the same family for several generations. Dan's Place is a tradition in town, and you will feel right at home there.

Dan's serves home-cooked Italian meals. Nothing fancy here, just good spaghetti and ravioli, a few veal dishes, and thick minestrone, all served in huge, family-style portions.

DAN'S PLACE, *Virginia Street, one block above Route 1; you can see the sign from the highway. (415) 728-3343. Lunch and dinner daily. Inexpensive to moderate.*

MOSS LANDING   ✓ **The Whole Enchilada.**   As you might expect, this is a Mexican restaurant. As you might not expect, it is a rather attractive and ambitious place that not only serves good food but also offers jazz concerts on Sunday afternoons.

The Whole Enchilada is right off the highway, so it attracts many of the tourists driving by, along with a good mix of locals. It's apt to be jumping. The food is fairly standard Mexican-American fare, with good-sized portions.

THE WHOLE ENCHILADA, *Route 1. (408) 633-3038. Open 11:30 A.M. to 9 P.M. Wednesday through Sunday. Inexpensive to moderate.*

PACIFICA   ✓ **La Vita Café.**   If you are just getting under way on a trip south and find yourself in need of a quick lunch or snack, let me recommend La Vita. This is a tiny spot with just a few tables and a rather limited menu. But as Spencer Tracy once said about Katharine Hepburn, "There ain't much meat, but what's there is cherce." At La Vita you will get "cherce" salads, homemade soups, thick sandwiches, good desserts, and an espresso machine that turns out a mighty fine cappuccino.

In an area where it's easier to find franchised food than the real thing, this café is a welcome stop.

LA VITA CAFÉ, *164 Reina del Mar. (415) 359-7927. Open 8:30 A.M. to 6 P.M. daily. Inexpensive.*

PESCADERO   ✓ **Duarte's.**   There's not a whole lot to the charming town of Pescadero, so you might wonder how so many people happen to be at a restaurant called Duarte's. There are several reasons. The food is good, if not great; the prices are right; and they serve one item for which they are justifiably famous: artichoke soup.

Yes, people come from all over to try this creamy, rich soup made from the thorny vegetable. Duarte's is located in the heart of artichoke country, and they've made the most of this delicacy. The rest of the menu features fresh fish, omelets, burgers, and items you might find in a lot of roadside cafés. My best meal there was one lunch in which I skipped an entree and went for the soup, a lightly fried fresh squid appetizer, and a piece of wonderful pecan pie. They bake all their pies daily, and they're great. If it's a beautiful day and there are lots of motorists along the neighboring coastline, be prepared to wait in line; on weekends, reservations are advised.

DUARTE'S, *202 Stage Road, in the center of town. (415) 879-0464. Breakfast, lunch, and dinner daily. Inexpensive to moderate.*

✔ **The Shore Bird.**   Set on a harbor in a lovely village filled with restaurants, The Shore Bird is billed as a bit of "Cape Cod on the California coast." Don't expect lobster or other New England delicacies, though. What you will find is an attractive, busy, tourist-oriented restaurant serving reasonably well prepared fresh fish and seafood in a Cape Cod–style building.

Indeed, the atmosphere is better than the food, although if you try the appetizers in the café and bar, you can have a delightful light lunch at moderate prices.

THE SHORE BIRD, *390 Capistrano Road. (415) 728-5541. Lunch and dinner daily, plus Sunday brunch. Moderate to expensive.*

PRINCETON-BY-THE-SEA

✔ **Casa Blanca.**   Of all the restaurants in Santa Cruz, you wouldn't be making a mistake if you walked into this one, even though the name is misleading. There will be no ceiling fans, no piano player named Sam, and very little intrigue.

What you will find is a very romantic spot in a white hotel overlooking the water. The selection offers something for every taste. Fresh fish, pasta, steak, and chicken are prepared in a style that blends classic continental cooking with California cuisine. Reservations are advised.

CASA BLANCA, *101 Main Street. (408) 426-9063. Dinner nightly, plus Sunday brunch. Moderate.*

SANTA CRUZ

✔ **Ferrell's Donuts.**   If you have any memories of fresh doughnuts, before the proliferation of franchised shops, you know what a hot-from-the-fryer treat at Ferrell's is like. This is a student hangout for the gang at the university up the hill. For years late study hours have been interrupted by jaunts down to the 24-hour doughnut kingdom. You can call ahead to find out what time your favorite kind will be ready.

FERRELL'S DONUTS, *2229 Mission Street. (408) 432-3448. Open 24 hours. Inexpensive.*

✔ **India Joze.**   One of the most eclectic yet satisfying restaurants I've come across in my travels is India Joze. As the name might indicate, they offer many foods from India and other Asian countries. They also serve a variety of fish, chicken, and meat dishes and hold an annual squid festival. Desserts are sky-high creations that appeal to typical American tastes, especially the range of chocolate specialties. This is a very attractive place, open and airy, with modern art adorning the walls. It is also a very popular place, and during the height of the dinner hour you may have to wait awhile for a table. But it's worth it.

INDIA JOZE, *1001 Center Street. (408) 427-3554. Lunch and dinner daily. Moderate.*

✔ **Pontiac Grill.**   One of the glitziest specimens of the re-created 1950s diner look is the Pontiac Grill. However, it comes by its name honestly. Situated in a former auto showroom, the grill of an actual Pontiac is built into the wall above the counter.

The food is the trendy version of classic diner cuisine: meatloaf, burgers, and milkshakes. But there's also the veggie breakfast burrito, hot apple soufflé pancake, cappuccino, and premium wines. It's all very good.

Be prepared to mingle with big crowds from the university and to listen to a nonstop jukebox.

PONTIAC GRILL, *429 Front Street. (408) 427-2290. Breakfast, lunch, and dinner daily. Inexpensive.*

✔ **Sea Cloud Restaurant and Social Club.**   If you have just one mealtime to spend in Santa Cruz, make it at the Sea Cloud. Despite the silly name, this is a terrific place for fresh fish, imaginatively prepared. I had the best salmon in my life here. They also have wonderful entrees for non–fish eaters.

The restaurant is quite attractive, situated on the municipal pier overlooking the Santa Cruz beach and boardwalk. You can drive your car out on the pier and park with relative ease.

Just about anything you order will be first-rate, including the luscious desserts. It's a big restaurant, but reservations are advised.

SEA CLOUD RESTAURANT AND SOCIAL CLUB, *Municipal Pier. (408) 458-9393. Lunch and dinner daily. Moderate to expensive.*

SOQUEL   ✔ **Greenhouse at the Farm.**   A truly beautiful and relaxing spot for a meal, especially on a nice day, is this restaurant situated on a working farm. The greenhouse is a large Victorian building where you can sit indoors near the salad bar. Or, weather permitting, you can sit outside on a garden patio.

The food features produce grown on the farm, plus items like quiche, omelets, seafood, and homemade soups and breads. The salad bar is well stocked, and you could easily let your salad bar creation become your entire meal. The food is not spectacular, but it is wholesome, and the atmosphere can't be beat.

Also, this is a gardener's paradise. My wife, Catherine, dashed off to the farm's nursery between courses, and we left the restaurant with a brand-new cactus collection.

GREENHOUSE AT THE FARM, *5555 Soquel Drive (a few minutes south of Santa*

Cruz on Route 1). (408) 476-5613. Lunch Monday through Saturday, dinner daily, plus Sunday brunch. Moderate.

✔ **Mansion House Restaurant.**   One of my nicest surprises on a trip from Santa Cruz to the Monterey Peninsula was lunch in this historic Victorian hotel. Located in the center of town, this place serves very good food with all the taste and flourishes you might expect to find only in larger-city restaurants.

The dining room is very comfortable, which is yet another bonus on the frequent days when the temperature climbs into the 90s. The menu features locally grown artichokes and avocados in salads, as well as nicely prepared grilled dishes and fresh pasta.

MANSION HOUSE RESTAURANT, *414 Main Street. (408) 724-2495. Lunch Monday through Saturday, dinner daily, plus Sunday brunch. Moderate.*

East Bay

The East Bay cities of Berkeley and Oakland are justifiably well known for their restaurants. Some of the finest and best-known places to eat in the entire Bay Area are here, including the world-famous Chez Panisse, where the California cuisine craze began. These restaurants are easy to find and are not on the back roads. So, in keeping with the theme of the book, the restaurants recommended here are those less likely to be found in other guidebooks. They are also chosen for proximity to destinations included in the main text of this book.

✔ **Beau Rivage.**   At the end of a road leading to a marina in Alameda stands a rather ornate French restaurant. I can't figure out what it's doing there, except serving very good traditional French food.

One afternoon my cameraman and I, both clad in jeans, lunched by candlelight with fine linen and china at a table overlooking the Bay. The other couple in the room didn't even notice us. Apparently, dinners are more crowded and formal.

I should mention that this is not a quasi-French restaurant. Both the chef and our waiter were French and very charming.

BEAU RIVAGE, *1042 Ballena Boulevard. (415) 523-1660. Lunch Monday through Friday, dinner daily. Moderate to expensive.*

✔ **Chevy's.**   If you want crowds and action, the hottest place to go in Alameda is a semi-Mexican place called Chevy's. This is a big operation, with lots of glitz and a kitchen that produces Americanized versions of south-of-the-border cooking. It's attractive and a lot of fun, and the food is decent.

CHEVY'S, *2400 Mariner Square. (415) 521-3768. Lunch and dinner daily. Moderate.*

ANTIOCH ✔ **Potato Barge.**   I don't think I will insult the town of Antioch if I report that there are not a lot of places to eat here. But how could I resist checking out a place called the Potato Barge? As it turns out, it's a small restaurant that doesn't really serve a lot of potato dishes. The name comes from the waterfront location: Barges moving potatoes used to pass by.

This is a burger and salad bar place, and the food is pretty good. If you stop by and need to use the rest room, be forewarned about the wallpaper in the men's room; it's rated X.

POTATO BARGE, *105 F Street. Open for lunch and dinner Monday through Friday. Inexpensive.*

BENICIA ✔ **First Street Foods.**   Down near the waterfront and antique row is a cozy place for people with light appetites. First Street Foods offers items like pastas, salads, and a pâté or two, served in an atmosphere that is conducive to perhaps just having a cappuccino and reading the paper for a while. Their desserts are good, too, and take-out service is available.

FIRST STREET FOODS, *440 First Street. (707) 745-4404. Opens 9:30 A.M. Tuesday through Sunday; closes 5 P.M. Tuesday, Wednesday, Saturday, and Sunday, 9 P.M. Thursday and Friday; closed Monday. Moderate.*

✔ **Mabel's.**   Many hearts were broken a few years ago when a restaurant in Benicia called Doña Francesca was forced to close because the landlord wanted to use the space for something else. But there was a silver lining to that cloud when some of the crew from Doña Francesca opened Mabel's.

Mabel's serves good, wholesome food in a comfortable re-created 1950s diner, complete with booths and a counter. You can get typical diner entrees, such as omelets and burgers, plus daily specials, which show some of the imaginative touches of the earlier restaurant. One of the specialties is their version of a Philly cheese steak sandwich, oozing with cheese and peppers. The desserts are wonderful, and you get plenty to eat for your money.

MABEL'S, *635 First Street. (707) 746-7068. Breakfast, lunch, and dinner daily, plus Sunday brunch. Inexpensive to moderate.*

CONCORD ✔ **Hot Dog Palace.**   For a quick bite you will find a very good selection of hot dogs and other sandwiches at the Hog Dog Palace. Service is quick, and you can sit and listen to the buzz from the courthouse crowd to find out what's going on in town. As for the decor, the place is more like a large coffeeshop than a hot dog stand or a palace.

HOT DOG PALACE, *1990 Grant Street. (415) 676-8723. Lunch and dinner daily. Inexpensive.*

✓ **Lippz Bistro.**   In a little house that stands in the shadow of a sparkling new Bank of America complex is a lovely restaurant combining continental and California cuisine. Lippz's menu features items like chicken marinated in lime and chiles, homemade sausages with corn and cheese timbales, plus a daily pasta and a daily calzone. The crowd from the bank is very well fed.

LIPPZ BISTRO, *2211 Clayton Street. (415) 827-1363. Lunch Monday through Friday, dinner Tuesday through Saturday, and Sunday brunch. Moderate.*

✓ **T.R.'s.**   *T.R.* stands for Teddy Roosevelt. I'm not sure why, but it really doesn't matter. This is a very large restaurant and bar that serves very good food. The menu offers a little something for everybody, from meat-and-potatoes eaters to those who prefer leaner cuisine. You can also get a great burger and fries, grilled chicken or fish, and specials like spinach linguine or a marinated pork sandwich with mustard sauce. Everything is prepared skillfully.

At lunchtime this is a popular spot for nearby business people. At cocktail time the bar is jumping, and there are TV sets everywhere for sports fans.

T.R.'S, *2001 Salvio Street. (415) 827-4660. Serving lunch and dinner daily, and Sunday brunch. Moderate.*

✓ **Nantucket Fish Company.**   Sitting out on the Crockett Marina, under the shadow of the Carquinez Bridge, is a bit of New England in the form of a restaurant called the Nantucket Fish Company. To get there, it's almost as difficult as driving to New England, as you have to negotiate a dirt hill and then cross some railroad tracks after you park your car. Once inside you'll think you've stepped into a lost corner of Cape Cod.

CROCKETT

The fresh catches of the day are written on a blackboard on a wall. There are also daily seafood entrees, and some dishes for non–fish eaters. The best thing to order, I think, is the fresh fish, and ask them to broil it without any sauce. In other words, the simpler the better is your best bet. The New England chowder is also quite good.

NANTUCKET FISH COMPANY, *at the foot of Port Street at the pier. (707) 557-9200. Lunch and dinner daily. Moderate.*

✓ **L'Ultima**.   Located in a large old house with an inviting front porch, this place bills itself as a "New Mexican" restaurant. That means that L'Ultima serves Mexican food like tacos and enchiladas (dishes in which the chile pepper is quite prominent) and Southwestern dishes like grilled meats and gourmet stews. It's all quite good.

DANVILLE

If you're feeling truly adventurous, have their ultimate dessert: piles of ice cream and chocolate sauce over pastry, a feast for the eyes as well as the sweet tooth.

L'ULTIMA, *263 South Hartz Avenue. (415) 838-9705. Lunch and dinner daily, plus Sunday brunch. Moderate.*

✔ **Vally Medlyn's.**   This is a diner named after the original proprietor, and it still looks like the typical coffeeshop of the 1940s and 1950s. A counter runs the length of the restaurant, plus there are several plastic booths.

As for the food, it, too, is like what you'd find in a typical coffeeshop of days past. This is Middle American diner food, and it is prepared faithfully. You'll find soup, tuna salad, grilled cheese, and the perennial hamburger. What's more, the waitresses like to joke with you, and everybody there seems to be having a good time.

VALLY MEDLYN'S, *184 North Hartz Avenue. (415) 837-4040. Breakfast and lunch daily. Inexpensive.*

FAIRFIELD   ✔ **Fairfield Landing.**   Overlooking Route 80 is a strangely nautical-looking place called the Fairfield Landing. This restaurant would look right at home at San Francisco's Fisherman's Wharf, but here it is a long way from the water. Anyway, it is an attractive operation, serving fresh fish, plus selections for meat and chicken eaters. The food is not great, but it's adequate, and there are not a lot of choices in this part of the world.

FAIRFIELD LANDING, *2440 Martin Road. (707) 429-2370. Lunch weekdays, dinner daily, and brunch Sunday. Moderate.*

✔ **Joe's Buffet.**   If you want a quick meal or a very good sandwich, try Joe's in downtown Fairfield. This is a friendly, informal spot that has been a Fairfield tradition for years. As you walk in the door you will be greeted by the sight of huge slabs of roast beef and corned beef sitting behind a steam table. There will probably be a pasta dish or two. Place your order and prepare to eat a huge sandwich or platter of pasta accompanied by a salad.

JOE'S BUFFET, *834 Texas Avenue. (707) 425-2317. Open 10 A.M. to 7 P.M. weekdays, to 4 P.M. Saturday; closed Sunday. Inexpensive.*

FREMONT   ✔ **Lucia's.**   I'm usually wary of fish houses in places that are not known for good restaurants. My fish is either fried in a heavy batter, or broiled until it's inedibly dry. Fortunately, they know what to do with fish at Lucia's. At lunch, a nice piece of halibut was broiled to juicy perfection, accompanied with soup or salad, potato, vegetables, and good sourdough bread . . . all for under $7. A real find.

Across the street, there's a companion Italian restaurant, featuring pizza, but I haven't tried it yet.

LUCIA'S, *681 Mowry Avenue. (415) 794-7247. Open daily for lunch and dinner. Inexpensive for lunch. Moderate to expensive for dinner.*

✔ Mission Peak Foods.

A block or so from Mission San Jose is a very congenial, family-run Mexican restaurant that happens to be one of the only places to eat near the mission. Fortunately, the food is quite good, with a menu offering items we have come to expect from Mexican-American restaurants. Portions are large, and there is a home-cooked quality to the chicken and beef that fills their tacos and burritos.

MISSION PEAK FOODS, *129 Anza Street. (415) 651-7112. Lunch and dinner Monday through Saturday. Inexpensive.*

✔ A Street Café and Wine Bar.

A Street Café is a very stylish California cuisine restaurant located in an area more familiar with fast-food franchises and Mexican cafés. The menu, which changes monthly, features such things as light pastas, warm chicken salad, and fresh fish. All the food is remarkably fresh and tasty and moderately priced.

The decor is stark white walls with blond wood tables and attractive overhead lamps. Counter service is available for those who hate to occupy a table when eating alone; in the evening the counter doubles as a bar for wine tasting.

A STREET CAFÉ AND WINE BAR, *1213 A Street. (415) 582-2558. Lunch Monday through Friday, dinner Tuesday through Saturday. Moderate.*

✔ Eden Express.

This is the sort of place you can go to feel better about the world. Eden Express is a very pleasant coffeehouse that also serves light meals and is staffed by mentally retarded employees who are learning to interact with society. The food is good and the menu large. Lunch might be a quiche or a homemade soup, breakfasts feature fresh-baked pastries, and there is an espresso machine for cappuccino and caffè latte. A wide variety of teas is also available.

EDEN EXPRESS, *799 B Street. (415) 886-8765. Breakfast and lunch daily. Inexpensive.*

✔ Old South Bar-B-Q.

Barbecue fans can be very discriminating and will argue over which of the many spots in the Bay Area serve the most authentic, best-tasting ribs. Old South always gets a lot of votes.

This is a small place, but they put out a lot of ribs, chicken, and links, all accented by their secret sauce. (All respectable barbecue joints have their own secret sauce.) You have your choice of spiciness, and if you go for the hottest you are likely to shed a tear or two.

OLD SOUTH BAR-B-Q, *27941 Manon Street at West Tennyson. (415) 782-1163. Lunch and dinner Tuesday through Sunday. Inexpensive.*

✓ **Rue de Main.**   French cuisine in Hayward? You bet, and it's good, too. Rue de Main is run by a former Berkeley chef, and he puts out classic French dishes like coq au vin and boeuf bourguignonne in a very charming little spot in the center of town.

RUE DE MAIN, *22622 Main Street. (415) 537-0812. Lunch and dinner Tuesday through Friday, dinner Saturday. Moderate.*

✓ **Val's Burgers.**   Wanna see where the Fonz hangs out? This must be the place because it looks like the set of *Happy Days*. Val's started in the 1950s and never left. The place has remained unchanged, except for occasional price hikes. (Nobody can survive selling hamburgers for 30 cents anymore.)

But this wonderful diner is run by Val and his sons, and you can get huge burgers, fries, and one of the best milkshakes in the world (I taste-tested three of them on one visit, all in the name of research, you understand).

VAL'S BURGERS, *2115 Kelly, at B Street. (415) 889-8257. Breakfast, lunch, and dinner Tuesday through Saturday. Inexpensive.*

LAFAYETTE   ✓ **Tourelle.**   Here you'll find the best food east of the Caldecott Tunnel, which separates Berkeley and Oakland from Contra Costa County. Tourelle is situated in a new building that looks like it was transported from nineteenth-century France, and it features a fancy dining room and an informal café.

In the dining room the emphasis is on California French cooking, using the finest ingredients and offering entrees with wonderful sauces. The menu changes often, determined by what ingredients are freshest.

Across a lovely courtyard from the dining room is the café, where it feels like you've suddenly crossed the border into Italy. Here you can have pizza, fresh pasta, grilled entrees, and salads in the style of a Milanese trattoria.

TOURELLE, *3565 Mount Diablo Boulevard. (415) 284-3565. Restaurant serves lunch and dinner Monday through Friday, dinner Saturday, lunch Sunday. Café serves lunch and dinner daily. Restaurant: expensive; café: moderate.*

LIVERMORE   ✓ **El Lorito Restaurant and Taqueria.**   A real surprise in Livermore is El Lorito. Not that it's so surprising to find a good, authentic Mexican restaurant in this area but that it is so well disguised in a nondescript shopping center near the downtown section of town.

When you enter, it appears that this is another quickie place where you place your order and then take your taco or burrito to your table. That's true . . . in the front. But if you go into the rear of the place you'll find a spacious and attractive dining room offering a more varied menu.

Along with the usual Mexican-American dishes you can have a more complete meal, such as a wonderfully roasted pork, and camarones (shrimp) with a spicy sauce. Even the rice, beans, and tortillas are especially good and are freshly made.

EL LORITO RESTAURANT AND TAQUERIA, *1316 Railroad Avenue. (415) 455-8226. Lunch Monday through Saturday, dinner daily, plus Sunday breakfast. Taqueria, inexpensive; restaurant, moderate.*

✔ Wente Brothers Sparkling Wine Cellars Restaurant.

Once you get past Berkeley and Oakland there are only a handful of restaurants to compete with the best in the Bay Area. Certainly by the time you get to the rolling agricultural land in the Livermore area you will find nothing to compare with the grand style of the Wente Brothers' showcase.

Nestled in one of the buildings in the Sparkling Wine complex (see Chapter 6, entry 16), Wente's features an elegant dining room with attentive service, as if to say, "You are not in the sticks out here."

As for the food, it is quite expensive but it is also quite good. The chefs do imaginative things with duck, lamb, and fish. They also feature fresh vegetables and often offer such hard-to-get items as stuffed zucchini blossoms. A wide range of California wines is available, but they seem to smile a lot when you order the house brand.

WENTE BROTHERS SPARKLING WINE CELLARS RESTAURANT, *5050 Arroyo Road. (415) 447-3023. Lunch and dinner Wednesday through Monday. Reservations strongly advised. Expensive.*

✔ Al's Diner.

LOCKE

As mentioned in our story about the town of Locke (see Chapter 9, item 5), Al's is a must stop. It's as much a part of visiting Locke as the old buildings.

Al's is also known as Al the Wop's, a nickname developed before our more enlightened time of ethnic sensitivity, and it seems to have stuck. As you enter the bar you will notice dollar bills hanging from the ceiling. Ask the bartender about them, but be prepared to pay for the answer. The tradition of the joint is that it costs you a buck to find out how the dollars all got up there.

In the dining room you will sit down at a table that has not only shakers of salt and pepper but also jars of peanut butter and jelly. That's because the specialty of the house is steak and peanut butter, and now they've added chicken to the menu. Either way, you will also get a side of buttered French bread. What happens with the peanut butter and jelly is up to you.

AL'S DINER, *Main Street. (916) 776-1800. Lunch and dinner daily. Inexpensive.*

MARTINEZ ✓ **Amato's.** If you are into politics and you also like Italian food, head to Amato's, which is in downtown Martinez.

Local politicians gather here for lunch, and since Martinez is the county seat, an eavesdropper can get an earful. As for the food, it's of the Southern Italian variety: pastas with red sauces, veal parmigiana, and garlic bread. Not great, but certainly adequate.

AMATO'S, *414 Ferry Street. (415) 228-3727. Lunch and dinner Monday through Friday. Inexpensive to moderate.*

✓ **Hot Dog Depot.** For a quick bite, the in spot in town is the Hot Dog Depot, right across from the railroad station. They serve many varieties of good, juicy hot dogs, plus items like frozen yogurt, pastries, and an occasional salad. If the weather's right, and the weather is usually warm here, you can sit outside and watch for the train while you look out at the Bay.

HOT DOG DEPOT, *400 Ferry Street. (415) 372-7177. Open 7 A.M. to 6 P.M. daily. Inexpensive.*

POINT RICHMOND ✓ **The Baltic.** This comfortable and friendly Italian restaurant is a hangout for many of the folks who work in the Point Richmond area. The Baltic is an informal place, where you can roll up your shirtsleeves and dig into large portions of middle-of-the-road Italian food (such as ravioli and spaghetti with meat sauce), plus sandwiches and soups. The menu is a bit more elaborate at dinner.

THE BALTIC, *135 Park Place. (415) 235-2532. Lunch and dinner daily. Moderate.*

✓ **Hotel Mac.** The fanciest place in Point Richmond, with prices to match, is the venerable old Hotel Mac dining room. The Mac menu features prime ribs and steak, fish dishes, and a few items designed to appeal to the gourmet palate. Portions are ample; reservations are advised. Atmosphere and food both rate high.

HOTEL MAC, *50 Washington Avenue. (415) 233-0576. Lunch Monday through Friday, dinner Tuesday through Saturday, plus Sunday brunch. Moderate to expensive.*

RIO VISTA ✓ **Henry's.** Restaurants really are few and far between in this neck of the woods, but at least Henry's is there 24 hours a day. This is a standard American diner, serving items like burgers, patty melts, and, for iron stomachs, the Monte Cristo —a deep-fried sandwich with cheese and ham inside; it's tasty, but hardly for the cholesterol-conscious.

But if you are really in the mood for letting go, you might as well save room for one of their cream pies. I can personally vouch for the chocolate and the coconut cream.

HENRY'S, *1000 Highway 12. (707) 374-6304. Open 24 hours. Inexpensive.*

✔ **The Point.**   The nicest spot in town is called The Point, which overlooks a lovely marina. Frankly, there is nothing special about the food, but the view is delightful and the options in town are limited. If you put away any comparisons with what you can get in San Francisco, Napa Valley, or Berkeley, I think you will enjoy your meal. The menu is standard American fare.

THE POINT, *120 Marina Drive. (707) 374-5400. Lunch and dinner Tuesday through Sunday. Moderate.*

✔ **Chatillon Restaurant.**   Good French restaurants are beginning to crop up in the suburbs, establishments that would have only been found in San Francisco 10 years ago. Chatillon fits into this category. Nestled in a small shopping center, it looks like a throwback to an older type of design, the kind of French restaurant you might find in most American cities, with candles, white linen, and waiters in tuxedos flaming dishes in front of your table.

The trick is to go here for lunch, when the no-nonsense waitresses take over, and when the prices are almost half the cost of dinner.

As for the food, it's excellent. This is not nouvelle or California cuisine, but traditional French and continental cooking with wonderful sauces.

CHATILLON, *21314A San Ramon Valley Boulevard. (415) 828-7910. Open daily for lunch and dinner. Moderate at lunch. Expensive at dinner.*

✔ **China Panda.**   Restaurants change hands often in the burgeoning suburbs, which might explain the unusual decor of the China Panda. Situated in yet another nondescript shopping center, the place was once an Italian restaurant; you dine in what looks like a cross between Peking and Palermo. Make no mistake about the kitchen, though. This is very good Chinese food, on a par with many of the better places in San Francisco. Service is gracious and leisurely in this family-run operation. If you're concerned that all you can get in a suburban Chinese restaurant is chow mein and egg foo yung, don't worry; the menu here offers a broad selection.

CHINA PANDA, *2211-H San Ramon Boulevard. (415) 838-8044. Lunch Monday through Friday, dinner daily. Moderate.*

✔ **Mudd's.**   Mudd's is the restaurant component of the Crow Canyon Institute (see Chapter 7, destination 4). It is an architectural gem, featuring a graceful, curved wooden ceiling and windows overlooking the gardens. On nice days you can dine on the patio.

SAN RAMON

The menu features the produce grown in the gardens, offering unusual combinations of vegetables with fish, chicken, beef, or fresh pasta. Certainly you will find at least one edible flower on your plate. The salads are a specialty of the house.

MUDD'S, *10 Boardwalk, on the grounds of the Crow Canyon Institute. (415) 837-9387. Lunch Monday through Friday, dinner Wednesday through Sunday, and Sunday brunch. Moderate to expensive.*

SUISUN CITY   ✔ **Josiah Wings.** Just when you think there is nothing good to eat for miles around, you bump into a place called Josiah Wings. The decor is nothing to write home about, but the food is a pleasant surprise. At dinner the chef, imported from France, gets creative, and the result, usually involving such things as chicken or pasta, is wonderful.

JOSIAH WINGS, *627 Main Street. (707) 429-2828. Dinner Tuesday through Sunday. Inexpensive to moderate.*

VALLEJO   ✔ **City Lights Café.** This is a genuine surprise in Vallejo, a place not known for epicurean delights. Situated right in the center of town in an old PG&E building, this spacious and bright café offers wonderful California cuisine. Fresh fish, chicken, pasta, and other staples of light dining are featured, and the chef knows what to do with them. Truly a spot worth going out of the way for.

CITY LIGHTS CAFÉ, *415 Virginia Street. (707) 557-9200. Open 11 A.M. to 8 P.M. Monday through Friday. Moderate.*

✔ **House of Soul.** With all the various types of cuisine available in the greater Bay Area, there are surprisingly few soul food restaurants. The House of Soul helps fill that gap nicely.

This is a friendly, rather small spot a few blocks from Highway 80, run by a family that knows the food of the South well. Wonderful fried chicken, chicken fried steak, greens, and biscuits are usually available. The only item that doesn't measure up is the ribs, only because they have to cook them in a kitchen oven instead of over an open fire. But don't let that keep you away from their other delicious offerings.

HOUSE OF SOUL, *1526 Solano Avenue. (707) 644-3792. Lunch and dinner Monday through Saturday. Inexpensive.*

WALNUT CREEK   ✔ **Spiedini.** The chain that operates successful restaurants like Prego and MacArthur Park in San Francisco has a real winner in Walnut Creek. Spiedini is a modern, sleek Italian restaurant offering an extensive menu of interesting dishes. The emphasis is on Northern Italian cooking, along with the ubiquitous pizzas, calzone, and fresh pasta. This is a touch of Milan in Contra Costa County.

There's also a touch of Beverly Hills as Spiedini is in a bank building, and offers valet parking.

SPIEDINI, *101 Ygnacio Valley Road. (415) 939-2100. Lunch and dinner Monday through Friday, dinner only Saturday and Sunday. Moderate.*

WOODLAND

✔ **Jody's Café**.   On Main Street in Woodland it is hard to miss a pink place called Jody's Café; though it doesn't look it, this is the home of very good, authentic Mexican food. Several years ago Jody's Café was a typical small-town coffeehouse. Then a Mexican-American family bought it and changed the menu to cuisine from their homeland. They just didn't bother to change the name or the decor.

Though there are quite a few Mexican restaurants in the area, this appears to be the favorite spot for locals. A woman at the Woodland Opera House told me that when her daughter comes to visit from San Francisco, she insists there's not a Mexican place in the big city as good as Jody's. Certainly there are none as inexpensive.

JODY'S CAFÉ *1126 East Main Street, to the east of Route 113. (916) 662-9857. Open 4 to 10 P.M. Monday through Saturday. Inexpensive.*

✔ **Morrison's Upstairs**.   A real culinary surprise is to be found on the third floor of a renovated nineteenth-century luxury apartment building in the town of Woodland. Morrison's Upstairs is a very attractive, cosmopolitan spot for lunch or dinner.

Lunch is a real bargain. The regular menu features fish, chicken, pasta, vegetarian items, and burgers; specials can include swordfish, grilled chicken, and a pasta dish. I ordered the chicken and was served a very nicely grilled boneless breast with a lovely herb sauce on the side, oven-fried potatoes, and fruit. The homemade desserts are also recommended.

MORRISON'S UPSTAIRS, *428½ First Street. (916) 666-0500. Lunch Sunday through Friday, dinner daily. Lunch, inexpensive to moderate; dinner, moderate.*

Gold Country

AVERY

✔ **Larry's 4 Ks Drive-In**.   Outside of Murphys is a small town called Avery where you'll find a very friendly café-diner that's a family operation. There really is a Larry, and the four Ks are his wife and three daughters: Karen, Kathryn, Kathleen, and Karla, I think. They all moved up here from Berkeley a few years ago to set up a dream life in the Gold Country, a dream that included having their own restaurant. This old converted drive-in serves burgers, hot dogs, and milkshakes, but these are really good burgers, hot dogs, and milkshakes, plus home-made fried chicken, a fishwich made from real fish, soup, or spaghetti—what-ever they feel like cooking up that day. There are a surprising number of items on the menu, and there's a real family feeling about the place.

LARRY'S 4 KS DRIVE-IN, *Highway 4. (209) 795-2661. Breakfast, lunch, and dinner daily. Inexpensive.*

COLUMBIA ✔ **City Hotel.** Considered by many to be the finest dining room in the Gold Coun-try, the City Hotel serves elegant French meals in a beautifully restored Victo-rian inn. Reservations must be made well in advance.

CITY HOTEL, *Main Street. (209) 532-1479. Lunch and dinner Tuesday through Sunday. Expensive.*

EL DORADO ✔ **Poor Red's.** This is one of the best barbecue spots in Northern California, in a town just south of Placerville on Route 49. Poor Red's is a bar with a huge brick barbecue built into the back wall. Their ribs and chicken are worth a trip out of the way.

POOR RED'S, *Main Street. (916) 622-2901. Lunch and dinner Monday through Saturday, 2 to 11 P.M. Sunday. Inexpensive.*

GRASS VALLEY ✔ **Michael D's.** This is a good place to eat when you're in the mood for a leisurely dinner cooked by a chef whose specialty is California and French cooking. Fish, veal, beef, and chicken dishes are based on the freshest ingredients available. The atmosphere is relaxed formality, and reservations are advised.

MICHAEL D'S, *155 Mill Street. (916) 272-7000. Dinner Wednesday through Sunday. Moderate to expensive.*

✔ **Tofanelli's.** This is a spacious downtown café that is a paradise for vegetar-ians. The meat eaters in your party can be well fed, too. While one gets a juicy hamburger, the other can have a tofu burger, and the cholesterol-conscious per-son can have a turkey burger. Several casserole-type vegetarian entrees are also offered, and the huge garden salads are a feast for eyes and palate.

TOFANELLI'S, *302 West Main Street. (916) 273-9927. Breakfast and lunch daily, dinner Monday through Friday. Inexpensive to moderate.*

JACKSON ✔ **Theresa's.** This is where the locals eat in the Sutter Creek–Jackson area. Theresa's is a friendly Italian restaurant, serving pasta dishes, chicken, veal, and fresh seafood in sizable quantities. Although the family is from Genoa and usually offers a Northern Italian pesto dish or two, the sauces run to the South-ern Italian tomato-and-oregano variety.

THERESA'S, *1235 Jackson Gate Road. (209) 223-1786. Dinner Friday through Tuesday. Moderate.*

✔ **Jack's for Dinner.**   If you have time for an adventure, call and make a reservation at Jack's. At 5 P.M. they stop taking calls; if only two people have called to make a reservation, that's how many people they'll shop for; if 12 people call, they shop for 12. What you will get is a five-course dinner served on fine china, with crystal and silver at the place settings. Jack really knows how to cook. The cuisine is generally continental, but the exact menu will depend on the season and the chef's mood.

JACK'S FOR DINNER, *101 Sacramento Street. (916) 265-3405. Dinner Wednesday through Saturday. Moderate to Expensive.*

✔ **Mama Su's Squeeze Inn.**   You really do have to squeeze into this little diner with a counter and a few tables. You may also have to wait for a seat because people all around Nevada City know that Mama Su is going to cook a great breakfast or lunch. This is a real folksy joint, where a lot of friendly teasing goes on, and everybody seems to know everybody. Folks with appetites big and small will get plenty of home-cooked grub.

MAMA SU'S SQUEEZE INN, *108 South Pine Street. (916) 265-5408. Breakfast and lunch daily. Inexpensive.*

✔ **Michael's Garden Restaurant.**   In a small house in the main section of town, Michael's Garden serves continental dishes and prepares them quite well. Features of the restaurant include chicken wrapped in phyllo and hot and spicy prawns. This is a relaxed place with small dining rooms for intimacy.

MICHAEL'S GARDEN RESTAURANT, *216 Main Street. (916) 265-6660. Lunch and dinner Monday through Saturday. Moderate.*

✔ **Café Zoë.**   Right in the center of Placerville is a charming place featuring homemade soups and fresh-baked breads, scrumptious desserts, and an espresso bar. It's a good stop for lunch if you're in the central Gold Country or on the way back from South Tahoe.

CAFÉ ZOË, *301 Main Street. (916) 622-9681. Lunch Monday through Saturday, dinner Friday through Sunday, plus Sunday brunch. Inexpensive to moderate.*

✔ **Good Heavens—A Restaurant!**   The name gives you an idea of the good humor behind this café that will win you over. The owner and his helpers are so exuberant while extolling the virtues of their homemade quiche, soups, salads, sandwiches, and daily specials that you will want to try everything. Then just wait until they tell you about their cakes. . . . Supposedly *Gourmet* magazine has

NEVADA CITY

PLACERVILLE

SONORA

been trying to coax the recipes out of them. It's good-natured fun, and the food is good in a wholesome, tearoom fashion.

GOOD HEAVENS—A RESTAURANT!, *51 North Washington Street. (209) 532-3663. Lunch Wednesday through Monday, dinner Saturday and Sunday. Inexpensive to moderate.*

Road to Yosemite

GROVELAND ✔ **Coffee Express.**   On the way to or from Yosemite on Route 120, you will pass through the town of Groveland. By all means, plan to have lunch at the Coffee Express. Two delightful ladies opened this small café after their children were old enough to take care of themselves, and they offer salads and sandwiches and home-cooked meals that are wholesome and delicious. I will go there again and again, hoping for another piece of their chocolate cream pie, which is the best I've ever eaten. They also have an espresso machine.

COFFEE EXPRESS, *18765 Main Street. (209) 962-7393. Open 7 A.M. to 3 P.M. daily. Inexpensive.*

MANTECA ✔ **The Milk House.**   It looks very ordinary from the outside, but this is a real find. If you are heading to Yosemite, the Gold Country, or the Delta via Manteca, plan a meal at The Milk House.

The regular menu offers steaks, pasta, chicken dishes, and daily specials. I can vouch for a wonderfully fresh king salmon with lemon and capers, a chicken breast amandine, and a great, thick pea soup. Manteca is not what you'd call a "gourmet ghetto," but the food here would stack up favorably anywhere.

THE MILK HOUSE, *4480 West Yosemite Avenue. (209) 239-5221. Lunch Monday through Friday, dinner Monday through Saturday. Moderate.*

MODESTO ✔ **B Fisheries.**   Seafood lovers will find this a worthwhile stop in Modesto. This is a fish market and restaurant; you go to the fish counter, pick whatever you'd like, and they will cook it to your specifications, be it broiled, fried, sautéed, or poached. They also sell fish to take home and prepare yourself. The atmosphere is very informal, like a deli with tables in front of the counter. Even though Modesto is a bit landlocked, the fish is very fresh with deliveries from the Bay Area several days a week.

B FISHERIES, *1501 Coffee Street, in the Atherton Plaza, a few minutes east of Route 132. No phone. Lunch and dinner Monday through Saturday. Inexpensive to moderate.*

✓ **Mallards.**   On your way to or from Yosemite, you will probably want something to eat. The best place in town to suit all tastes is Mallards, a very large and attractive place on the old Yosemite Road, Route 132.

Surrounded by just about every franchised restaurant you can name, Mallards caters to every trend. They have an oyster bar, a mesquite grill, and several dishes they say are recommended by the American Heart Association for low-cholesterol diets. My advice is to stick to the most simply prepared grilled dishes and avoid the attempts to be fancy. Also, if you happen to use the rest rooms, you will notice they are labeled for "Drakes" and "Hens." Brush up on your farm terminology before nature calls.

MALLARDS, *1700 McHenry Street (Route 132). (209) 522-DUCK. Lunch and dinner daily. Inexpensive to moderate.*

✓ **Mountain Room Broiler.**   In Yosemite National Park, you are at the culinary mercy of the Curry Company, which runs all the food services. Their most famous restaurant is the dining room in the Ahwahnee Hotel. It is a gorgeous room that serves mediocre, expensive dinners. I enjoy the surroundings more at a less costly meal, like breakfast.

Instead, the best dinner to be had in Yosemite is in the Mountain Room Broiler at Yosemite Lodge. Here you have simply broiled steak or fish, and when the weather is good you can dine outdoors in a beautiful courtyard. Another advantage is that you can also dress informally at the Mountain Room Broiler, whereas the Ahwahnee dining room requires gentlemen to wear a jacket to dinner. (By the way, they keep a supply of jackets on hand for those who forgot to pack a dinner jacket, which is why so many diners in the Ahwahnee look like Pee-wee Herman.)

MOUNTAIN ROOM BROILER, *Yosemite Lodge. Open for dinner May to October, on an irregular schedule the rest of the year. For information and reservations, call (209) 232-4848. Moderate to expensive.*

YOSEMITE

Lake Tahoe

CARNELIAN BAY

✓ **Old Post Office Restaurant.**   Before you hit the slopes or head out on a hike, you might want to stoke up on breakfast at the Old Post Office. This place is a North Lake Tahoe tradition, and even if you are not a huge eater, you might enjoy watching others wolfing down stacks of pancakes, biscuits with country gravy, and various egg dishes. The food is pretty good here, but the emphasis is on volume.

OLD POST OFFICE RESTAURANT, *5245 North Lake. (916) 546-3205. Open 6 A.M. to 3 P.M. daily. Inexpensive.*

EMERALD BAY   ✔ **Cantina Los Tres Hombres.**   If you are looking for a place that is filled with people out for a good time, head for the Cantina. This mammoth Mexican-American restaurant has many rooms and serves enormous portions of decent enchiladas, tacos, and burritos. Atmosphere is king, however, and the big draw seems to be the huge pitchers of margaritas. Many folks never make it past the drinks and appetizers in the lounge. The nachos alone could satisfy a normal appetite.

CANTINA LOS TRES HOMBRES, *Emerald Bay Road at Tenth Street. (916) 544-1233. Open 11:30 A.M. to 10:30 P.M. Moderate.*

SQUAW VALLEY   ✔ **Perkins' Pretty Good Grocery.**   Named by a Garrison Keillor fan, Perkins' Grocery is much better than pretty good. This is an oasis of wonderful food right in the shadow of the Squaw Valley ski area. Here you can pick up food to take out or eat at one of their tables. One winter's day I sat in the warm sun and watched the snow show while eating a terrific chicken salad with a side of tabbouleh, great French roast coffee, and a luscious chocolate mousse cake. You will find a wonderful selection of food, wine, and other beverages crammed into this tiny store and restaurant.

PERKINS' PRETTY GOOD GROCERY, *1602 Squaw Valley Road. (916) 581-3663. Last time we checked, hours were 10 A.M. to 2 P.M. in summer, 8 A.M. to 6 P.M. November through April, and closed during May, June, and parts of September and October. Better call ahead. Moderate.*

TAHOE CITY   ✔ **Lakehouse Pizza.**   Here you have a pizza parlor, Tahoe-style. The jukebox is blaring, everyone is beautifully tanned and in great shape, and the waitresses are incredibly bubbly because they have either just returned from the lake or the slopes or are heading that way.

The food is also geared for active people. They serve enormous portions of pasta, gigantic hero sandwiches, pretty good pizza, and other dishes you can enjoy as you look out on the lake. At lunch, Lakehouse Pizza is a good place to relax; at dinner and into the night, the joint is jumping.

LAKEHOUSE PIZZA, *120 Grove Street, on the lake in the center of Tahoe City. (916) 583-2225. Inexpensive to moderate.*

✔ **Wolfdale's.**   Probably the best meal available in the North Tahoe area is to be had at Wolfdale's, which offers what it calls "cuisine unique." It can best be described as California cuisine with a Japanese influence. Every plate will be beautifully arranged and presented, the ingredients will be fresh and seasonal, and the food will be perfused with subtle combinations of tastes. Be sure to have a reservation.

WOLFDALE'S, *640 North Lake Boulevard. (916) 583-5700. Dinner Wednesday through Monday. Moderate to expensive.*

✔ **The Restaurant.**   It may appear a bit presumptuous to name one's business The Restaurant, but it turns out to be very appropriate here in Fort Bragg. This is the one spot in town that caters to just about every taste, serving fresh fish, chicken, beef, and vegetarian dishes and doing them all very well. With a fishing harbor nearby, you are likely to find a good choice of seafood. I had a perfect salmon steak, simply broiled, with crisply cooked vegetables and a good salad. Nothing fancy, just reliably good food.

THE RESTAURANT, *418 North Main Street. (707) 964-9800. Lunch and dinner Thursday through Tuesday. Moderate.*

✔ **Little River Restaurant.**   I must admit that I have never been in the area when the Little River Restaurant is open, but I include it in the book because locals keep telling me how great it is. This is a tiny place located behind the Little River post office a few miles south of Mendocino and serving gourmet California French cooking. There are two seatings for dinner, and what they serve depends on what's fresh and the whims of the chef.

LITTLE RIVER RESTAURANT, *7750 North Highway 1. (707) 937-4945. Dinner Thursday through Sunday. Moderate to expensive.*

✔ **Café Beaujolais.**   This homey café near the main tourist action in Mendocino is a Bay Area favorite, garnering a lion's share of local and national publicity. Most food writers wax ecstatic about the café's breakfast, with its offerings of ranch-fresh eggs, homemade muffins and pastries, and a cup of coffee as good as you'll find anywhere in San Francisco.

Lunch features salads made with vegetables grown out in back of the restaurant or on nearby farms, plus sandwiches and daily specials. Dinner is a bit more adventurous, but all meals emphasize fresh ingredients prepared skillfully. This is a popular place with locals and visitors, so be prepared to wait.

CAFÉ BEAUJOLAIS, *961 Ukiah Street. (707) 937-5614. Breakfast and lunch daily, dinner Thursday through Sunday in spring and summer. Call first to be sure. Inexpensive to moderate.*

✔ **Carine's Fish Grotto.**   Just south of Fort Bragg, and about 20 minutes north of Mendocino, is a little fishing harbor with several seafood restaurants. My favorite is Carine's, though I've never tried any of their fish. I go to Carine's for the hamburger, an entire pound of good ground beef on a huge bun, accompanied by a sky-high mound of french fries—all for $5 (in 1986). You can sit inside or, weather permitting, outside at picnic tables on a dock overlooking the harbor where working fishing boats putt out and in.

Carine's posts outrageous-looking prices for their dinners, but don't be discouraged. When I asked Mama Carine about an entree with a $35 price tag, she assured me it is enough to feed a party of five or six.

CARINE'S, *32420 North Harbor Drive. (707) 964-2429. Lunch and dinner daily. Inexpensive to moderate.*

Redwood Empire

EUREKA   ✔ **Ramone's Café.**   Ramone's is *the* spot for imaginative cuisine in the city of Eureka. Located in a tiny alley in the Old Town section, it's a charming little place that succeeds in its attempts to present good food that is out of the ordinary.

For example, on one visit, the adventurous cameraman had to try the special of the evening called "Chicken Mamoo," which was advertised as being very spicy. We all tasted it and agreed it was the hottest dish any of us had ever eaten. It was also excellent. Other specials included an unusual stuffed steak, some more traditional veal and chicken dishes, and fresh fish. Everything was good and plentiful.

RAMONE'S CAFÉ, *Opera Alley, off E Street. (707) 444-3339. Lunch Monday through Friday, dinner Tuesday through Saturday, plus brunch Sunday. Moderate.*

✔ **Samoa Cookhouse.**   Everybody who comes to the Eureka area crosses the bridge to the village of Samoa to eat in the historic cookhouse that was once the commissary for lumberjacks before they headed out into the forest. The cookhouse still serves up lumberjack-sized meals for hearty appetites. Part of the building is now a museum of the early logging industry, but there is still room to serve hundreds of people simultaneously.

Everything is served family-style, and you get what they happen to be serving that day. Breakfast might be as many eggs as you can eat, potatoes, sausages, biscuits, juice, and coffee, with maybe a few pancakes thrown in. Lunch might feature endless plates of fried chicken, mashed potatoes, vegetables, rolls—you get the idea. The food is not what you would call nouvelle cuisine, but it's a real value.

SAMOA COOKHOUSE, *across the Samoa Bridge from Eureka. Follow the signs on Samoa Boulevard; once you get to Samoa, you cannot miss the cookhouse. (707) 442-1659. Breakfast, lunch, and dinner daily; closed Thanksgiving and Christmas. Inexpensive.*

✔ **Becker's Pool Hall.**   This is a real hangout for the citizens of Ferndale. In the front part of the room there's a lunch counter, a few tables, and some books and magazines. In the back there's always a card game in progress and a group of kibitzers huddled around the action. The only thing missing at Becker's Pool Hall is a pool table.

Lunch is sandwiches and whatever the cook happens to make that day; it might be chili, an elaborate casserole, or good old spaghetti. It really doesn't matter because the real reason to come here is the atmosphere and the chance to meet the townspeople, who are very devoted to and opinionated about their town.

BECKER'S POOL HALL, *409 Main Street. No phone. Open 6 A.M. to 3 P.M. Monday through Saturday, 6 to 9 A.M. Sunday. Inexpensive.*

✔ **Ferndale Meats.**   For a wonderful and wonderfully huge sandwich sliced from big slabs of beef or ham right before your eyes, stop in at this butcher shop downtown. The sandwich is served on fresh-baked bread, and you can eat it there or take it on a picnic.

FERNDALE MEATS, *376 Main Street. (707) 786-4501. Open 8 A.M. to 5:30 P.M. Monday through Saturday. Inexpensive.*

✔ **The Cheesecake Lady.**   If you like desserts, stop in here. You'll find a tempting assortment on display, a few tables where you can sit and relax, and a counter espresso bar. This small café is the front section of a huge wholesale bakery operation that provides cheesecakes and other goodies to bakeries and restaurants as far away as San Francisco and Sacramento. I have personally sampled at least five of their offerings (in the name of research, of course), and I can tell you they are sensational. The chocolate mousse cake is too good to be real. At breakfast you can get a croissant or muffin and a good cup of coffee.

THE CHEESECAKE LADY, *right on Route 101, next door to the Hopland Brewery. (707) 744-1441. Open 7:30 A.M. to 6 P.M. weekdays, 9:30 A.M. to 5 P.M. weekends. Inexpensive.*

✔ **Hopland Brewery, Tavern, Beer Garden, and Restaurant.**   For a very good lunch or light dinner, this brewery/pub puts out a very respectable spread. You can get homemade soups, salads, juicy burgers, and daily specials. When the weather is warm, you can sit outside in the beer garden. They make their own beer, and it is very good. Non–beer drinkers might enjoy the pub's homemade mineral water, and there is a full supply of nonalcoholic beverages (see Chapter 14, destination 1).

HOPLAND BREWERY, TAVERN, BEER GARDEN, AND RESTAURANT, *13351 South*

Highway 101. (707) 744-1015. They are open on a very complicated schedule, so it's best to call ahead. Inexpensive.

✓ **Joel's Restaurant.**   The best place for a complete meal in Hopland is Joel's Restaurant, which is located in a high school building that has been remodeled into the Fetzer Winery complex called Hopland Station. Joel's serves fresh fish, pasta, and the rest of the items that have become the standard bill of fare for California cuisine. The important thing to know is that they use top ingredients and the chef really knows how to cook. The dining room is attractive and informal.

JOEL'S RESTAURANT, *right on Highway 101 in Hopland Station. (707) 744-1328. Dinner Wednesday through Sunday, plus Sunday brunch; lunch is available at the deli next door Monday through Saturday. Moderate.*

TRINIDAD   ✓ **Larrupin' Café.**   About a half hour north of Eureka in the lovely coastal town of Trinidad is a terrific restaurant run by a woman named Dixie. That ought to be a clue to what you'll get here. Larrupin' is a Southern term for good eating, and that's what Dixie offers at her café.

The menu features barbecue and Louisiana dishes. Everything is great. Dixie even bottles her secret sauces and sells them around the area. Larrupin' has a real following, so be sure to call ahead.

LARRUPIN' CAFÉ, *1150 Westhaven Drive. (707) 677-0230. At last report, dinner was served Friday, Saturday, and Sunday only; call ahead to see if the schedule has changed. Moderate.*

Monterey and Big Sur

Because this is such a busy tourist center, there are almost as many restaurants on the Monterey Peninsula as there are in the San Francisco area. An entire guidebook would be necessary for a complete listing.

In general, the huge fish houses near the wharf in Monterey are overpriced and tend to overcook their fish. Then there are the celebrity joints, such as Clint Eastwood's Hog's Breath Inn in Carmel; the food there is OK, but don't get your hopes up about running into Mayor Eastwood.

I will limit my recommendations to the few places I think are special.

BIG SUR   ✓ **Deetjen's Big Sur Inn.**   This is a very rustic, homey dining room in an equally rustic, even funky, inn next door to the Henry Miller Library. The food is homemade, with a limited menu offering steak, a vegetarian plate, and daily specials. The food is very fresh and wholesome. There's likely to be a fire in the fireplace, adding to the woodsy charm of the place. There are two seatings each night for dinner, and reservations are advised.

DEETJEN'S BIG SUR INN, *Route 1, 19 miles north of Lucia Lodge, one-half mile south of Nepenthe. (408) 667-2377. Breakfast, lunch, and dinner daily. Moderate.*

✔ **Nepenthe.**   As mentioned (see Chapter 15, entry 6), Nepenthe is a must stop for visitors to the area. In a dramatic setting overlooking the ocean, you can have burgers and homemade soups, baked chicken, steak, or vegetarian specialties. The food is simple and good.

If the wait for a table is too long, go down the outdoor steps to the Café Amphora and have a light snack or a great dessert with cappuccino. The view is the best part of the visit anyway.

NEPENTHE, *Route 1, 1 mile south of the Ventana Inn. (408) 667-2345. Lunch and dinner daily. Moderate.*

✔ **La Bohème.**   If the line is not too intimidating, you might like the adventure of eating in this small café. The menu changes daily, and the diner is not given a choice: what they cook, you eat, all served family-style. The cuisine is European peasant food, and I should add that the peasants seem to eat better than the royalty. I suggest calling first to see what's being served.

LA BOHÈME, *Dolores Street at Seventh Street. (408) 624-7500. Dinner daily; no reservations. Moderate.*

CARMEL

✔ **L'Escargot.**   For a classic French meal served in an elegant, quiet setting, L'Escargot offers a place of refuge from the bustle of downtown Carmel. There is nothing trendy about this place. For years L'Escargot has been serving dishes with rich cream sauces and truffles to satisfied customers. And yes, they do serve snails, à la Burgundy. Reservations are advised.

L'ESCARGOT, *Mission Street at Fourth Street. (408) 624-4914. Dinner Monday through Saturday. Moderate to expensive.*

✔ **Rio Café.**   Owned by the group that brought us Mustard's in the Napa Valley and the Fog City Diner in San Francisco, the Rio Café is my favorite of the bunch. This is the kind of menu many places copy when they want to offer California cuisine. Here you will get wonderful salads, fresh pasta, grilled fish and chicken, and a great burger, all served with imaginative sauces and made from the freshest ingredients.

CARMEL VALLEY

The decor is simple, with blond wood tables set against white walls; the atmosphere is calm. This is quite an accomplishment, since the Rio is in the center of a busy shopping center off the main highway. Reservations are advised.

RIO CAFÉ, *101 Crossroads Boulevard, in the Crossroads Shopping Center. (408) 625-5436. Lunch and dinner daily. Moderate.*

MONTEREY ✔ **Hammerhead's.** Even though I have never eaten here, I mention it because it has one feature I have never seen anywhere else: a chocolate bar. It's like a salad bar, except instead of lettuce, croutons, and the like, you will find chocolate in every form of cake and mousse and in every shade from light to dark— enough to send a chocoholic straight to seventh heaven.

Judging by what I saw on people's plates, the rest of the menu seems to be the meat, potatoes, and chicken sort of fare. Because just looking at the chocolate bar made me feel a change in my complexion, I can't offer any firsthand knowledge of how any of it tastes. But I like the fact that it's there, and I thought that chocolate fans would want to know about it. In 1986 the price was $5.95 for all you could eat.

HAMMERHEAD'S RESTAURANT, *414 Calle Principal. (408) 373-3116. Breakfast, lunch, and dinner Monday through Friday, dinner Saturday and Sunday. Inexpensive to moderate.*

Lodgings

This book is based on my personal travels. I have visited every destination and eaten at every restaurant, unless otherwise noted. But when it comes to hotels, motels, inns, and other overnight accommodations, my opportunities have been more limited.

Producing the *Bay Area Backroads* television program seldom requires an overnight trip. Most of our stories are shot during day trips from San Francisco; only rarely do I need to spend the night anywhere.

In addition, while I have no problem recommending places to eat or a destination where people will spend only an hour or two, recommending a place to spend the night seems much trickier. Overnight accommodation means an investment of more time and more money, and individual needs and wants come more into play. For example, I care more about having a good feather pillow than whether there is room service. I am more interested in an inn that does not allow smoking than whether there is a hot tub. You may prefer a bed and breakfast where you can get really chummy with the proprietors; I prefer privacy.

So in this book I cannot address all the questions you might have, and thus I will not attempt to provide you with a complete guide to overnight accommodations. However, I can tell you about a few of my favorite places. These have been selected because they are unusual or ambitious and because I have been personally satisfied with my stay there. Since it is impossible to pin down a price that will be the same by the time you read this, I'll limit my choices to places that fit in the moderate category based on the going rates in the area.

On the next page you will find some services and agencies preceding my few recommendations. These can be used to get information and make reservations.

✔ **American Family Inn/Bed and Breakfast.** This service makes arrangements for visitors to stay in private houses around San Francisco, the wine country, and the Monterey Peninsula. Write P.O. Box 349, San Francisco, CA 94101, or call (415) 931-3083.

✔ **Carmel Room Finders.** This operation is a reservation house for hotels, motels, inns, and condos on the Monterey Peninsula. They also have a working relationship with a bed-and-breakfast service in Sonoma. Write P.O. Box 7430, Carmel, CA 93921, or call (408) 624-1711.

✔ **Mendocino Inns Referral Service.** They will help you find a place to stay in the Mendocino area. Write P.O. Box 647, Mendocino, CA 95460, or call (707) 961-0140.

✔ **Napa Valley Tourist Bureau.** They will make reservations for you at inns, hotels, and bed and breakfasts. Write P.O. Box 3240, Yountville, CA 94599, or call (707) 252-1985.

✔ **Lake Tahoe.** In Lake Tahoe two services will help you find an available condo or private cabin. For North Tahoe, phone (800) 822-5959; for South Tahoe, phone (800) 822-5922.

Marin County

INVERNESS

✔ **MacLean House.** The small town of Inverness has several very nice bed and breakfasts, but my favorite is the MacLean House. Located on a hill overlooking town, this small inn has only two rooms for rent. Unlike many bed-and-breakfast inns, they are good-sized, in addition to being nicely decorated, and they have private baths. Reserve well in advance.

MACLEAN HOUSE, *Hawthorne Way, off Inverness Way. (415) 669-7392.*

✔ **Golden Hinde Motel.** If you prefer the anonymity motel rooms can offer, check out this place, which is right on the way in Inverness. Accommodations are hardly lavish; it's like spending the night in someone's beach cabin. But there is a swimming pool, fireplaces in most rooms, and others have little patios overlooking Tomales Bay. There is a certain funky charm to the place, and the motel's restaurant, Barnaby's, has a pleasant and airy dining room where you can get good appetizers and fresh fish.

GOLDEN HINDE MOTEL, *Sir Francis Drake Boulevard, just north of the main part of Inverness. (415) 669-1389.*

✓ **The Estate.** As you drive a few minutes out of Guerneville on Route 116, you'll come to what I think is the best place to stay in the Russian River resort area. The Estate is the former country home of a wealthy banker that has been taken over by two gentlemen from San Francisco and converted to a bed-and-breakfast inn. The 10 bedrooms are elegantly furnished, and each has a private bath. In addition, there are two large common rooms for socializing or reading by the fireplace. A full-course breakfast is served in the morning.

The big crowds arrive on the weekends, so if you can visit during the week you'll have lots of privacy and the room will be discounted 40 percent from the weekend rate.

THE ESTATE, *13555 Highway 116. (707) 869-9093.*

✓ **Hope-Merrill and Hope-Bosworth Houses.** Two of the nicest Victorian inns in the Sonoma wine country are in the town of Geyserville and are run by the Hope family. They have converted two mansions, the old Merrill and Bosworth homes, into lovely bed-and-breakfast inns across the street from each other. They also offer an unusual feature called "Stage-a-Picnic," horse-drawn stagecoach rides to nearby wineries complete with a lavish picnic lunch.

HOPE-MERRILL HOUSE, *21253 Geyserville Avenue. (707) 857-3945.*
HOPE-BOSWORTH HOUSE, *21238 Geyserville Avenue. (707) 857-3356.*

✓ **Stone Tree Ranch.** By telling you about this place I am probably never going to get to stay here again. This is a unique bed and breakfast in the Sonoma hills that fits my definition of getting away from it all. The Stone Tree Ranch has just one cabin to rent, upstairs above what was once a stable. The Gavigans, who live in the ranch house close by, will stock the place with everything you will need for breakfast, including fresh coffee beans and a grinder, then leave you to your own devices. You can use the hot tub on their deck if you like, and you can roam around the ranch, which affords a sweeping view of the valley. It's a good idea to make your reservation for this place well in advance.

STONE TREE RANCH, *7910 Sonoma Mountain Road. (707) 996-1114.*

✓ **Healdsburg Inn.** On the plaza in the center of town, the Healdsburg Inn is in a lovely old building. This bed and breakfast offers large rooms, fireplaces, antiques, and a rooftop garden and solarium. It's also within walking distance of three good restaurants and a short ride from the beautiful wineries on West Side Road.

HEALDSBURG INN, *116 Matheson Street. (707) 433-6991.*

Napa County

ST. HELENA   ✓ **El Bonita Motel.**   If you are nostalgic about traveling in the 1940s and 1950s, you will enjoy a stay at the El Bonita Motel, right on the main highway in the Napa Valley. El Bonita has an art deco exterior, tastefully decorated rooms, and a swimming pool. And the rates are inexpensive compared to similar accommodations in the area.

EL BONITA MOTEL, *Highway 29, one mile south of St. Helena. (707) 963-3216.*

✓ **Meadowood.**   There are many luxury resorts in the wine country. If you want to splurge for the weekend, I recommend staying at Meadowood, which features tennis courts, a pool, a nine-hole golf course, and beautifully decorated and spacious rooms, all tucked away in a secluded section of Napa Valley. It truly is a special place.

MEADOWOOD, *900 Meadowood Lane, near St. Helena. (707) 963-3646.*

South Bay Inland

FREMONT   ✓ **Lord Bradley's Inn.**   Fremont is not a place you would expect to find a charming old country inn, but in the mission district of town, just down the street from the Mission San Jose, is such a place. Lord Bradley's Inn is a turn-of-the-century farmhouse, and it's a good, inexpensive spot for a getaway. Breakfast is served to overnight guests, and there are lovely grounds out in back of the inn for strolling or just relaxing.

LORD BRADLEY'S INN, *43344 Mission Boulevard. (415) 490-0520.*

SAN JUAN BAUTISTA   ✓ **San Juan Inn.**   Just outside of town is a modern and quiet motel with spacious bedrooms and a swimming pool. The San Juan Inn is a good value, especially when you have the entire family along.

SAN JUAN INN, *410 The Alameda. (408) 623-4380.*

South Bay Coast

✓ **American Youth Hostels.**   As mentioned earlier (see Chapter 5, item 3), anyone willing to endure hosteling can stay right along the ocean at Montara Lighthouse or Pigeon Point Lighthouse. Reservations can be made through the San Francisco office of American Youth Hostels.

AMERICAN YOUTH HOSTELS, *Building 240, Fort Mason, San Francisco. (415) 771-4647.*

✔ **San Benito House.**   There are several bed-and-breakfast inns in Half Moon Bay, most of them quite expensive. I prefer the San Benito House, which was built as the Mosconi Hotel in 1904, then was converted in the 1970s into a 10-room inn. There is a sundeck and sauna, plus a dining room and deli downstairs, which are recommended for lunch and dinner.

SAN BENITO HOUSE, *Main Street and Mill. (415) 726-3425.*

✔ **Asilomar Conference Center.**   If you want to save money but stay in beautiful surroundings near Carmel, try to get a room at Asilomar. This is a real bargain. Although most of the large facility is booked by groups for meetings, a few rooms are usually available for individuals or families. The rooms are adequate, if not elaborate, but the grounds and the neighboring beach are spectacular. And it's located just a few minutes' drive from Carmel and Monterey.

ASILOMAR CONFERENCE CENTER, *800 Asilomar Boulevard. (408) 372-8016.*

East Bay

See "Hotels of Pleasanton" (Chapter 6, entry 18).

Gold Country

✔ **National Hotel.**   There seems to be a National Hotel in every major town in the Gold Country, but probably none is more historic than the one in Nevada City. This is said to be the oldest continuously operating hotel in California, and it's now a state historic landmark.

Rooms are comfortable and nicely furnished. My wife and I stayed in the room where the papers that created the Pacific Gas and Electric Company were signed; my cameraman had the room young Herbert Hoover used to stay in when he was a mining engineer.

NATIONAL HOTEL, *211 Broad Street, in the center of town. (916) 265-4551.*

✔ **Hanford House.**   Though the Hanford House is a fairly modern bed-and-breakfast inn, the nine spacious rooms are decorated with antiques. Because the operation is subject to certain zoning restrictions, the nice folks there can't cook eggs and bacon in the morning, but they do provide a substantial continental breakfast with lots of fresh fruit and pastries.

HANFORD HOUSE, *Highway 29. (209) 267-0747.*

✓ **Sutter Creek Inn.**   Hostess Jane Way was one of the West Coast bed-and-breakfast pioneers, and she has done everything right. Her New England–style Sutter Creek Inn offers comfortable, interesting rooms, insulated from such modern appliances as the telephone and the television set. Breakfast is a full-blown meal with eggs, fresh-baked pastries, juice, and good coffee. For me, the best touch of all was the pillow on the bed. Jane sends away to France for her feather pillows. This is a nice place for a romantic getaway; no children under 15 or pets allowed.

SUTTER CREEK INN, *75 Main Street. (209) 267-5606.*

Yosemite

See Chapter 11.

Lake Tahoe

NORDEN   ✓ **Clair Tappan Lodge.**   For hostel-like accommodations for the whole family, this lodge run by the Sierra Club is a popular spot. The facility offers some large common rooms for conversation and reading by the fire, plus a library, hot tub, and Ping-Pong table. Sleeping accommodations are either same-sex dorm-style or in small family rooms. They provide cots and bunk beds plus three good meals a day; you provide the bedding and soap and towels, and you pitch in on chores, such as clearing the table in the communal dining hall.

Even though this lodge is huge and can accommodate 140 people, it is usually booked well in advance, especially during ski season. The rate is very inexpensive.

CLAIR TAPPAN LODGE, *on Old Highway 40. (916) 426-3632.*

Mendocino County

MENDOCINO   ✓ **Big River Lodge.**   A bit south of town is a former motel that has been converted into a large, antique-and-art-filled bed-and-breakfast inn. Each bedroom has a wood-burning fireplace and a deck; some rooms have a view of the ocean, others a view of Mendocino. A nice touch: Bicycles are available to guests free of charge.

BIG RIVER LODGE, *also called Stanfords by the Sea, Comptche-Ukiah Road, about 3 miles south of Mendocino. (707) 937-5615.*

Redwood Empire

✔ Eureka Inn. This is a fine place to stay if you want to be in the center of town. The inn is a blocklong 1920s English Tudor building, now a historic landmark. Though the bedrooms are nothing special, the rest of the hotel is a throwback to an era of stately elegance that is hard to find these days. The lobby with its huge roaring fireplace is particularly inviting. The inn offers many hotel-type services, including a pool, Jacuzzi, sauna, and a very large dining room.

EUREKA INN, *Seventh and F streets. (707) 442-6441.*

✔ Gingerbread Mansion. Usually a cute name like this would be a turnoff to me, but after I saw the place I realized I could never come up with a better name to describe this splendid Victorian inn. It is truly an incredible building, and the innkeepers who run it make sure every touch is just right. One of the interesting design features is the unusual bathrooms. If it's available, reserve the downstairs room with the two clawfoot bathtubs facing each other. Very romantic. Afternoon tea is served in the four large parlors, and in the morning a tray of coffee, tea, or juice is placed in the hallway and you can take your wake-up beverage into your room. Then a full breakfast is served in the formal dining room, overlooking one of the gardens.

GINGERBREAD MANSION, *400 Berding Street. (707) 786-4000.*

✔ Scotia Inn. The grandest building in the company town of Scotia (see Chapter 14, destination 4) was built as a tourist attraction for the wealthy. In recent years the class distinction has eroded somewhat, but the elegant old hotel stands and offers overnight accommodations for all. Rooms are attractive, and the dining room is a classic from a bygone era. But I should warn you that the company whistle goes off to wake the entire town—including hotel guests—at 6:30 A.M. each workday.

SCOTIA INN, *corner of Main and Mill streets. (707) 764-5683.*

Monterey Peninsula

✔ Ripplewood Resort. Accommodations in Big Sur can run from the very expensive and stylish, such as the Ventana Inn, to the funky, like the Big Sur Inn. Ripplewood falls somewhere in between, offering a variety of rooms in separate cabins or in a main lodge. It's woodsy but clean and functional.

RIPPLEWOOD RESORT, *Route 1. (408) 667-2242.*

Index

An asterisk (*) indicates a restaurant or hotel.